MAN TO MAN

Chuck Swindoll Selects His Most
Significant Writings FOR MEN

MAN TO MAN

Chuck Swindoll Selects His Most
Significant Writings FOR MEN

CHARLES R. SWINDOLL

ZondervanPublishingHouse
Grand Rapids, Michigan

A Division of HarperCollinsPublishers

Man to Man
Copyright © 1996 by Charles R. Swindoll, Inc.

Requests for information should be addressed to:

ZondervanPublishingHouse
Grand Rapids, Michigan 49530

Library of Congress Cataloging-in-Publication Data

Swindoll, Charles R.
   Man to man : Chuck Swindoll selects his most significant writings for men / Charles R. Swindoll.
      p.   cm.
      ISBN: 0-310-21056-9
   1. Men—Religious life. 2. Christian life. 3. Men—Conduct of life. I. Title.
BV4528.2.S95 1996
248.8' 42-dc 20

                                                  96-2369
                                                  CIP

International Trade Paper Edition 0-310-21075-5

This edition printed on acid-free paper and meets the American National Standards Institute Z39.48 standard.

Unless otherwise indicated, all Scripture references are from the New American Standard Bible, © The Lockman Foundation 1960, 1962, 1963, 1968, 1971, 1972, 1973, 1975, 1977.

Verses marked NIV are from the Holy Bible: New International Version, copyright ©1978 by the International Bible Society.

Verses marked TLB are taken from The Living Bible, © 1971 by Tyndale House Publishers, Wheaton, Ill.

Verses marked MLB are from the Modern Language Bible, The New Berkeley Version in Modern English, © 1945, 1959, 1969 by Zondervan Publishing House.

Verses marked GNB are from the Good News Bible, © American Bible Society 1976.

Verses marked Amplified Bible are from The Amplified New Testament, © 1954, 1958 by The Lockman Foundation.

Material in this book has appeared in the previous Charles R. Swindoll volumes *Make Up Your Mind, Standing Out, The Strong Family, The Quest for Character, Strike the Original Match,* and various Charles R. Swindoll booklets published by Zondervan Publishing House.

Published in association with Sealy M. Yates, Literary Agent, Orange, CA

Interior design by Sue Vandenberg Koppenol

Printed in the United States of America

---

96 97 98 99 00 01 02❖ DH/ 10 9 8 7 6 5 4 3 2 1

Contents

Introduction

Macho. Sensitive. Wild. Caring.
A mighty warrior. A best buddy. A strong leader. One who stands alone—and inspires. One who cries—and bonds. One who innovates—and risks.

Which of those '90s' descriptions of a man are you? Which describes your partner, or father, or brother, or friend?

Today there are many voices telling men how to be men. Some say we need to go out into the wilderness, hole up in a sweat lodge, and wait till that primal urge roars up from within. Others say we need to be tenderized by life and group-hugged toward a sensitivity that would erase our Neanderthal attitudes. Still others say there's a question over whether maleness is even needed anymore. Masculinity is out. Period.

> Men in general, and fathers in particular, are increasingly viewed as superfluous to family life: either expendable or as part of the problem. Masculinity itself, understood as anything other than a rejection of what it has traditionally meant to be male, is typically treated with suspicion and even hostility in our cultural discourse.[1]

The old descriptions of men just don't seem to be working, either. Men used to take pride in calling themselves assertive, confident, ambitious, decisive, independent, and competitive. Now we better be sure that along with those adjectives we sprinkle in words like *sympathetic, kind, helpful, affectionate, tender,* and *compassionate.*

It seems that the most positive changes in the character of men in the '90s have nothing to do with job behaviors or personal accomplishments. When both men and women were polled to determine what set the '90s man apart from his predecessors, the top two characteristics chosen in today's men were (a) being more family-oriented, and (b) being more able to display feelings in public.[2]

At the same time, almost 90 percent of the women polled in the same survey (a) like it when a man opens the door for them, and (b) feel protected when they're with their husbands/boyfriends.[3]

Is it just me, or were we going in one direction and got passed by the bus coming the other way? Obviously there are a lot of differing opinions out there on the masculine identity.

So exactly what does it mean to be a man? And is it important?

The movements, marches, and mood today cry out for men to fill roles from which they've significantly disappeared. For men to be responsible for families and homes. For men to step up to their commitments—and follow through with them.

But how?

I knew a man who didn't really have a father, growing up. And his brother was always one step beyond him. The man's friends were many, but they weren't the kind who were close. As my acquaintance went through life, he wondered what it meant to be a man. Although this man truly had no model of masculinity from his father, many of us would probably agree that learning to be a man from within our families or without seems to be a lost art. And yet we can learn, when we open up to God's patterns for men found in His Word.

In this book I want to talk with you one-on-one. I've done a lot of looking through my writings to come up with what I consider my best counsel on the subject of being a man. They're not "the final words," but they have been seasoned with time and shaped by over sixty years of experiences (including more than forty years of marriage).

I'm giving you some longer chapters on big issues like integrity, anger, adversity, commitment, stress, and purity. But then I've salted in some of the smaller issues—which today are big issues—like holding things loosely, building memories, acting medium, becoming models, and starting over.

We're going to look at the problems and responses to those problems that lead us to wrong attitudes, wrong actions, and wrong ways of living. But we're going to look at successful ways to meet life head-on and enjoy it to its fullest. (Anybody who knows me will tell you I believe that we can learn—and have fun—at the same time. I'll go so far as to say that if we're not laughing at ourselves and with one another, then we're not learning some of God's greatest lessons.)

This book is not a right-angle approach to defining what a man should be. I'm not qualified to make that declaration. There isn't a formula, no matter how many books, seminars, speakers, and conventions promise otherwise. So rather than punching out a boiler-plate pattern, I've chosen to rough out the framework with some general characteristics that men need. (Oddly enough, when we hook up with the qualities we need as men, we find out they're the traits our wives and family members and friends want us to have.) I'll fill in the gaps with several stories and some memories along with a few suggestions that will help further describe the truly successful man—the authentic *Christian* man—of the '90s.

But I'm not going to unload one lecture after another. I'm going to talk with you as if you and I were together, somewhere easy. Maybe sitting on the lowered tailgate of a pickup truck, gazing at the orange horizon of a Texas sunset, trading stories about our kids and wives that bring back laughter and maybe some tears. It's possible we could be out in one of our yards, sitting with our knees propped up and our backs against the fence after a morning of lawn cutting and car washing. And we're talking about our jobs and the pressures from the boss, or the seductive magnetism of success and beautiful cars, or the temptations to forget our marriage vows, even for a few flirting minutes.

I'd like to see this as our book, yours and mine. You and I will share the moment as we consider those things that might make us laugh, or might make us think, or might make us tear up ... but hopefully will make us better. I invite all readers, but I hope that this volume will find its way especially into the hands of fathers, and their sons, young men and older men, brothers and friends.

As man to man, we can learn more what it means simply to be a man.

Being Real

D ave Cowens, star basketball center for the Boston Celtics, dis-appeared. Without warning, he walked off the practice court, showered, dressed, and drove away. Alone.

He kept driving to . . . somewhere. His only explanation was the familiar comment, "I need to get my head together." He added that it could take as little as two weeks or as much as ten years. The sports-casters, management, team, spectators, and fans couldn't imagine what he was looking for.

I could.

The Carpenters did a number that helps explain the superstar's puzzling reaction. It's a peaceful soul-song that talks about needing a place to hide away . . . to be quiet . . . to think things through . . . to reflect.

Perhaps that's what the Boston superstar was trying to say. He had everything imaginable—fame, possessions, job security, a strong body, lots of bucks—but maybe at that moment in his life he lacked some-thing far more important. Something like a sense of purpose and inner fulfillment. Something which basketball and all its benefits could never provide. An inner itch that couldn't be scratched by achievement or people or things or activities. To scratch it required a great deal of internal searching, which the athlete felt he couldn't do and still keep pace with the maddening NBA schedule.

To "find yourself" requires that you take time to look. It's essen-tial if you want to be a whole person, real to the core.

Now I'm not advocating that one suddenly stop everything else so he can work the hide-and-seek process. That's rather unrealistic even if you aren't the starting center for an NBA franchise. It's a lit-tle like removing an anthill in your backyard with six sticks of TNT. Or like setting your car on fire because the engine knocks. Learn-ing to be whole isn't prompted by copping out. But there are times in all our lives when we need to back away, slow down, stay quiet, think through, be still.

"I'd rather burn out than rust out!" shouts the zealot. Frankly, neither sounds very appealing to me. Either way you're *out*. People who are burning out may start a lot of fires and stir up a lot of noise and smoke. But who cares—if everything turns to ashes? People who are rusting out may move about as slowly as a sloth and live to be 130. But so what—if all they accomplished in life is paying bills and staying out of jail?

There *has* to be more to life than just doing. There is! It's *being*. Becoming whole . . . believable . . . purposeful . . . lovable. The word is *real*. It takes time, and it usually hurts.

The Velveteen Rabbit is a classy book for children with a message for adults. In it is a revealing nursery dialogue between a new toy rabbit and an old skin horse. As they are lying side by side one day, Rabbit asks Horse:

> "What is REAL? Does it mean having things that buzz inside you and a stick-out handle?"
>
> "Real isn't how you are made," said the Skin Horse. "It's a thing that happens to you. When a child loves you for a long, long time, not just to play with, but REALLY loves you, then you become REAL."
>
> "Does it hurt?" asked the Rabbit.
>
> "Sometimes," said the Skin Horse, for he was always truthful. "When you are REAL you don't mind being hurt."
>
> "Does it happen all at once, like being wound up," he asked, "or bit by bit?"
>
> "It doesn't happen all at once," said the Skin Horse. "You become. It takes a long time. That's why it doesn't often happen to people who break easily, or have sharp edges, or have to be carefully kept. Generally, by the time you are Real, most of your hair has been loved off, and your eyes drop out and you get loose in the joints and very shabby. But these things don't matter at all, because once you are Real you can't be ugly, except to people who don't understand."[4]

Take a long look at *you*, suggests Skin Horse. Going through a lot of activities? Staying busy? In a hurry most of the time? Spinning around the squirrel cage? Seldom pausing to ask why? Still reluctant to be loved . . . to be real? Still keeping a distance between yourself and your family members? Still substituting *doing* for *being?*

It'll never satisfy. You cannot play cover-up forever. What does God suggest? Having a heart of compassion, being kind, tender, transparent, gentle, patient, forgiving, loving, and lovable. All those things spell R-E-A-L.

I'm convinced that's what Cowens was looking for. He may not have found it in a few weeks, but it sure was worth the effort. Losing your hair takes time, and it's pretty painful to have your eyes drop out and your joints get loose. But in the long run, that's the only way to be.

REAL.

Masculine Model of Leadership

◆

Remember when men were men? Remember when you could tell by looking? Remember when men knew who they were, liked how they were, and didn't want to be anything but what they were? Remember when it was the men who boxed and wrestled and bragged about how much they could bench-press? Remember when it was the women who wore the makeup, the earrings, and the bikinis? Remember when it was the men who initiated the contact and took the lead in a relationship, made lifelong commitments, treated a woman like a lady, and modeled a masculinity that displayed security and stability?

I'm not thinking about the half-crazed Rambo types who suffer from macho mania . . . those who look for a fight, walk with a swagger, never apologize, and give that "make my day" stare. Those guys may be able to destroy half of North Vietnam single-handedly, but they make terrible neighbors, horrible business partners, and brutal husbands and dads. Being a man is not the same as living like a panther ready to pounce.

Neither do I have in mind the Archie Bunker-type loudmouth who slouches in his chair, barks out orders, and thinks the world gravitates around him. Since when do dogmatism, prejudice, and selfishness mean masculinity? This type of fellow lives in a fantasy world, only imagining he's running the show. In actuality, he's a frightened child inside a man's body, the object of sarcastic ridicule among friends and family alike.

True manhood calls for discipline of character, strong determination to set a course of action, and courage to stay at a task. But brutality? Vulgarity? Lack of courtesy? Hardly. Authentic men aren't afraid to show affection, release their feelings, hug their children, cry when they're sad, admit it when they're wrong, and ask for help when they need it. Vulnerability fits beautifully into mature manhood. So does integrity.

I am concerned about a vanishing masculinity that was once in abundance. I mean honest-to-goodness *men* who are distinctly that—discerning, decisive, strong-hearted men who know where they are going and are confident enough in themselves (and their God) to get there. They aren't afraid to take the lead, to stand tall and firm in their principles even when the going gets rough.

Such qualities not only inspire the respect of women, they engender healthy admiration among younger men and boys who hunger for heroes. We need fewer spineless wimps who've never disentangled themselves from mama's apron strings, and more clear-thinking, hard-working, straight-talking men who, while tender, thoughtful, and loving, don't feel the need to ask permission for taking charge. I'm convinced that most single ladies would love to have men like that to spend time with ... and most wives long to have men like that to share life with. Children especially like having dads like that.

Over the last three decades there has been an assault on masculinity. The results are well represented in the arts, the media, the world of fashion, and among those who have become our youths' heroes. There are exceptions, I realize, but therein lies the problem ... they are *exceptions*. Androgynous individuals now prance to and fro on rock-concert stages across America. Poster-size portraits of male celebrities paper the walls in thousands of boys' bedrooms. Many performers no longer even pretend to be masculine. Sex roles are deliberately being blended. Female impersonators are the hot ticket in show places all around the world, performing before mainly male audiences.

A number of years ago, *People* magazine included a dialogue between a psychologist and his seven-year-old nephew. The professional asked the boy, "Is Michael Jackson a boy or a girl?" The boy thought for a moment, then answered, "Both." If you don't think it's now cool to wrap both sexes into one package, you've not checked out the stores that handle the chic designer labels. We're talking "Who's What?"

This reminds me of a book I read about on being a man.[5] The author, Weldon Hardenbrook, referred to a line of women's lingerie released by Calvin Klein. The lingerie is modeled after men's undershirts and jockey shorts. The ladies' undies are not slinky satin or frilly nylon, but 100 percent cotton, available in six varieties of tops, eight types of bottoms, in twenty-five colors. And get this: The briefs are cut high on the leg, but the string bikini resembles a jockstrap, and the boxer shorts actually have a fly. Was there any question whether or not it would sell? Are you kidding? That line of Klein's underwear line was expected to gross $70 million in its first fourteen months. Unisex used to be limited to a few kinky beauty salons and off-the-wall jewelry stores— now it's as close to us as undergarments. Don't kid yourself; gender blending is not a passing fad on society's bizarre edge. It is here, and it is neither subtle nor silent.

Author Alvin Toffler saw all this happening years ago in his book, *The Third Wave*, in which he announced:

> The role system that held industrial civilization together is in crisis. This we see most dramatically in the struggle to redefine sex roles. In the women's movement, in the demands for the legalization of homosexuality, in the spread of unisex fashions, we see a continual blurring of traditional expectations for the sexes.[6]

Toffler is on target but too soft.

The separate distinction of male and female is not merely a "traditional expectation," it's a biblical precept ("male and female He created them," Genesis 1:27b). And it isn't simply a "role system that held industrial civilization together." It is a foundational block upon which any healthy civilization rests. When the roles get sufficiently blurred, confusion and chaos replace decency and order. When effeminate men begin to flood the landscape, God's longsuffering reaches the length of its tether, ushering in the severest judgment imaginable ... à la Sodom and Gomorrah. Romans 1:24–27 is still in the Book, isn't it? Worst of all, because more and more men care less about being men, the family is thrown into confusion. Leadership is shifted to the wife and mother, and the children understandably reverse the roles, tragically perpetuating the unnatural trend.

A PORTRAIT WORTH EXAMINATION

Tucked away in Paul's first New Testament letter, we find one of those biblical pen portraits no one could improve. Even though the original purpose of the writer was not to describe the role of a father in the family, I think there is room for us to apply his words along those lines.

Read the following paragraph slowly and deliberately. I want to use it as the basis of some suggestions on how we men can become the kind of dads that wives appreciate and children admire.

> But we proved to be gentle among you, as a nursing mother tenderly cares for her own children. Having thus a fond affection for you, we were well-pleased to impart to you not only the gospel of God but also our own lives, because you had become very dear to us. For you recall, brethren, our labor and hardship, how working night and day so as not to be a burden to any of you, we proclaimed to you the gospel of God. You are witnesses, and so is God, how devoutly and uprightly and blamelessly we behaved toward you believers; just as you know how we were exhorting and encouraging and imploring each one of you as a father would his own children, so that you may walk in a manner worthy of the God who calls you into His own kingdom and glory (1 Thessalonians 2:7–12).

I don't know if you observed a rather bold contrast at the beginning and end of those verses. Paul, the writer, initially admits he was gentle "as a nursing *mother*," then later he writes that he exhorted, encouraged, and implored them "as a *father.*" When I first saw that contrast, it occurred to me there might very well be some hints for the home in a context that mentions both mother and father. In fact, I find no fewer than five wonderful traits in this portrait of a father in the home.

A Fond Affection

Having thus a fond affection for you . . . (v. 8).

Paul had at his fingertips a half dozen or more Greek terms of affection he could have used that were familiar to the people in that day. He picked one, however, that is found nowhere else in all the New Testament. Gerhard Kittel, in his massive, nine-volume set on New Testament words, tells us that the term translated *affection* means "to feel oneself drawn to something or someone."[7] There is a strong intensity implied in the term. Zahn, a Greek scholar of German descent, says it is a term of endearment taken from the nursery, one that is both masculine and tender. It is the picture of a father who holds and treats a child tenderly, feeling himself affectionately drawn to that little one.

As I write these words, I remember (as many of you who are dads also remember) the first time I held our first child in my arms. Ours happened to be a curly-haired little boy whom we named Curtis. That was way back in September of 1961. I remember carefully holding that little fella, afraid I would break him—or drop him. I had this incredible fear he would somehow fall out of my arms. I noticed right away he couldn't hold his head up. It kept falling. I said stuff like, "Hold your head up, Curt!" and "Straighten up, boy!" It didn't help a bit. You see, I had never held a baby that tiny and fragile before. It's amazing how mothers have a built-in knack for knowing how to do all the right things. Even though Cynthia had never had her own baby before Curt, she seemed to know what to do. Moms know, but dads don't! And so what do we do? We hold them very carefully, very tenderly . . . at least at first. Unfortunately, much of our tender affection fades rapidly if we're not careful.

As the years pass, work increases, pressures mount, and the demands and deadlines grapple for more of our time and energy. In the meantime our child grows—no longer little and able to be held in our arms. Before we know it, he's about our height or even taller. In fact, we find our arms are no longer able to reach around his broad shoulders.

But don't kid yourself. That "fond affection" is still needed! And, I would add, it is especially needed from dad. I don't mean that we simply think it, but that we *demonstrate* it. That is especially true as our children spread their wings and begin to break close ties with their parents. Such attempts at independence require a great deal of wisdom on the parents' part.

I am reminded of the prodigal son. It's the story of a boy who reaches the age when he says, "I'm going to make it on my own. Give me what I've got coming, Dad, because I'm leaving." Off he goes. Perhaps it was a rather stormy, rapid departure. The young man hits the streets and lives there for an undetermined period of time. While he's away, there is no contact with home. The boy doesn't write. He doesn't attempt to get in touch. Who knows how long he stayed away. As times got hard the boy sank lower and lower. He wound up humiliated, bankrupt, and depressed. Finally, at the very bottom, he comes to his senses and says to himself:

> How many of my father's hired men have more than enough bread, but I am dying here with hunger! I will get up and go to my father . . . (Luke 15:17–18).

By the way, he never once thought his father would not let him return home. Interesting, isn't it? Our kids know us. They can usually predict our response.

> I will get up and go to my father, and will say to him, "Father, I have sinned against heaven, and in your sight; I am no longer worthy to be called your son; make me as one of your hired men" (vv. 18–19).

Sounds to me like he is rehearsing his speech. He is now living with the scars of all those terrible memories. Awash in feelings of guilt, he tries to imagine stumbling back to the front door of his home, facing a dad who is liable to be ashamed of him. So he plans to say with sincerity, "I'm not worthy to be called your son." He expects to encounter the wrath of Khan. But that's not what he finds back home. The boy's return is one of the most moving scenes imaginable! I never tell this story without having to fight back the tears.

> And he got up and came to his father. But while he was still a long way off, his father saw him, and felt compassion for him, and ran and embraced him, and kissed him (v. 20).

Wow! That's what I call demonstrating tender affection. No hesitation. No inquisition. No probation. Only compassion. In fact (if you read the rest of the story), there was a celebration!

To those of us who bear the name "Dad," I cannot impress upon you enough how imperative it is that we show our affection. We can do that in two ways. First, we affirm who our child is; and second, we appreciate what our child does. This twofold assurance, however, must be given in more than words. Affection—the nonverbal communication of closeness, touching, and even kissing—is among the most important experiences we share with one another.

Many a young woman who opts for immoral sexual relationships does so because she can scarcely remember a time when her father so much as touched her. Unaffectionate dads, without ever wishing to do so, can trigger a daughter's promiscuity. All this leads me to write with a great deal of passion, dads . . . *don't hold back your affection!* Demonstrate your feelings of love and acceptance to both sons and daughters, and don't stop once they reach adolescence. They long for your affirmation and appreciation. They will love you for it. More important, they will emulate your example when God gives them their own families.

Between 1961 and 1970, God gave Cynthia and me four children. The one ingredient she and I have discovered that has held us close together has been the open expression of our affection for one another. Interestingly, what we demonstrated to our children, they began to demonstrate to one another. The investment of "fond affection" throughout their growing-up years has resulted in wonderful dividends. It is a great delight to see our married kids now carrying on the same affectionate tradition with their little ones.

A Transparent Life

Next, we read of the value of giving ourselves—our whole lives.

> Having thus a fond affection for you, we were well-pleased to impart to you not only the gospel of God but also our own lives, because you had become very dear to us (1 Thessalonians 2:8).

Talk about being transparent! Look at the words, my fellow father. "Not only the gospel, but our own lives."

Question: Isn't the gospel important? *Absolutely.* Well then, when it comes to the Christian family, isn't the gospel *alone* enough? *Absolutely not!* To hear the gospel is a necessity for children. If they are to come to know the Savior whom you love, Dad, they need to have you tell them of Him. I have no greater joy than the memory that our four children heard early in their lives the gospel concerning Jesus Christ from their dad's lips. They heard that God loved them through His Son and sent the Savior for them. And that He died for them, paying the penalty for their sins. And if, as a child, they would simply trust themselves to the Savior, by faith in His death and resurrection, they would be given the gift of eternal life.

They heard . . . and each one responded. That is imparting the gospel. How terribly important it is to impart the gospel! But when it comes to rearing those children, how valuable it is to impart our own lives to them as well. The term *impart* carries with it the idea of making a contribution, sharing fully.

What would that include? I can think of several things that might be "imparted." Our children want to learn a proper scale of values from us. They also want to discover how to make good decisions. It intrigues them to think we are able to stand alone and unintimidated. They want to know the techniques of such security (not just that you do it, but *how* you do it). They want to know how to handle their finances. They also need your approval . . . the assurance that you value them. I would also include a well-exercised sense of humor, a positive, contagious attitude toward life. Few memories are more pleasant than a father who laughed and had fun with his family. And how about including freedom from worry and stress? Or when stress comes, admitting your struggle with it. They'll understand. In fact, you'll be amazed. Your stock will go up several points in their minds whenever they see you under stress and observe your willingness to talk about it. Our children learn from our failures as well as from our successes. This is all part of living a transparent life.

Few experiences are more endearing than having one of your children lean over and tell you he loves you . . . that he understands and cares. Children find great security in finding us open and vulnerable. My kids, hopefully, are learning through a transparent life that their dad has needs. Sometimes my need is to be forgiven—so I must be willing to admit failure and wrong. Then and only then do I become *real!* Do not fear that transparency will cause a child to lose respect for you.

Several years ago an understandably proud father slipped into my study. His daughter had written a letter that had won a blue ribbon prize at school. She had written a paper on her dad. Among other things, she wrote:

> My dad has not always been "Pop" to us. We, my brothers and sister, as well as Mom, called him "Daddy" when we were young. He was able to make even folding clothes on Saturday fun with

tickle fights amidst freshly washed garments strewn all over the living room floor. He would roll and pretend at vulnerability on the carpet and grab each tiny, groping hand that attempted to tweak his ribs. We seldom won, of course. Daddy could mercilessly tickle the toes off a dead giant, not to mention take on four lively kids.

And, yes, there were serious times as well. We knew of them, too. He could spank the tears out of any of us, not because the physical pain was so incredible, but because it hurt us to think that we had brought him pain by having earned that spanking.

Looking back, I can see that my parents, by joint effort, have done an exceptionally good job raising us. High moral values, spiritual priorities, academic excellence—all these have been held out to us as important. My pop has instilled in us kids a sense of trust. He's been available, especially in emergencies. He has done what he thinks best for us, even when we might not agree. My dad has a corner on the upper echelons of fatherhood.

There is no question in my mind that this girl's dad is imparting his life, not just the gospel.

A fond affection . . . a transparent life; two qualities a family needs in a dad. There is a third, according to this biblical passage.

An Unselfish Diligence

Hardworking men will especially appreciate this verse:

> For you recall, brethren, our labor and hardship, how working night and day so as not to be a burden to any of you, we proclaimed to you the gospel of God (v. 9).

Focus your attention on eleven words: "working night and day so as not to be a burden. . . ." It's an obvious picture of hard work, responsible diligence.

Many of you who read this page have no better memory (perhaps for some, no other memory!) of your father than that he was a hard worker. But before you pooh-pooh that mental image, pause long enough to appreciate it in contrast to an irresponsible, indolent father. Those of us fortunate enough to have had a dad who was a diligent model of hard work have much for which to be grateful. Dads sometimes get the blast of preachers and authors who decry all that time at work. While it can certainly be taken to an unwholesome extreme, many a family has a hardworking dad to thank for their survival.

And so I say to you men who are models of diligence in your work, stay at the task ... but don't quit there. Help your child discover what it means to be diligent and devoted and dedicated to a job. Help him know what motivates you. Help her know what spurs you on to do a quality piece of work and to get the job done. There are numerous lessons to be learned from hard work. Happy is the family who has a model of diligence in the man of the home. And *happier* is the family whose dad keeps the right perspective on his diligence.

When former Chaplain of the Senate Richard Halverson wrote his book *Perspective*, he dedicated it "to faithful Christian laymen who with silent heroism under relentless secular pressure fight the economic battle as stewards of the living God." I join Dr. Halverson with a hearty round of applause.[8]

Hats off to you guys! And to all of you with fathers who have distinguished themselves as men of diligence and commitment, I urge you to say, "Thank you. Thanks for the years you invested that we might have a few things. Maybe you didn't give us all of yourself, and maybe we don't know you as well as we would like, but how greatly we've benefited from your work. You have taught us to appreciate what it means to be responsible. We love you, Dad!"

It is easy to let things you buy for your family take the place of giving yourself. In our affluent era, how easy to provide too much too soon! Maybe a simple principle I learned will help you, too. Your child will not fully appreciate something unless he knows he deserves it. He won't assess its value and have fun with something if it is just dumped on him. So help your child work hard, too. There are times you would be wise to restrain yourself—to keep your hands off and allow the child to work things through on his own.

A little fella was sitting at the kitchen table, trying to draw a pony. (If you've ever tried to draw a pony, you know how difficult it is, especially if you're not an artist.) To make matters worse, his dad, standing near, was blessed with artistic skill. He found himself biting his lip as he watched his son struggle to make the legs look like legs, to put the ears in just the right places, and make it all look proportionate. The kid just about wore the eraser down to zip as he reworked his drawing. Finally, the father could restrain himself no longer. In a moment of impatience, he grabbed the paper, flipped it over, and drew a beautiful young colt, running at full gallop. He included some shading, even added a few leafy trees in the background, then pushed the paper across the table and said, "Here, Son, here's your pony."

The boy looked down, frowned, and said rather dejectedly, "But, Daddy, . . . I wanted a pony *I* drew."

For all the right reasons, diligent dads can lavish upon their children so many things that the child becomes indulged and, ultimately, irresponsible. We need to work at keeping the balance.

There is yet another quality worth our consideration.

A Spiritual Authenticity

> For you recall, brethren, our labor and hardship, how working night and day so as not to be a burden to any of you, we proclaimed to you the gospel of God. You are witnesses, and so is God, how devoutly and uprightly and blamelessly we behaved toward you believers (vv. 9–10).

Pay close attention to the one side, "we proclaimed," followed by the other side, "we behaved." Like a coin, a life needs both sides before it is considered authentic. When it comes to being a father, few things are more significant than authenticity.

As difficult as it is to write the words that follow, I must. How rare are those families where the father is truly the spiritual leader! Usually, it's the mother. Isn't it about time we changed that, men? It is refreshing when the dad is the one who sets the pace, who takes the lead, who, more than anyone in the family, "hungers and thirsts after righteousness." I'm not thinking about big talk and little walk, not that . . . but rather a life that is lived in beautiful balance, where Christ is truly living out His life in the man of the house . . . where the wife and the children learn from the man's example what it means to truly love God.

Cynthia and I are very close friends with a family who live in another state. There are four girls in that family, all very close in age and relationships. They attended the same high school, even the same university. All four are now happily married. What stands out in all four young women's minds is the authentic model of true Christianity they witnessed in their dad. No question, if you asked any one of them, each would say their father set the pace, spiritually, in their home.

To give you an idea of his leadership, I want to quote from a letter he wrote them during their college years.

Dear girls of mine:

I'm enclosing this article I've read. It is one of the finest I have seen with regard to pinpointing the necessity for proper family relationships. I am hopeful that it will be worth your time to not only read it but also study and keep it for future use.

Now listen to his counsel. Notice how obviously yet graciously he takes the leadership:

The men you girls marry need to fit into the mold of the husband as outlined in this article. I don't know of the author's spiritual understanding, but he is using biblical principles in describing the family relationships.

Now, your heart can play tricks on you with regard to looking for a husband. There is so much romanticism beamed at you from every direction, it is easy to fall prey to the secular version of the husband and happiness. I am confident that each of you girls will allow the Lord to choose your husband. He will pick a man who fulfills the scriptural mandates for the head of the house.

I love each of you.
Daddy

That's what I'd call being spiritually authentic. Isn't it amazing, men? We watch our daughters grow, begin to date, move closer and closer to making life's second most significant decision—marriage—and we virtually take hands off the whole thing. It is our tendency to back away and leave most (if not all) of the counsel up to the wife . . . when, in fact, the girl is marrying one like us—a man. And because she doesn't quite know how to ask for our input, she waits for us to take the initiative. She longs to have that behavior that is marked by devoutness and uprightness of heart. It is so easy to let the eternal slip by unnoticed, isn't it? We can do the same with our sons. I thought of that when I read these lines from a modern translation of *Augustine's Confessions*, as he speaks of his own father:

No one had anything but praise for my father who, despite his slender resources, was ready to provide his son with all that was needed to enable him to travel so far for the purpose of study. Many of our townsmen, far richer than my father, went to no such trouble for their children's sake. Yet this same father of mine took no trouble at all to see how I was growing in your sight or whether I was chaste or not. He cared only that I should have a fertile tongue, leaving my heart to bear none of your fruits, my God, though you are the only Master, true and good, of its husbandry.[9]

A Positive Influence

Just as you know how we were exhorting and encouraging and imploring each one of you as a father would his own children, so that you may walk in a manner worthy of the God who calls you into His own kingdom and glory (vv. 11–12).

Paul refers to his ministry in Thessalonica as being one of active encouragement, "as a father." Isn't that interesting? When the apostle searched for an example of someone who brought a positive influence, "a father" came to his mind.

Would you think of a father as best fulfilling this role? Does *your* dad come to mind, for example? It has been my observation that fathers in our generation seem to have lost sight of this trait. More often than not, we focus on the negative, the wrong, rather than the positive.

Dan Benson, in his book *The Total Man*, verifies that fact with a rather disturbing statistic. After an extensive survey was taken, it was found that for one positive statement made in the homes that were surveyed, there were ten negatives—ten to one![10]

Let me refer to Charlie Shedd's words again. He is addressing the importance of a positive influence in a home. In another promise to his son, Peter, he writes:

I promise you that I will never say "No" if I can possibly say "Yes."

We see it often. Babies raised in a positive atmosphere develop much better personalities than those who constantly hear the words "No," "Stop," "Don't."

Let me show you what I mean. This has to do with a dirty old bale of binder twine. When we moved from Nebraska to Oklahoma, we brought it along. I had used it there to tie sacks of feed and miscellaneous items. It cost something like $1.15. So I said, "Now, Philip, you see this binder twine? I want you to leave it alone." But it held a strange fascination for him and he began to use it any time he wanted. I would say, "Don't," "No," and "You can't!" But all to no avail.

That went on for six or eight months. Then one day I came home, tired. There was the garage, looking like a no-man's land with binder twine across, back and forth, up and down. I had to cut my way through to get the car in. And was I provoked! I ground my teeth as I slashed at that binder twine. Suddenly, when I was halfway through the maze, a light dawned. I asked myself, "Why do you want this binder twine! What if Philip does use it?" So when I went in to supper that night, Philip was there and I began, "Say, about that binder twine!" He hung his head, and mumbled, "Yes, Daddy." Then I said, "Philip, I've changed my mind. You can use that old binder twine any time you want. What's more all those tools out in the garage I've labeled 'No' you go ahead and use them. I can buy new tools, but I can't buy new boys." There never was a sunrise like that smile. "Thanks, Daddy," he beamed. And guess what, Peter? He hasn't touched that binder twine since![11]

It's amazing, isn't it, how kids are put together. We scream, "Quit!" "Stop!" "Don't!" and they do. Then we finally learn to relax and say, "Go ahead, it's fine, do!" and, lo and behold, they're no longer interested.

Oh, dads, when will we learn? How long will it take? Each day of our lives we make deposits into the memory banks of our children. By remembering that, I find I am more likely to work on the qualities that build a lasting relationship between my children and me. Naturally, there are times when I blow it, and my family must forgive me. But when I focus on the traits I've mentioned in this chapter, I'm motivated to become the dad God wants me to be.

Looking Back . . . Looking Ahead: A Plea

As you look back and stand in the shadow of *your* father, what one word would you use to describe him? As you remember the man, what do you call him? Think back. . . .

If he's wealthy and prominent, and you stand in awe of him, call him "Father." If he sits in his shirt sleeves and suspenders at a

ball game and picnic, call him "Pop." If he wheels the baby car-
riage and carries bundles meekly, call him "Papa" (with the
accent on the first syllable). If he belongs to a literary circle and
writes cultured papers, call him "Papa" (with the accent on the
last syllable).

If, however, he makes a pal of you when you're good, and
is too wise to let you pull the wool over his loving eyes when
you're not; if, moreover, you're quite sure no other fellow you
know has quite so fine a father, you may call him "Dad."[12]

Now it's your turn. What do you call yours? Or if he's gone on
to glory, what did you call him? A lot of people I know would answer
without hesitation, "Absent." Much as I would prefer to soften the
blows or speak in defense of all dads, there's a growing number of
folks who refuse to be ignored any longer. They miss their dad! They
don't want substitutes: things to play with, a car for graduation, their
own room, money for tuition, or a Hawaiian honeymoon. No, not
nearly as much as they want the presence and influence of a dad. Not
all day, you understand (they're realistic enough to realize that can't
be), but time with him . . . to talk to, listen to, laugh with, mess around
with, learn from, and grow alongside the man who loved their mother enough to conceive them.

"Where is he now?" they ask.

I hear more loneliness than bitterness in their voices. More "I
wish" than "I hate." Somehow, some way . . . there's a longing for
those strong arms and that familiar voice. Emotional distance does
a number on relationships, even when adulthood replaces adolescence. Singer Barry Manilow sang of that in a song of yesteryear.

> *We walked to the sea, just my father and me;*
> *And the dog played around on the sand.*
> *Winter cold cut the air, hangin' still everywhere,*
> *Dressed in gray . . . did he say "hold my hand"?*
> *I said, Love's easier when it's far away;*
> *We sat and watched a distant light.*
> *We're two ships that pass in the night,*
> *We both smile and we say it's all right;*
> *We're still here—it's just that we're out of sight*
> *Like those ships that pass in the night.*
> *There's a boat on the line where the sea meets the sky,*

There's another that rides far behind;
And it seems you and I are like strangers
A wide ways apart as we drift on through time.
He said, it's harder now, we're far away,
We only read you when you write;
We're two ships that pass in the night. . . . [13]

Dad, it is possible you've gotten overly committed, so involved in your work or some away-from-home project or hobby that it is draining your time and energy with your family. I understand, believe me, I do. Maybe it is hard for you to come up close and be vulnerable, even with your kids. You may really prefer "Father" to "Pop" or "Dad." Again, I can't fault you for the way you've been put together. You can't be someone you're not . . . nor should you try to fake it. But surely between a distant patriarch and a down-home, easy-goin' daddy there's a common ground . . . a place to meet, time to be, room to hear, to feel, to care, to touch. Yes, I'm pleading.

How easy to get squeezed into a system that began with the Industrial Revolution. A mass migration brought people from quiet, family-oriented farms to busy cities, big factories, and tight living quarters. Urban fathers left home early and returned late. By the mid-twentieth century, even the grandfathers, once the revered, wise sages of homesteads, were shunted off to retirement villages or old folks' homes. Imperceptibly, dads have become shadows in dark rooms, leaving home before dawn and returning after bedtime.

Instead of challenging fathers to give of themselves, the system encourages them to give the stuff their increased salaries can buy: a better education, a membership at the club, material possessions, nicer homes, extra cars, personal TVs, credit cards, and computers—the list goes on.

But what about Dad himself? And that priceless apprenticeship learned in his presence? And that healthy masculine influence? And that integrity which rubs off the older onto the younger? It's gotten lost in the shuffle. The Adversary has won a tragic victory, which no church, no school, no occupation, no coach, no therapy group, no hobby can fully overcome. The Absent Father has emerged. It's time for you and me to cut a new course.

C'mon, dads, let's lead a revolt! Let's refuse to take our cues from the system any longer. Let's start saying no to more and more of the things that pull us farther and farther away from the ones who need us the most. Let's remember that the greatest earthly gifts we can provide are our presence and influence while we live and a magnificent memory of our lives once we're gone.

You're not perfect? So, what else is new?

You don't know exactly how to pull it off? Welcome to the club!

A piece of graffiti usually comes to my mind when I hear such excuses: "Life ain't no exact science." Which, interpreted, means, "You ain't Clark Kent, so don't sweat it." Your family doesn't expect profound perfection, command performances, or a superhuman plan. Just you—warts and all—your smile, your affirmation, your gentleness, your support, your leadership, your involvement... *you!*

C'mon, dads! Let's get started before all our children have is a memory of us—the shadowy memory in the back of their minds of two ships that once passed in the night.

A LOOK AT ANOTHER MODEL

While we're looking at the role of the father in a family, how about the role of a husband? What does that model look like according to the Scriptures?

There's a good picture—no, a perfect picture—of the ideal husband in letters from Paul and Peter in the New Testament. Now, nobody's perfect. But guys, our marching orders are pretty clear if we focus in on these passages as goals to aim for. In Ephesians 5, Paul gives us the big picture. In 1 Peter 3, Peter moves in closer to give us the details.

No one can claim he has done a thoroughly biblical study of marriage without dealing with Ephesians 5:22–33. In these verses, Paul first speaks to wives (vv. 22–24) and then to husbands (vv. 25–33). Let's look at the husband's role and the analogy Paul makes to underscore its significance (v. 25).

> Husbands, love your wives, just as Christ also loved the church and gave Himself up for her.

This isn't complicated. The husband's basic role is adoration . . . and the analogy is " . . . as Christ also loved the church and gave Himself up for her." (I'm talking to the men here. I take a look at both the man's and the woman's role, side by side, in my book on marriage, *Strike the Original Match*, published by Zondervan.)

Coming to grips with Ephesians 5 for the husband boils down to this one question: "Do I love my wife enough to *die* for her?" The world today doesn't talk about this kind of sacrificial love. Mention it on any TV talk show and listen for the razzing from host and audience alike. But this is our role—loving our wives enough to die for them. And Christ's willing death for the church He loved is our example.

In the first nine verses of 1 Peter 3, there are practical suggestions for the wife (vv. 1–6), the husband (v. 7), and a brief wrap-up (vv. 8–9). Again, we center in on the verses penned for the husband (vv. 7–9):

> You husbands likewise, live with your wives in an understanding way, as with a weaker vessel, since she is a woman; and grant her honor as a fellow heir of the grace of life, so that your prayers may not be hindered. To sum up, let all be harmonious, sympathetic, brotherly, kindhearted, and humble in spirit; not returning evil for evil or insult for insult, but giving a blessing instead; for you were called for the very purpose that you might inherit a blessing.

Living with Your Wife

The first instruction for the husband is obvious: *Live with your wife.* "Hey, I do! Come home every night. We have the same address, eat at the same table, sleep in the same bed, and even use the same bathroom." But that's not all this verse is talking about. The original term translated "live" means "to dwell down," and it suggests being closely aligned, being completely at home with. The little word *with* is a term calling for close companionship, deep-down togetherness.

Many a husband looks to the wife to maintain this. "My job's the office, her job's the home. I earn the bucks, she handles the bills. The business is mine and all its headaches. The home is hers and all those needs related to it." That may be the way you were raised, my friend, but it isn't the way God originally designed it for husbands. No way. On the front end of everything the Lord says in this verse, "living with your wife" is paramount. It is our task to lay the groundwork for domestic harmony, husbands. We are the ones who should be cultivating an in-depth partnership with our mates. We are to initiate the action, encourage the process.

Cynthia and I came across this truth many years ago. It began to haunt me that I was becoming much more passive (like my own father) in matters pertaining to the home. I was leaving more and more decisions up to her, unconsciously turning over the reins of leadership. It was *convenient*, frankly. I could always use the excuse of pressures related to the church I was serving or demands on my time from people in great need for spiritual counsel. It was also a lot *easier*. Being the hotshot down at the church was a downhill slide in comparison to the nitty-gritty leadership of the home. It was much more glamorous, far more ego-satisfying, and certainly "more spiritual" to care for the flock as a shepherd than to establish and embellish a partnership with my wife.

Then God shot a right jab to my jaw with 1 Timothy 3:4–5, where He writes to pastors who are also husbands:

> He must be one who manages his own household well, keeping his children under control with all dignity (but if a man does not know how to manage his own household, how will he take care of the church of God?).

See the word *manage*? It's mentioned twice. It means, literally, "to preside over, to lead," but it's much broader. Listen to this excellent explanation:

> A good manager knows how to put other people to work.... He will be careful not to neglect or destroy his wife's abilities. Rather, he will use them to the fullest.... He does not consider her someone to be dragged along. Rather, he thinks of her as a useful, helpful, and wonderful blessing from God....
>
> A manager has an eye focused on all that is happening in his house, but he does not do everything himself. Instead, he looks at the whole picture and keeps everything under control. He knows everything that is going on, how it is operating, and only when it is necessary to do so steps in to change and to modify or in some way to help.[14]

That really convicted me! Since making the discovery and implementing some changes, I have traveled to one seminary and Bible school after another underscoring the importance of the home life of the minister. Not infrequently, it is the *first* time many of the men have ever considered the vital link between their relationship with their wives and families and the congregations they serve.

It is absolutely imperative, men, that we fight our tendency to be passive in matters pertaining to the home. The passive husband continues to be one of the most common complaints I hear from troubled homes. Men, *get with it!* Your wife will grow in her respect for you as soon as she sees your desire to take the leadership and management of the home.

Knowing Your Wife

A second instruction for husbands could be put in these words: *Know your wife.* Again, this might sound like something you are already doing. The original expression, however, will help you determine if you are. Literally, the expression means "dwell together according to knowledge." The success of your dwelling with your wife, my friend, will be in direct proportion to your knowledge of her.

Knowing your wife includes those things about her that others don't and won't know. Her deep fears and cares. Her disappointments as well as her expectations. Her scars and secrets and also her thoughts and dreams. That's *knowing* your wife. It calls for a sensitive spirit, a willingness to be involved, to listen, to communicate, to care. Husbands—if your marriage is eroding, this is one of the most important issues you can give yourself to. It will do as much to heal her hurts and calm the storm as anything I could suggest. Your wife longs to be understood and to know you desire that.

Honoring Your Wife

Finally, Peter says, *honor your wife.*

. . . and grant her honor as a fellow heir of the grace of life (1 Peter 3:7).

The term rendered "grant" means "to assign," and here the husband "assigns" her a place of honor. Interestingly, the term "honor" and the previously used word "precious" are from the same Greek root. Husband, what place have you "assigned" your wife? Maybe you really value her and appreciate her. It's quite likely you genuinely view her as a precious treasure, a person you might esteem and honor.

Does *she* know it? Have you told her? Do you demonstrate that honor you claim to have for her? Guys like us tend to assume our wives know how much they mean to us. But there is nothing like telling her. Sometimes with well-chosen words. Other times with flowers. With small, elegant gifts. With letters we mail to her while we're away. With little notes here and there. With a meal for two at one of her favorite spots. With a surprise weekend trip where new surroundings and room service and relaxing around a pool offer undeniable proof that she is significant and worth a lot to you. On the way back home, believe me, your wife won't have as much difficulty believing that you really *want* to be close to her, to know her, to honor her.

I just spent forty-five minutes on a long-distance phone call with a man whose wife wants him gone—"Outta here … now!" Through tears, he admitted he was responsible for her feeling that way. He had just finished reading the same things you just read, except, for him, it's now "too late" (his words). Let's learn from that broken man. Don't wait to become the husband your wife needs. Start now!

Relaying
the Truth

It was late afternoon when the boat's engine sputtered, stalled, and refused to restart. Gallons of water surged into the craft as it pitched on sickening, six-foot swells. The five Jaegers had done all they knew to do, but it wasn't enough. An exciting fishing trip was now a thing of horror. They were going under.

Grim-faced, George Jaeger, his three sons, and his elderly father methodically tightened the buckles on their life jackets, tied themselves together with a rope, and slipped silently into a black and boiling Atlantic.

George glanced at his watch as the boat finally disappeared—6:30 P.M. Very little was said. It grew dark. First one boy and then another swallowed too much saltwater, gagged, and strangled on the brine as they fought to keep their heads up. The helpless father heard his sons, one by one, and then his dad choke and drown. But George couldn't surrender. After eight nightmarish hours, he staggered onto the shore, still pulling the rope that bound him to the bodies of the other four. Pause and try to imagine the sight!

"I realized they were all dead—my three boys and my father—but I guess I didn't want to accept it, so I kept swimming all night long," he later told reporters. "My youngest boy, Clifford, was the first to go. I had always taught our children not to fear death because it was being with Jesus Christ." Before Cliff died, his dad heard him say, "I'd rather be with Jesus than go on fighting."

In that vivid Atlantic memory, George Jaeger had a chance to witness the impact of his fifteen years as a father. The boys died quietly, with courage and dignity. Up to the very last minute, one by one they modeled the truth passed on by their father: When under pressure, stay calm ... think ... even if death is near, keep under control. So they did, and so they died. When the ultimate test was administered in an angry sea, they handed in perfect scores.[15]

In her best-seller, *What Is a Family?*, Edith Schaeffer devotes her longest chapter to the idea that a family is a *perpetual relay of truth*.[16] A place where principles are hammered and honed on the anvil of everyday living. Where character traits are sculptured under the watchful eyes of moms and dads. Where steel-strong fibers are woven into the fabric of inner constitution.

The relay place. A race with a hundred batons.

- *Determination*. "Stick with it, regardless."
- *Honesty*. "Speak and live the truth—always."
- *Responsibility*. "Be dependable, be trustworthy."
- *Thoughtfulness*. "Think of others before yourself."
- *Confidentiality*. "Don't tell secrets. Seal your lips."
- *Punctuality*. "Be on time."
- *Self-control*. "When under stress, stay calm."
- *Patience*. "Fight irritability. Be willing to wait."
- *Purity*. "Reject anything that lowers your standards."
- *Compassion*. "When another hurts, feel it with him."
- *Diligence*. "Work hard. Tough it out."

And how is this done? Over the long haul, believe me. This race is not a sprint, it's a marathon. There are no 50-yard dash courses on character building. Relays require right timing and smooth handoffs—practiced around the track hour after hour when nobody is looking. And where is this practice track? Where is this place where rough edges cannot remain hidden, must not be left untouched? Inside your own front door. *The home* is God's built-in training facility.

That's why He urged all the dads in Moses' day to relay the truth:

> ... and you shall teach them diligently to your sons and shall talk of them when you sit in your house and when you walk by the way and when you lie down and when you rise up (Deuteronomy 6:7).

That's the plan—the inimitable strategy that makes winners out of runners. Relay the truth—diligently, consistently. One final warning, however. If you determine to make this your goal, you'll have to outdistance two relentless foes: slow starts and sloppy handoffs. Keep in mind, dads, you really don't have forever. Negligence will catch you from behind and beat you in the stretch if you let up. And don't think your kids will let you get away with faking it, either.

I just read about a salesman who knocked on the door of a run-down apartment house in a low-rent district. The mother didn't want to talk to the guy, so she told her little boy to tell him she couldn't come to the door because she was in the bathtub. Her son answered the door this way: "We ain't got no bathtub, but Mom told me to tell you she's in it."[17]

Furthermore, it won't work for you to play catch-up by dumping a truckload of truth once or twice a year. The secret of good parenting is consistency. Never forget that.

Got the game plan, now? Stay at it, day in and day out. And make sure your handoffs are crisp and sharp throughout this race against time. Relays are won or lost at that critical moment when a young hand reaches back and gropes for the baton.

Ask George Jaeger.

Doing What You Know Is Right

With big boulders rumbling across life's landscape—like Bosnia, Whitewater, the national debt, corporate downsizing, and unemployment—who's concerned about a distant, almost-forgotten pebble of the past? Like *Watergate*. Haven't we beaten that drum enough? I mean, names like Segretti and Dean and Mitchell and Magruder and Ehrlichman and Haldeman and Kalmbach and Kleindiendst are now political relics of yesteryear. The whole sick scene has been put to bed, hasn't it? Along with the U-2, the Bay of Pigs, the Gulf of Tonkin incident, and Chappaquiddick, shouldn't we be realistic enough to admit that Watergate happened, wrong occurred, consequences followed, and we'll never know all the story?

Yes, I suppose. Far be it from me to go snooping around for a few harmless skeleton bones . . . if indeed they are harmless. But if there's another lesson to be learned from that national embarrassment, maybe it's worth the effort of exhuming and examining the remains yet again.

Part of my reason for doing so is prompted by a nagging desire to learn everything possible from previous blunders. In that sense, history alone is a wise pedagogue. But another reason I'm intrigued is brought about by a book written by Leo Rangell, M.D., a psychiatrist who explores what he calls "the compromise of integrity" in his careful, articulate analysis of the inner workings within the head and psyche of Richard M. Nixon and several of his closest confidants. It's appropriately called *The Mind of Watergate*. Within the book is the transcript of a verbal investigation between Senator Baker and young Herbert L. Porter. Because the question-and-answer dialogue sets forth a basic issue worth pursuing, I'll repeat a segment of the account exactly as it transpired.

> Baker: Did you ever have any qualms about what you were doing?... I am probing into your state of mind, Mr. Porter.
>
> Porter: [Uncomfortably] I was not the one to stand up in a meeting and say that this should be stopped ... I mean ... I kind of drifted along.

The questioning continued.

> Q: At any time did you ever think of saying, "I do not think this is quite right, this is not quite the way it ought to be." Did you ever think of that?
> A: Yes, I did.
> Q: What did you do about it?
> A: I did not do anything.
> Q: Why didn't you?
> A: [After evidence of much inner thought on his face] In all honesty, probably because of the fear of group pressure that would ensue, of not being a team player.[18]

Porter's answer comes back to haunt us. How much of that whole, ugly nightmare between the break-in in June of 1972 to the resignation of the President over two years later would have never happened if there had been the courage to stand alone?

What if, for example, the fear of doing wrong had been *greater* than "the fear of group pressure"? Or—the refusal to compromise one's personal integrity had been *stronger* than the desire to be loyal to the man at the top? This quality—peer courage—has to do with the retention of the capacity to think and to act as a separate individual while under the influence of the surrounding group.

Easy to say, but hard to do? Certainly! It's one thing to write stuff like this later after the fog has cleared and anybody can see the black-and-white issues. Hindsight is always 20-20. Monday-morning quarterbacks and armchair generals have the same two things in common: clear perspective and correct decisions. But given the same pressures, fears, insecurities, uncertainties, and group intimidation at the time everything is caving in, it's terribly hard to stand pat and buck the tide. Few are the Joshuas who will stand up and say, "As for me and my house...." Especially when nobody else is saying it. Or even thinking it.

All this strikes much closer to home than a break-in in D.C. or a breakdown in the Oval Office. It's a major motivation behind experimentation with drugs or sexual promiscuity or wholesale commitment to some cult or cooperation with an illegal financial scheme. Group pressure is terribly threatening. The screams and shouts of the majority have a way of intimidating integrity.

If it can happen among the upper crust of a nation, it should surprise no one that it can happen with ordinary folks like you and me. Be on guard! When push comes to shove, think independently. Think biblically. Do everything possible to lead with your head more than your feelings. If you fail to do this, you'll lose your ethical compass somewhere between your longing to be liked and your desire to do what is right. "Do not be misled," warns the apostle who often stood alone, "bad company corrupts good character" (1 Corinthians 15:33, NIV).

Watergate is well over two decades old. But a timeless lesson lingers: It is not so hard to know what is right to do as to do what you know is right. If being a "team player" requires doing what is wrong, you're on the wrong team.

Integrity

Let's face it. People we can trust are hard to find. Ask any businessman and he'll tell you that good personnel is one of his greatest needs—and rarest discoveries. The same is true in the political arena. Or the church, for that matter. Such terms as "rip-off" and "phony" and "con artist" are commonly used against a leader or some so-called "public servant."

What's missing? Integrity.

We seldom even hear the term anymore. As a result, we are becoming increasingly more suspicious, less trusting . . . fearful of those who once received our full support.

But trust is something we must earn. Not being an automatic virtue, it is solid, authentic character learned and earned in the trenches of life, in the crucible of pressure. That's what this booklet is all about. If you genuinely desire to be different—part of the answer rather than part of the problem—in our dishonest and deceitful world, you will be encouraged by these words.

You *can* become one of those hard-to-find individuals we can trust.

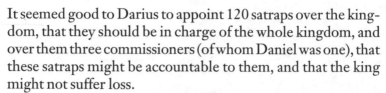

It seemed good to Darius to appoint 120 satraps over the kingdom, that they should be in charge of the whole kingdom, and over them three commissioners (of whom Daniel was one), that these satraps might be accountable to them, and that the king might not suffer loss.

Then this Daniel began distinguishing himself among the commissioners and satraps because he possessed an extraordinary spirit, and the king planned to appoint him over the entire kingdom.

Then the commissioners and satraps began trying to find a ground of accusation against Daniel in regard to government affairs; but they could find no ground of accusation or evidence of corruption, inasmuch as he was faithful, and no negligence or corruption was to be found in him.

Then these men said, "We shall not find any ground of accusation against this Daniel unless we find it against him with regard to the law of his God."

Then these commissioners and satraps came by agreement to the king and spoke to him as follows: "King Darius, live forever!

"All the commissioners of the kingdom, the prefects and the satraps, the high officials and the governors have consulted together that the king should establish a statute and enforce an injunction that anyone who makes a petition to any god or man besides you, O king, for thirty days, shall be cast into the lions' den.

"Now, O king, establish the injunction and sign the document so that it may not be changed, according to the law of the Medes and Persians, which may not be revoked."

Therefore King Darius signed the document, that is, the injunction.

Now when Daniel knew that the document was signed, he entered his house (now in his roof chamber he had windows open toward Jerusalem); and he continued kneeling on his knees three times a day, praying and giving thanks before his God, as he had been doing previously.

Then these men came by agreement and found Daniel making petition and supplication before his God.

Then they approached and spoke before the king about the king's injunction, "Did you not sign an injunction that any man who makes a petition to any god or man besides you, O king, for thirty days, is to be cast into the lions' den?" The king answered and said, "The statement is true, according to the law of the Medes and Persians, which may not be revoked."

Then they answered and spoke before the king, "Daniel, who is one of the exiles from Judah, pays no attention to you, O king, or to the injunction which you signed, but keeps making his petition three times a day."

Then, as soon as the king heard this statement, he was deeply distressed and set his mind on delivering Daniel; and even until sunset he kept exerting himself to rescue him.

Then these men came by agreement to the king and said to the king, "Recognize, O king, that it is a law of the Medes and Persians that no injunction or statute which the king establishes may be changed."

Then the king gave orders, and Daniel was brought in and cast into the lions' den. The king spoke and said to Daniel, "Your God whom you constantly serve will Himself deliver you" (Daniel 6:1–16).

A VERY FAMILIAR STORY

There are some stories in the Bible that are so familiar we have given them titles. These titles are so familiar, even a part of that title is all we need to complete it. For example:

"Noah and _____."

"The Ark," sure.

Good! Then there's "David and _____."

"Goliath."

All right, let's try some more: "Jonah and _____."

"The Whale."

"The Patience of _____."

"The Patience of Job."

"Moses Crossing" what?

Why, "the Red Sea," of course.

The "Destruction of Sodom and _____."

"Gomorrah" is the place.

One more, how about "Daniel and _____."

I'm sure you thought, "the Lions' Den." Now, I find that a very interesting title.

The book of Daniel has twelve good-sized chapters filled with events, stories, and vast prophetic scenes. But, to the public, the most familiar topic in all the book is "Daniel and the Lions' Den."

I remember, as a little boy in Sunday school (when they kept me quiet enough to listen), hearing the story of "Daniel and the Lions' Den." Two things always bothered me as a kid. First, who threw old Daniel in a dangerous place like that, and second, what had he done that was so bad that they put him in a dungeon where the king of the jungle lived? One of the reasons I was curious about all that was because I did not want to wind up there myself!

As I got older and began to study the story for myself, I was surprised. I found out that Daniel was not in the lions' den because he had done something *wrong*, but because he had done something *right*. That confused me all the more! As a matter of fact, it still confuses many Christians today. We are under the impression that when we do what is wrong, we will be punished for it; but, when we do what is *right*, we will be rewarded for it soon afterward. Now that makes good, logical, common sense . . . but, *it isn't always true*. Sometimes, when you do things wrong, you are rewarded for it (as far as this world is concerned); and occasionally, when you do what is *right*, you pay a terrible price for it. Invariably, that throws us a curve.

I had a man come to me following a morning worship service in our church in Fullerton, California, and share with me how he had done what was right on his job. He had diligently done his work. As a man of strong conviction, he stood by his guns, believing what he was doing was right. He had been both careful and consistent to do all this with wisdom. But, the very next Monday morning, he faced the threat of losing his job because of doing what was right. As a matter of fact, the following day he *did* lose his job.

That was his "lions' den," so to speak. Daniel was certainly not the last man to suffer for doing what is right.

DARIUS' SEARCH FOR INTEGRITY

Let's turn to Daniel 6—the lions' den chapter. But our interest will be on what happened *before* Daniel was dumped into the dungeon.

This chapter revolves around the decision of an exceedingly powerful man named Darius, the sixty-two-year-old king, the man to whom Daniel answered. Notice the first verse of Daniel 6.

It seemed good to Darius to appoint 120 satraps. . . .

We don't know what "satraps" means, because we do not use the term today. Some translations have rendered it "overseers." These were 120 men who shared Darius' delegation of authority over his kingdom. They were governmental officials who served under the king in charge of large sections of the kingdom. Darius set up 120 "overseers" to whom he delegated some of the authority of his responsibility. However, as soon as authority is delegated, a king runs the risk of corruption, and that's *exactly* what Darius feared, so he placed over those "satraps" an upper echelon. They were called "commissioners." Look at the verses with me.

> It seemed good to Darius to appoint 120 satraps over the king-
> dom, that they should be in charge of the whole kingdom, and
> over them three commissioners (of whom Daniel was one), that
> these satraps might be accountable to them, and that the king
> might not suffer loss (vv. 1–2).

The commissioners were responsible for the activity of the overseers. Daniel was one of the three commissioners (v. 2). This accountability arrangement was set up so the king would not suffer loss. The second verse clearly states that fact. It was to guard against financial rip-offs, quite frankly. Those 120 overseers or governors could otherwise make off with a lot of illegal revenue and get away with all sorts of illegal acts if they were not kept accountable.

And so these three men, who were apparently the most trusted in the kingdom, were given authority over the whole kingdom. What a responsible position Daniel held! He was, by this time, in his eighties. Even though in his eighties, Daniel wasn't shelved. He wasn't a useless, retired, dust-collecting, rocking-chair type. He was involved. (Was he ever!) He not only had seniority, he had superiority over many others. Look at verse 3.

> Then this Daniel began distinguishing himself among the com-
> missioners and satraps because he possessed an extraordinary spir-
> it, and the king planned to appoint him over the entire kingdom.

DANIEL'S INTEGRITY—THE MARKS OF GODLINESS

Now, I want you to study verse 3 very carefully. In our world, it's not what you know, it's *whom* you know that usually brings about a promotion. But in God's world, it's what you *are*, not who you know. It's what you are in your character. God saw fit, because of the marks of godliness—the integrity in Daniel's life—to move in the heart of King Darius to plan a promotion. Notice his extraordinary spirit. The Berkeley Version of the Bible calls it a "surpassing spirit."

Our tendency is to think in terms of the spiritual life—that he was a Spirit-filled man. That's true, but I don't take it to mean just that here in verse 3. I take it to refer to his *attitude*.

An Excellent Attitude

The first mark of godliness in the life of Daniel was an excellent attitude. Now, if you want to be a person of integrity, you must begin down deep within. With your attitude. It's so easy to mask our lives and look as though our attitude is good when in reality it isn't. One of the first places it shows up is in the realm of our work.

It's significant that there was no jealousy in Daniel's heart against those other two men who were appointed as commissioners. He could have been threatened, he could have been competitive, he could have been rather nasty and ugly in his responsibilities, because he had the longest time in the kingdom. Long before those men had even come upon the scene, he had been in authority under previous monarchs. But, because he possessed that "extraordinary spirit," the king planned to appoint him over the entire kingdom.

Let me pause right here and ask you about *your* attitude. How is it? Perhaps it's good right now, but what about tomorrow morning when you punch in at the time clock? Or what about by the end of the day tomorrow evening? How will your eight to ten hours have been? As you work shoulder to shoulder with people in your shop, in your office, among the sales force where you are employed, or in the secretarial pool, what kind of attitude will you have? An excellent attitude means so much!

You might wonder, "Will my boss notice if I have a good attitude?" Don't worry about that. He'll stumble all over it! He'll be amazed by it. In fact, he'll be *terribly* impressed. Maybe I should warn you ahead of time—your trouble won't come from your employer. Your main troubles will come from your fellow workers, who are often lazy and dishonest and bothered that you're not like them. And because you won't be like they are, you will discover they will become envious and jealous and so petty that you might even begin to endure what Daniel experienced.

Read on and you'll see that's exactly what happened. Look at the plot that took place against our eighty-year-old friend. First, there were attempted accusations:

> Then the commissioners [that is, the other two—Daniel's peers] and the satraps began trying to find a ground of accusation against Daniel in regard to government affairs . . . (v. 4).

Now, isn't that significant? Here's a man who was doing a splendid job, who had an excellent attitude, and who was apparently working very hard for his superior and among his peers. And yet those who were working around him and under him set up a spying program against him. They began to search for something they could use as accusations against him. It says they searched in the realm of "government affairs." And what did they find? Well, verse 4 continues:

> . . . they could find no ground of accusation or evidence of corruption. . . .

Wow! How would you like *your* work to come under that kind of close scrutiny? I mean, out there where you make a living—not the way you are on Sunday, but the way you are where you earn your living. How would you make out if for some reason a group of secret investigators began to examine your work? What would they find? Would it make you nervous? Would you have to burn or destroy some evidence? Or hide some of the skeletons you have tucked away in the closet? Daniel was investigated to see if they could find *anything* with regard to his work—that's government affairs—in the realm of occupation. And the remarkable thing is that they could not find one ground of accusation. They could not find one shred of damaging evidence . . . no corruption! That's not only remarkable, today it seems impossible.

Some of us are going through a time of real rethinking about our total trust in government. We who love this country and love it dearly (and would fight to the last day to preserve it) are becoming increasingly more concerned about integrity at the higher levels of our government. I think it speaks with immediate relevance when it says that Daniel was not found guilty of any accusation or corruption.

Faithful in His Work

Here is the second mark of godliness: Daniel was faithful in his work. Now, be careful here. We often use the word *faithful* only as it relates to the spiritual life, the religious life. But it's not talking about faithfulness at church or in the temple, as if referring to worship. They are investigating *his occupation*. They are looking for something they could criticize in his faithfulness at work. This passage says that when Daniel was investigated, he was found to be faithful in his work. There was an absence of negligence. The Berkeley Version of the Bible says he was faithful "in the discharge of his official duties" (Daniel 6:4).

Look at Proverbs 20:6–7. Verse 6 reads:

Many a man proclaims his own loyalty, but who can find a trustworthy man?

It's asked with the answer in mind. Trustworthiness is rare. Only on very few occasions will you find an individual who is completely trustworthy. I had a man tell me recently that in his business it isn't the public that gives him trouble; it's his employees. It isn't just the public that steals his goods; it's often those who work for him. It has come to the place where many an employer will no longer hire a Christian! As a matter of fact, when we were living in Texas, we were close friends with the president of a bank, and the highest risk for bank loans were preachers! Isn't that significant? Those who gave our banker friend the most difficulty were those who were engaged continually in the ministry of God's Word.

It's time again to appraise your personal life. Are you trustworthy? Can others count on you to get the job done when the boss isn't around? Are you a faithful employee?

Verse 7 goes on to say:

A righteous man who walks in his integrity—how blessed are his sons after him.

A righteous man walks where? He walks in his *integrity*. Now, that's what Daniel 6 is talking about. Daniel was faithful in his work. There was no negligence, no corruption found in him. What a man! Faithful in his work.

Personal Purity

I find in the last part of Daniel 6:4 yet another mark of godliness: personal purity. A life of purity that can stand up under the most intense scrutiny. Today, we would say that they "tailed" Daniel. They followed him, spied on him, searched through his personal effects, and they discovered after that examination that there was nothing lacking. No hanky-panky. No hidden dirt. Zero! He was a man of personal purity. They could dig all they wished and Daniel came out smelling like a rose.

Wouldn't you love to hire a person like that? Wouldn't that be great? I am continually hearing from employers that their number one problem is personnel; that is, finding trustworthy personnel. I mean through and through.

Some time ago, I heard about a fellow in Long Beach who went into a fried chicken place to get some chicken for himself and the young lady he was with. She waited in the car while he went in to pick up the chicken. Inadvertently, the manager of the store handed the guy the box in which he had placed the proceeds of the day instead of the box of chicken. You see, he was going to make a deposit and had camouflaged it by putting the money in a fried chicken box.

The fellow took his box, went back to the car, and the two of them drove away. When they got to the park and opened the box, they discovered they had a box full of money. Now that's a very vulnerable moment for the average individual. He realized there must have been a mistake, so he got back in the car and drove back to the place and gave the money back to the manager. Well, the manager was elated! He was so pleased that he told the young man, "Stick around, I want to call the newspaper and have them put your picture in it. You're the most honest guy in town."

"Oh no, don't do that!" said the fellow.

"Why not?" asked the manager.

"Well," he said, "you see, I'm married, and the woman I'm with is not my wife!"

Now, I think that is a perfect illustration of how *on the surface* we may look like people of honesty and great integrity. It looks like others can count on folks to be so thoroughly honest they'd give the dime back at the phone booth . . . but underneath, it isn't unusual to find a lot of corruption there.

Not Daniel! They found he was incredible—an excellent attitude, faithfully doing his job at work, an honest man who was personally pure. No hypocrisy. Nothing to hide.

Now, that so frustrated those who were investigating him that verse 5 tells us they set up a devastating plan. After their earlier plot began to run its course and they couldn't find an accusation, they then determined to do something worse. They would have an injunction written against him.

Notice how they appealed to the vanity of the king.

> Then these men said, "We shall not find any ground of accusation against this Daniel unless we find it against him with regard to the law of his God" (Daniel 6:5).

One thing they had discovered about Daniel when they investigated him was that he was a man of God. They said, "Look, this man is so consistent in his walk that the only place we're going to trip him up is to use his faith in God against him." Go on to the next verse:

> Then these commissioners and satraps came by agreement to the king . . . (v. 6).

Interesting, "by agreement." It was all a conspiracy. It was a well-planned program to sell Daniel down the river. Then they appealed to the vanity of the king.

King Darius, live forever! All the commissioners of the kingdom . . . have consulted together. . . .

Wait a minute! That's a lie!! All but *one* of the commissioners of the kingdom. Daniel didn't know anything about it, but they acted as though Daniel was part of this plan. Here's the way it reads:

> "All the commissioners of the kingdom, the prefects and the satraps, the high officials and the governors have consulted together that the king should establish a statute and enforce an injunction that anyone who makes a petition to any god or man besides you, O king, for thirty days, shall be cast into the lions' den" (v. 7).

Now, *that* is the basis of the lions' den. By the way, they didn't want to throw him in a fiery furnace, because they were Zoroastrians by faith. That religion believed fire to be sacred, and to have cremated him would have been to make a god out of him. So many who dedicated their living being to fire did it as a worship to the gods. They didn't want to put him into a fire, because that would be worshiping their god through sacrifice. So they said, "Let's put into a den of lions anyone who doesn't worship Darius for thirty days." How interesting.

Many years ago, there was a program on television entitled, "Queen for a Day." You may remember that the lady who won got top treatment for that entire day! Well, in this case, they were suggesting that Darius be made "God of the Month"! That's exactly what they said. "For these thirty days, if anybody worships anyone else but you, O king, they will be thrown into the lions' den." How flatteringly cruel!

> "Now, O king, establish the injunction and sign the document so that it may not be changed, according to the law of the Medes and Persians ..." (v. 8).

We have that same phrase today. You know how it goes: "the law of the Medes and Persians"—it will never be changed.

"'... which may not be revoked.' Therefore King Darius signed the document." That is, the injunction. Darius thought it was a great idea. Naturally, he would. Now what happens? Don't forget that our man Daniel isn't deserving of *any* of this. This sneaky conspiracy against him was because he had done what was right, remember? Now, verse 10:

> When Daniel knew that the document was signed....

That's significant. He knew nothing of it until the document was signed. Dirty deal! Not only had they tried raking through his life to find some slipup in his service record, but they concocted a law that Daniel's honest and pure lifestyle would automatically violate. And they did it behind his back. Some reward for having nothing to hide!

Consistent Walk with God

But suddenly we learn what Daniel did when he heard that the document was signed.

> Now when Daniel knew that the document was signed, he entered his house (now in his roof chamber he had windows open toward Jerusalem); and he continued kneeling on his knees

three times a day, praying and giving thanks before his God, as he had been doing previously (v. 10).

I submit to you, that's an incredible response to one's own death warrant. I find here his fourth mark of godliness—his consistent walk with God.

I think the last part of that verse is the most remarkable: ". . . as he had been doing previously."

Daniel did not turn to prayer in panic. He had been consistently on his knees three times a day before his God, day in, day out, year after year. By the way, remember, he was one of the top officials in the land, yet he had time with God regularly. The psalmist writes:

> Evening, and morning, and at noon, will I pray, and cry aloud: and he shall hear my voice (Psalm 55:17 KJV).

Isn't that a great verse? Evening, morning, noon, I will pray. Daniel was no stranger to prayer. But still he didn't flaunt the fact that he was a man of prayer. Notice his windows were *already* open. He didn't suddenly bang them open so that everyone would know he was praying and be impressed with his piety.

There was an advertisement some time ago from one of the airlines. It said, "When you've got it, flaunt it." That may work for an airline, but it doesn't work for an authentic man or woman of God. When you've got it, you *don't* flaunt it. Why? Because when you flaunt it, you really don't have it.

Daniel just quietly walked up to the chamber in his home and again before God he poured out his fear, his concern, his future, his life. Daniel is phenomenal. Just very near unreal. We Christians have a low threshold of pain, don't we? When things run along pretty well, we can stay fairly consistent; but a little ripple comes in the water, and we plunge! We pray at those times, but they are usually panic prayers, "Help-me-out-of-this-mess" prayers. Not Daniel! The remarkable thing about him is that he simply went back to God as before. I think if they had had an electrocardiogram, it would have read just the same as always, like those astronauts of years gone by. Just before the blastoff, scientists and medical specialists did an electrocardiogram on them and the results were just like the morning before when they were having breakfast. "What else is new? Going around the earth, ho hum." And off they went.

And Daniel? "Well, what else is new? What do you expect from the world?" So he heard about this news and he just went right back to God and told God about them. He had a place to meet. By the way, will you observe that he got on his knees. I want to suggest that kneeling is a good way to pray, because it's *uncomfortable*. Our problem is that we pray in such a comfortable position that we just sort of drift off after a few sentences. Try that. Jim Elliot has said:

> God is still on His throne and man is still on his footstool. There's only a knee's distance in between.

How is *your* time in prayer? What does it take to get you on your knees? A tragedy? A real emergency? This man had been doing this as a habit of his life. He had a place to meet with God and he met. He consistently kept his life and his burdens at the throne. Please don't excuse yourself because you're too busy. Not a person reading this page is busier than Daniel could have been as one of the three top men in the country. You can't get busier than that. But somehow, his consistent walk with God was so important, he simply stayed before His presence. I don't think he spent hours there, but I think he spent significant periods of time just punctuating his needs of the day, week in and week out.

INTEGRITY: HOW TO DEVELOP IT

Let's review the marks of Daniel's godliness: He had an excellent attitude. He was faithful at work. He maintained a high level of personal purity. He had a consistent walk with God.

The public arrest came as the result of that godly life.

> Then these men came by agreement and found Daniel making petition and supplication before his God (Daniel 6:11).

Isn't that significant? They interrupted him in prayer. That's where they found him "doing wrong." And the final result? The lions' den, that's what.

> Then the king gave orders, and Daniel was brought in and cast into the lions' den (Daniel 6:16a).

How about that? A more godly influence could not be found in the entire kingdom of Persia, and he was the man who was thrown into the lions' den. A man with four great marks of godliness was dumped into the dungeon.

As we wrap up our thoughts on this passage, let me share with you three lessons that I have learned.

1. *You will seldom get what you deserve from people, so don't expect it.* That applies to both criticism and honor. When you are genuinely deserving of honor, you will seldom get it from people; and when you are genuinely deserving of criticism, you will seldom get it as you should. You will seldom get direct confrontation at the time you need it. Usually, when you do receive it, you'll get it at the wrong time. When the world administers its reproach, it's frequently wrong. You'll get promoted when you don't deserve it. You'll even get demoted when it isn't fair. You'll seldom get what you deserve from people, so don't expect it. Perhaps because Daniel knew this, he wasn't blown away when his enemies accused him.

2. *You will always get what is best from God, so don't doubt it.* The interesting thing about it is that it won't come in the package you expect, and it usually will be delivered late according to your timing expectations. God plans His best for us . . . and then He delivers it according to His timescale.

You'll seldom get what you deserve from people. Don't expect it. You will always get what is best from God. Don't doubt it, even though it may come slowly.

3. *Your ability to handle both is directly related to the consistency of your walk with the Lord.* And that's the crux of this entire story. Daniel could handle the final blow, because he had been consistently walking with God. You cannot handle the honors, nor can you handle the attacks if your walk with God is inconsistent. You will begin to think you really are deserving of honor or you will begin to doubt in the midst of a trial because you think you are deserving of something else.

Dr. Ralph Byron is one of the most interesting and outstanding Christian surgeons in the Los Angeles area. Early in his medical profession he sought for a way to make life count. Professionally and personally, he wanted to be a man of God. One day in his search for godliness, he came across Ezekiel 22:30:

> And I searched for a man among them who should build up the wall and stand in the gap before Me for the land, that I should not destroy it; but I found no one.

Dr. Byron pondered this kind of question: "Would God find me standing in the gap?" Here he was a young surgeon with the press of responsibility all around him, and he answered the question honestly, "No, not right now." He concluded that in order for him to be a man of God, he must continually place a priority on prayer. At first, it was very difficult, because his duties were numerous. He decided that in order for him to have time with God, he would personally have to get up very early. He set aside the time of 5:30 A.M., which he called "an unearthly hour." But he did it. It was the best time, in light of his busy schedule. Week after week. The remarkable thing he discovered was that within just two weeks, he began to have a quality of life he had never known before. He saw two men trust Christ. He discovered that a major conflict in their church had been resolved—*dissolved* is a better word—as he committed it faithfully to God in prayer. And so he concluded, "It was apparent to me that I must give prayer top priority, even if it means getting less than six hours of sleep every night."

Now, I'm not demanding, necessarily, that you get up at 5:00 or 5:30 every morning. Some of us function a lot better later on and are a lot more effective when we are wide awake. It's not the time of day that's important, it's that *there is a top priority every day for God.* That's what this is all about. We don't read that Daniel got up at 3:00 in the morning and prayed until daybreak. We just read that he prayed three times a day. There was a priority for prayer in his life.

If the truth were known, in many of our lives, there is not that priority, and I freely confess that it has not been on a number of occasions in my own life. At one of those "low tide" experiences in my life, I saw this quotation hanging on a wall:

> When you're faced with a busy day, save precious time by skipping your devotions.
> Signed, Satan.

That's what some of you have done, isn't it? That's why you are very relieved to know it was Daniel who was placed into the lions' den and not you, right?

Have you come to the place in your life where you are not getting what you deserve from people? If the truth were known, some of you could say, "That's the story of my life. I have been misunderstood; I have been misused; I have been wrongly criticized."

It's time to take account of God's hand in your life. Some of you have begun to doubt it. Some of you have begun to let the busy day crowd out your time with God. You can't remember the last time you had a meaningful encounter on your knees, apart from an emergency. No wonder you're having trouble with relationships! No wonder your attitude is poor at work! No wonder you're suffering from this emptiness of heart at home, at work, within yourself!

Daniel had no corner on integrity. The marks of godliness are available to you. Make plans to meet with God. Don't announce it, just do it. Be consistent. Watch it work.

The Lonely Hitchhiker

Everybody says they want it, but most people run right by it. Contentment is the lonely hitchhiker back somewhere in the rearview mirror as the transfixed driver hurdles by on the expressway. Few bother to notice they've sped past the very thing they kept saying they were looking for. And even if they did notice a blurred object in their peripheral vision, there was really no time to slow down and investigate. Went by too fast. And the traffic moves on.

Books on contentment decorate the windows of a thousand bookstores. And keep right on selling. Isn't it strange that we need a book to help us experience what ought to come naturally? No, not really. Not when you've been programmed to compete, achieve, increase, fight, and worry your way up the so-called "ladder of success" (which few can even define). Not when you've worshiped at the shrine of PROMOTION since infancy. Not when you've served all your life as a galley slave on the ship of *Public Opinion*. To you, contentment is the unknown "X" in life's equation. It is as strange to you as living in an igloo or raising a rhinoceros in your backyard.

Face it. You and I are afraid that if we open the door of contentment, two belligerent guests will rush in—loss of prestige and laziness. We really believe that "getting to the top" is worth *any* sacrifice. To proud Americans, contentment is something to be enjoyed between birth and kindergarten, retirement and the rest home, or (and this will hurt) among "those who have no ambition."

Stop and think. A young man with keen mechanical skills and little interest in academics is often counseled against being contented to settle for a trade right out of high school. A teacher who is competent, contented, and fulfilled in the classroom is frowned upon if she turns down an offer to become principal. The owner of *El Taco Loco* on the corner has a packed-out joint everyday—and is happy in his soul, contented in his spirit. But chances are, selfish ambition won't let him rest until he opens ten other places and gets rich—leaving contentment in the lower drawer of forgotten dreams. A man who serves as an assistant (or any support personnel in a ministry, company, or the military) frequently wrestles with feelings of discontent until he or she is promoted to the top rung of the scale—regardless of personal capabilities.

Illustrations are legion. This applies to nuclear scientists, plumbers or cops, engineers or seminary students, caretakers or carpet layers, artists or waiters. This ridiculous pattern would be hilarious if it weren't so tragic . . . and common. Small wonder so many get frostbitten amidst the winter of their discontent.

"Striving to better, oft we mar what's well," wrote ye olde Shakespeare.[19] It's a curious fact that when people are free to do as they please, they usually imitate each other. I seriously fear we are rapidly becoming a nation of discontented, incompetent marionettes, dangling from strings manipulated by the same dictatorial puppeteer.

Listen to Jesus: ". . . be content with your wages" (Luke 3:14b).

Hear Paul: "I am well content with weaknesses . . . if we have food and covering . . . be content!" (2 Corinthians 12:10; 1 Timothy 6:8).

And another apostle: ". . . let your life be free . . . being content with what you have" (Hebrews 13:5).

Now I warn you—this isn't easy to implement. You'll be outnumbered and outvoted. You'll have to fight the urge to conform. Even the greatest of all apostles admitted, "I have learned to be content" (Philippians 4:11). It's a learning process, often quite painful. And it isn't very enjoyable marching out of step until you are convinced you are listening to the right drummer.

When you are fully convinced, two things will happen: (1) Your strings will be cut, and (2) you'll be free, indeed! And funny thing: You'll find that lonely hitchhiker you left miles back sitting in the passenger seat right beside you . . . smiling every mile of the way.

The Gift
That Lives On

In our pocket of society, where pampered affluence is rampant, we are often at a loss to know what kind of gifts to buy our friends and loved ones on special occasions. For some people (especially those who "have everything") the standard gift won't cut it. Nothing in the shopping mall catches our fancy.

I have a suggestion. It may not seem that expensive or sound very novel, but believe me, it works every time. It's one of those gifts that has great value but no price tag. It can't be lost, nor will it ever be forgotten. No problem with size either. It fits all shapes, any age, and every personality. This ideal gift is *yourself*. In your quest for character, don't forget the value of unselfishness.

That's right, give some of yourself away.

Give an hour of your time to someone who needs you. Give a note of encouragement to someone who is down. Give a hug of affirmation to someone in your family. Give a visit of mercy to someone who is laid aside. Give a meal you prepared to someone who is sick. Give a word of compassion to someone who just lost a mate. Give a deed of kindness to someone who is slow and easily overlooked. Jesus taught: " . . . to the extent that you did it to one of these brothers of Mine, even the least of them, you did it to Me" (Matthew 25:40).

Teddy Stallard certainly qualified as "one of the least." Disinterested in school. Musty, wrinkled clothes; hair never combed. One of those kids in school with a deadpan face, expressionless—sort of a glassy, unfocused stare. When Miss Thompson spoke to Teddy, he always answered in monosyllables. Unattractive, unmotivated, and distant, he was just plain hard to like. Even though his teacher said she loved all in her class the same, down inside she wasn't being completely truthful.

Whenever she marked Teddy's papers, she got a certain perverse pleasure out of putting *X's* next to the wrong answers, and when she put the *F's* at the top of the papers, she always did it with a flair. She should have known better; she had Teddy's records and she knew more about him than she wanted to admit. The records read:

1st Grade: Teddy shows promise with his work and attitude, but poor home situation.

2nd Grade: Teddy could do better. Mother is seriously ill. He' receives little help at home.

3rd Grade: Teddy is a good boy but too serious. He is a slow learner. His mother died this year.

4th Grade: Teddy is very slow, but well-behaved. His father shows no interest.

Christmas came, and the boys and girls in Miss Thompson's class brought her Christmas presents. They piled their presents on her desk and crowded around to watch her open them. Among the presents there was one from Teddy Stallard. She was surprised that he had brought her a gift, but he had. Teddy's gift was wrapped in brown paper and was held together with Scotch tape. On the paper were written the simple words, "For Miss Thompson from Teddy." When she opened Teddy's present, out fell a gaudy rhinestone bracelet, with half the stones missing, and a bottle of cheap perfume.

The other boys and girls began to giggle and smirk over Teddy's gifts, but Miss Thompson at least had enough sense to silence them by immediately putting on the bracelet and putting some of the perfume on her wrist. Holding her wrist up for the other children to smell, she said, "Doesn't it smell lovely?" And the children, taking their cue from the teacher, readily agreed with "oohs" and "ahs."

At the end of the day, when school was over and the other children had left, Teddy lingered behind. He slowly came over to her desk and said softly, "Miss Thompson... Miss Thompson, you smell just like my mother... and her bracelet looks real pretty on you, too. I'm glad you liked my presents." When Teddy left, Miss Thompson got down on her knees and asked God to forgive her.

The next day when the children came to school, they were welcomed by a new teacher. Miss Thompson had become a different person. She was no longer just a teacher; she had become an agent of God. She was now a person committed to loving her children and doing things for them that would live on after her. She helped all the children, but especially the slow ones, and especially Teddy

Stallard. By the end of that school year, Teddy showed dramatic improvement. He had caught up with most of the students and was even ahead of some.

She didn't hear from Teddy for a long time. Then one day, she received a note that read:

Dear Miss Thompson:
> I wanted you to be the first to know.
> I will be graduating second in my class.

Love,
Teddy Stallard

Four years later, another note came:

Dear Miss Thompson:
> They just told me I will be graduating first in my class. I wanted you to be the first to know. The university has not been easy, but I liked it.

Love,
Teddy Stallard

And four years later:

Dear Miss Thompson:
> As of today, I am Theodore Stallard, M.D. How about that? I wanted you to be the first to know. I am getting married next month, the 27th to be exact. I want you to come and sit where my mother would sit if she were alive. You are the only family I have now; Dad died last year.

Love,
Teddy Stallard

Miss Thompson went to that wedding and sat where Teddy's mother would have sat. She deserved to sit there; she had done something for Teddy that he could never forget.[20]

What can *you* give as a gift? Instead of giving only something you buy, risk giving something that will live on after you. Be really generous. Give yourself to a Teddy Stallard, "one of the least," whom you can help to become one of the greats.

Attitudes

◆

The colorful, nineteenth-century showman and gifted violinist Niccolò Paganini was standing before a packed house, playing through a difficult piece of music. A full orchestra surrounded him with magnificent support. Suddenly one string on his violin snapped and hung gloriously down from his instrument. Beads of perspiration popped out on his forehead. He frowned but continued to play, improvising beautifully.

To the conductor's surprise, a second string broke. And shortly thereafter, a third. Now there were three limp strings dangling from Paganini's violin as the master performer completed the difficult composition on the one remaining string. The audience jumped to its feet and in good Italian fashion filled the hall with shouts and screams, "Bravo! Bravo!" As the applause died down, the violinist asked the people to sit back down. Even though they knew there was no way they could expect an encore, they quietly sank back into their seats.

He held the violin high for everyone to see. He nodded at the conductor to begin the encore and then he turned back to the crowd. With a twinkle in his eye, he smiled and shouted, "Paganini . . . and one string!" After that he placed the single-stringed Stradivarius beneath his chin and played the final piece on one string as the audience (and the conductor) shook their heads in silent amazement. "Paganini . . . and one string!" *And*, I might add, an attitude of fortitude.

Dr. Victor Frankl, the bold, courageous Jew who became a prisoner during the Holocaust, endured years of indignity and humiliation by the Nazis before he was finally liberated. At the beginning of his ordeal, he was marched into a Gestapo courtroom. His captors had taken away his home and family, his cherished freedom, his possessions, even his watch and wedding ring. They had shaved his head and stripped his clothing off his body. There he stood before the German high command, under the glaring lights being interrogated and falsely accused. He was destitute, a helpless pawn in the hands of brutal, prejudiced, sadistic men. He had nothing. No, that isn't true. He suddenly realized there was one thing no one could ever take from him—just one. Do you know what it was?

Dr. Frankl realized he still had the power to choose his own attitude. No matter what anyone would ever do to him, regardless of what the future held for him, the attitude choice was his to make. Bitterness or forgiveness. To give up or to go on. Hatred or hope. Determination to endure or the paralysis of self-pity. It boiled down to "Frankl . . . and one string!"[21]

Words can never adequately convey the incredible impact of our attitude toward life. The longer I live the more convinced I become that life is 10 percent what happens to us and 90 percent how we respond to it.

How else can anyone explain the unbelievable feats of hurting, beat-up athletes? Take Joe Namath, for instance; at age thirty he was a quarterback with sixty-five-year-old legs. Although he might have difficulty making one flight of stairs, it was attitude that kept the man in the game.

Or take Merlin Olsen and his knees. In an interview with a sports reporter, the former Los Angeles Ram all-pro defensive lineman admitted:

> That year after surgery on my knee, I had to have the fluid drained weekly. Finally, the membrane got so thick they almost had to drive the needle in it with a hammer. I got to the point where I just said, " . . . get the needle in there, and get that stuff out."[22]

Joe Namath . . . Merlin Olsen . . . *and one string!*

ATTITUDES ARE ALL-IMPORTANT

This may shock you, but I believe the single most significant decision I can make on a day-to-day basis is my choice of attitude. It is more important than my past, my education, my bankroll, my successes or failures, fame or pain, what other people think of me or say about me, my circumstances, or my position. Attitude is that "single string" that keeps me going or cripples my progress. It alone fuels my fire or assaults my hope. When my attitude is right, there's no barrier too high, no valley too deep, no dream too extreme, no challenge too great for me.

Yet, we must admit that we spend more of our time concentrating and fretting over the strings that snap, dangle, and pop—the things that can't be changed—than we do giving attention to the one that remains, our choice of attitude. Stop and think about some of the things that suck up our attention and energy, all of them inescapable (and occasionally demoralizing).

- The tick of the clock
- The weather . . . the temperature . . . the wind!
- People's actions and reactions, *especially* the criticisms
- Who won or lost the ball game
- Delays at airports, waiting rooms, in traffic
- Results of an X-ray
- Cost of groceries, gasoline, clothes, cars—everything!
- On-the-job irritations, disappointments, workload

The greatest waste of energy in our ecologically minded world of the 1990s is not electricity or natural gas or any other "product"; it's the energy we waste fighting the inevitables! And to make matters worse, *we* are the ones who suffer, who grow sour, who get ulcers, who become twisted, negative, and tightfisted fighters. Some actually die because of this.

Dozens of comprehensive studies have established this fact. One famous study, called "Broken Heart," researched the mortality rate of 4,500 widowers within six months of their wives' deaths. Compared with other men the same age, the widowers had a mortality rate 40 percent higher.[23]

Major F. J. Harold Kushner, an army medical officer held by the Vietcong for over five years, cites an example of death because

of an attitudinal failure. In a fascinating article in *New York* magazine this tragic yet true account is included:

> Among the prisoners in Kushner's POW camp was a tough
> young marine, twenty-four years old, who had already survived
> two years of prison-camp life in relatively good health. Part of
> the reason for this was that the camp commander had promised
> to release the man if he cooperated. Since this had been done
> before with others, the marine turned into a model POW and
> the leader of the camp's thought-reform group. As time passed
> he gradually realized that his captors had lied to him. When the
> full realization of this took hold he became a zombie. He refused
> to do all work, rejected all offers of food and encouragement,
> and simply lay on his cot sucking his thumb. In a matter of weeks
> he was dead.[24]

Caught in the vice grip of lost hope, life became too much for
the once-tough marine to handle. When that last string snapped,
there was nothing left.

THE VALUE OF ATTITUDES: SCRIPTURE SPEAKS

In the little letter Paul wrote to the Christians in Philippi, he
didn't mince words when it came to attitudes. Although a fairly
peaceful and happy flock, the Philippians had a few personality skir-
mishes that could have derailed them and hindered their momen-
tum. Knowing how counterproductive that would be, he came right
to the point: their attitudes.

> If therefore there is any encouragement in Christ, if there is any
> consolation of love, if there is any fellowship of the Spirit, if any
> affection and compassion, make my joy complete by being of
> the same mind, maintaining the same love, united in spirit,
> intent on one purpose (Philippians 2:1–2).

What does all this mean? Well, let's go back and take a look.
There *is* encouragement in the Person of Christ. There *is* love.
There is also plenty of "fellowship of the Spirit" for the Christian
to enjoy. Likewise, affection and compassion. Heaven is full and
running over with these things even though earth is pretty barren
at times. So Paul pleads for us to tap into that positive, encouraging
storehouse. How? By "being of the same mind." He's telling us to
take charge of our own minds; clearly a command. We Christians

have the God-given ability to put our minds on those things that build up, strengthen, encourage, and help ourselves and others. "Do that!" commands the Lord.

Attitude of Unselfish Humility

Paul gets specific at verses 3 and 4 of Philippians 2:

Do nothing from selfishness or empty conceit, but with humility of mind let each of you regard one another as more important than himself; do not merely look out for your own personal interests, but also for the interests of others.

This is a mental choice we make, a decision not to focus on self ... me ... my ... mine, but on the other person. It's a servant mentality the Scriptures are encouraging. I have written an entire book on this subject,[25] so I'll not elaborate here except to say that few virtues are more needed today. When we strengthen our grip on attitudes, a great place to begin is with humility—authentic and gracious unselfishness.

Our example? Read on:

Have this attitude in yourselves which was also in Christ Jesus, who, although He existed in the form of God, did not regard equality with God a thing to be grasped, but emptied Himself, taking the form of a bond-servant, and being made in the likeness of men.

And being found in appearance as a man, He humbled Himself by becoming obedient to the point of death, even death on a cross (Philippians 2:5–8).

Maybe you have never stopped to think about it, but behind the scenes it was an attitude that brought the Savior down to us. He deliberately chose to come among us because He realized and valued our need. He placed a higher significance on it than His own comfort and prestigious position. In humility, He set aside the glory of heaven and came to be among us. He refused to let His position keep us at arm's length.

Attitude of Positive Encouragement

Listen to another verse in the same chapter:

Do all things without grumbling or disputing (v. 14).

Ouch! If ever a generation needed that counsel, *ours* does! It is virtually impossible to complete a day without falling into the trap of "grumbling or disputing." It is so easy to pick up the habit of negative thinking. Why? Because there are so many things around us that prompt us to be irritable. Let's not kid ourselves, life is *not* a bed of roses!

For my birthday one year, my sister Luci gave me a large scroll-like poster. Since our humor is somewhat similar, she knew I'd get a kick out of the stuff printed on it. She suggested I tack it up on the back of my bathroom door so I could review it regularly. It's a long list of some of the inescapable "laws" of life that can make us irritable "grumblers and disputers" if we let them. They are commonly called "Murphy's Laws." Here's a sample:

- Nothing is as easy as it looks; everything takes longer than you think; if anything can go wrong it will.
- Murphy was an optimist.
- A day without a crisis is a total loss.
- The other line always moves faster.
- The chance of the bread falling with the peanut-butter-and-jelly side down is directly proportional to the cost of the carpet.
- Inside every large problem is a series of small problems struggling to get out.
- 90% of everything is crud.
- Whatever hits the fan will not be evenly distributed.
- No matter how long or hard you shop for an item, after you've bought it, it will be on sale somewhere cheaper.
- Any tool dropped while repairing a car will roll underneath to the exact center.
- The repairman will never have seen a model quite like yours before.
- You will remember that you forgot to take out the trash when the garbage truck is two doors away.
- Friends come and go, but enemies accumulate.
- The light at the end of the tunnel is the headlamp of an oncoming train.
- Beauty is only skin deep, but ugly goes clear to the bone.[26]

Every item on the list is an attitude assailant! And the simple fact is that they are so true we don't even have to imagine their possibility—*they happen.* I have a sneaking suspicion they happened in Paul's day too. So when he wrote about grumbling and disputing, he wasn't coming from an ivory tower. A positive, encouraging attitude is essential for survival in a world saturated with Murphy's Laws.

Attitude of Genuine Joy

Joy is really the underlying theme of Philippians—joy that isn't fickle, needing a lot of "things" to keep it smiling . . . joy that is deep and consistent—the oil that reduces the friction of life.

Finally, my brethren, rejoice in the Lord (Philippians. 3:1a).

Therefore, my beloved brethren whom I long to see, my joy and crown, so stand firm in the Lord, my beloved. . . . Rejoice in the Lord always; again I will say, rejoice! Let your forbearing spirit be known to all men. The Lord is near. Be anxious for nothing, but in everything by prayer and supplication with thanksgiving let your requests be made known to God. And the peace of God, which surpasses all comprehension, shall guard your hearts and your minds in Christ Jesus (Philippians 4:1, 4–7).

There it is again—*the mind.* Our minds can be kept free of anxiety (those strings that snap) as we dump the load of our cares on the Lord in prayer. By getting rid of the stuff that drags us down, we create space for joy to take its place.

Think of it like this: Circumstances occur that could easily crush us. They may originate on the job or at home or even during the weekend when we are relaxing. Unexpectedly, they come. Immediately we have a choice to make . . . an attitude choice. We can hand the circumstance to God and ask Him to take control, or we can roll up our mental sleeves and slug it out. Joy awaits our decision. If we do as Philippians 4:6–7 suggests, peace replaces panic and joy moves into action. It is ready, but it is not pushy.

AGGRESSIVE-PASSIVE ALTERNATIVES

Let's not kid ourselves. When we deliberately choose not to stay positive and we deny joy a place in our lives, we'll usually gravitate in one of two directions, sometimes both—the direction of blame or self-pity.

Blame

The aggressive attitude reacts to circumstances with blame. We blame ourselves or someone else, or God, or if we can't find a tangible scapegoat, we blame "fate." What an absolute waste! When we blame ourselves, we multiply our guilt, we rivet ourselves to the past (another "dangling" unchangeable), and we decrease our already low self-esteem. If we choose to blame God, we cut off our single source of power. Doubt replaces trust, and we put down roots of bitterness that can make us cynical. If we blame others, we enlarge the distance between us and them. We alienate. We poison a relationship. We settle for something much less than God ever intended. And on top of all that, we do not find relief!

Blame never affirms, it assaults.
Blame never restores, it wounds.
Blame never solves, it complicates.
Blame never unites, it separates.
Blame never smiles, it frowns.
Blame never forgives, it rejects.
Blame never forgets, it remembers.
Blame never builds, it destroys.

Let's admit it—not until we stop blaming will we start enjoying health and happiness again! This was underscored as I read the following words recently:

> . . . one of the most innovative psychologists in this half of the twentieth century . . . said recently that he considers only one kind of counselee relatively hopeless: that person who blames other people for his or her problems. If you can own the mess you're in, he says, there is hope for you and help available. As long as you blame others, you will be a victim for the rest of your life.[27]

Self-pity

The passive attitude responds to circumstances in an opposite manner, feeling sorry for oneself. I find this just as damaging as blaming, sometimes more so. In fact, I'm ready to believe that self-pity is "Private Enemy No. 1." Things turn against us, making us recipients of unfair treatment, like innocent victims of a nuclear mishap. We neither expect it nor deserve it, and to make matters worse, it happens at the worst possible time. We're too hurt to blame.

Our natural tendency is to curl up in the fetal position and sing the silly little children's song:

> Nobody loves me, everybody hates me,
>   I think I'll eat some worms.

Which helps nobody. But what else can we do when the bottom drops out? Forgive me if this sounds too simplistic, but the only thing worth doing is usually the last thing we try doing—turning it over to our God, the Specialist, who has never yet been handed an impossibility He couldn't handle. Grab that problem by the throat and thrust it skyward!

There is a familiar story in the New Testament that always makes me smile. Paul and his traveling companion, Silas, had been beaten and dumped in a dungeon. It was so unfair! But this mistreatment did not steal their joy or dampen their confidence in God. Their circumstance, however, could not have been more bleak. They were there to stay.

> But about midnight Paul and Silas were praying and singing hymns of praise to God, and the prisoners were listening to them (Acts 16:25).

I would imagine! The sounds of confident praying and joyful singing are not usually heard from a stone prison. But Paul and Silas had determined they would not be paralyzed by self-pity. And as they prayed and sang, the unbelievable transpired.

> And suddenly there came a great earthquake, so that the foundations of the prison house were shaken; and immediately all the doors were opened, and everyone's chains were unfastened.
>
> And when the jailer had been roused out of sleep and had seen the prison doors opened, he drew his sword and was about to kill himself, supposing that the prisoners had escaped.
>
> But Paul cried out with a loud voice, saying, "Do yourself no harm, for we are all here!" (vv. 26–28).

With calm reassurance, Paul spoke words of encouragement to the jailer. He even promised there would be no attempt to escape. And if you take the time to read the full account (vv. 29–40), you will find how beautifully God used their attitude to change the entire face of their situation. I love such stories! They stand as monumental reminders that the right attitude choice can literally transform our circumstance, no matter how black and hopeless it may appear. And best of all, the right attitude becomes contagious!

I was sharing some of these thoughts at a large gathering in Chicago some time ago. It was Founders' Week at Moody Bible Institute, the annual time of celebration when Christians from all over the United States come to the school for a week of Bible teaching, singing, and interaction together. Following one of my talks, a lady I never met wrote me this letter.

Dear Chuck,

I want you to know I've been here all week and I've enjoyed every one of your talks. I know they will help me in my remaining years . . .

I love your sense of humor. Humor has done a lot to help me in my spiritual life. How could I have raised 12 children starting at age 32 and not have had a sense of humor! I married at age 31. I didn't worry about getting married, I just left my future to God's will. But every night I hung a pair of men's pants on the bed and knelt down and prayed:

> *"Father in heaven, hear my prayer*
> *And grant it if you can,*
> *I've hung a pair of trousers here,*
> *Please fill them with a man!"*

I had a good laugh. In fact, I thought it was such a classic illustration of the right mental attitude toward life that I read it to my congregation in Fullerton, California, when I returned. Mom and a sick daughter were home, but Dad and an older son in his twenties were present and heard me read the letter. The mother (who knew nothing of the letter) wrote me a note a couple weeks later. She was brief and to the point. She was concerned about her older son. She said that for the last week or so he had been sleeping in his bed with a bikini draped over the footboard. She wanted to know if I might know why . . . or if this was something she needed to worry about.

FOOD FOR THE RIGHT ATTITUDE

Since our choice of attitude is so important, our minds need fuel to feed on. Philippians 4:8 gives us a good place to start:

> Finally, brethren, whatever is true, whatever is honorable, whatever is right, whatever is pure, whatever is lovely, whatever is of good repute, if there is any excellence and if anything worthy of praise, let your mind dwell on these things.

Good advice: "Let your mind *dwell* on these things." Fix your attention on these six specifics in life. Not unreal far-fetched dreams, but things that are *true*, real, valid. Not cheap, flippant, superficial stuff, but things that are *honorable*; i.e., worthy of respect. Not things that are wrong and unjust, critical and negative, but that which is *right*. Not thoughts that are carnal, smutty, and obscene, but those that are *pure* and wholesome. Not things that prompt arguments and defense in others, but those that are *lovely*, agreeable, attractive, winsome. Finally, not slander, gossip, and put-downs, but information of *good report*, the kind that builds up and causes grace to flow.

Do you do this? Is this the food you serve your mind? We are back where we started, aren't we? The choice is yours. The other discouraging strings on your instrument may snap and hang loosely—no longer available or useful, but nobody can *make* you a certain way. That is strictly up to you.

And may I take the liberty to say something very directly? Some of you who read these words are causing tremendous problems because of your attitude. You are capable. You are intelligent. You are qualified and maybe even respected for your competence. But your attitude is taking a toll on those who are near you—those you live with, those you work with, those you touch in life. For some of you, your home is a battleground, a mixture of negativism, sarcasm, pressure, cutting comments, and blame. For others, you have allowed self-pity to move in under your roof, and you have foolishly surrendered mental territory that once was healthy and happy. You are laughing less and complaining more. You have to admit that the "one string" on which you can play—if you choose to do so—is out of tune.

As your friend, let me urge you to take charge of your mind and emotions today. Let your mind feast on nutritious food for a change. Refuse to grumble and criticize: Reject those alien thoughts that make you a petty, bitter person. Play that single string once again!

Let it yield a sweet, winsome melody that this old world needs so desperately. Yes, you *can* if you *will.*

I was sitting at the Christian Bookseller's Association's final banquet the last evening of the convention in 1981. My mind was buzzing as I was arranging my thoughts for the speech. I was a bit nervous and my attitude was somewhere between blame ("Why in the world did you say 'yes,' Swindoll?") and self-pity ("There are a dozen or more people sitting among those thousands out there who could do a lot better job than you, dummy!") when the spotlight turned from the head table to a young woman sitting in a wheelchair off to the side. She was to sing that evening.

I was greatly encouraged to see her. I was strengthened in my spirit as I thought back over Joni Eareckson's pilgrimage since 1967—broken neck; loss of feeling from her shoulders down; numerous operations; broken romance; the death of dreams; no more swimming, horseback riding, skating, running, dancing; not even an evening stroll, ever again. All those strings now dangled from her life. But there sat a radiant, remarkable, rare woman who had chosen not to quit.

I shall never forget the song she sang that quieted my nerves and put things in perspective:

> *When peace, like a river, attendeth my way,*
> *When sorrows like sea billows roll;*
> *Whatever my lot, Thou has taught me to say,*
> *"It is well, it is well with my soul."*
> *Though Satan should buffet, tho' trials should come,*
> *Let this blest assurance control,*
> *That Christ has regarded my helpless estate,*
> *And hath shed His own blood for my soul.*[28]

Do you know what all of us witnessed that evening? More than a melody. More than grand and glorious lyrics. Much, much more. In a very real sense, we witnessed the surpassing value of an attitude in a life that literally had nothing else to cling to. Joni Eareckson . . . and one string.

Holding Things Loosely

Letting go.
Turning loose.
Releasing the squeeze.

Being better at smothering than loving, we are blown away with the thought of relaxing our gargantuan grip. Releasing introduces the terror of risk, the panic of losing control. The parting cannot happen without inward bleeding. The coward heart fears to surrender its prized toys, even though it must say good-bye eventually.

Like losing a mate or a child. Experts tell us our first response is denial: "No!" In a rather extensive psychosomatic research project, the Holmes-Rahe Stress Test, I learned that most of us cannot cope with the full blast of 300 "life-change units" in any given twelve-month period without the possibility of severe repercussions. Interestingly, among the stress experiences, losing a mate (100), losing a marriage (73), and losing a close family member (63) rated right at the top.[29] It's hard to let go. Turning loose heightens our stress.

Like releasing a dream; or allowing a child space to grow up; or letting a friend have the freedom to be and to do. What maturity that requires! What a test on our insecurity!

We are often hindered from giving up our treasures out of fear for their safety. But wait. Everything is safe that is committed to our God. In fact, nothing is really safe which is *not* so committed. No child. No job. No romance. No friend. No future. No dream.

Need some proof? Check out Abraham with his almost-adult son Isaac. Genesis 22. The old man's treasured delights rested in that boy. That relationship could well have bordered upon the perilous—if father would not come to grips with releasing son. But it was at that juncture that Jehovah-turned-pedagogue taught the patriarch a basic lesson in life.

"Take now your son, your only son, whom you love, Isaac, and go to the land of Moriah; and offer him there as a burnt offering . . ." (Genesis 22:2).

It was time to turn him loose. Abraham might have started pleading or bargaining or manipulating, but that would not have caused the Almighty to choose an alternate course. No—Abraham had to open his hands and surrender on that ancient altar the one thing that eclipsed the Son from his heart. It hurt cruelly—beyond imagination. But it was effective.

The greater the possessiveness, the greater the pain. The old miser within us will never lie down quietly and die obediently to our whisper. He must be torn out like a Cypress taproot. He must be extracted in agony and blood like a tooth from the jaw. And we will need to steel ourselves against his piteous begging, recognizing it as echoes from the hollow chamber of self-pity, one of the most hideous sins of the human heart.

What is it God wants me to do?

To hold all things loosely. That He might reign within without a rival. With no threats to His throne. And with just enough splinters in my pride to keep my hands empty and my heart warm.

Building Memories

Y ou guys go on without me. You'll have a great time—I'm sure of that. Sorry, family, but I have to work."

The place? Montgomery, Alabama.

The time? Several years ago.

The situation? A dad, who really loved his family and wanted them to enjoy a summer vacation, had to work. The press of business kept him tied to the office. But being committed to their happiness, he assured them of his desire that they take the trip and enjoy the fleeting summer days.

He helped them plan every day of the camping trip. They would load up the family station wagon, drive to California, camp up and down the coast, then travel back home together. Each day was carefully arranged—even the highways they would travel and the places they would stop. Dad knew their whole route, the time they would reach each state—planned almost to the hour—even when they would cross the Great Divide.

It's what he didn't tell them that made the difference.

The father took off work (he'd planned it all along) and arranged to have himself flown to an airport near where his family would be on that particular day of the trip. He had also arranged to have someone pick him up and drive him to a place where every car on that route had to pass. With a wide grin, he sat on his sleeping bag and waited for the arrival of that familiar station wagon packed full of kids and camping gear. When he spotted the station wagon, he stood up, stepped out onto the shoulder of the road, and stuck out his thumb.

Can you visualize it?

"Look! That guy looks just like . . . DAD!"

The family assumed he was a thousand miles away, sweating over a stack of papers. It's amazing they didn't drive off into a ditch or collapse from heart failure. Can you imagine the fun they had the rest of the way? And the memories they stored away in their mental scrapbook—could they ever be forgotten?

When later asked by a friend why he would go to all that trouble, the unusually creative father replied, "Well . . . someday I'm going to be dead. When that happens, I want my kids and my wife to say, 'You know, Dad was a lot of fun.'"[30]

Talk about a unique domestic game plan! What an outstanding model of a father who wants to be remembered for more than just the basics—the bare essentials:

"Turn out the lights."
"Did you get that bed made?"
"Get out there and cut the grass."
"No, we can't. I gotta work."
"How much does it cost?"
"That's too much trouble, dear. Let's be practical."
"Hold it down—I can't hear the news."

Oh—but there's so much more in life! The beautiful music of living is composed, practiced, and perfected in the harmony of home. The freedom to laugh long and loudly; the encouragement to participate in creative activities; the spontaneity of relaxed relationships that plant memories and deepen our roots in the rich, rare soil of authentic happiness. Couldn't this be included in the "all things" Paul mentioned in Romans 8:32 and 1 Timothy 6:17? The apostle tells us that our God "richly supplies us with all things to enjoy."

We're missing it—God's best—if the fun memories are being eclipsed by the fierce ones. The world outside the family circle is dark enough. When the light goes out *within* the circle . . . how great is the darkness.

If life with Mom and Dad has become more of an endurance course than a refreshing catalyst, then your prime-time project isn't too tough to identify. Too many of us are beginning to resemble stern-faced customs officials guarding the border rather than approachable, believable parents building happy memories. And maybe even a few crazy ones too. Don't worry, God can handle it. He's got a great sense of humor. He made *you*, didn't He?

I'd much rather my brood remember me as the dad who tossed their mother fully clothed into the swimming pool—and lived to tell the story—than the preacher who frowned too much, yelled too loud, talked too long . . . and died too young.

Impossibilities

"**T**his is absolutely impossible. No way, friend."
"Won't work . . . just won't work, period!"
"Him change? Are you kidding? That guy will never change."
"My situation is a dead-end street. An impossibility."

Do those lines sound familiar? They certainly should! We hear them almost daily. Unfortunately, we sometimes say them ourselves. Week after week those negative lines are reinforced in our minds.

In our world of human opinion and limited thinking, impossibilities are commonplace. We are fed a verbal diet of them through the media, from those we work with, and in the books we read. If we are hesitant to "accept the inevitable," we are labeled unrealistic, people who live in a dreamworld—fantasy freaks.

Here are a few words that offer another perspective. Without making foolish and fanatical promises, these pages take us back to the timeless truths of Scripture and dare us to trust instead of panic . . . to believe God more than any other voice . . . to walk confidently by faith rather than fearfully by sight.

If that sounds like the plan you would prefer to discover instead of the one you have been following, these words should bring some encouragement you have been lacking. Best of all, they will help you focus more of your attention on the living Lord and less on yourself.

When that happens, it's amazing how inevitable impossibilities turn into incredible opportunities.

We often find ourselves bogging down in our spiritual growth simply because the challenges before us look absolutely impossible. Such frustrations are not new. The one who composed this little chorus must have experienced those feelings too.

> *Got any rivers you think are*
> *uncrossable;*
> *Got any mountains you can't*
> *tunnel through?*
> *God specializes in things tho't*
> *impossible;*
> *He does the things others cannot do.*[31]

If you are not currently in such a bind, it will not be long until you will be. If things seem a little difficult today, just wait: they'll soon be impossible! Uncrossable rivers, untunneled mountains, and impossible circumstances really aren't unusual. How do you handle them? Where do you get the faith to meet them?

"IMPOSSIBLE" SCRIPTURES

To put everything into the right perspective, I would like us to begin by looking at four key passages of Scripture that address the subject of impossibilities. Two of them are in Jeremiah 32 and two are in the Gospel of Luke. The prophet Jeremiah wrote:

> Ah Lord God! Behold, Thou hast made the heavens and the earth
> by Thy great power and by Thine outstretched arm! Nothing
> is too difficult for Thee (Jeremiah 32:17).

Read that sentence again: "Nothing is too difficult for Thee."

Do you realize that whatever thing or things you're calling "impossibilities" could be superimposed over what God says is "nothing" to Him? *Nothing!*

It's difficult to reconstruct in the English language the full color and impact of the Hebrew words used in this verse. The best we can do is: "No, absolutely nothing for You is extraordinary or surpassing." The text begins with the strongest negative known to the Hebrew language. "No, nothing, absolutely nothing for You, Lord, is extraordinary." What a statement to ponder!

Jeremiah 32:27 is the second verse I want you to see.

> Behold, I am the LORD, the God of all flesh; is anything too difficult for Me?

Look at the last part of that verse a second time: "Is anything too difficult for Me?" God is asking you to substitute your impossibilities for the word *anything*. You fill in the blank. "Is _____ too difficult for Me?" The implied answer, of course, is: "Absolutely not, Nothing is too difficult for Me."

You may be sitting there thinking, *Yeah, that may be true for Christians who have a lot of past miracles in their repertoires. But you don't know my situation.*

I don't have to know your situation. All I need to know—and all you need to know—is God and His promises. He is Lord, the bottom line of life, and nothing is too difficult for *Him*.

Next, look at Luke 1:37. I want you to connect those passages in Jeremiah with this message in Luke. It is an answer to Mary's question concerning her conception. An angel appeared to her and said, "You are going to bear the Christ-child."

She asks, "How can this be, since I am a virgin? How is that possible?"

Do you recall the answer given to her? It's what we just read in Jeremiah—"For nothing will be impossible with God." To make that statement practical, the word *nothing* can be replaced with your situation. Whatever it is, it is not impossible with God.

In Luke 18:27, Jesus Christ said, "The things impossible with men are possible with God." Close your eyes for a moment. I want you to think about that which seems most impossible. You have seen and read these four promises of God. Each has said virtually the same thing: Nothing is impossible with God. That includes your river, your mountain, any impossibility. Is it your business? Or your school? Or your marriage? How about keeping the house clean, keeping up with the wash, having a ministry with others, or healing strained relationships with people? Will you ask the Lord to handle that specific impossibility, and then leave it with Him in a faith that simply will not doubt?

DO THAT RIGHT NOW . . . PLEASE!

ONE "IMPOSSIBLE" EVENT

In John 6 we find not only a familiar event, but a unique one, for several reasons.

First, it is the only miracle mentioned in all four Gospels, so it seems to be extremely significant to the Gospel writers, and certainly to the Lord Himself.

Second, it is the only account in which Jesus asked the advice of someone else.

Third, it is the only time Jesus performed a miracle before such a huge crowd.

Fourth, it is an "absolute" miracle. That is, it is not some natural thing that was altered slightly on a sliding scale. In fact, I have chosen this miracle because it seems so impossible.

John 6 begins with three words that are of importance to the setting: "After these things . . ." When you read these words in your Bible, always ask yourself, "What things?" John's account of this miracle is preceded by five other chapters, and if you suddenly come into the midst of the story it is like beginning a novel in the middle. So we need to ask, "After *what* things?"

Jesus has chosen His disciples and sent them out for ministry. According to Matthew, they have gone to every village in the area and proclaimed the gospel of the kingdom, the message of repentance. Now they are back with Jesus, tired and weary. They've preached in every nook and cranny. They are physically exhausted, emotionally worn, and the Lord desires to be alone with them and to rest. (It is important for all of us in our work—and the Lord Jesus is an illustration of this—to have times of refreshment.) He wanted to provide His hardworking men the opportunity to get away from the crowd.

> After these things Jesus went away to the other side of the Sea of Galilee (or Tiberias). And a great multitude was following Him. . . . And Jesus went up on the mountain, and there He sat with His disciples (John 6:1–3).

Picture the scene. Jesus and His twelve are alone on the mountain. They are there for some "R and R." Then, in John 6:5, we read:

> Jesus therefore lifting up His eyes, and seeing that a great multitude was coming to Him . . .

They are tired and weary, and they want to be alone. Jesus looked up and saw an enormous crowd approaching. According to verse 10, the number was about five thousand. Matthew 14:21 tells us it was five thousand *plus* the women and children. So it would be safe to say there could have been eight to ten thousand people coming up that mountain. That's a lot of folks—and a lot of needs!

Here they are in a barren place, and wouldn't you know, the tribe is hungry. And no Safeway store! The disciples don't know anyone, and they aren't aware of any source of food. It's an *impossible* situation.

But *that's how Jesus wanted it*, because those disciples are just like you and me. "Oh no, Lord. What on earth can we do?" That's the way we disciples look at it, but Jesus saw it as a perfect opportunity for a Class-A miracle. He had explained to them that He was God's Son, God in the flesh. They had learned that theory back in their boot camp days. Now was their chance to see Him in action. It was time for sterile theory to be replaced with solid reality.

So He gave them a test. The first one to take the exam was Philip. He is mentioned by name in verse 5.

> Jesus therefore lifting up His eyes, and seeing that a great multitude was coming to Him, said to Philip, "Where are we to buy bread, that these may eat?"

Philip was probably not the smartest one in the group. (I personally believe Judas was the sharpest of the Twelve. That is often true of wolves and false prophets, by the way.) And Philip was not the one in charge of supplies. Judas was treasurer, but He didn't ask Judas. Why?

Before we answer that, let's look at the next verse. It takes all the pressure off.

> And this He was saying to test him; for He Himself knew what He was intending to do (v. 6).

Jesus knew what He was intending to do. He always does! The learning process is for *our* benefit. He knows how we're going to wind up, but He doesn't put us in some cosmic time machine and catapult us to the end. He lets us grind through the experience. Remember, He wants us to persevere *through* the pressure, trusting Him during impossible situations.

So He said to Philip, "Where are we going to find bread to feed them?" Why Philip? To test him. He wanted to ascertain the depth of his faith. He wanted to determine, "Has Philip learned how to trust Me? Will Philip focus on My ability while standing neck-deep in *his* impossibility?"

I want to give you just a little insight into Philip. It makes you appreciate even more that Jesus asked *him*. Philip was the one who later said to the Lord, "Just let us see God and we won't have any more questions." Philip was the fellow who had to *see* everything. He was what I call a "statistical pessimist." He had a slide rule for a mind, and if he could figure it out—great.

How easy it is to dress up doubt in neat-sounding, logical, sophisticated garb! Philip never even answered Jesus' question. He said, "Two hundred denarii worth of bread is not sufficient for them, for everyone to receive a little."

That's not the question! The Lord had asked, "Where are we going to go to get bread to feed these eight to ten thousand people?" And Philip said, "Two hundred denarii worth of bread will not feed them." That's two different conversations: the Lord asked him, "Where do we go?" and Philip's answer was "How much?"

A denarius, by the way, was worth about seventeen cents. It equaled a man's daily wage. (How about that, you who think you have it rough.) Seventeen cents times two hundred is thirty-four dollars in our terms. Thirty-four dollars wouldn't give each person a crumb and a cup of tea.

The statistical pessimist! All the Lord wanted Philip to say was, "I don't know. It's impossible with *me*, but it's nothing to You, and I'm going to wait and see what You're going to do. You are a specialist, Lord, in situations like this." But that's not what Philip said.

The testing was not over. Another fellow, who is of still more interesting significance to us, came on the scene. His name was Andrew. He was as different from Philip as night and day. Philip saw only the *situation*, the size of the problem. He did not remember how big God is. He was more convinced of what could *not* be done than what could be done.

If you are a Philip, that's the way you are. When someone suggests a new idea, you say, "Oh no. That won't work." Or when some situation gets worse and you cannot handle it any longer, it never dawns on you to simply trust God. All you can see is what can't be done. There are a lot of people like that in God's family.

I once heard about a farmer who was continually optimistic, seldom discouraged or blue. He had a neighbor who was just the opposite. Grim and gloomy, the neighbor faced each new morning with a heavy sigh.

The happy, optimistic farmer would see the sun coming up and shout over the roar of the tractor, "Look at that beautiful sun and the clear sky!" And with a frown, the negative neighbor would reply, "Yeah—it'll probably scorch the crops!"

When clouds would gather and much-needed rain would start to fall, our positive friend would smile across the fence, "Isn't this great—God is giving our corn a drink today!" Again, the same negative response, "Uh huh . . . but if it doesn't stop before long it'll flood and wash everything away."

One day the optimist decided to put his pessimistic neighbor to the maximum test. He bought the smartest, most expensive bird dog he could find. He trained him to do things no other dog on earth could do—impossible feats that would surely astound anyone.

He invited the pessimist to go duck hunting with him. They sat in the boat, hidden in the duck blind. In came the ducks. Both men fired and several ducks fell into the water. "Go get 'em!" ordered the owner with a gleam in his eye. The dog leaped out of the boat, walked *on* the water, and picked up the birds one by one.

"Well, what do you think of that?"

Unsmiling, the pessimist answered, "He can't swim, can he?" Philip was that kind of guy, pessimistic to the core.

John 6:8 says: "One of His disciples, Andrew, Simon Peter's brother, said to Him . . ." (I feel a little sorry for Andrew. Every time he is mentioned, he is called Simon Peter's brother. Ever thought about that?)

Andrew had one strong thing going for him, however. Any man who can talk a little fella out of his lunch must have some degree of persuasion! He said, "There is a lad here who has five barley loaves and two fish." How did he know that? Well, he must have been inside his lunch sack, that's how he knew. He had probably been rustling through the crowd, seeing who had what. He approached the Lord and said, "Here are five loaves and two fish."

But he didn't stop there. He went on, "But what are these for so many people?" Too bad he didn't stop when he was ahead. He volunteered information he wasn't even asked. It is almost as though he put the lunch sack down and walked away with a shrug. The Lord didn't even answer him. Such "little thinking" turned Him off!

This is applicable for all of us "Andrews" who are hardworking and diligent, but who are shot down by the prospect of the odds being against us.

You hear of the needs of the unreached multitudes. A whole world out there is aching to know Christ. You tuck the little ones in at night—two, three, four children. "Lord, they are Yours, but what are these among so many?"

You don't have a whole lot of money, so you are able to give just forty-five dollars month after month. You begin to calculate, "What's this among so many needs?"

You don't have a lot of time. Your work takes up ten or twelve hours a day, and you think, "I often don't have but five or ten minutes for prayer. That hardly counts."

The woman who composed the hymn "O Zion, Haste" must have had the Andrews in mind when she wrote:

> *Give of thy sons to bear the message glorious;*
> *Give of thy wealth to speed them on their way;*
> *Pour out thy soul for them in prayer victorious;*
> *And all thou spendest Jesus will repay.*[32]

Maybe you don't have a lot to give, but that's all that little fellow had, and that's all Andrew could find, and that's all the Lord needed. *Just that.*

Now, the miracle. Remember the story? It's as simple a miracle as it can be. In quiet, unobtrusive fashion, Jesus said to the disciples, "Have the people sit down" (John 6:10). You see, the Twelve are going to be personally involved in carrying out the miracle, because the miracle was basically for *their* benefit, not the multitude's. He could have fed the thousands anything they wanted any time of the day, but He used the disciples as ushers.

The people sat down as they were told. Then Scripture says:

Jesus therefore took the loaves; and having given thanks, He distributed to those who were seated; likewise also of the fish as much as they wanted (John 6:11).

You can't fully appreciate this unless you understand that the word *fish* was the word used for little pickled fish, like a sardine, not a great big sea bass or salmon. And barley loaves were the size of large pancakes—flat, hard, and brittle, the bread of poor people.

Jesus took these brittle loaves and tiny fish in His hands and pulled off the impossible. The multitudes were sitting along the slopes of the mountain, and those disciples were busy passing out the food to dozens, then hundreds, then thousands!

Remember Philip, who was figuring in minimums? John 6:11 concludes: "as much as they wanted." You can just picture some old fellow who had not eaten for a long time—"Hey, Philip, a little more bread over here." So Philip brings the bread—*all they* wanted.

"And when they were filled . . ." (v. 12). That's just like the Lord. Not only does He do the impossible, He does abundantly beyond all anyone could ask or think. He gave to those people until they had plenty. He performed His specialty; He did the impossible.

The river was crossed, the mountain was tunneled, the impossible was accomplished. And to Him, it was as nothing! You'll notice that when the people were filled, He said to the disciples: "Gather up the leftover fragments that nothing may be lost" (v. 12). They gathered them up and filled twelve baskets with fragments from the five barley loaves.

How many disciples? Twelve. How many baskets? Twelve. Can't you picture Philip? He's way down the hill, his basket full. And all the way back up the hill he is saying, "I can't believe it!" It was more than they could ever use. Andrew, the "little thinker," must have been stunned!

RELEASING OUR GRIP

You know the lesson I think the disciples learned, or at least should have learned? *When you face an impossibility, leave it in the hands of the Specialist.* Refuse to calculate. Refuse to doubt. Refuse to work it out by yourself. Refuse to worry or encourage others to worry. Stand against that.

Instead, say, "Lord, I'm carrying around something I cannot handle. Because You are not only able but also willing and anxious, take this off my hands. It's impossible to me, but it is as nothing with You." Persevering through the pressures of impossibilities calls for *that* kind of confidence.

Now, our problem is that we hold onto our problems. If your Swiss watch stops working, you don't sit down at home with a screwdriver and start working on it yourself. You take it to a specialist.

What if you do work on that watch and *then* you take it to a specialist? "Sir, my watch stopped working."

"Oh, really. Let me take a look at it. What in the world have you done to this lovely watch?"

The problem is that the Lord gets all the leftovers. We make all the mistakes and get things tied into nineteen granny knots, then dump it in His lap and say, "Here, Lord."

No! Right at first, say, "It's impossible: I can't handle it. Lord, before I foul it up, it's Yours." He is able to handle it.

I remember reading an exciting book called *Say It with Love*, by my good friend Dr. Howard Hendricks. You need to read it. In the book he tells the most marvelous true story.

> We had a lovely couple in Dallas a number of years ago. He sold his business at a loss, went into vocational Christian work, and things got rather rough. There were four kids in the family. One night at family worship, Timmy, the youngest boy, said, "Daddy, do you think Jesus would mind if I asked Him for a shirt?"
>
> "Well, no, of course not. Let's write that down in our prayer request book, Mother."
>
> So she wrote down "shirt for Timmy" and she added "size seven." You can be sure that every day Timmy saw to it that they prayed for the shirt. After several weeks, one Saturday the mother received a telephone call from a clothier in downtown Dallas, a Christian businessman. "I've finished my July clearance sale and knowing that you have four boys it occurred to me that you might use something we have left. Could you use some boys' shirts?"
>
> She said, "What size?"
>
> "Size seven."
>
> "How many do you have?" she asked hesitantly.
>
> He said, "Twelve."

Many of us might have taken the shirts, stuffed them in the bureau drawer, and made some casual comment to the children. Not this wise set of parents. That night, as expected, Timmy said, "Don't forget, Mommy, let's pray for the shirt."

Mommy said, "We don't have to pray for the shirt, Timmy."

"How come?"

"The Lord has answered our prayer."

"He has?"

"Right." So, as previously arranged, brother Tommy goes out and gets one shirt, brings it in, and puts it down on the table. Little Timmy's eyes are like saucers. Tommy goes out and gets another shirt and brings it in. Out—back, out—back, until he piles twelve shirts on the table, and Timmy thinks God is going into the shirt business. But you know, there is a little kid in Dallas today by the name of Timothy who believes there is a God in heaven interested enough in his needs to provide boys with shirts.[33]

But we don't usually give God those kinds of chances. We are so totally (and sinfully) confident in ourselves that we don't give God the chance to do what He is a real specialist at doing. If something is humanly impossible, then what in the world are we doing trying to pull it off?

There's a conclusion to this subject I don't want us to miss. It has to do with "personalizing" what we have been reading about. Because it revolves around a father and his son, it won't be difficult for most of us to identify with it. The man (like many of you) had reached the end of his rope.

BELIEVING THE UNBELIEVABLE

And they brought the boy to Him. And when he saw Him, immediately the spirit threw him into a convulsion, and falling to the ground, he began rolling about and foaming at the mouth. And He asked his father, "How long has this been happening to him?" And he said, "From childhood. And it has often thrown him both into the fire and into the water to destroy him. But if You can do anything, take pity on us and help us!" And Jesus said to him, "'If You can!' All things are possible to him who believes" (Mark 9:20–23).

The only place I know of in the Scriptures where Jesus made that kind of statement is in this passage. The father looked at his son, then turned to Jesus and said, "Lord, if You can help . . ." And Jesus said, "'If You can!' Why, I'm a specialist in that kind of thing. It's impossible with you, but with Me that's nothing."

The father's response is commendable. When he realized his need to trust completely and not fret any longer, he cried out, "I do believe; help me in my unbelief" (v. 24).

Sure enough, some of you who read these words are facing some of the most unbelievable problems anyone could imagine. You've come to the absolute end. There is nothing you can do—zero.

What's God saying to you now? "All things are possible to him who worries"? No. "All things are possible to him who attempts to work it out"? No. "All things are possible to him who *believes*." The story in Mark 9, of course, is that He saves the boy's life, freeing him from this unclean spirit and providing healing.

The work God wants to accomplish is not going to take place while you sit here reading. It's going to take place when the pressure of impossibility rests upon your shoulders. Child of God, learn a family secret. God specializes in things we think are totally impossible. But being a gentleman, He won't grab them out of your hands if you insist on holding on to them. " . . . The Lord longs to be gracious to you," says Isaiah, "and . . . He waits on high to have compassion on you . . ." (Isaiah 30:18).

Your impossible situation may be a marriage that is almost or altogether on the rocks. It may be a destroyed romance that's left you disillusioned. It may be a terrible habit that you just cannot conquer. It may have to do with your work or your career, or perhaps your schooling. You may be at rock bottom financially. It may be a relationship that is now so strained and pressured that you cannot handle it. If it seems impossible to you, TAKE YOUR HANDS OFF! Ask God, in absolute faith, to take over.

Let me end with a statement I'd like you to memorize. Really. Before you press on, commit it to memory. Repeat it orally several times. It's a statement I say to myself almost every week of my life. It never fails to bring those so-called "impossibilities" into proper focus.

We are all faced with a series of great opportunities brilliantly disguised as impossible situations.

Got any rivers? Any mountains?

Back Home

Of all life's pressures, none is harder to bear than trouble at home. Financial pressure is tough, but not impossible to work through. Physical pain is bad—sometimes *horrible*—but usually not without hope. The loss of a job or failure at school may bring to the surface feelings of desperation, but this too will pass.

There is, however, nothing to compare with the lingering, agonizing, tortuous heartache brought on by a rebellious and wayward child. Too big to spank. Too angry to reason with. Too volatile to threaten. Too stubborn to warn. Determined to run free of authority . . . regardless. The rebel has one great desire in life (borrowing from Sinatra's hit): to say, "I did it *my* way."

Maddened with an adventurous lust for excitement, anxious to burst from the tight cocoon of parental control, the young anarchist creates havoc in a home before finally deciding to fly wild and free. Soon it occurs with the slam of a door. "I'm gone forever!"

At that moment, both sides feel a measure of bittersweet relief. But not for long. At home, peace returns. Along with silence. Which mates with memories. Bearing crippled offspring: guilt, grief, shame.

> A foolish son is a grief to his father, and bitterness to her who bore him (Proverbs 17:25).

If you have been there, no one needs to elucidate. The brokenhearted mom and dad need a comforter, not a commentator. It is agony at its highest peak. Imagination, like the rebel, runs wild, as worry, fear, and empathy play mental music in a minor key.

Time crawls. No word. The chill of winter and the rains of spring merely widen the chasm of silence. No word. Summer's furnace and fall's colors do little to temper the edge of parental anxiety. No word.

Prayer becomes a lonely vigil—at times, the empty, hopeless repetition of sounds struggling out of a swollen face. Thoughts are confused. And endless.

Where did we go wrong . . . ?
Will we ever see each other again . . . ?
Is he/she safe . . . ?
If we had it to do over again . . . .
How did it all start . . . ?
Should we . . . could we . . . ?

Still, no word.

Winter returns, but not the wayward. The icy blast pushes its way through windows and doors, but the phone doesn't ring and a knock doesn't come. No familiar voice breaks the silence.

And then. Unannounced. Suddenly. At the least expected moment, the prodigal comes back . . . back to where life makes up its mind: Home.

A lean profile can be seen on the horizon. Shoulders stooped. Head bowed. Long lines of remorse, disgrace, humiliation stretch across that once-defiant face. Wasted and repentant, with only a few soft-spoken whispers of apology, the wayward one slumps into the arms of the waiting dad. As time momentarily stops. And two hearts beat together again. One forgiving, the other forgiven.

And God smiles.

It happens every day.

Taking Time

Eight words are brashly smeared across the dashboard of the speedboat tied up at Gulf Shores, Alabama. They reflect the flash and flair of its owner whose fast life has often been publicized in sporting news across America. In the off-season, the left-handed Gulf of Mexico speedster resembles a shiftless, beachcombing drifter with his stubble beard, disheveled hair, and darting eyes, rather than one of the highest-paid quarterbacks in Oakland Raider history. If his profession doesn't fit his looks, his nickname certainly does. *SNAKE.* As swift and sneaky in a swamp as he is on the field, Ken Stabler knows one speed . . . full throttle.

So we shouldn't be surprised to read the saucy sign on his dashboard that warns all passengers:

GET IN, SIT DOWN, SHUT UP, HANG ON.

If you plan to ride with Snake Stabler, be ready for one sustained roar during the trip. Somehow there's this itch inside him that isn't scratched, apart from that scream of an engine and the blur of saltwater waves rushing beneath to the tune of eighty plus miles per hour. Once you get in and sit down, you have the distinct feeling that shutting up and hanging on comes naturally. Once you've committed yourself to such an accelerated velocity, nothing short of survival really matters.

All that's okay if survival is the only thing that matters. If, however, the things that make life rich and meaningful to us (and those traveling with us) involve more than survival, then speed is an awfully thin wire to hang from. In other words, if we really want some things to count, if we genuinely desire some depth to emerge, some impact to be made, some profound and enduring investment to cast a comforting shadow across another's life (your child, a friend, whomever), it is essential that we slow down—at times, stop completely. And think. Now . . . not later. Don't you dare put this off another day!

My oldest son and I were lingering in a local gift shop some time ago. Our eyes fell upon a row of large posters that were framed and stacked together. We laughed at some nutty ones, we studied some serious ones—but one stood alone as our favorite. When Curt found it, he said nothing at first, then moments later he whispered quietly, "Wow, Dad, that's good!" It was a picture of a misty morning on a calm lake. In a little skiff were a father and his son looking at two corks floating at the ends of their fishing lines. The sun was tipping its hat over the mountains in the distance. Stretching across the scene was peace, refreshment, easygoing small talk. Two wistful words beneath the border appropriately released the message:

TAKE TIME.

In my younger years I was irritated with the well-worn tune attached to the old-fashioned sounding words of William Longstaff:

Take time to be holy,
Speak oft with thy Lord;
Take time to be holy,
The world rushes on. . . .

Twenty-five years, four children, many miles and mistakes later, those words make a lot of sense. They are like the psalmist's plea in Psalm 46:10: "Cease striving and know that I am God." Or our Lord's counsel in Matthew 11:28: "Come to me . . . I will give you rest."

Eight calm words from David. Eight restful words from Jesus. How unlike those eight panic words from the speedboat!

Listen . . . please listen! Is all your activity *that* important? Is it really necessary that you move *that* fast or that you drive at such breakneck speed? Why must you say yes to so many things that should be answered with a no? Could it be that your speed, your hurry-up lifestyle, is nothing more than a cheap narcotic to numb the pain of an empty life? Does *insecurity* require of you such intense acceleration? Is it *guilt* that drives your boat at full throttle? Maybe it's just a habit you've fallen into of choking down your food, talking too much and too fast (often without thought), and simply planning too many things in your schedule. All of this communicates volumes as you ricochet through your day. People get the definite impression that the only way to get next to you is to get in, sit down, shut up, and hang on.

An incredible observation regarding Jesus Christ came to my attention some time back. Not once does the Bible report that He *rushed* anywhere. He was often busy, but never in a mad dash. And yet He perfectly accomplished all the Father designed for Him to do. When you stop to think it over, His greatest accomplishment occurred the day He silenced the message of the snake.

Sensuality

Red-blooded, healthy Americans struggle with the same savage— lust. Non-Christians and Christians alike wrestle with its presence and its persistence throughout their lives. Some think that getting married will cause temptation to flee. It doesn't. Others have tried isolation. But sensual imagination goes with them, fighting and clawing for attention and gratification. Not even being called into vocational Christian service helps. Ask any whose career is in the Lord's work. Temptation is there, relentlessly pleading for satisfaction.

"How do I cope with moral temptation? How do I say *no* when lust screams *yes?* Is there life? Can I conquer this sensual savage?" These are questions most people ask . . . but they go unanswered. We reach out for help, but we seldom find it. To make matters worse, we are surrounded by folks who believe the only way to handle temptation is to *yield* to it. Stupid advice!

The Bible doesn't dodge the tough issues. It offers plain and achievable counsel that works. It promises hope, power, and assurance for those who are weary of losing the battle and living with guilt.

Olympic hockey hero Jim Craig thought he had his hands full during the Americans' gold-medal-winning performance. The pressure of the 1980 Winter Olympics was immense for the goalie and his teammates . . . but the *real* ordeal began afterward.

People demands from all over the country increased with crushing impact. His name became a household word in the homes of sports fans around the world. Offers and opportunities were an almost-everyday occurrence. And the temptations were also frequent. A local newspaper reported:

> ". . . Craig now admits that the pace was so frantic that he developed an ulcer. . . ."
>
> Jim Naughton of the New York Times wrote: "There was the time in Chicago when he unlocked his hotel room to find a nude woman lying on his bed (Craig said, 'Please leave.'). . . .
>
> "There was an occasion in Chicago when he awoke with the feeling that someone was watching him, and glancing to the door, he saw four female hotel employees peering around the door. ('I always use the bolt now.') There was the time in Atlanta when a girl who said she had been speaking to God about him kissed him passionately . . . and then passed out."[34]

No one is immune to temptation. Not even a hero. Not even a nobody. Not even people like you and me. Lust is never very far away. And just when you least expect it, there it is again.

TEMPTATION IN THREE DIMENSIONS

Temptations come packaged in varied shapes, sizes, and colors . . . but most of them fall into one of three categories:

1. *Material Temptation.* This is lust for things. The things may be as large as a house or as small as a ring, as bright and dazzling as a new sports car or as dull and dusty as a two-hundred-year-old antique dresser.

2. *Personal Temptation.* This is lust for status. Special recognition. The status of fame, fortune, power, or authority. Having a title that makes heads turn, like "top executive" or "president" or "executive director" or even "doctor."

3. *Sensual Temptation.* This is lust for another person. The desire to have and enjoy the body of an individual, even though such plea-

sure is illegal and/or immoral. We'll limit our thoughts to this third category. Even though we shall do that, don't think for a minute that this one area is all there is to temptation. Sensuality is a large part of the battle, but it is by no means the whole story of the conflict within.

HISTORICAL SITUATION: A MAN NAMED JOSEPH

Rather than skate on the ice of theory and try to analyze temptation from an abstract viewpoint, let's plunge into the life of one who faced it head-on. His name is Joseph. His story is told in the book of Genesis, chapters 37 through 50. Of special interest to us is chapter 39, when lust paid the man an unexpected and unforgettable visit.

Joseph became the trusted slave of a high-ranking Egyptian official named Potiphar. Joseph was Jewish, a handsome young man who earlier had been hated and rejected by his brothers. They, by the way, had sold him into slavery, if you can believe it. Although a man of high principle and true godliness, Joseph became a common slave in Egypt.

Listen to the story as it unfolds:

> Now Joseph had been taken down to Egypt; and Potiphar, an Egyptian officer of Pharaoh, the captain of the bodyguard, bought him from the Ishmaelites, who had taken him down there.
>
> And the LORD was with Joseph, so he became a successful man. And he was in the house of his master the Egyptian.
>
> Now his master saw that the LORD was with him and how the LORD caused all that he did to prosper in his hand.
>
> So Joseph found favor in his sight, and became his personal servant; and he made him overseer over his house, and all that he owned he put in his charge.
>
> And it came about that from the time he made him overseer in his house, and over all that he owned, the LORD blessed the Egyptian's house on account of Joseph; thus the LORD's blessing was upon all that he owned, in the house and in the field.
>
> So he left everything he owned in Joseph's charge; and with him there he did not concern himself with anything except the food which he ate. Now Joseph was handsome in form and appearance (Genesis 39:1–6).

Potiphar had a very responsible position. As "captain of the bodyguard," he was in charge of that elite group of men who surrounded the pharaoh and other Egyptian officials with protection.

Perhaps it could be compared to our director of the Federal Bureau of Investigation. He was a respected, busy, well-paid officer. With a discerning eye, he had bought Joseph off the slave market, having seen in this fine young man the marks of maturity and responsibility. As time passed, Joseph was promoted to the very important position of "overseer." By and by he was put in charge of *all* that Potiphar owned.

Two things stand out in these six verses that give us such a clear, historical backdrop:

1. *The Lord was with Joseph.* Joseph didn't talk about it, but the truth couldn't be ignored. His master saw it. Whatever Joseph was given to do got done, and got done well.

2. *Because of Joseph the Lord prospered Potiphar.* Scripture states " . . . the LORD blessed the Egyptian's house on account of Joseph; thus the LORD's blessing was upon all that he owned . . ." (v. 5).

Promotions were well-deserved. Finally, the top spot was granted to Joseph—house steward—Potiphar's personal and trusted confidant. He was the reason Potiphar had no worries.

Let it also be remembered that this series of promotions made Joseph increasingly more vulnerable. With greater success come greater privileges and privacy. Wise is the old saint who wrote:

> We may expect temptation in days of prosperity and ease rather than in those of privation and toil. Not on the glacier slopes of the Alps, but in the sunny plains . . . not where men frown, but where they smile sweet exquisite smiles of flattery—it is there, it is there, that the temptress lies in wait! Beware! If thou goest armed anywhere, thou must, above all, go armed here.[35]

Joseph was a "sitting duck" for the appealing and flattering lure of lust. Perhaps it is because of this that the passage we've been looking at ends with the words,

> Now Joseph was handsome in form and appearance (Genesis 39:6).

The Living Bible renders it:

> Joseph, by the way, was a very handsome young man.

The New International Version says:

> . . . was well-built and handsome.

Please understand that there is nothing wrong with a man being handsome and well-built. (It isn't fair! But there's nothing evil about it.) It is like being wealthy—not necessarily wrong, it just intensifies the battle, for there will always be others who notice and drop the bait of lust—which is precisely what happened to Joseph.

SENSUAL TEMPTATION: ENTER MRS. POTIPHAR

And it came about after these events that his master's wife looked with desire at Joseph, and she said, "Lie with me" (Genesis 39:7).

Now that's what you could call the *direct* approach. The Hebrew says the woman "lifted up her eyes," which conveys the thought of paying close or special attention to him. She had been watching Joseph, imagining how enjoyable it would be to have him hold her and make love to her. With time on her hands, Mrs. Potiphar allowed lust to dominate her mind. She put the moves on this handsome, muscular young man and fully expected him to melt into her arms with passion.

Egyptologists and archaeologists alike verify that ancient Egyptian women were among the first to consider themselves liberated. Egyptian monuments offer mute testimony to the extreme laxity of the morals of Egyptian women. This may explain her bold and shameless proposition.

Joseph's response must have shocked the woman. Look at verses 8 and 9:

But he refused and said to his master's wife, "Behold, with me here, my master does not concern himself with anything in the house, and he has put all that he owns in my charge.

"There is no one greater in this house than I, and he has withheld nothing from me except you, because you are his wife. How then could I do this great evil, and sin against God?"

As abrupt as her invitation had been, Joseph rejected. No way would he yield! But how could he? She was available. They could easily have guaranteed their secrecy. He was unmarried—and certainly a man with a strong sexual drive. How could he reject her offer?

Look closely at those verses you just read.

• He rejected her offer on the basis of *reason*. How foolish to break the trust he had been building for years! (v. 8.)

- He rejected on the basis of *conscience* as well. It was unthinkable that he could violate the name of his God by yielding to her advances (v. 9).

Do you think she gave up? Not on your life. The next verse states she poured it on—"day after day." And it also tells us he kept on refusing her persistent appeals. It even says he stopped listening to her and that he stopped being with her. He stayed away.

We admire the man. He was so determined not to yield that he took practical steps to keep lust at arm's length. Smart move!

Anyone who has played with lust can testify that it plays for keeps. Like fire, it will finally burn you. Here's why:

> In our members there is a slumbering inclination towards desire which is both sudden and fierce. With irresistible power desire seizes mastery over the flesh. All at once a secret, smoldering fire is kindled. The flesh burns and is in flames. It makes no difference whether it is sexual desire, or ambition, or vanity, or desire for revenge, or love of fame and power, or greed for money, or, finally, that strange desire for the beauty of the world, of nature. Joy in God is . . . extinguished in us and we seek all our joy in the creature. At this moment God is quite unreal to us, he loses all reality, and only desire for the creature is real; the only reality is the devil. Satan does not here fill us with hatred of God, but with forgetfulness of God. . . . The lust thus aroused envelops the mind and will of man in deepest darkness. The powers of clear discrimination and of decision are taken from us. . . . It is here that everything within me rises up against the Word of God.[36]

Joseph was smart enough to realize that his "slumbering inclination" would indeed become a sudden and fierce savage, demanding gratification, if he listened to her offers. He would simply "forget God" for awhile and enjoy. No, he stood his ground.

She still didn't quit. Read on.

> Now it happened one day that he went into the house to do his work, and none of the men of the household was there inside.
> And she caught him by his garment, saying, "Lie with me!" And he left his garment in her hand and fled, and went outside (Genesis 39:11–12).

The Hebrew says he left her and fled "to the street." I mean, *he split!* He had tried to reason with her, and she ignored his rationale.

He had tried to avoid her and spurn her advances, and she refused to honor his determination to remain pure. Now the only thing left to do was run. Literally, he ran.

You may be surprised to know that every time the subject of sensual lust is discussed in the New Testament, there is one invariable command—RUN! We are told to get out, to flee, to run for our lives. It is impossible to yield to temptation while running in the opposite direction.

THE PRICE TAG FOR PURITY

We've all heard the saying, "Heaven hath no rage like love to hatred turned, nor hell a fury like a woman scorned." And Mrs. Potiphar is certainly no exception! Not only scorned, she had been humiliated. Enraged and furious, she manufactured a lie with circumstantial evidence in her favor.

> When she saw that he had left his garment in her hand, and had fled outside, she called to the men of her household, and said to them, "See, he has brought in a Hebrew to us to make sport of us; he came in to me to lie with me, and I screamed.
>
> "And it came about when he heard that I raised my voice and screamed, that he left his garment beside me and fled, and went outside" (Genesis 39:13–15).

Claiming to have been raped, she says that Joseph forced himself upon her and then ran. Her husband believes her (perhaps not completely, since he did not have Joseph killed) and locked him up in prison. Joseph did not remain there, however . . . but that's another part of this incredible story we haven't the time or space to tell.

What are the personal ramifications of all this for us living in today's world? How does it apply? Rather than pass it off with a vague "Lord, help us all" prayer, let me declare four "musts" based on Joseph's experience. These "musts" are to be applied if you expect to resist sensual temptations in your life.

1. *You must not be weakened by your situation.* Economically, Joseph was secure, respected, trusted, and stable. Personally, he was handsome and desirable. He was also in charge of the entire house, so getting alone posed no problem. On top of all that, it wasn't his idea; the woman thought it up! And he was also unmarried.

Your flesh, creative and cool as it is, will invariably remind you of a dozen ways to rationalize around the wrong of your lust. And there is a name for those who listen to those reasons: *victim*. You *will* yield if you allow yourself to be weakened.

2. *You must not be deceived in the persuasion.* Remember Bonhoeffer's words? When lust reaches fever pitch, "God is quite unreal to us" and Satan fills us with "forgetfulness of God." This is a classic example of our adversary's deceptive methods. He attempts to cancel out tomorrow's consequences by emphasizing today's delights.

Joseph could have allowed himself to listen to the wrong voice. Men filled with lust do so every day:

"Her husband doesn't meet her needs like I can."

"Who will ever find out? We're safe."

"Look, we're going to be married soon."

"I'm so lonely. God will understand and forgive."

"Just this once—never, ever again."

Don't be deceived by such persuasive thoughts. Rivet into your mind God's very clear command:

> For this is the will of God, your sanctification; that is, that you abstain from sexual immorality (1 Thessalonians 4:3).

3. *You must not be gentle with your emotions.* Look again at Joseph's model (Genesis 39):

Verse 8: *He refused.*

Verse 9: *How then could I do this great evil . . . ?*

Verse 10: *He did not listen to her to lie beside her, or be with her.*

Verse 12: *He left . . . and fled. . . .*

Be tough on yourself; boldly reject the bait! Think of it as a brutal savage, ready to pounce and devour.

> . . . Lust is committed to wage war against your soul—in a life-and-death struggle—in hand-to-hand combat. Don't stand before this mortal enemy and argue or fight in your own strength—run for cover. . . . Lust is one flame you dare not fan. You'll get burned if you do.[37]

When it comes to your emotions, be tough rather than tender. Refuse to let your feelings dominate your mind when lust craves satisfaction.

4. *You must not be confused with the immediate results.* Do you recall what happened to our friend Joseph? Even though he resisted the woman's advances, she kept coming back. Instead of those advances tapering off, they intensified. Instead of being immediately rewarded for his self-control, he was falsely accused and dumped into a dungeon. Talk about confusing!

But Joseph kept his eyes fixed on the Lord. He refused to be disillusioned. How often I've seen people withstand a barrage of temptation for awhile. Then in a weak moment fall because of confusion! The enemy does not surrender easily. Keep standing firm, even though you feel strangely alone and forgotten by the Lord. Ultimately, He will reward every act of moral restraint.

SCRIPTURAL ANALYSIS OF TEMPTATION

Three New Testament passages come to mind when I think of any temptation, including sensuality: Matthew 4:1–11, 1 Corinthians 10:13, and James 1:13–16. Each one emphasizes an important truth that helps us counteract our tendency to yield when tempted. By analyzing each we'll get a better handle on the problem.

Matthew 4:1–11

This is the familiar account of the time when the devil tempted Christ. He launched his full-scale attack on the Son of God. But Jesus never yielded. Why? What was it that gave Him such inner strength? Read these eleven verses in your Bible, slowly and aloud. You will hear yourself saying the same words three times,

> . . . it is written . . . (v. 4)
> . . . it is written . . . (v. 7)
> . . . it is written . . . (v. 10).

Following those words, each time Jesus referred back to verses of Scripture from the Old Testament—Deuteronomy 8:3, Deuteronomy 6:16, and Deuteronomy 6:13. When the Lord Jesus Christ was tempted, He used the Word of God, which He quoted aloud from memory.

Interestingly, only one offensive weapon is part of our armor described in Ephesians 6:10–17, "the sword of the Spirit, which is the word of God." The Greek term translated "word" is the term meaning "saying." It has reference to something that is *spoken*.

Let's take that literally! Christ did. He actually *stated* the words from Scripture. He "wielded" the sword of the Spirit in the face of the tempter. God honored His truth. We read in Matthew 4:11— immediately following the third time Jesus had quoted Scripture— *then the devil left Him....*

If you want to stand strong against the magnetic, powerful lure of lust, quote aloud the Word of God. The psalmist is correct:

> *How can a young man keep his way pure?*
> *By keeping it according to Thy word.*
> *With all my heart I have sought Thee;*
> *do not let me wander from Thy commandments.*
> *Thy word I have treasured in my heart,*
> *that I may not sin against Thee (Psalm 119:9–11).*

A pure heart is directly linked to "treasuring God's Word" there.

First Corinthians 10:13

The apostle Paul gives us hope in this verse of Scripture:

> No temptation has overtaken you but such as is common to man; and God is faithful, who will not allow you to be tempted beyond what you are able, but with the temptation will provide the way of escape also, that you may be able to endure it.

A close look at these words reveals something we tend to forget when we are tempted: *God is there through it all.* He is faithful. We may feel alone, but we are not alone. He places definite limitations on the attack, not allowing the magnet to be stronger than we can bear. And He also promised to provide "the way of escape" so that we aren't totally surrounded and consumed by the temptation. Left completely to ourselves, abandoned and forgotten by God, we would have no hope of victory. But God is faithful. He doesn't leave us in the lurch. Never!

I once heard a father tell of his son's first serious conflict at school. His boy was being picked on by two or three bullies. They punched the youngster a time or two, pushed him over when he was riding his bike home from school, and generally made life miserable for the lad. They told him they would meet him the next morning and beat him up.

That evening the dad really worked with the boy at home. He showed him how to defend himself, passed along a few helpful techniques, and even gave him some tips on how he might try to win them over as friends. The next morning the lad and dad prayed together, knowing that the inevitable was sure to happen. With a reassuring embrace and a firm handshake, the father smiled confidently and said, "You can do it, Son. I know you'll make out all right."

Choking back the tears, the boy got on his bike and began the lonely, long ride to school. What the boy did *not* know was that every block he rode he was under the watchful eye of his dad . . . who drove his car a safe distance from his son, out of sight but ever ready to speed up and assist if the scene became too threatening. The boy thought he was alone, but he wasn't at all. The father was there all the time.

But this does not mean that God is actually involved in setting us up. In no way is He responsible for those temptations that fling themselves across our path. This brings me to the third significant biblical passage.

James 1:13–16

James, practical Christian that he is, spells out the downward spiral that occurs when we yield to temptation.

> Let no one say when he is tempted, "I am being tempted by God"; for God cannot be tempted by evil, and He Himself does not tempt anyone.
>
> But each one is tempted when he is carried away and enticed by his own lust.
>
> Then when lust has conceived, it gives birth to sin; and when sin is accomplished, it brings forth death.
>
> Do not be deceived, my beloved brethren.

As we think over these descriptive words, three facts emerge:

1. *Temptation is inevitable.* Did you notice the word *when* (v. 13)? No way can we ever find a place that will secure us from all temptations. Not even the monk in the remotest monastery is safe. He may think he's protected, but his mind is there, ready to paint the most colorful (and sensual) mental pictures imaginable. We cannot ever get completely away from temptation.

2. *Temptation is never prompted by God.* He says this clearly in verse 13. He neither is tempted by evil nor does He tempt another. He is holy, remember. Infinitely pure. Totally separate from sin.

The next time you find yourself ready to implicate God in battle with lust, don't waste your time. You have been "drawn away" and "enticed" by your *own* lust. It's like those bank robberies we've read about—it's always an "inside job." You'll have to take the rap because you alone are responsible. Verse 14 makes that painfully clear.

3. *Lust always follows the same process.* As you read verses 14 and 15, it is not difficult to see the downward spiral:

Step 1: The bait is dropped.

Step 2: Your inner desire (lust) is attracted to that bait.

Step 3: As you yield, sin occurs. It happens when you bite the bait.

Step 4: Tragic consequences are set in motion. Like the hooked fish, we end up fried.

James 1:13–16 provides us with this thought. *Wake up! Realize that yielding to lust always results in tragic consequences.* This passage takes the fun 'n' games out of sensuality.

I find it extremely significant that the Greek term translated "entice" in verse 14 is a fishing term. It means "to lure by a bait." And anybody who's done much fishing quickly gets the picture. In order to attract the fish, the right lure is needed—with just the right eye-catching color or shape or sparkle. And it must be handled just the right way in order for the fish to be "lured" out of his safe hiding place. The more skilled and experienced the angler, the greater his success.

And so it is in life. Our enemy, crafty and clever and experienced as he is, knows which lure best attracts each one of us. Our unique inner "itch" longs to be satisfied by that particular outer "scratch." And unless we draw upon the all-conquering power of Christ, unless we consciously apply the same biblical techniques Joseph applied, we'll yield. We'll bite the bait, and we'll suffer the horrible consequences.

Small wonder James ends his counsel with the warning: "Do not be deceived."

Let's rivet into our minds these wise words:

Matthew 4:1–11 Use the memorized Word of God. Quote it aloud. Openly wield the sword before the enemy.

1 Corinthians 10:13 You are not alone. Call out for help and the Lord Jesus Christ will help you endure and escape.

James 1:13–16 Don't be deceived. The bait will inevitably drop. Do not yield. If you do, you will experience tragic consequences. If you refuse, you will remain secure and safe.

As I stated earlier, God will reward your every act of moral restraint.

TAKE CHARGE OF YOUR THOUGHTS!

My Christian friend, let me level with you. You and I are surrounded by a continual stream of sexually suggestive stimuli. The world of advertisement, the newsstand, the soap operas and prime-time television, the film industry, many of the new fashions and fads. Even much that falls within the category of the arts appeals to our sensuous appetites. Obviously, we are not called to clean up our world . . . but to be salt in it, to shine the light within it.

Salt loses its bite and light becomes dim when we allow these stimuli to hold our attention and find lodging in our minds. The longer this continues to be tolerated, the less discriminating we remain and the less self-control we retain. Silently and slowly our moral fiber erodes, leaving us an easy prey to the subtle lure of lust. Like pounding ocean waves that finally wear smooth the sharp edges of huge seawall boulders, the endless assault takes a terrible toll on our internal standards. And if allowed to penetrate deeper and deeper, these alien thoughts will find refuge within us, dulling the once-keen edge of our spiritual sensitivity.

On the authority of God's Word, I warn you: *Take charge of your thoughts!* Be extremely careful about what you allow your eyes to observe and your ears to absorb. Ask the Spirit of God to assist you as you apply a filter to everything that enters your mind. Trust Him to provide you with the discipline and discernment you will need. And take it one day at a time. If the Lord could give Joseph the strength he needed to withstand the sensual assault of a woman centuries ago, He will do the same for you today.

Take charge of your thoughts, I repeat. If you do not, I can assure you it will be only a matter of time before you fall, a piece of soft putty in the hands of lust. God offers a better way, the *only* way to live victoriously:

> . . . walk by the Spirit, and you will not carry out the desire of the flesh (Galatians 5:16).

Gumption

We don't hear much about gumption anymore. Too bad, since we need it more than ever these days. I was raised on gumption (sometimes called "spizzerinctum") and to this day I will use the word around the house . . . especially when trying to motivate the kids. I ran across it again while reading Robert Pirsig's *Zen and the Art of Motorcycle Maintenance* (now there's a great book title), as he was singing the praises of all that gumption represents. He writes:

> I like the word "gumption" because it's so homely and so forlorn and so out of style it looks as if it needs a friend and isn't likely to reject anyone who comes along. It's an old Scottish word, once used a lot by pioneers, but . . . seems to have all but dropped out of use. . . .
>
> A person filled with gumption doesn't sit around dissipating and stewing about things. He's at the front of the train of his own awareness, watching to see what's up the track and meeting it when it comes.[38]

A little later Pirsig applies it to life. Hiding his comments behind the word picture of repairing a motorcycle:

> If you're going to repair a motorcycle, an adequate supply of gumption is the first and most important tool. If you haven't got that you might as well gather up all the other tools and put them away, because they won't do you any good.
>
> Gumption is the psychic gasoline that keeps the whole thing going. If you haven't got it, there's no way the motorcycle can possibly be fixed. But if you have got it and know how to keep it, there's absolutely no way in the whole world that motorcycle can keep from getting fixed. It's bound to happen. Therefore the thing that must be monitored at all times and preserved before anything else is gumption.[39]

Seems a shame the old word has dropped through the cracks, especially since quitting is now more popular than finishing. I agree with that author, who'd like to start a whole new academic field on the subject. Can't you just see this entry in some college catalog: "Gumptionology 101." That'll never be, however, since gumption is better caught than taught. As is true of most other character traits, it is woven so subtly into the fabric of one's life that few ever stop and identify it. It is hidden like thick steel bars in concrete columns supporting ten-lane freeways. Gumption may be hidden, but it's an important tool for getting a job done.

Gumption enables us to save money rather than spend every dime we make. It keeps us at a hard task, like building a tedious model or completing an add-on or practicing piano or losing weight—and keeping it lost—or reading the Bible all the way through in a year's time. Most folks get a little gumption in their initial birth packet, but it's a tool that rusts rather quickly. Here's some sandpaper.

1. *Gumption begins with a firm commitment.* Daniel "made up his mind" (1:8) long before he was dumped in a Babylonian boot camp. Joshua didn't hesitate to declare his commitment in his famous "as for me and my house" speech (24:15) before the Israelis. Isaiah says he "set his face like flint" (50:7), which is another way of saying he firmly decided. Instead of starting with a bang, it's the human tendency to ponder, to rethink, to fiddle around with an idea until it's awash in a slimy swamp of indefiniteness. An old recipe for a rabbit dish starts out, "First, catch the rabbit." That puts first things first. No rabbit, no dish. You want gumption to continue to the end? Start strong!

2. *Gumption means being disciplined one day at a time.* Rather than focusing on the whole enchilada, take it in bite-size chunks. The whole of any objective can overwhelm even the most courageous. Writing a book? Do so one page at a time. Running a marathon? Those 26 plus miles are run one step at a time. Trying to master a new language? Try one word at a time. There are 365 days in the average year. Divide any project by 365 and none seem all that intimidating, do they? It will take daily discipline (à la Proverbs 19:27), not annual discipline.

3. *Gumption includes being alert to subtle temptations.* Robert Pirsig referred to our being at the front of the train of our own awareness, looking up the track and being ready to meet whatever comes. Gumption plans ahead . . . watching out for associations that weaken us (Proverbs 13:20), procrastination that steals from us (Proverbs 24:30–34), and rationalizations that lie to us (Proverbs 13:4; 25:28).

People who achieve their goals stay alert. Our adversary is a master strategist, forever fogging up our minds with smoke screens, which "thicken" our senses. If it were possible for God to die and He died this morning, some wouldn't know it for three or four days. Gumption stabs us awake, keeps us wide-eyed and ready.

4. *Gumption requires the encouragement of accountability.* People—especially close friends—keep our tanks pumped full of enthusiasm. They communicate "You can do it, you can make it" a dozen different ways. At David's low-water mark, Jonathan stepped in. Right when Elijah was ready to cash in everything, along came Elisha. With Paul was Timothy . . . or Silas or Barnabas or Dr. Luke. People need people, which is why Solomon came on so strong about iron sharpening iron (Proverbs 27:17).

5. *Gumption comes more easily when we remember that finishing has its own unique rewards.* Jesus told the Father He "accomplished" His assignment (John 17:4). On more than one occasion Paul referred to "finishing the course" (Acts 20:24; 2 Timothy 4:7). Those who only start projects never know the surge of satisfaction that comes with slapping hands together, wiping away those beads of perspiration, and saying that beautiful four-letter word, *Done!* Desire accomplished is sweet to the soul.

Do you desire to have the character of Christ formed in you? No quest is more important. Are you under way? Good for you! If the journey seems extra long today, enjoy a gust of wind at your back from these words out of *The Living Bible.* It's one of those spizzerinctum Scriptures:

> . . . let us not get tired of doing what is right, for after a while we will reap a harvest of blessing if we don't get discouraged and quit (Galatians 6:9).

Tough Days

You've heard them. Those all-too-familiar cries of exasperation. Maybe a couple have crossed *your* mind today sometime between the too-early clang of the alarm and the too-late racket of the neighbors next door.

Going from bad to worse.

Jumping from the frying pan into the fire.

Between a rock and a hard place.

He said, "Cheer up, things could get worse," so I cheered up—and sure enough, things got worse!

"My mother told me there would be days like these, but she never said they would run in packs."

Tough days. We all have them. Some are worse than others. Like the one the hard-hat employee reported when he tried to be helpful. Maybe you heard about it too; the account actually appeared on a company accident form. Bruised and bandaged, the workman related this experience:

> When I got to the building I found that the hurricane had knocked off some bricks around the top. So I rigged up a beam with a pulley at the top of the building and hoisted up a couple barrels full of bricks. When I had fixed the damaged area, there were a lot of bricks left over. Then I went to the bottom and began releasing the line. Unfortunately, the barrel of bricks was much heavier than I was—and before I knew what was happening the barrel started coming down, jerking me up.
>
> I decided to hang on since I was too far off the ground by then to jump, and halfway up I met the barrel of bricks coming down fast. I received a hard blow on my shoulder. I then continued to the top, banging my head against the beam and getting my fingers pinched and jammed in the pulley. When the barrel hit the ground hard, it burst its bottom, allowing the bricks to spill out.
>
> I was now heavier than the barrel. So I started down again at high speed. Halfway down I met the barrel coming up fast

and received severe injuries to my shins. When I hit the ground, I landed on the pile of spilled bricks, getting several painful cuts and deep bruises. At this point I must have lost my presence of mind, because I let go of my grip on the line. The barrel came down fast—giving me another blow on my head and putting me in the hospital.

I respectfully request sick leave.

Yeah, I would imagine!

Some days you honestly wonder why you ever crawled out from under the covers that morning—and later, if you will ever make it back to bed that night. Most of us have little difficulty fielding two or three problems during the day, but when they start coming down like hail, with no relief, rhyme, or reason, we get jumpy. More often than not we also get grumpy. Invariably, there are those who love us and really want to help. But try all they like, tough days are usually solo flights. Others only complicate matters.

Take the four guys who decided to go mountain climbing one weekend. In the middle of the climb, one fella slipped over a cliff, dropped about sixty feet and landed with a thud on the ledge below. The other three, hoping to rescue him, yelled, "Joe, are you okay?"

"I'm alive . . . but I think I broke both my arms!"

"We'll toss a rope down to you and pull you up. Just lie still!" said the three.

"Fine," answered Joe.

A couple of minutes after dropping one end of the rope, they started tugging and grunting together, working feverishly to pull their wounded companion to safety. When they had him about three-fourths of the way up, they suddenly remembered he said he had broken *both* of his arms.

"Joe! If you broke both your arms, how in the world are you hanging on?"

Joe responded, "With my TEEEEEEEEEEETH. . . ."

No, other people can't help much on tough days. They may be good companions, but they sure can't stop the pain. Holding hands and singing during an earthquake is small comfort.

Some would advise, "Just get in there and keep busy—work harder." But that doesn't help much either. When the barn's on fire, slapping a coat of paint on the other side doesn't make much sense. If the tires are flat, driving faster is pretty dumb.

So, what's the answer? How can we handle tough days when the enemy works overtime to persuade us that God doesn't care? Just recently, I have found solid encouragement from four threads woven into the fabric of Galatians 6. See if you don't agree.

1. *Let us not lose heart* (v. 9). On tough days, you gotta have heart. Don't quit, whatever you do. Persevere. Stand firm. Be strong, resilient, determined to see it through. Ask God to build a protective shield around your heart, stabilizing you.

2. *Let us do good* (v. 10). Our tendency will be anything but that. Instead of good, we will feel like doing evil. Fume. Swear. Scream. Fight. Pout. Get irritated. Burn up all kinds of emotional BTUs. Rather than parading through that shopworn routine, stay quiet and consciously turn it *all* over to the Lord.

3. *Let no one cause you trouble* (v. 17). Superb advice! Refuse to allow anyone (or any*thing*) to gain mastery over you. That throne within you belongs only to the Lord Jesus Christ. Stop leasing it out!

4. *Let grace be with your spirit* (v. 18). Allow the full impact of grace to flow through your thoughts, your attitudes, your responses, your words. Open the gates and let those good things stampede freely across your tough day. You sit on the fence and relax.

It works. It *really* does. Even at home.

Even on sick leave.

Anger

From mild irritation to uncontrolled rage, anger wears many faces and plays numerous roles in our life. Sometimes justified, often not, anger is one of our emotions that must be kept under the dominating control of the Holy Spirit. Like fire, it can either be of benefit or cause permanent damage. Something *that* powerful deserves our full attention. And God's full control.

This discussion is dedicated to helping victims of anger get a grip on the problem. Without condemning, it offers straight-from-the-Scripture counsel that is sure to help. And best of all, it holds out hope to those who have struggled for years with an internal burning fuse of hostility.

Do you need encouragement and assistance?
Are you tired of losing the war with wrath?
Have you been more irritated in recent days?
Is your initial reaction to opposition a clenched fist?
Would you rather fight than switch?

If so, these pages contain information that is essential to your spiritual survival. You *can* know victory in the hot arena of everyday demands, difficult people, and irritating circumstances. Through God's help, a new beginning can start today!

A great American statesman, Thomas Jefferson, worked out a way to handle his anger. He included it in his "Rules of Living," which describes how he believed adult men and women should live. He wrote this:

> When angry, count ten before you speak; if very angry, a hundred.[40]

Author Mark Twain, about seventy-five years later, revised Jefferson's words. He wrote:

> When angry, count four. When very angry, swear.[41]

I don't know of anything more frustrating to deal with than anger (it makes me mad!). It has a way of disarming us, of robbing us of our testimonies. It injures our home lives and our relationships with co-workers.

Some time ago a man sat in my study and poured out his anguish. He had battered his wife the night before. She was too humiliated (and bruised) to come with him. Both, by the way, are Christians.

I sat in the Orange County jail with a young father, his face buried in his hands. Tears ran through his fingers as he told me of his temper. He had just killed his infant daughter with his own hands—in an uncontrollable rage. He had been irritated by the baby's crying as he was listening to music.

No, anger isn't a humorous matter. It's something that must be understood, admitted, and kept under control, or it will literally slay us.

WHAT IS ANGER?

Let me begin by defining what anger is, and that's not easy. I've woven together several different resources and have come up with this definition:

> Anger is an emotional reaction of hostility that brings personal displeasure, either to ourselves or to someone else.

People who study psychology tell us that there are various phases of anger. All of us have experienced some of them.

Anger can begin with *mild irritation*, which is nothing more than perhaps an innocent experience of being upset, a mild feeling of discomfort brought about by someone or something.

Then anger can turn from irritation to *indignation*, which is a feeling that something must be answered; there must be an avenging of that which is wrong. But both irritation and indignation can go unexpressed.

If fed, indignation leads to *wrath*—which *never* goes unexpressed. Psychologists tell us that wrath is a strong desire to avenge.

Then, as it increases, anger becomes *fury*. The word suggests violence, even a loss of emotional control.

The last phase of anger is *rage*. Obviously, rage is the most dangerous form of anger.

In Los Angeles some time back, a man drowned his children—four of them. He admitted it happened in a fit of rage. Rage is a temporary loss of control involving acts of violence; the angry person scarcely realizes what he has done.

THE SCRIPTURES MAY SURPRISE YOU!

In Ephesians 4:26–27 we have two verses that have to do with anger.

> Be angry, and yet do not sin; do not let the sun go down on your anger, and do not give the devil an opportunity.

The Amplified Bible renders those verses this way:

> When angry, do not sin; do not ever let your wrath—your exasperation, your fury or indignation—last until the sun goes down. Leave no [such] room or foothold for the devil—give no opportunity to him.

The New English Bible says it this way:

> If you are angry, do not let anger lead you into sin; do not let sunset find you still nursing it; leave no loophole for the devil.

The very first time I looked at this verse in depth, I did a doubletake. Do you realize that God is saying to you, "Get mad!" That's right. If that were the end of verse 26, we would put an exclamation point after the word *angry*. Be angry! How about that! When's the last time you obeyed the Scriptures and "blew your cool"?

I see three important things in these verses.

1. *Anger is a God-given emotion.* There's something inhuman about a person who never gets angry. He has a strange makeup. We

would be quick to say that one who does not show compassion really does not have a heart. And one who doesn't love—well, there's something terribly wrong with him. These emotions are God-given, and He says to express them. The same is true of anger. God says, "Be angry."

2. *Anger is not necessarily sinful.* God says, "Be angry, and yet do not sin." Not every expression of anger is wrong. It's as though I were to say to one of my children, "Now, when you go out tonight, enjoy yourself. Really have a good time. But don't misuse your humor." Or it's like the Lord when He says, "I want you to love, but don't love the world. Don't even love the things of the world. I want you to love, but restrict that love to certain things." This is the same thought. Be angry, but don't carry that anger to the point where it becomes sin.

Some of you may be questioning whether or not it is *ever* right to be angry. Did you know that in the Old Testament "the anger of the Lord" is mentioned no less than eighteen times?

And in the New Testament we have some classic examples of Jesus' anger! When those money changers were in the temple, He didn't walk in and say, "Now listen, guys, I don't want to offend you, but what you are doing isn't very good." Rather, he plaited together a whip of thongs and physically drove them out of the temple. His was an expression of real indignation. He got mad!

And Jesus never spoke more angrily and forthrightly to anyone than He did to the religious hypocrites in Matthew 23, where in one case after another He said, "Woe to you." He even called them "whitewashed tombs" and "serpents"! There are times when anger is very appropriate. I'll say more about that later.

3. *Anger must have safeguards.* Notice the two safeguards Paul gave us right in this passage?

Safeguard number one:

Do not let the sun go down on your anger (Ephesians 4:26).

Don't prolong anger into the night. In Paul's day, the setting of the sun was the closing of the day and the beginning of the next. By the end of the day, make sure your anger problem is solved.

I believe this is to be taken very literally. We practice this in our home; perhaps you do in yours. If there have been times of disagreement or anger throughout the day, clear them up by evening.

When you lay your head on your pillow, make sure those feelings of anger have been resolved. Be certain that there is forgiveness, a clearing out of that conscience. Husbands and wives, don't go to sleep back to back. Don't allow yourself the luxury of feeling you can take care of it later on.

Every once in a while, a Christian brother or sister tells me of an experience when they flew off the handle. They were in the wrong. And they will say something like, "You know, as I turned in that night, things just didn't settle right." Maybe you've had that experience. I certainly have. Then they say, "I had to get up, turn the light on, and make a phone call . . . or get dressed, go over to this person's house, and talk with him face-to-face to clear it up." It's a real encouragement to hear things like that.

Safeguard number two:

Do not give the devil an opportunity (Ephesians 4:27).

That means just what it says. Don't allow your anger to be expressed in such a way that you are weakened and the devil reproduces his character through you.

You see, Jesus Christ loves to reproduce His character through us. When we are under the control of the Holy Spirit, then the character of Christ flows freely—His love, His gentleness, His compassion, His joy, His concern for others. But the devil is a master of counterfeit, and when we are given over to the things of Satan, he aims to make us behave like him.

That's Paul's whole point. Don't let anger get hold of you and weaken you so that other areas of sin, or even satanic involvement, can come into your life. Keep that in mind if you are prone to get angry. Sustained, uncontrolled anger offers the enemy of our souls an open door. It's serious.

WHEN IS ANGER JUSTIFIED?

When can we actually say it is right to be angry? That's an important question. I find there are three specific situations in Scripture when anger is justifiable.

1. *Anger is justified when God's Word and God's will are knowingly disobeyed by God's people.* Something should happen in the heart of the child of God who sees other believers sinning openly, ignoring and disobeying the will of God. It's not good for us to look on pas-

sively. Something's wrong! When Moses saw what was going on around that golden calf, he couldn't handle it. He got downright indignant (see Exodus 32:19–20).

Further, there is an instance in Solomon's life that shows us the Lord does not overlook acts of carnality. First Kings 11 is the very tale of Solomon's last years. He had been blessed with riches, the likes of which the world has never known. The late J. Paul Getty would look like a bum compared to Solomon. He was loaded. And he had more wives and concubines, it seems, than any other man who has ever lived. He had more wisdom than anyone else in Scripture. But look at the latter part of his life.

> Now King Solomon loved many foreign women along with the daughter of Pharaoh: Moabite, Ammonite, Edomite, Sidonian, and Hittite women, from the nations concerning which the LORD had said to the sons of Israel, "You shall not associate with them, neither shall they associate with you, for they will surely turn your heart away after their gods."
> Solomon held fast to these in love.
> And he had seven hundred wives, princesses, and three hundred concubines, and his wives turned his heart away. For it came about when Solomon was old, his wives turned his heart away after other gods; and his heart was not wholly devoted to the LORD his God, as the heart of David his father had been (1 Kings 11:1–4).

The next four verses describe his idolatrous practices. Then we read:

> Now the LORD was angry with Solomon because his heart was turned away from the LORD, the God of Israel, who had appeared to him twice, and had commanded him concerning this thing, that he should not go after other gods; but he did not observe what the LORD had commanded (1 Kings 11:9–10).

Anger is justified not only on man's part, but on the Lord's part when we openly and knowingly disobey His Word. On some fronts, grace has been twisted to convey the idea that God no longer has any standards, or that a godly quality of life is not expected of us, now that we're under grace. That is a perversion and a lie right out of the pit of hell!

There are other occasions in the Bible in which anger is justified.

2. Anger is justified when God's enemies assume positions of jurisdiction outside their rights. The prophet Isaiah records an example of the Lord's enemies moving into a realm outside their rights. The Lord rebuked them for it.

> *Woe to those who call evil good, and good evil;*
> *Who substitute darkness for light and light for darkness. . . .*
> *Woe to those who are wise in their own eyes,*
> *And clever in their own sight!*
> *Woe to those who are heroes in drinking wine,*
> *And valiant men in mixing strong drink;*
> *Who justify the wicked for a bribe* [and now here's the phrase],
> *And take away the rights of the ones who are in the right!*
> [Woe to them!]
> *Therefore, as a tongue of fire consumes stubble . . .*
> *So their root will become like rot and their blossom blow away*
>   *as dust;*
> *For they have rejected the law of the LORD of hosts,*
> *And despised the word of the Holy One of Israel.*
> *On this account the anger of the LORD has burned against*
>   *His people*
> *(Isaiah 5:20–25).*

The little phrase in verse 23 attracts my attention. "Those who take away the rights of the ones who are in the right!" My point is this: Anger is justified when enemies of the Lord take away rights outside their realm of jurisdiction.

Several examples of this could be shown from Scripture.

In 1 Samuel 11, Saul is the anointed king when the enemy comes to invade the land. We read in 1 Samuel 11:6 that "the Spirit of God came upon Saul mightily when he heard these words, and he became very angry." Literally, his anger became intense, because war was being declared against the land of God and the people of Israel. Their freedom was being threatened.

I think this is very applicable for our day and our view of war. I can assure you that I am not a warmonger. No one hurts more than I do to see the results of war. No doubt, you feel the same. But this is not to say that when an enemy desires to come in and remove the freedom of our land that we should sit passively by and say, "Well, we just had better live with it. It's just one of those problems of life. Evil is on the earth." The Scriptures declare that when people take away the rights of those who are in the right, the Lord becomes angry . . . and so should we. Defending these treasured rights is our responsibility.

3. *Anger is justified when children are dealt with unfairly by parents.* Here, we are no longer dealing with theory or some distant war or some court of law. We are now talking about justified anger in the home. I want to be very careful how I express myself, so that I won't be misunderstood.

> Children, obey your parents in the Lord, for this is right. Honor your father and mother (which is the first commandment with a promise), that it may be well with you, and that you may live long on the earth. And, fathers, do not provoke your children to anger; but bring them up in the discipline and instruction of the Lord (Ephesians 6:1–4).

The parallel verse in Colossians is:

> Fathers, do not exasperate your children, that they may not lose heart (Colossians 3:21).

It is interesting that in both passages, the apostle Paul specifically addressed *fathers*. We fathers often are given to impatience; to a lack of real understanding of the feelings of our little ones, our teenagers, or our young adults still living at home. When we exasperate our children by dealing with them unfairly and they respond in anger, this anger is justified. Do not provoke your children to anger!

And children, be careful that you do not look upon every word from your father's lips as provoking you to anger. I'm talking about those things fathers do that really bring about feelings of unfair hurt and irritation.

I want to say something that might be misunderstood, but I am still going to say it. I think some of us are twisting the teaching of the "chain of command" in the home way beyond its proper bounds. Anyone can take a good truth and pervert it, and I know of cases where this has been done.

Be careful as a husband, a father, a man of God, that your dealings with your family are *fair* and that you can, before God, support them scripturally and logically. Be sensitive to your wife and children. Don't use the concept of the "chain of command" as a brutal, bloody club, lording it over your family. Instead, be an authority that *serves*. (This topic is discussed at length in two of my books, *You and Your Child* and *Improving Your Serve*.)

Are you given to unjustified anger? Have doors been slammed closed in your home or with your friends simply because you lost your temper? Ephesians 4:31–32 reads:

> Let all bitterness and wrath and anger and clamor and slander be put away from you, along with all malice. And be kind to one another, tender-hearted, forgiving each other, just as God in Christ also has forgiven you.

The wrath of God was poured out on Jesus Christ at Calvary. All His anger at sin was, at that point in time, poured out on the Savior. He knows what anger is like; you can pour yours out upon Him. He wants to take that weakness, that area of sin, and give you victory in it.

UNJUSTIFIED ANGER

Let's dig deeper. We can't leave the subject until we look at the other side of the coin. When is anger unjustified?

1. *Anger is unjustified when it comes from the wrong motive.* We've all studied the prodigal son, but we usually miss the prodigal that stayed home! He is the one who illustrates an anger that was not justified because it sprang from a wrong motive. When the younger brother came to himself, he was, you will recall, in a swine pen. He was at the end of his rope, and the Scripture says:

> But when he came to his senses, he said, " . . . I will get up and go to my father, and will say to him, '... I am no longer worthy to be called your son; make me as one of your hired men'" (Luke 15:17–19).

And he did that. You know the rest of the story. The father greeted him with open arms, delighted to have him there. But this joy was not shared by the wayward son's older brother.

> Now his older son was in the field, and when he came and approached the house, he heard music and dancing. And he summoned one of the servants and began inquiring what these things might be. And he said to him, "Your brother has come,

and your father has killed the fattened calf, because he has received him back safe and sound" (Luke 15:25–27).

Now notice the *jealous motive* that resulted in anger.

But he became angry, and was not willing to go in; and his father came out and began entreating him. But he answered and said to his father, "Look! For so many years I have been serving you, and I have never neglected a command of yours; and yet you have never given me a kid, that I might be merry with my friends; but when this son of yours came [notice he doesn't call him "my brother"; he was tremendously angry], who has devoured your wealth with harlots [How does he know that? The Bible never tells us his brother visited prostitutes. It's possible, but when you're angry and jealous, you exaggerate the story.], you killed the fattened calf for him."

And he [the father] said to him, "My child, you have always been with me, and all that is mine is yours. But we had to be merry and rejoice, for this brother of yours was dead and has begun to live, and was lost and has been found" (Luke 15:28–32).

When we are jealous of some other person, our response is frequently one of anger, especially when that other person receives some kind of commendation or promotion or attention from other people. "It isn't fair! That's my right to enjoy, not his!" That anger is unjustified.

The thing we must ask ourselves when anger begins to come is, "What is the motive behind my feelings?"

2. Anger is unjustified when things don't go your way. The book of Jonah contains the most extensive revival recorded in history. The entire city of Nineveh—believed by many Old Testament scholars to be half a million or more in population—repented of their sins and turned to the Lord.

Jonah, of course, was a bigoted racist. He was a prophet, indeed, but he was a man who really wanted to see Nineveh destroyed, something of an ancient Archie Bunker! That is why he didn't go to Nineveh when God told him to the first time. He did not want Nineveh to repent; he wanted it blasted away. And he got angry because things didn't go his way.

When God saw their deeds, that they turned from their wicked way, then God relented concerning the calamity which He had declared He would bring upon them. And He did not do it. But it greatly displeased Jonah, and he became angry (Jonah 3:10–4:1).

Notice that the reason for his anger was that he didn't get his way—he wanted destruction, but God gave deliverance.

And he prayed to the LORD and said, "Please LORD, was not this what I said while I was still in my own country? ["This is why I didn't want to go in the first place."] . . . Therefore now, O LORD, please take my life from me, for death is better to me than life."
And the LORD said, "Do you have good reason to be angry?" (Jonah 4:2–4).

Jonah went out to a hillside, refusing to answer the Lord. He sat down under a nice, leafy gourd vine to enjoy a little shade. Sitting comfortably there on that hill, the wind blowing softly, he thought, *My, this is living*. Here, he could quickly forget about Nineveh. Then a little worm came and ate up that gourd plant, and it wilted. Jonah got hot and bothered, and begged God to take his life.

Then God said to Jonah, "Do you have good reason to be angry about the plant?" (Jonah 4:9).

This brings us to a very practical point: We really do like to have our own way. For example, you work hard all week and you think, "I will have a nice evening out with my wife on Friday night." You get it all arranged, and you drive to your favorite restaurant. There's a long line, but you are not worried. You walk up to the front and say, "I called in reservations for tonight."
The hostess says, "I'm sorry, sir, but I don't have your name written down here."
How do you respond? Unless I miss my guess, you become angry. Rather than saying, "Lord, what can I learn through this?" you think, "Listen, I've got my rights!"
"But I called in two days ago," you protest.
"Sorry."
So you wait in line. Steaming. Frowning. When you finally are seated, you get a bad table (it's near the door and the legs are uneven) and your waitress is irritable. Your food is cold. The candle goes out. The people around you are loud and boisterous.

This is where Christianity is put on the block. The real test is not in a Sunday service. It's in a Friday night restaurant when things don't go our way.

One of the best ways I know to keep from getting angry when we don't get our way is to have a good sense of humor. Turn the bad times into a little fun.

When we were living in Texas, our family planned for months to go to a state park for a camping vacation. We looked forward to it, but before we left we prayed, "Lord, whatever happens, we're going to have a good time."

It was a good thing we prayed that, because the place was a rat-hole. There were wall-to-wall people. It was hot—the weather was terrible! It was a great disappointment. We spent one night with spiders and scorpions, laughed it off, and headed back home. On the way, we stopped off at another state park where there wasn't a soul. I still can't understand it. We checked in and spent almost two full weeks in a place that was marvelously quiet and delightful, unseasonably cool and picturesque.

God seems to reward us with good, delightful experiences when we move with joy through those times when we didn't get our own way. The choice is ours. If we choose to be offended when we don't get our own way, then we're going to live constantly on the edge of anger. But if we say to ourselves, "A merry heart does good like a medicine," it'll make all the difference in the world.

3. *Anger is unjustified when you react too quickly without investigating the facts.*

> The end of a matter is better than its beginning; patience of spirit is better than haughtiness of spirit. Do not be eager in your heart to be angry, for anger resides in the bosom of fools (Ecclesiastes 7:8–9).

> But let everyone be quick to hear, slow to speak and slow to anger (James 1:19).

If we have a *patient* spirit, if we *hear a matter out*, it is better than just hearing its beginning. If we are eager in our hearts to be angry, we're foolish.

It's a real concern to me that we have to live at such a hurried, harried pace. When the schedule is not met, the instant response of the foolish one is anger. Retaliate. Fight back. The writer of Ecclesiastes is saying, "If you do that, you're a fool."

This struck me during a past family vacation. It was amazing how much more patient we were when we got some times of sustained quietness. We were camping deep in the heart of the giant redwoods up near the Oregon border. Beneath the glow of our little red Coleman lantern, we sat around a fire each night. Quietness was all around. Each morning we arose to the chirp of birds and the river's rippling rapids. I don't think we'll ever forget it! As I recall, we didn't have one bout with anger during the whole three weeks.

Develop the art of quietness. Turn off the appliances, including the TV. In fact, wean yourself from it for an entire evening. Leave it off. Honestly, we will never become men and women of God without experiencing some solitude.

WINNING OVER ANGER

What do we do about anger? *When it comes from a wrong motive, when we don't get our own way, when we act in haste*—anger is sin. What practical things does God say about dealing with anger? Scripture offers four specific directives in the book of Proverbs. Let's cover them quickly.

1. *Learn to ignore petty disagreements.*

A man's discretion makes him slow to anger, and it is his glory to overlook a transgression (Proverbs 19:11).

Perhaps it is better rendered in the Berkeley Version.

It is prudent for a man to restrain his anger; it is his glory to overlook an offense (MLB).

In God's eyes, it is *glory* if you are big enough to overlook an offense. Don't look for a fight, Christian. Keep the chip off your shoulder. Don't be defensive about your point or your right. Be willing to give.

Proverbs 17:14 says essentially the same thing. I like this verse.

The beginning of strife is like letting out water, so abandon the quarrel before it breaks out.

Just as in the tango, it takes two to quarrel. If you see that there is an angry disagreement coming, back off; leave it. Learn to ignore petty differences.

2. *Refrain from close association with anger-prone people.* Don't hang around them.

> Do not associate with a man given to anger; or go with a hot-tempered man, lest you learn his ways, and find a snare for yourself (Proverbs 22:24–25).

It's true: We become like those we spend our time with. If you spend time with a rebel you will become rebellious and angry. If I hang around people who are negative, you know what happens to me? I become negative. (And by nature, I'm a positive person.) But it's amazing—the more I'm around people who talk about how things won't work, and how this isn't good, and how even though there were ten very fine things, two things went wrong, the more I begin to think, "You know, a lot of things are wrong." Then I get petty and negative in other areas.

Are you becoming an angry person because you're associating closely with angry people? The Scripture says, "Don't do it!"

3. *Keep very close check on your tongue.* More than any slanderous event, any immoral act, any unwise financial dealings, that which breaks up a church quickest is an unchecked tongue. The longer I live, the more I realize that.

> A gentle answer turns away wrath, but a harsh word stirs up anger (Proverbs 15:1).

Washington Irving made this statement:

> The only edged tool that gets sharper with use is the tongue.[42]

It isn't your leg muscle that's the strongest muscle in your body; it's the muscle in your mouth. Control your tongue. It will literally "turn away wrath."

4. *Cultivate honesty in communication—don't let anger build up.* Take a close look at Proverbs 27:4–6:

> *Wrath is fierce and anger is a flood,*
> *But who can stand before jealousy?*
> *Better is open rebuke*
> *Than love that is concealed.*

Faithful are the wounds of a friend,
But deceitful are the kisses of an enemy.

The New Testament counterpart to this passage is Ephesians 4:25:

Therefore, laying aside falsehood, speak truth, each one of you, with his neighbor, for we are members of one another.

There is no substitute for total honesty, spoken in love. Allowing anger to seethe on the back burner will lead to a very large lid blowing off a very hot pot. Let me encourage you to pick up a copy of David Augsburger's fine book, *Caring Enough to Confront.*[43] In that little volume you'll find an excellent treatment of this whole subject. Augsburger offers some outstanding guidelines on how to communicate honestly, yet lovingly.

Well, you've done enough thinking about anger. Enough of theory! Now it's time to put it into action. Not as Mark Twain suggested, or even as Thomas Jefferson . . . but as the Bible directs.

Restraint

Yesterday I got drunk.

Now wait a minute! Before you pick up your phone and notify six of your closest friends, let me explain. I was the victim of a dentist's drill. As he was about to do his thing on my ivories, he inserted eighty milligrams of Nembutal into my innocent bloodstream—resulting thereafter in a flow of words and actions that were *anything* but innocent, I am told. I have been informed that a tape recording was made that probably would call into question my ordination as well as cause my old Marine Corps drill instructor to blush. I am sure that the entire dental office—that group of rascals!—has sufficient information to blackmail me. But they are sworn to secrecy. I hope.

My neighbors probably raised some eyebrows when my dear wife helped me out of the car and I staggered to the door, singing loudly. She informed me that I saw a mosquito and took a rather exaggerated swing at it. That led to a few other verbal expressions totally unlike a man of the cloth. When I awoke on the patio three hours later, my children were still giggling and snickering over my irresponsible homecoming. They also are sworn to secrecy. *They better be!*

Isn't it amazing what happens when the clamps of restraint are loosened? In some cases, it's unbelievable! I would never, under normal conditions, declare: *"Dentistry is a rip-off!"* But I did yesterday. Right in front of my dentist and his drill team. I would not say to a young lady, *"You talk too much—get out!"* But that's exactly what I said to one of his capable assistants.

Thanks to Nembutal, I became an open book with no secret sections or hidden chapters containing guarded, private feelings and thoughts. For several unrestrained hours, my emotions ran rampant, and there's no way to recover the damage or remove the raw facts from that page of my life.

Of course, I was under the influence of a painkilling drug, so I'm automatically excused, or so they assure me. Because of the circumstances, it's nothing more than a funny, harmless episode that makes us chuckle.

But that isn't always so.

The removal of restraint is usually neither excusable nor amusing. In fact, restraining ourselves is so important that God lists it as a fruit of the Spirit in Galatians 5:22–23. "Self-control," another word for restraint, is honored by the Lord as the "anchor virtue" on His relay team that runs life's race for His glory. Many other voices are saying "Let it all hang out" and "Tell it like it is" and "Hold nothing back" and "Be open. Express your feelings without restraint!" It's easy to buy that kind of advice. But when I go to my Bible, I find contrary counsel being marketed.

When we are angered, God instructs us to restrain ourselves. For proof, ponder Proverbs 14:29, 15:1, and 29:11, along with Ephesians 4:26–27. He further tells us not even to associate with one given to anger (Proverbs 22:24–25) or place him into leadership in the church (1 Timothy 3:2–3).

When we are tempted, He admonishes us to say no to lust and restrain our carnal nature (1 Corinthians 9:26–27; 2 Timothy 2:22).

When we are prompted to talk too much, He says, "Hold it! Better keep that to yourself!" (Proverbs 17:28; Job 13:5; Ephesians 4:29). Restraint of the tongue is a mark of wisdom. It is a slippery eel in need of being held in check between our cheeks.

When food is stacked before us, God is pleased when we restrain ourselves from gluttony (Proverbs 23:1–2; 1 Corinthians 10:31–32). Being fat is generally a telltale sign that control is lacking.

When money is to be earned, spent, saved, or invested, the use of restraint is the order of the day (Matthew 6:19–21; Luke 14:28–30; Romans 13:7–8).

Removing restraint from your life may seem like an exciting adventure, but it inevitably leads to tragedy. It's a lot like removing the brakes from your car. It may be daring and filled with thrills for awhile, but injury is certain. Take away the brakes and your life, like your car, is transformed into an unguided missile—destined for disaster.

Let's all learn a lesson from my extracurricular escapades this week.

When medicine is needed
To dull the pain you're in,

Your actions may be silly
Yet they really are not "sin."
But when you willfully lose control
And set restraint aside,
Your actions then are sinful
And pain is multiplied.

Backing Off

Kids are nutty.

Some friends of ours in Texas have two little girls. The younger child is constantly on the move, rarely winding down by bedtime. So the nightly affair has become something of a familiar routine. A story from her favorite book. A drink of water. A prayer. A song. Her doll. Another drink of water. A kiss. A hug. A third sip of water. A trip to the bathroom. A warning. Another kiss. You know, the whole bit.

One night her dad decided he'd be Mr. Nice Guy, the epitome of patience and tolerance. He did it all. Not once did he lose his cool. When Miss Busybody finally ran out of requests, her daddy slipped out of the room, heaved a sigh of relief, and slumped into his favorite chair by the fireplace. But before he could stretch out and relax, there was a piercing scream from the jitterbug's room. Startled, he dashed down the hall and rushed to her bedside. Great tears were rolling down the little girl's face.

"What's wrong? What happened?"

"I burnt my tongue."

Baffled, he tried again. "You what?"

"I burnt my *tongue!*" she yelled.

"How in the world did you do that?" he asked.

"I licked my night-light."

That really happened. She couldn't control her curiosity. She simply had to discover how it would feel to lick that little thing that glowed so warmly and serenely by her bed. Rude was her awakening to the fact that lights are strictly for lighting . . . not licking. And tongues are made for tasting . . . not testing. You and I realize that the best thing our little friend could have done was to stay in bed, keep her tongue to herself, and allow the light to fulfill its appointed function. But she didn't—and she got burned.

In the book of Ecclesiastes, Solomon, the wise, passes along to us a list of various types of "appointed times" on earth. Among them he mentions a time to heal, a time to shun embracing, a time to give up as lost, a time to be silent.

I see in these words of counsel one strong undercurrent of advice: BACK OFF! It is often wise to relax our intensity, refuse to force an issue, allow nature to take its course, "let sleeping dogs lie." Backing off, says Solomon, provides opportunity for healing to occur, opportunity for perspective to break through the storm clouds of emotion and illuminate a difficult situation with a fresh understanding.

When the time is right, things flow very naturally, very freely. To rush or force creates friction—scars that take years to erase. Intensity leads to futility. Like the little boy who plants the seed and then nervously digs it up every day to see if it is growing. Waiting is as necessary as planting and fertilizing.

When the fish aren't biting, banging on the water with an oar won't help. You can't get sap out of a hoe handle. Nor can a relationship be corrected by legislation and force. Remember, God says there is a "time to shun embracing" just as there are times to embrace. "Giving up as lost" may, on some occasions, be the wisest response, though extremely painful. Sometimes that means simply being silent and allowing God to work. In other words, *back off* so God can move in. This is never more essential than among family members in a home. Allowing some loose slack in the rope is, at the right time, a mark of real wisdom.

What a difficult pill for uptight parents to swallow! Kept edgy by impatience, rigidity, and unbending determination, they foolishly rush in where angels loathe to tread. The result? Exasperated kids. Rooms choked with threats and irritating pressure.

Young guys can do this with girls they date. She wants room to breathe, some space to think things out for herself, but he continues to smother. We can do this with people we have offended. They need time to reason, freedom to forgive without being hurried. To push for a quick closure is like a hard-sell salesman pressing you to buy when you are trying to decide what's best. The faster he talks and the harder he pushes, the less interested you become in buying. Even something you *need*. The wise salesman knows when to allow you the privilege of deciding for yourself—when to back off and leave you alone.

Nobody is able to eat while they're weeping. Serving more food isn't the answer. The appetite will return when the agony subsides . . . and not until. That takes time.

Stop and think. Think first about your family. Then your other friends. Are you being wise or foolish? Are you using force or providing freedom? Are you being pushy or patient? Are you intimidating by your intensity . . . or backing off and relaxing? Are you allowing the ground fog to roll back or are you launching blindly into dangerous flight?

Take it from one who has learned this difficult lesson the hard way—keep a tight bridle on your tongue, relax and settle for a good night's sleep. Otherwise, you're going to get pushy, you're going to get caught with your tongue in the wrong place . . . and you're going to get burned.

Adversity

To most people pain is an enemy . . . nothing more than an invading, adversary force that takes unfair advantage of its victims. Stop and think. Who ever thought of affliction as a friend? How many folks do you know who would encourage you to learn from God's messages, even though they come wrapped in discomfort?

The following pages are based on the scriptural suggestion that we are not to be disturbed and demoralized when our comfort zone gets the squeeze. Why? Because during and following those times of distress, our God deposits some of His best lessons into our lives.

So then, as you read what I have written, take time to put *yourself* in the scene. Think of your particular circumstances, especially those that seem unusually difficult. Ask the Lord to give you the patience and the perspective to glean much wisdom as you apply what you are reading.

May you *grow* rather than simply *groan* through it all!

We sent Timothy . . . to strengthen and encourage you as to your faith, so that no man may be disturbed by these afflictions; for you yourselves know that we have been destined for this (1 Thessalonians 3:2–3).

Physician Scott Peck calls it "the road less traveled." Scholar C. S. Lewis refers to it as "God's megaphone." Contemporary author Philip Yancey says that it is "the gift nobody wants." English poet Byron referred to it as "the path to truth." But no one ever said it better than Isaac Watts. While writing the lyrics for a hymn that Christians still sing today, he asked direct and searching questions: "Am I a soldier of the cross, a follower of the Lamb?" And again, "Must I be carried to the skies on flowery beds of ease, while others fought to win the prize and sailed thru bloody seas?"

What is this "road less traveled"? Where is that "path to truth"? I'm referring to pain. It's in pain that God speaks to us through His megaphone. *Suffering* is "the road less traveled." *Affliction* is "the path to truth." *Hardship* and *adversity*—these are the gifts nobody wants. Just the presence of these things in our lives creates tension.

For example, you go to your physician for an annual checkup. He takes your X ray. Within a few days he contacts you and says, "We'll need to do a biopsy." After the biopsy, he faces you with that horrible piece of information: you have cancer. There's no getting around it. Enter high-level tension.

One part of us responds, "I will accept this. There is no such thing as a mistake in the life of the child of God. This is a 'road less traveled,' and I want to travel it carefully and well. I want to learn all that God is saying to me through this affliction."

But another part of us says, "I will fight this to the end, because I am a survivor and because I believe there may well be a cure around the corner. So I will not succumb. I will not lie down in my bed, give up hope, and die an early death."

It is the tension between acceptance and resistance. The conflict is actually a mental struggle between seeing God as a God of sovereign control and viewing Him as a God of gracious mercy. There are lessons to be learned that can only be learned along the road of affliction, hardship, and pain.

SUFFERING IS INEVITABLE

There's no getting around it, pain and suffering are inevitable. Our parents did not escape it, you and I will not escape it, and neither will our children. According to Philippians 1:29, suffering is here to stay.

> For to you it has been granted for Christ's sake, not only to believe in Him, but also to suffer for His sake.

There are some today who say, "All suffering is wrong. All who suffer are out of the will of God. If you suffer, you are in sin. And since you are in sin, if you will deal correctly and sufficiently with your sin, your suffering will go away." That is simply not the truth. Scripture does not support such teaching. To be sure, all suffering is rooted in the fact that sin has entered the human race; however, not only has it been granted that we believe in Christ, but it has also been planned that we suffer.

Second Corinthians 4:7–10 presents a similar set of facts:

> But we have this treasure in earthen vessels, that the surpassing greatness of the power may be of God and not from ourselves; we are afflicted in every way, but not crushed; perplexed, but not despairing; persecuted, but not forsaken; struck down, but not destroyed; always carrying about in the body the dying of Jesus, that the life of Jesus also may be manifested in our body.

This represents one of the deep mysteries of God. By "carrying about in the body the dying of Jesus," we enter into the true lifestyle of Christ—real living.

A few verses later in 2 Corinthians 4, we read,

> Therefore we do not lose heart, but though our outer man is decaying, yet our inner man is being renewed day by day (v. 16).

Again, notice we are decaying. And yet deep within we are being renewed.

First Peter 4:12–13 assures us that suffering should never surprise us.

> Beloved, do not be surprised at the fiery ordeal among you, which comes upon you for your testing, as though some strange thing were happening to you; but to the degree that you share the sufferings of Christ, keep on rejoicing; so that also at the revelation of His glory, you may rejoice with exultation.

Look at that, Christian! Are you, right this moment in your life, being reviled? Are you currently under attack as a soldier of the cross? Here's a new way to look at such treatment: You are blessed! Rejoice! It's part of the package. It is inevitable.

> By no means let any of you suffer as a murderer, or thief, or evil-doer, or a troublesome meddler; but if anyone suffers as a Christian, let him not feel ashamed, but in that name let him glorify God (vv. 15–16).

Now that's one side of the coin. Suffering is inevitable.

PAIN IS ESSENTIAL

There's another side to this same coin . . . and that's the part that says suffering and pain are also essential. In Psalm 119 there are three verses separated from each other but connected by the same thought—Psalm 119:67, 71, and 75:

> Before I was afflicted I went astray, but now I keep Thy word. . . .
> It is good for me that I was afflicted, that I may learn Thy statues. . . . I know, O LORD, that Thy judgments are righteous, and that in faithfulness Thou hast afflicted me.

A man told me recently, "God never had my attention until He laid me on my back. Since then, I've been listening!" This strong-willed and stubborn man was fighting back the tears as he spoke those words. And he's only been in the crucible less than two weeks.

Suffering is essential if we hope to become effective for God. A. W. Tozer said it like this: "It is doubtful whether God can bless a man greatly until He has hurt him deeply."[44]

Solomon, in his journal named Ecclesiastes, wrote:

> Consider the work of God, for who is able to straighten what He has bent? In the day of prosperity be happy, but in the day of adversity consider—God has made the one as well as the other . . . (7:13–14).

"Consider." In Hebrew, the term means "to inspect." It was used by Moses in Exodus 3, verse 3. When the bush began to burn, he said, in effect, "I will now turn aside and *consider* why the bush is not consumed." It was his way of saying, "I will make an investigation." The term includes the idea of perceiving. And when it is used of oneself, it's the idea of revealing to oneself the truth, examining for the purpose of evaluating.

Let's go back.

> Consider the work of God, for who is able to straighten what
> He has bent? In the day of prosperity be happy, but in the day
> of adversity consider [inspect, examine, gain some objective
> instruction, slow down and listen]—God has made the one as
> well as the other. . . .

Suffering is essential, not only because it softens our spirits, making us sensitive to the voice of God, but also because it reveals to us the true nature of ourselves. It shows us the truth about ourselves.

Although this journey along the avenue of affliction is unpleasant and unappealing, it is both inevitable and essential. No one in God's family can remain a stranger to pain and suffering.

AN ANCIENT EXAMPLE

Centuries ago, there was a fine group of Christians in the Macedonian church at Thessalonica. The man who was responsible for founding that church wrote them a letter of encouragement when he heard of the hard times they were enduring. Even though his missionary travels forced him to press on into other regions, his heart was still moved over their plight . . . so he sent his capable companion, Timothy, to check up on how they were doing.

Unable to get them off his mind, the apostle Paul decided to have his friend travel back to Thessalonica and determine the truth of what he'd been hearing. He wondered how they were doing in the storm of suffering that had followed his departure. He had been concerned about them long enough. It was time for action. The opening statement of 1 Thessalonians 3 reveals his plan:

> Therefore when we could endure it no longer, we thought it best
> to be left behind at Athens alone; and we sent Timothy our
> brother [to find out how you're doing]. . . .

If one of your kids attended Kent State University or was a student at the University of California in Berkeley in the late 1960s, you understand such concern. If you had a son or daughter in the Vietnam War in the late '60s and early '70s, you understand the *"therefore"* of chapter 3, verse 1.

There is something about being in a context that is marked by panic and adversity and the vicious treatment of individuals that causes you as a parent to be uneasy. You don't sleep well. You mentally imagine what they're going through. And you, on occasion, find yourself unable to endure. You have to have information about how your son or daughter is doing.

Exactly what was it Timothy was sent to do? Paul states that he sent Timothy for two reasons: (1) to strengthen the believers and (2) to encourage them, as to their faith.

To help you understand the importance of those reasons, let's briefly examine those two terms. The word *strengthen* means "to shore up, to buttress." That's an old word we don't use today—"buttress." One man says, "It's to put a ramrod down one's back to enable him to stand straight and erect, come what may."

"I sent Timothy to put a ramrod down your back, so that you wouldn't slump and shuffle around as though you were being mistreated but would stand tall during the hard times . . . you'd stand erect, like a steer in a blizzard. You'd refuse to bend against the odds. I sent him to add strength to you."

They taught us in the marines that when you are preparing for combat, you should dig a hole big enough for two. There's nothing quite like fighting a battle all alone. There's something strengthening about having a buddy with you in battle that keeps you from panic. Paul says, "You needed somebody alongside to buttress you, to keep you from surrendering."

Now the second word, "encourage," is a comforting word. *Parakaleom* is the Greek term. We get the word *Paraclete* from it, one of the titles of the Holy Spirit. It's often translated "comfort" in the New Testament, but here it is rendered *"encourage."* It is the idea of standing alongside another person to put courage into him or her. There is a loving, confident hug of reassurance in the word.

If you have ever gone through the valley, perhaps you could testify that you were able to make it only because a Timothy came to your side. Timothy, in your case, might have been a physician or a counselor or a neighbor or perhaps your own parents. But when the Timothy came, whoever he was, he brought strength and courage to you.

Notice, the encouragement had a target—to "encourage you as to your faith." Timothy didn't come just to say, "Buck up! You can handle it! Suck it up—that's the way it is in life! Others have made it and you can too!" He didn't come to be a motivational cheerleader.

That's not it. Timothy came to examine and to help strengthen the Thessalonians in their faith.

Let me show you an example of this from the Old Testament, back in 1 Samuel 23. One of my favorite stories, when it comes to relationships, is about Jonathan and David. Young David was hunted by King Saul. Saul was in this crazed state of mind. The paranoid king was convinced that young David was trying to usurp the throne, so Saul forgot all about fighting Philistines and decided his greater need was to fight David, and ultimately to kill him. But in the meantime, Jonathan, Saul's son, had developed a warm and supportive relationship with David, his brother in the faith. Imagine the scene:

> And David stayed in the wilderness in the strongholds, and remained in the hill country in the wilderness of Ziph. And Saul sought him every day, but God did not deliver him into his hand. Now David became aware that Saul had come out to seek his life while David was in the wilderness of Ziph at Horesh (vv. 14–15).

You know, it's bad enough to have somebody on your tail, but it's even worse when you *find out* that they are. News reached David in his hiding place: "Saul is out to get you. He's got his men searching for you. They know what you look like. You'd better watch out." Look what happened according to the next verse:

> And Jonathan, Saul's son, arose and went to David at Horesh, and encouraged him in God (v. 16).

You talk about meeting a need! Jonathan became David's single source of earthly support. Stop and imagine how much David treasured that meeting with Jonathan.

We would be amazed if we could find out who the Davids are today. Feeling overwhelmed and pressured, one former pastor's wife in the Northeast writes: "My husband and I have occasionally felt on the edge of an ill-defined despair. Those were times when we felt a variety of things: a desire to either quit or run, a feeling of anger, the temptation to fight back at someone, the sense of being used or exploited, the weakness of inadequacy, and the reality of loneliness." She adds, "Such attitudes can easily conspire to reduce the strongest and the most gifted to a state of nothingness."[45]

Now back to the Thessalonians' situation. They needed a Timothy—a century-one Jonathan.

> For this reason, when I could endure it no longer, I also sent to find out about your faith . . . (1 Thessalonians 3:5a).

Remember, it wasn't just to see how they were doing. It wasn't a nosy curiosity—"I wanted to see how you were doing." Then, why?

> . . . for fear that the tempter might have tempted you, and our labor should be in vain (v. 5b).

That is so practical!

One of the great battles within young Christians occurs when the adversary strikes during a time of suffering. The adversary finds that weak link or that chink in the armor, and he pushes his way in. That's when our comfort zone *really* gets the squeeze!

"When you can't endure it any longer, you pick up the phone and you call." That's a modern-day paraphrase of verse 5, I guess we can say. "When I could endure it no longer, I sent a friend. I wrote a letter. I took time from my schedule to check up on how you were doing."

We're not isolated islands of solid granite, living out our lives like rocks of Gibraltar. We are eroding pieces of soil on the seashore, especially when we are traveling the road of pain. When those age-old waves of affliction are beating against us, we need each other! Timothy's presence must have been a great encouragement to the Thessalonian believers.

Let me add here that on occasion it's wise to trace your churnings. Sometimes you will churn over someone during the night. When you awaken, you'll still be churning over the same individual . . . just can't seem to get the person out of your mind.

This was Paul's situation: "When I could endure it no longer, I also sent to find out." Want a little advice for no extra charge? *Don't ignore your churnings.* Trace them. Ask yourself why. Why can't I get so-and-so off my mind? Check up and find out! At the heart of Paul's concern was a "fear that the tempter might have tempted you, and our labor should be in vain." Paul didn't want to look back and say, "All of those hours we spent together were spent in vain."

THEOLOGICAL PERSPECTIVE

To keep the right perspective in all of this, we need a solid dose of theology. Back to verses 3 and 4—same chapter, same subject of suffering. Paul has been concerned about the Thessalonians. Look at the theology behind the suffering. He sent Timothy to encourage, to strengthen them, "so that no man may be disturbed by these afflictions . . ." (v. 3a).

Before I go any further, I want to analyze that first part of verse 3. Paul states a fact that we can rely on. It is this: *Affliction need not unsettle God's people.*

A very interesting Greek term translated "disturbed" is used only here in all of the New Testament. Paul draws it from extrabiblical literature and has inserted it here, under the guidance of the Holy Spirit, to grab the attention of the reader.

Originally it was used to describe the wagging of a dog's tail. The whole idea was "to be shaken back and forth." The term later grew to mean more than the idea of a dog's wagging its tail. Finally, as you come up closer to it, the creature *bites!* And if you are a runner, you know exactly what I'm talking about. Rule number one . . . never trust a dog that wags its tail. Why? It's gonna bite ya! It's going to catch you off guard. AND YOU'RE GOING TO BE DECEIVED! That's the word here.

"I don't want you, in the midst of the wagging of all of this experience, to be bitten, shaken, and hurt." A child of God need not be unsettled by affliction.

You know how it happens? It often begins with *questions.* See if these sound familiar: Doesn't God care about me anymore? Isn't He the One who promised to help me? How can He be good and permit this to happen to me? Why doesn't He answer my prayer—is He deaf? And then it intensifies into *doubt:* Maybe I've believed wrongly all my life. These questions cause us to start rethinking our bottom-line convictions.

Do you know somebody who's struggling through those thoughts right now? You know why they are? They have been *deceived* by affliction.

Paul realized how subtle the enemy is, so he dispatched Timothy. "I sent him to strengthen and encourage you, so that you wouldn't be full of doubt from these afflictions." That's the idea.

Now there is a logical and practical question we would be wise to ask: How can I keep from being disturbed by affliction? How can I keep from having those doubts that unsettle my faith? First of all, I remember that I have been destined for this.

> . . . so that no man may be disturbed by these afflictions; for you yourselves know that we have been destined for this (v. 3).

God, in His sovereign and inscrutable plan, realized that pain had to be a part of our training program, so He destined it for us.

And, second, I keep in mind that I have been warned ahead of time. Look at verse 4:

> For indeed when we were with you, we kept telling you in advance that we were going to suffer affliction; and so it came to pass, as you know.

As I mention warning someone about something important in advance, I recall a familiar scene. I prepared my children for marriage as best I could. And one of my pieces of counsel was this: Falling in love is wonderful. Courtship is great. The wedding ceremony is a memory you'll never forget. The honeymoon is . . . well, it's *pretty good!* But when all of that has taken place and you begin to live the real life, roll up your sleeves and tighten your belt. It's tough. So when they go—not if, but *when* they go—through the difficulties in marriage, they have been forewarned. Both have thanked me, by the way, for the previous "warning."

By being forewarned, we are forearmed to handle the pressures and challenges of married life. It helps to have some advance warning.

It's the same in the Christian life. There's no reason to be scandalized or shocked, because we have been warned ahead of time—unless you were led to Christ and discipled by someone who told you a lie; namely, "Trust Christ and all your problems will be solved." Then you are in for a real shocker! But if you have been faithfully and realistically trained, you have been equipped to handle this part of God's training program. You can stand firm through your journey along the avenue of affliction. When your comfort zone gets the squeeze, you're not blown away. You can handle it with remarkable inner peace.

By the way, you can't if you don't have Christ. Without Christ, you can no more enter into this life that I'm describing than you can fly by flapping your arms. In order for there to be that ramrod in your back, in order for you to be able to stand firm against times of adversity, Christ must remain in first place. And before that can occur, it is essential that you have the Lord Jesus in your life. That isn't automatic simply because you were born into a Christian home. You aren't a Christian just because you have moved into a Christian community or because you attend a church that preaches the truth of the gospel. You individually and independently must make that decision on your own. Only then can you *know* you're in God's family. And only then can you take life's blows on the chin without being knocked out.

REACTIONS TO AFFLICTION

You see, when we succumb to those overwhelming feelings of adversity, we tend to have three very normal and human reactions: first, resentment toward a former authority figure; second, isolation from Christian friends; and third, indifference regarding former teaching—we begin to doubt what we were once taught.

Interestingly, all three of those feelings were withstood by the Thessalonians. "But now . . ." See the contrast? "I was concerned. I sent Timothy. *But now* Timothy has come back, and he's brought us good news of your faith and love."

Isn't that just like Paul? The man was never petty. He was never nosy. He was sincerely concerned about how they were coming along in their walk with Christ. And he says, "You're doing great." How affirming!

Now note: " . . . and that you always think kindly of us . . ." (v. 6). You might think, why did he put that in there? Because one of the signs of a twisted response to affliction is resenting a former authority. Guess who gets the business when a Christian in a congregation defects? The defecting Christian will often come back at the teacher. Sometimes it's the pastor. Sometimes it's the one who counseled him or her. But the Thessalonians didn't respond in that way. "I got word that you still love me! You still think kindly of me." So they passed the first test; they weren't resentful of Paul. "I'm encouraged to know that you still think kindly of us. You *always* think kindly of us, so you're doing well. You refuse to blame me for what you're going through."

They also passed the second test . . . remember the second reaction? It's the tendency to isolate oneself from former friends. Look at what he says: "You long to see us, just as we also long to see you."

So often, when people are in a time of distress amidst afflictions, they tend to go to the other side of the street when they see someone familiar approaching. They don't want to answer their phone calls. They don't want to relate to anyone else. They want to be aloof, distant, isolated.

The worst place in the world to be, when going through doubts, is all alone. You need a friend—someone close, like a Jonathan—to support you. The Thessalonian Christians continued reaching out to Paul. They didn't isolate themselves even though their comfort zone had been invaded. They genuinely desired Paul's encouragement.

They passed the third and final test as well: they had a firm commitment to spiritual truth.

> For this reason, brethren, in all our distress and affliction we were comforted about you through your faith (v. 7).

There it is again. "We were so encouraged to know you're still believing in prayer, you're still trusting in God, you're still counting on Him to be glorified."

Now don't miss something that Paul quietly drops in toward the end of this paragraph. He says, "For now we really live, if you stand firm in the Lord" (v. 8).

Does that surprise anybody else? You'd think Paul had really lived no matter what. No, that's not true. Nothing helped him stand firm and "really live" like knowing his children in the faith were doing the same—in spite of affliction.

PRACTICAL THOUGHTS TO CONSIDER DURING AFFLICTION

I want to point out a couple of things that I've been saving until now. These two truths will make all the difference, if you will keep them in mind when assaulted by affliction.

1. *As Christians, having our comfort zone invaded is essential, not unfair.* You know a good example of that? The same reason people say, "It's best not to have just one child. It's better to have several in the family." Why? Because when you have brothers or sisters, they invade your comfort zone. They get under your skin. (They also get into your closet!) They have a way of dirtying dishes that you have to clean. They are notorious for messing up a house that you have to vacuum. And we who came from large families would agree that

it was best—now that we look back. Rather than being unfair . . . it was essential.

2. *As soldiers, suffering hardship in battle is expected, not unusual.* If you lived back in the days of the Second World War, as I did, you will remember a phrase that was often repeated: "There's a war on." Remember hearing that? Remember saying that? Someone would ask you about something you were doing that seemed a little extravagant. They would say, "How can you do that? There's a war on!"

I remember reading the gasoline rationing sticker that my dad had stuck on the right corner of the windshield of our car. It had a little statement on it that read, "Is this trip really necessary?" And with gasoline rationed as it was, if we were out just taking a drive and it looked like we weren't really going anywhere, someone had the right to say, "Why are you doing that? This trip isn't essential. There's a war on!" Restrictions and warfare go hand in hand. Suffering hardship is par for the course when we are traveling down the avenue of affliction.

Tertullian, in his *Address to Martyrs*, wrote, "No soldier comes to the war surrounded by luxuries, nor goes into action from a comfortable bedroom, but from the makeshift and narrow tent, where every kind of hardness and severity and unpleasantness is to be found." He understood the austerity that accompanies the battle.

I began with a quote from Scott Peck. I want to conclude with another one:

> Truth . . . is avoided when it is painful. We can revise our maps only when we have the discipline to overcome that pain. To have such discipline, we must be totally dedicated to truth. That is to say that we must always hold truth . . . to be more important, more vital to our self-interest, than our comfort. Conversely, we must always consider our personal discomfort relatively unimportant and, indeed, even welcome it in the service of the search for truth. . . . [And] what does a life of total dedication to the truth mean?" [Dr. Peck lists three essentials:] (1) "Continuous, and never-ending stringent self-examination." (2) "Willingness to be personally challenged." (3) "Total honesty." (None of these things comes painlessly!)[46]

God has used every means conceivable to get your attention. Perhaps He has not yet gotten it. He will not quit until He does. And

He will bring you to a knowledge of the truth, as He invades your comfort zone and escorts you down the road less traveled.

For some of you, the road means coming to faith in Christ. And you know it. You just can't dodge it any longer. Today is the day for you to submit to Him. Quit putting it off—there is no better time to turn to Him. For others, it means turning over the controls of your life to the Lord your God. It means full surrender.

Testing Our Balance

There are two extreme tests that disturb our balance in life. Each has its own set of problems. On one side is *adversity*. Solomon realized this when he wrote:

> If you faint in the day of adversity, your strength is small (Proverbs 24:10, RSV).

The Good News Bible paraphrases that verse:

> If you are weak in a crisis, you are weak indeed.

Adversity is a good test of our resiliency, our ability to cope, to stand back up, to recover from misfortune. Adversity is a painful pedagogue.

On the other side is *prosperity*. In all honesty, it's a tougher test than adversity. The Scottish essayist and historian, Thomas Carlyle, agreed when he said:

> Adversity is sometimes hard upon a man; but for one man who can stand prosperity, there are a hundred that will stand adversity.[47]

Precious few are those who can live in the lap of luxury ... who can keep their moral, spiritual, and financial equilibrium ... while balancing on the elevated tightrope of success. It's ironic that most of us can handle a sudden demotion much better than a sizable promotion. Why?

Well, it really isn't too difficult to explain. When adversity strikes, life becomes rather simple. Our need is to survive. But when prosperity occurs, life gets complicated. And our needs are numerous, often extremely complex. Invariably, our integrity is put to the test. And there is about one in a hundred who can dance to the tune of success without paying the piper named Compromise.

Now, before we get too carried away, let's understand that being successful isn't necessarily wrong. Being promoted, being elevated to a place of prominence can come from God Himself.

> *For not from the east, nor from the west,*
> *Nor from the desert comes exaltation;*
> *But God is the Judge;*
> *He puts down one, and exalts another*
> *(Psalm 75:6–7).*

Asaph, the guy who wrote those words, was correct. It is the Lord's sovereign right to demote as well as to promote . . . and we seldom know why He chooses whom.

Any biblical proof that some have been snatched from obscurity and exalted to prosperity without losing their integrity? Any examples of prosperous people who kept their balance while walking on the wire? Sure, several of them.

- Daniel was lifted from a lowly peon in a boot camp at Babylon to a national commander in charge of one-third of the kingdom (Daniel 6:1–2).
- Amos was promoted from a fig-picker in Tekoa, nothing more than an ancient sharecropper, to the prophet of God at Bethel, the royal residence of the king (Amos 7:14–15).
- Job was a rancher in Uz when God prospered him and granted him financial independence (Job 1:1–5).

And not one of the three lost his integrity in the process.

But the classic example is David, according to the last three verses of Psalm 78:

> *He also chose David His servant,*
> *And took him from the sheepfolds;*
> *From the care of the ewes with suckling lambs*
> *He brought him,*
> *To shepherd Jacob His people,*
> *And Israel His inheritance.*
> *So he shepherded them according to the integrity of his heart,*
> *And guided them with his skillful hands.*

As Jehovah scanned the Judean landscape in search of Saul's successor, He found a youth in his midteens who possessed a unique combination: the humility of a servant, the heart of a shepherd, the hands of skill.

And by his thirtieth birthday, Jesse's youngest held the premier office in his nation. King. At his fingertips was a vast treasury, unlimited privileges, and enormous power.

And how did he handle such prosperity? Read that final verse again. He shepherded the nation "according to integrity." He was Carlyle's "one in a hundred."

Are *you?*

If so, when you give your word, you do it. Exactly as you said you would. Because integrity means you are verbally trustworthy. Furthermore, when the bills come due, you pay them. Because integrity means you are financially dependable. Also, when you're tempted to mess around with an illicit sexual affair, you resist. Because integrity means you are morally pure. You don't fudge because you're able to cover your tracks. Neither do you fake it because you're now a big shot. Being successful doesn't give anybody the right to call wrong right. Or the okay to say something's okay if it isn't okay.

Adversity or prosperity, both are tough tests on our balance. To stay balanced through adversity, resiliency is required. But to stay balanced through prosperity—ah, that demands *integrity*. The swift wind of compromise is a lot more devastating than the sudden jolt of misfortune.

That's why walking on a wire is harder than standing up in a storm. Height has a strange way of disturbing our balance.

Lifelines

Today I had another birthday.

No big deal . . . just another stabbing realization that I'm not getting any younger. I know that because the cake won't hold all the candles. Even if it could, the frosting would melt before I'd be able to blow all of them out. My kind and thoughtful secretary suggested another approach. She gave me a birthday card depicting a wizened old codger tottering beside a cake *covered* with candles. On the front it reads:

> Don't feel you're getting old if you can't blow out all the candles . . .

and inside:

> . . . just beat 'em out with your cane.

If I was hoping for comfort and encouragement from my children . . . I shouldn't have. In all seriousness my youngest asked me recently if they had *catsup* when I was a boy. I tried not to look offended—he could have asked if they had the *wheel*. But I took pains to inform him that we not only had catsup . . . but also electricity, talking movies, the radio, cars, and indoor plumbing. He gave me that you-gotta-be-kidding look and walked out of the room, shaking his head. I suddenly felt the need to lie down and take a nap.

But birthdays are milestones. Significant points in the passing of time. Specific yet mute reminders that more and more sand has passed through our hourglass. They do, however, give us a handle on the measurement of time which, when you boil it down into minutes, gets up and *moves*. There are 60 of them every hour . . . 1,440 every day . . . over 10,000 of them each week . . . about 525,000 per year. As of today—I've experienced over 34 million of them. Talk about feeling old!

But they pass so quietly, so unobtrusively, so consistently they fool you. That's part of the reason C. S. Lewis used to say:

The safest road to Hell is the gradual one—the gentle slope, soft underfoot, without sudden turnings, without milestones, without signposts.[48]

The long, dull, monotonous years of middle-aged prosperity or middle-aged adversity are excellent campaigning weather [for the devil].[49]

We mark our calendars with *deadlines*—dates that set limits for the completion of objectives and projects. To ignore these deadlines brings consequences. To live without deadlines is to live an inefficient, disorganized life, drifting with the breeze of impulse on the fickle wave of moods. We set deadlines because they help us accomplish the essentials; they discipline our use of time; they measure the length of our leash on the clothesline of demands.

God, however, brings about birthdays . . . not as deadlines but *lifelines*. He builds them into our calendar once every year to enable us to make an annual appraisal, not only of our length of life but also our depth. Not simply to tell us we're growing older, but to help us determine if we are also growing deeper.

These lifelines are not like that insurance policy you invested in several years ago. There's no automatic promise of annual renewal. Obviously, if God has given you another year to live for Him, He has some things in mind, some very special plans to pull off through your life. Surely it includes more than existing 1,440 minutes a day!

It's been awhile since you've slowed down enough to take stock of where you are going, hasn't it? And how about an evaluation of the kids? Or your marriage? Or the direction your family is heading. Or your own future? You know what I mean. Trimming off the fat of lazy thinking and taking a lean, hard look at the years remaining. If Christ doesn't return (and I don't die in the meantime), I figure I've got about 20 remaining years of effective service. How old are you? Stop and figure how many years lie between now and when you turn 65 or 70 years of age. See what I mean?

If that doesn't grab you, consider your family in the next decade. In only ten years my wife Cynthia and I will have a son 44 years old, a daughter 42, another daughter 38, and our "baby" will be 35! It's possible that none of our brood will be living at home . . . in only ten short years. Seems impossible. Especially since our place today resembles a cross between the Indianapolis 500, O'Hare Airport, and the San Diego Zoo.

How we need those lifeline days for regrouping and evaluation! Even the sports world has its time-out, seventh-inning stretch, pit stop, and halftime, so why shouldn't we? Before the smoke from your birthday candles blends into the humdrum atmosphere of the day after, force yourself to pull off the road. Ask yourself some hard questions. Here are a few worth personal consideration:

1. Am I really happy, genuinely challenged and fulfilled in life?
2. In light of eternity, am I making any consistent investment for God's glory and His cause?
3. Is the direction of my life currently leading me toward a satisfying and meaningful future?
4. Can I honestly say that I am in the nucleus of God's will for me?

And how about the kids?

1. Am I spending sufficient time with my children? Do they have a firm grasp on the fact that I love them, accept them, and care very much about their future? Am I consistent in my discipline . . . maintaining the standards?
2. Am I communicating life goals, a proper value system, a model of moral purity, a drive for excellence, and commitment to loyalty, integrity, generosity, and honesty to my children? Do they really *know* how I feel about these things?
3. When they leave the nest, will they be able to stand alone?

What are you asking the Lord for on behalf of your life and children? I challenge you, stop long enough to think it over. But don't just think, get alone and *write down* your thoughts, your dreams, your aspirations. Refuse to let tonight's television programs or some insignificant activity interrupt this necessary discipline. Don't wait for your birthday. In God's economy, *today* is of the utmost importance.

HOME IS A LOT OF THINGS. . . . BUT MAINLY IT IS THE PLACE WHERE LIFE MAKES UP ITS MIND.[50]

The psalmist gives us the perfect prayer to pray every year our lifeline rolls around.

Teach us to number our days aright, that we may gain a heart of wisdom (Psalm 90:12 NIV).

Good advice! Socrates put it another way:

The life which is unexamined is not worth living.[51]

Now let me caution you. Don't expect wisdom to come into your life like great chunks of rock on a conveyor belt. It isn't like that. It isn't splashy and bold . . . nor is it dispensed like a prescription across a counter. Wisdom comes privately from God as a by-product of right decisions, godly reactions, and the application of scriptural principles to daily circumstances. Not from trying to do great things for God, but from being faithful in the small, obscure tasks few people ever see.

Are you just growing *old* . . . or are you also growing *up?* As you "number your days," do you just count years—the grinding measurement of minutes—or can you find marks of wisdom, character traits that were not there when you were younger?

Take a look. You really don't have a lot longer, you know. As a matter of fact, one of these years, your lifeline will be God's deadline.

Hope

O ur bodies have been constructed to withstand an enormous amount of pressure. God has made us to be fairly resilient people. We can survive the heat of the tropics or the icy winds of winter. With undaunted courage we can go through seasons of illness, financial reversals, domestic disappointments, unemployment, or the death of someone dear to us . . . *if.* If we don't lose the one essential ingredient—hope.

We can rebound against wind and weather, calamity and tragedy, disease and death, so long as we have our hope. We can live weeks without food, days without water, and even several minutes without air, but take away our hope and within the briefest amount of time, *we toss in the towel!*

Knowing that that is true about His creatures, God calls hope the "anchor of the soul," the irreplaceable, irreducible source of determination. He not only calls it our "anchor," He develops a helpful series of thoughts about hope in His Book, the Bible. But in one special section of Scripture, He concentrates direct attention upon this subject. That particular section is my major emphasis here.

For when God made the promise to Abraham, since He could swear by no one greater, He swore by Himself, saying, "I will surely bless you, and I will surely multiply you." And thus, having patiently waited, he obtained the promise. For men swear by one greater than themselves, and with them an oath given as confirmation is an end of every dispute. In the same way God, desiring even more to show to the heirs of the promise the unchangeableness of His purpose, interposed with an oath, in order that by two unchangeable things, in which it is impossible for God to lie, we may have strong encouragement, we who have fled for refuge in laying hold of the hope set before us. This hope we have as an anchor of the soul, a hope both sure and steadfast and one which enters within the veil, where Jesus has entered as a forerunner for us, having become a high priest forever according to the order of Melchizedek (Hebrews 6:13–20).

Somewhere along our many miles of southern California shoreline walked a young, twenty-year-old woman with a terminal disease in her body and a revolver in her hand. She had called me late in the evening and we had talked for a long time. A troubled young woman, her mind was filled with doubts. She had advanced leukemia. The doctors told her she would not live much longer. She checked herself out of a hospital because, as she put it, she "couldn't take another day in that terrible isolation." Her husband had left her; her two-month-old daughter had recently died; her best friend had been killed in an auto accident. Her life was broken. She'd run out of hope. I'll come back to this woman later on.

Doubts often steal into our lives like termites into a house. These termite-like thoughts eat away at our faith. Usually, we can hold up pretty well under this attack. But occasionally, when a strong gale comes along—a sudden, intense blast—we discover we cannot cope. Our house begins to lean. For some people it completely collapses. It is during these stormy times, during the dark days and nights of tragedy and calamity, that we begin to feel the destructive effects of our doubts.

MAXIMUM PRESSURE POINTS

For me, there are three times when the intensity of doubt reaches maximum proportions. One such time is when things I believe should never happen, happen.

There are times when my loving, gracious, merciful, kind, good, sovereign God surprises me by saying yes to something I was convinced He would say no to. When bad things happen to good people. When good things happen to bad people. When a lie is passed off as the truth and wins the hearing of the majority.

In his book, *When Bad Things Happen to Good People*, Rabbi Harold Kushner writes:

> There is only one question which really matters: why do bad things happen to good people? All other theological conversation is intellectually diverting.... Virtually every meaningful conversation I have ever had with people on the subject of God and religion has either started with this question, or gotten around to it before long.[52]

I once received a letter from a woman who heard over a radio program a talk that I had given entitled, "Riding Out the Storm." Little did she know how meaningful it would be to her, for as she was entering into the truth of that message, she arrived at home only to discover that her young, recently married daughter had been brutally murdered. *Why did God say yes to that?* Why did that bad thing happen to that good person? The effect of such termites within our soul is great. They eat away at us and doubt wins a hearing.

Doubts also increase when things I believe should happen, never happen (the other side of the coin). When I expected God to say yes but He said no. Numerous parents of young men and women have said good-bye and sent their children away to war, convinced that God would bring them home again. But sometimes He says no. How about the family of the policeman who was killed at the onion field outside Bakersfield? Think of their rage as they went the distance to see that the murderers were finally sent to the gas chamber—only to realize the inescapable fact that not only were the killers allowed to live, but one was actually set free.

Joni Eareckson Tada (and a thousand like her) may trust confidently for awhile that the paralysis will go away—that God will say, "Yes, I'll get you through this. I'll teach you some deep lessons and then I will use you with full health in days to come as I heal you completely." But God ultimately says no.

Evangelist Leighton Ford and his wife, Jean, members of the Billy Graham Evangelistic Association team, lost their twenty-one-year-old son, Sandy, on November 27, 1981. Four days after the funeral, Ford spoke to the Graham team. His conversation was recorded in part in *Decision* magazine, dated June 1982:

> A week ago yesterday, right before Thanksgiving, my stomach was so tied up in knots, so anxious that I had to get out and run. When I stopped, I prayed; I talked with God. I said, "Lord, I know You can heal Sandy through this surgery if You want to. If You don't want to, I can't imagine why You don't." I can't tell you everything I was feeling, but I remember that I finally prayed and said, "God, I just want to say one thing, be good to my boy tomorrow."
>
> I am conscious that almost every one of us has within our hearts—some openly, some secretly—a great gaping, grieving wound that we carry. And in the midst of it we say, "Why? Is God really good?"[53]

That father wanted a yes answer to his prayers. Sandy died. God said no. And he admits:

> I would be less than honest if I did not tell you that I wish I could just smile and say, "I'm thankful for this." For there is a part of me inside that says, "It is not right."
>
> . . . I say these things inside myself. They fight. There are hours of great peace and joy, and then there are times when it just closes in, and I say, " . . . Am I doubting God?"[54]

When we expect Him to say yes and He says no, doubts multiply.

There's a third situation where doubts grow. This takes place when things I believe should happen *now*, happen much, much later. Of all the doubts which "rap and knock and enter in our soul" (Browning), perhaps few are more devastating than those that happen when we are told by God, in effect, "Wait, wait, wait, wait . . . wait . . . wait!" All of us have wrestled greatly with His timing.

These "pressure points" provide a perfect introduction to the verses in Hebrews 6. This is that great chapter that begins with a strong warning, continues with words of affirmation, and closes with words of reassurance and ringing confidence. It addresses the

Christian hanging on by his fingernails as he feels himself sliding down the hill. It shouts: "Persevere! Hang tough! Be strong! Don't quit!" Even when God says no and you expected yes. Even when He says yes and you anticipated no. And especially when He says to wait and you expected it now.

A CLASSIC EXAMPLE: ABRAHAM

> ... when God made the promise to Abraham, since He could swear by no one greater, He swore by Himself, saying, "I will surely bless you, and I will surely multiply you." And thus, having patiently waited, he obtained the promise (Hebrews 6:13–15).

What's all that about? Well, maybe we should become acquainted with the warning that comes just before the mention of Abraham. Verse 12 says:

> ... that you may not be sluggish, but imitators of those who through faith and patience inherit the promises.

Imitate those strong-minded men and women in biblical history! They believed God. They said, in effect, "I will stand, no matter what occurs. I will believe God, even though my world crumbles and my house leans. No calamity will make me fall!"

As an illustration of just such an individual, Abraham is mentioned. Now if you don't know your Bible, you can't appreciate the extent to which Abraham and Sarah trusted God. The two of them had been married for years. She was sixty-five; he was seventy-five. And if you can believe this, God had said to the man that in the latter years of his life his wife was going to have a baby. God promised Abraham in no uncertain terms; He swore on the basis of His own integrity that Sarah would have a son. And then, after making that firm promise, God said, "Now you trust Me. You wait."

Abraham waited a year and nothing happened. By then Sarah had turned sixty-six. He waited another ten years and by that time she was seventy-six. Still nothing had happened. *Another* ten years— nothing at all. Then, when Abraham was nearing his one hundredth birthday (which means his wife was about ninety years old), God came back and said, "I'm here again. Guess what? You're still going to have that baby."

If we were to return to the original time when the first dialogue occurred, we would gain a whole new appreciation for God's faithfulness and consistency. It's a wonderful story because it proves how trustworthy God is in the waiting period. Let's pick up the story as God is speaking to His friend, Abraham:

> . . . "As for Sarai your wife, you shall not call her name Sarai, but Sarah shall be her name. And I will bless her, and indeed I will give you a son by her. Then I will bless her, and she shall be a mother of nations; kings of peoples shall come from her." Then Abraham fell on his face and laughed . . . (Genesis 17:15–17).

Can't you imagine Abraham's response? "Oh, I cannot believe this. God, here You are talking about this baby who is going to come into our home. Oh, God, how can it be? How can it be?" I love the man's honesty. I wonder if he was smiling, maybe chuckling, when he answered,

> ". . . Will a child be born to a man one hundred years old? And will Sarah, who is ninety years old, bear a child? . . . Oh that Ishmael might live before Thee!" (vv. 17–18).

"We have this other young man in our home, God. Have it happen through him"—that makes a lot of sense! No, God had not planned that the arrangement would be through Ishmael. See verse 19:

> ". . . No, but Sarah . . . shall bear you a son, and you shall call his name Isaac. . . ."

The name Isaac means "laughter" in Hebrew. "You laugh at Me; I'll laugh at you. I'll show you when that boy is born, that I keep My word."

Now you might think Sarah is waiting in the wings just as confident as she can be that it will be exactly as it was promised. Better take a close look at the Genesis account: chapter 18, verse 9. Three men have come for a visit, bringing the message from God to underscore what He had said earlier. Abraham is there; Sarah's listening through the tent flap.

> . . . "Where is Sarah your wife?" And he said, "Behold, in the tent." And he said, "I will surely return to you at this time next year; and behold, Sarah your wife shall have a son." And Sarah

was listening at the tent door, which was behind him.... Sarah was past childbearing. And Sarah laughed to herself... (vv. 9–12).

Ninety years old, why not? There's not much else to do but laugh at something like that, you know. After all, "I'm ninety years old and I'm going to get pregnant? I'm going to bear a son? You gotta be kidding!"

On our way back to Hebrews 6, let's stop off at Romans 4. We can't fully appreciate Hebrews or Genesis without the Romans 4 passage sandwiched in between. Here's our friend Abraham who might have laughed on the outside, but down deep was obviously confident God could do it. Romans 4:18:

In hope against hope he believed....

There it is, friends. That's what Hebrews 6 is talking about. "In hope against hope"—when it didn't make sense. When the physical body couldn't pull it off. When it was an impossibility to man:

... in order that he might become a father of many nations, according to that which had been spoken, "So shall your descendants be." And without becoming weak in faith he contemplated his own body, now as good as dead since he was about a hundred years old, and the deadness of Sarah's womb; yet, with respect to the promise of God, he did not waver in unbelief, but grew strong in faith, giving glory to God, and being fully assured that what He had promised, He was able also to perform (Romans 4:18–21).

That's a clear illustration of faith. That's believing even when doubts attack. That's being confident that God knows what He is doing regardless of the waiting period. That's being just as firm when there's a ten-year period to wait as when there's only one year ahead. He hoped against hope:

... with respect to the promise of God, he did not waver in unbelief, but grew strong in faith, giving glory to God....

That's a very important part of this sentence. While you wait, you give Him glory. While you trust Him, you give Him glory. While you accept the fact that He has you in a holding pattern, you give Him glory.

. . . Being fully assured that what He had promised, He was able also to perform. . . . It was reckoned to him as righteousness (vv. 21–22).

The man walked patiently through those years, trusting God.

TRUSTING . . . IN SPITE OF THE CIRCUMSTANCES

Now back to Hebrews 6. This isn't a lesson on Abraham's life; this is a lesson for us today. And the lesson has to do with trusting God when things don't work out our way. This is a lesson on how to deal with doubt. How to have hope when the answers haven't come. How to be confident in God when you cannot be confident in your circumstances or your future.

See the transition in verse 16? It all goes back to God's promising on His name that everything would occur just as He promised. Now to bring it into focus, men and women today, the writer adds:

[People today] swear by one greater than themselves, and with them an oath given as confirmation is an end of every dispute (v. 16).

Right hand raised, "Do you swear to tell the truth, the whole truth, and nothing but the truth, so help you God?" You've sworn on One greater than your name, and you are expected in the courtroom to tell the truth. There was none greater, so Almighty God swore on His own name. The writer says in this transitional principle: "Men swear by calling on a name greater than their own name."

In biblical days, before the day of attorneys, title companies, and other modern institutions, people settled their disagreements by coming to a mutual understanding and then confirming it with a promise. Such an oath or promise was final in its authority and settled disputes.

In those days there were many ways to signify that you had negotiated an agreement: You shook hands; or you raised your hand; or you put your thigh next to the thigh of the other person; or you put your hand under the thigh of one who was aged—a number of things were done. But you would swear when you touched the other person that you would do such and such, exactly as you had promised, and it was an oath based on a name greater than your own. Abraham had a promise that was based on God's name; it wouldn't fail. What hope it must have given that old man!

Now, verse 17. Look at how it all ties in:

> In the same way God, desiring even more to show to the heirs of the promise the unchangeableness of His purpose, interposed with an oath. . . .

With God, there is an unchangeable purpose. It is mysterious; it is unfathomable; there is no way, in this point of time, we can unravel all of the reasons behind His purpose. But it *is* unchangeable; it is so firm He has confirmed it by an oath. The passage goes on to say:

> . . . in order that by two unchangeable things, in which it is impossible for God to lie. . . .

The purpose He has planned for us and the oath He has taken, swearing that that purpose will be unchanged and ultimately right—those two things stand as God's confirmation to His people.

THE NEED TO THINK THEOLOGICALLY, NOT LOGICALLY

I confess to you, at times I doubt God's purpose and promise. I say that to my own embarrassment. When things haven't worked as I thought they would, when I received a no instead of a yes or a yes instead of a no, when I couldn't unravel a situation and fit it with the character of God . . . those have been times when I have said, "I know down inside this isn't right." The writer is coming to us on his knees, saying, "Please, rather than thinking logically, think *theologically!*" That's awfully good advice.

When the bottom drops out of your life, when hope starts to wear thin, when human logic fails to make much sense, think *theologically!* Go back and read Hebrews 6:17–18. The theological facts are: (1) there is an unchangeable purpose with God; and (2) that purpose is guaranteed with an oath.

It's at this juncture I should add: Don't try to explain it all to someone else. You can't. If you could, you would be God. The only thing you can explain theologically is that it is part of His unchangeable purpose, guaranteed with an oath, neither of which is a lie. That's theological thinking. As Solomon states so well: "[God] has made everything appropriate in its time" (Ecclesiastes 3:11a).

Let me give you a syllogism—a theological syllogism:

God is in control of the times and seasons.

Some times are hard and some seasons are dry. So the conclusion is:

God is in control of hard times and dry seasons.

We are quick to give God praise when the blessings flow—when the checking account is full and running over; when the job is secure, and a promotion is on the horizon; when the salary is good; when our health is fine. But we have a tough time believing when those things aren't true.

THREE BENEFITS OF THINKING THEOLOGICALLY

There are benefits that come from thinking theologically; you'll see three of them right here in these two verses in Hebrews 6. Look at verse 18:

> ... by two unchangeable things, in which it is impossible for God
> to lie, we may have strong encouragement ...

Logical thinking will discourage you; theological thinking will encourage you. That's the first benefit ... *personal encouragement*. Believe it. You will have "strong encouragement."

Read on:

> ... we who have fled for refuge in laying hold of the hope ...

That's the second benefit ... *a refuge of hope*. Encouragement is the opposite of discouragement. Hope is the opposite of despair. When you accept the fact that sometimes seasons are dry and times are hard and that God is in control of both, you will discover a sense of divine refuge, because the hope then is in God and not in yourself. That explains why Abraham gave glory to God during the waiting period. "I can't figure it out, I cannot explain it, but Lord, You promised me ... and I give You glory for the period of waiting, even though I'm getting up in years."

A strong encouragement, a refuge of hope, and for the ultimate benefit, read on:

> This hope we have as an anchor of the soul ...

That's the third benefit ... *an anchor for the soul*. The word *anchor* is used often in ancient literature, but it is only used once in the New Testament, right here in Hebrews 6. There are lots of hymns and gospel songs that make use of the anchor metaphor. Every one of them comes back to this verse that refers to the "anchor of the soul."

There's something beautiful in this word picture that I would have missed without the advice of one very capable scholar:

> The picture is that of an ancient sailing vessel finding its way through the narrow entrance to a harbor. This was one of the trickiest maneuvers the captain of a ship had to make. As his ship moved through the opening, he had to guard against a gust of wind running it onto a reef or a sandbar. The skeleton of many a ship could be seen on the rocks, giving testimony to the fact that its captain had failed his navigation test.
>
> To minimize the risk, the olden-day skipper would lower the ship's anchor into a smaller boat, which would then be rowed through the narrow entrance of the harbor. The anchor would then be dropped and this ship, with sails down, would be pulled past the obstacles, through the narrow opening, and into the safety of the harbor.[55]

I distinctly remember when our troop ship arrived (after seventeen days at sea!) at the harbor city of Yokohama, Japan. As we approached the harbor, the skipper stopped our ship and it sat silent in the deep sea, like an enormous, bloated whale. We marines waited on the deck in the hot sunshine as a tiny tugboat left the harbor and came out toward our huge vessel. Soon, a small Japanese gentleman came up the side of our ship and ultimately took the controls of our ship as he personally guided it until we were safely docked in the harbor. Someone later explained the reason to me: There were still mines in the Japanese harbor. That's a fun thought after seventeen days at sea: "Welcome to Japan; the mines are ready for you!" He guided us through the treacherous waters of the harbor and right up to the pier.

THE SPIRITUAL ANALOGY

The point of all of this, of course, is not anchors and skippers, ships and harbors. The point is this: That is *exactly* what Jesus Christ does when the bottom of life drops out. Look closely at the verse:

> ... We have as an anchor of the soul, a hope both sure and steadfast and one which enters within the veil. ...

The imagery of that verse may not be clear at first glance. Let me put it in today's terms. In the days of the Tabernacle, the Jews gathered around it and within it as a place of worship. Within the Tabernacle were veils; within the innermost veil was the holiest place on earth . . . the place we might call the "God-room." In this God-room the light (or, as it was called, the *shekinah*) of God resided. It's my understanding that the light of God was a brilliant, blazing light that shone down into the God-room. Within that room was an ark, or a small chest, much lower and smaller than most pulpits. On top of that chest was a grail, with golden cherubim on either end (angel-like creatures with their wings folded in front of them). That entire piece of unique furniture was too holy for words.

Once a year the high priest of the Jews would enter that God-room with a small pan of blood which, precisely as God required it in the Law, he poured out on the grail (which was called the "mercy seat") there between the golden cherubim. God, witnessing the spilling of the blood and pleased with the sacrifice that had been made correctly by the priest, graciously forgave the Jewish people. It was an annual event; it was the most sacred of all events. The Hebrews must have held their breath as the high priest went in with the pan, poured the blood, and came out of this room where God dwelled. The first-century Jews who read this word *veil* in Hebrews 6 understood all that. Look closely:

> This hope we have as an anchor . . . a hope both sure and stead-fast . . . one which enters within the veil, where Jesus has entered as a forerunner for us, having become a high priest forever according to the order of Melchizedek (vv. 19–20).

In other words, our Savior has gone through life, has taken all of life's beatings and buffetings, and He has gone before us. And now? Now He pulls us toward Himself! He invites His followers within the veil. He says, "Come in. Find here the rest that you need, the relief from the burdens and buffetings of doubt."

Doubt, you see, will always try to convince you, "You are all alone. No one else knows. Or cares. No one else really can enter in and help you with this." In Hebrews, however, the writer says that Christ is our constant priest—not once a year, but forever. He lives in the God-room. He is there, sitting alongside the Father, repre-senting your needs to Him. And, child of God, there is nothing so great for you to endure that He does not feel touched by it and stay by you through it.

SOME PERTINENT AND PRACTICAL REMINDERS

Now I want to say very practically, when you minister to people who have come to the end of their trail of despair, *logic won't cut it.* Logical thinking will not help you, nor will it help them. Sometimes, quite honestly, it will backfire. I'll give you an illustration:

> Writer Harriet Sarnoff Schiff has distilled her pain and tragedy in a book called *The Bereaved Parent.* She remembers that when her young son died during an operation to correct a congenital heart malfunction, her clergyman took her aside and said, "I know that this is a painful time for you. But I know that you will get through it all right, because God never sends us more of a burden than we can bear. God only let this happen to you because He knows that you are strong enough to handle it." Harriet Schiff remembers her reaction to those words: "If only I was a weaker person, Robbie would still be alive."[56]

Human logic, you see, breaks down. The mystery is enormous. And it is the enormity of it all that calls for faith. I'm sorry if that sounds like an overused bromide. But if we could unravel it, why would we need faith? If that were true, all we'd really need is the answer in the back of the book and someone to point it out to us; we'd read it and that's all there would be to it. But God's plan is that we walk by faith, *not* by sight. It is faith and patience that stretch us to the breaking point. Such things send doubt running.

When you find yourself dealing with doubt, let me give you three things to remember. First, *God cannot lie.* He can test, and He will. He can say no, and He sometimes will; He can say yes, and He will; He can say "wait," and occasionally He will—but God cannot lie. He must keep His word. Doubt says, "You fool, you're stupid to believe in a God who puts you through this." By faith, keep remembering that God cannot lie.

I appreciate very much the words of one survivor of Auschwitz:

> It never occurred to me to question God's doings or lack of doings while I was an inmate of Auschwitz. Although, of course, I understand others did. I was no less or no more religious because of what the Nazis did to us, and I believe my faith in

God was not undermined in the least. It never occurred to me to associate the calamity we were experiencing with God, to blame Him, or to believe in Him less, or cease believing in Him at all because He didn't come to our aid. God doesn't owe us that, or anything. We owe our lives to Him. If someone believes God is responsible for the death of six million because He didn't somehow do something to save them, he's got his thinking reversed. We owe God our lives for the few or many years we live. And we have the duty to worship Him and do as He commands. That's what we're here on earth for; to be in God's service and to do God's bidding.[57]

God cannot lie.

Here's the second piece of advice that helps me: *We will not lose.* Doubt says, "You lose if you trust God through this. You lose." If I read anything in this whole section of Hebrews 6, I read that in the mysterious manner of God's own timing, for some unexplainable and yet unchangeable purpose, those of us who trust Him ultimately win—because God ultimately wins.

There's a little chorus that Christians love to sing. It is quiet and tender, yet tough and true:

In His time, in His time,
He makes all things beautiful
In His time.
Lord, please show me every day,
As You're teaching me Your way,
That You do just what You say,
In Your time.[58]

God cannot lie. We will not lose. Your mate has walked away from you, an unfair departure—you will not lose, child of God. Your baby has been born and for some reason it has been chosen to be one of those special persons on this earth. You will not lose. You've waited and waited, and you were convinced that things would improve, yet things have only gotten worse—keep remembering, you will not lose. God swears on it with an oath that cannot change. You will not lose.

Third—and I guess it's the best of all—is that *our Lord Jesus does not leave.* To quote a verse from Scripture, He "sticks closer than a brother" (Proverbs 18:24).

. . . Jesus has entered as a forerunner for us, having become a high priest forever . . . (Hebrews 6:20).

That means He is there at any time . . . and always.

Remember the young woman I mentioned earlier? Remember her difficult circumstances? Advanced leukemia, daughter dead, husband gone, greater debt than she could even add up. She had checked herself out of a hospital, deciding that anything would be better than the isolation she was in as she endured that advanced stage of leukemia.

She and I spoke calmly and quietly about what was happening. I did a lot of listening. There were periods when there was silence on the phone for thirty to forty-five seconds. I didn't know where she was. I still don't know her full name. She spoke of taking her husband's revolver and going out on the beach to finish it all, and she asked me a lot of questions about suicide.

In what seemed an inappropriate moment . . . I felt peace, a total absence of panic. I had no fear that she would hang up and take her life. I simply spoke very, very quietly about her future. I made no special promise that she would immediately be healed. I knew that she might not live much longer, as her doctors were talking to her in terms of a very few weeks—perhaps days. I spoke to her about Christ and the hope He could provide. After a sigh and with an ache that was obvious, she hung up.

It was about thirty minutes later that the phone rang again. It was the same young woman. She had a friend who was a nurse, who used to come to our church in Fullerton, California. The nurse had given her a New Testament in which she had written my name and phone number and had said, "If you really are in deep need, I think he will understand." By the way, the nurse—her closest friend—was the one who had been killed in the auto accident. She had nothing to cling to from that friendship but memories and this Testament. She read from it. I said, "What does it say to you?" She said, "Well, I think the first part of it is biography and the last part is a group of letters that explain how to do what's in that biography." (That's a good analysis of the New Testament.) I said, "Have you done that?" And she had called back to say, "Yes, I've done that. I decided, Chuck, that I would, without reservation, give myself to Jesus Christ. I'm still afraid; I still have doubts. I still don't know what tomorrow's going to bring, but I want you to know that I have turned my life over to Jesus and I'm trusting Him through this. He has given me new hope ... the one thing I really needed."

It's very possible that someone reading these words right now feels the very same way. You're thinking thoughts that you have never entertained before, and you're thinking them more often and more seriously. Without trying to use any of the clichés on you, I would say that this hope Christ can bring, this "anchor of the soul," is the only way through. I have no answer other than Jesus Christ. I can't promise you healing, nor can I predict that your world will come back right side up. But I *can* promise you that He will receive you as you come in faith to Him. And He will bring back the hope you need so desperately. The good news is this: That hope will not only get you through this particular trial, it will ultimately take you "within the veil" when you die.

The Winsome Witness

Tonight was fun 'n' games night around the supper table in our house. It was wild. First of all, one of the kids snickered during the prayer (which isn't that unusual) and that tipped the first domino. Then a humorous incident from school was shared and the event (as well as how it was told) triggered havoc around the table. That was the begining of twenty to thirty minutes of the loudest, silliest, most enjoyable laughter you can imagine. At one point I watched my oldest literally fall off his chair in hysterics, my youngest doubled over in his chair as his face wound up in his plate with corn chips stuck to his cheeks . . . and my two girls leaning back, lost and preoccupied in the most beautiful and beneficial therapy God ever granted humanity: *laughter.*

What is so amazing is that everything seemed far less serious and heavy. Irritability and impatience were ignored like unwanted guests. For example, during the meal little Chuck spilled his drink twice . . . and even *that* brought the house down. If I remember correctly, that made six times during the day he accidentally spilled his drink, but nobody bothered to count.

All is quiet now, a rather unusual phenomenon around here. It's almost midnight and although my bones are weary, I'm filled and thrilled with the most pleasant memories a father can enjoy—a healthy, happy, laughing family. What a treasure! The load that often weighs heavily upon my shoulders about this time each week seems light and insignificant now. Laughter, the needed friend, has paid another dividend.

If you ask me, I think it is often just as sacred to laugh as it is to pray . . . or preach . . . or witness. But then—laughter *is* a witness in many ways. We have been misled by a twisted, unbalanced mind if we have come to think of laughter and fun as being carnal or even questionable. This is one of Satan's sharpest darts and from the looks and long lines on our faces, some of us have been punctured too many times. Pathetic indeed is the stern, somber Christian who has developed the look of an old basset hound through long hours of practice in restraining humor and squelching laughs.

Looking stern and severe is nothing new. The frowning fraternity of the sour set got started in the first century. Its charter members were a scowling band of religious stuffed shirts called Pharisees. I hardly need to remind you that Jesus' strongest words were directed at them. Their superserious, ritually rigid lifestyle nauseated our Lord. This brings me to a related point of contention I have with artists who portray Jesus Christ perpetually somber, often depressed. You simply cannot convince me that during thirty-three years as a carpenter and discipler of the Twelve He never enjoyed a long, sidesplitting laugh. Wouldn't it be refreshing to see a few pictures of Jesus leaning back with His companions, thoroughly enjoying a few minutes of fun with them? Surely that isn't heresy!

Picture in your mind Martin Luther, the reformer. What do you see? A stern-faced, steel-jawed, frowning fighter with his German fist clenched and raised against wrong? *Wrong!*

Several of his biographers inform us that he *abounded* in an unguarded, transparent sincerity . . . plain and pleasant honesty . . . playful humor and mirth. Small wonder he attracted the oppressed, browbeaten people of his day like flies to honey. The reformer, you see, wasn't afraid to laugh. In one word, surprising though it may seem, Luther was *winsome*.

Let's try another famous name: Charles Haddon Spurgeon, the great preacher of London. What do you see? A sober, stoop-shouldered pastor who dragged the weight of sinful England around with a rope? Try again!

Spurgeon was a character. His style was so loose he was criticized again and again for bordering on frivolity in the Tabernacle pulpit. Certain incensed fellow clergymen railed against his habit of introducing humor into his sermons. With a twinkle in his eye, he once replied: "If only you knew how much I hold back, you would commend me."

This preacher thinks it less a crime to cause a momentary laughter than a half-hour of profound slumber.[59]

Spurgeon dearly loved life. His favorite sound was laughter—and frequently he leaned back in the pulpit and *roared aloud* over something that struck him funny. He infected people with cheer germs. Those who caught the disease found their load lighter and their Christianity brighter. Like Luther, Spurgeon was *winsome*.

Winsomeness. That tasteful, appealing, ultra-magnetic quality ... that charisma ... that ability to cause joy and genuine pleasure in the thick of it all. When a teacher has it, students line up for the course. When a dentist or physician has it, his practice stays full. When a salesman has it, he gets writer's cramp filling out orders. When an usher has it, the church is considered friendly. When a college president has it, the public relations department has a downhill slide. When a coach has it, the team shows it. When a restaurant owner has it, the public knows it. When parents have it, kids grow it.

Winsomeness *motivates*. It releases the stranglehold grip of the daily grind. It takes the sting out of reality. Winsomeness *simplifies*. Things suddenly become less complicated ... less severe ... less bothersome. The hole at the end of the tunnel becomes far more significant than the dark passage leading to it. Winsomeness *encourages*. Without ignoring the wrong, winsomeness focuses on the benefits, the hope, the answers. Even when it must deal with jagged disappointment or inescapable negatives, winsomeness stands tall and refuses to spend the night in such dwellings.

Winsome humor is an asset beyond value in the life of a missionary. Indeed, it is a most serious deficiency if a missionary lacks the ability to find something to smile about in diverse and difficult situations. I recently read of a Swede who was urged by friends to give up the idea of returning to India as a missionary because it was so hot there. "Man," he was exhorted, "it's 120 degrees in the shade!" "Vell," countered the Swede in noble contempt, "ve don't always have to stay in the shade, do ve?"[60]

Some frowning, neurotic soul is reading this and saying, "Well, somebody's got to do the job. Life is more than a merry-go-round. Laughter is all right for schoolgirls—but adults, especially *Christian adults*, have a task to perform that's deadly serious." Okay, pal, so it's serious. So it isn't all a joke. Nobody's going to argue that life has its demands and that being mature involves discipline and responsibility. But who says we have to get an ulcer and drive ourselves (and each other) to distraction in the process of fulfilling our

God-given role? No one is less efficient or more incompetent than the person on the brink of a breakdown, who has stopped having fun, who is nursing a bleeding ulcer, who has become a pawn in the brutal hands of relentless responsibilities, who has begun a one-man crusade for *whatever*, who has lost the ability to relax and laugh and "blow it" without guilt. Our hospitals are full—literally jammed—with the victims of the let's-cut-the-fun philosophy of life. And today, quite frankly, they really aren't much of an asset to society—nor to the cause of Christ. That is not a criticism—it's reality.

By a sense of humor, I am neither referring to distasteful, inappropriate, vulgar jesting, nor foolish and silly talk that is ill-timed, offensive, and tactless. I mean that necessary ingredient of wit—enjoyable, delightful expressions or thoughts—which lifts our spirits and lightens our day.

How is such winsomeness cultivated—and communicated—in our homes and among our other contacts? What practical steps can be taken to yank us out of the doldrums? I suggest three specific projects:

1. *Start each day with pleasant words.* Your family will be the first to benefit (better have the glycerin tablets ready). No need to dance around like Bozo the clown or force jokes into your sleepy mate's ears. Just be pleasant in your remarks, cheerful with your greetings. As you are slipping out of bed, thank God for His love . . . His calm, fresh reminders that this new day is under His control. Quietly state the encouraging truth: God loves me.

2. *Smile more often.* I cannot think of many occasions when a smile is out of place. Develop a cheerful countenance. A frowning face repels. A smile reaches out and attracts. God gave you this gift that radiates encouragement. Don't fence it in . . . loosen up, break that concrete mask—*smile*. You might even release a laugh or two this month if you want to get fanatical about it.

3. *Express at least one honest comment of appreciation or encouraging remark to each person you are with during the day.* As a Christian, you want to share Christ's love. You want to lift up hearts that are heavy. Spot strengths—and say so. Steadfastly decline to camp on others' weaknesses. Ask the Lord to make you genuinely interested in others instead of so occupied with yourself. Ask Him to enable you to take the risk and reach out. Ask Him to be winsome through you.

In spite of bleak and serious surroundings about us, I firmly believe we need another good dose of Solomon's counsel. Listen to David's wisest son:

> A joyful heart makes a cheerful face, but when the heart is sad, the spirit is broken. . . . All the days of the afflicted are bad, but a cheerful heart has a continual feast (Proverbs 15:13, 15).

> A joyful heart is good medicine [the Hebrew says, ". . . causes good healing . . ."] but a broken spirit dries up the bones (Proverbs 17:22).

Honestly now . . . how's your sense of humor? Are the times in which we live beginning to tell on you—your attitude, your face, your outlook? If you aren't sure, ask those who live under your roof, they'll tell you! Solomon talks straight, too. He (under the Holy Spirit's direction) says that three things will occur in the lives of those who have lost their capacity to enjoy life: (1) a broken spirit, (2) a lack of inner healing, and (3) dried-up bones. What a barren portrait of the believer!

Have you begun to shrivel into a bitter, impatient, critical Christian? Is your family starting to resemble employees at a local mortuary? The Lord points to a better way—the way of joyful winsomeness. "A joyful heart" is what we need . . . and if ever we needed it, it is now.

Houdini's Secret

E hrich Weiss was a remarkable man.

By the time of his death he was famous around the world. Never heard of him, huh?

Maybe this will help. He was born of Hungarian-Jewish parentage in Appleton, Wisconsin, in 1894. He became the highest-paid entertainer of his day.

That still doesn't help much, does it? This will.

When he finally got his act together, Weiss adopted a stage name: *Harry Houdini.* The master showman, a distinguished flyer, a mystifying magician, and—most of all—an unsurpassed escapologist.

On March 10, 1904, the London *Daily Illustrated Mirror* challenged Houdini to escape from a special pair of handcuffs they had prepared. Are you ready? There were six locks on each cuff and nine tumblers on each lock! Seven days later, 4000 spectators gathered in the London Hippodrome to witness the outcome of the audacious challenge that Houdini had accepted.

At precisely 3:15 P.M., the manacled showman stepped into an empty cabinet that came up to his waist. Kneeling down, he was out of sight for a full 20 minutes. He stood up smiling as the crowd applauded, thinking he was free. But he was not. He asked for more light. They came on brighter as he knelt down out of sight. Fifteen minutes later he stood to his feet. Applause broke out—again, premature. He was still handcuffed. Said he just needed to flex his knees.

Down into the cabinet again went the magician. Twenty minutes passed slowly for the murmuring crowd before Houdini stood to his feet with a broad smile. Loud applause quickly stopped as the audience saw he was not yet free. Because the bright lights made the heat so intense, he leaped from the cabinet and twisted his manacled hands in front of him until he could reach a pocketknife in his vest. Opening the knife with his teeth, he held its handle in his mouth and bent forward to such a degree that the tail of his coat fell over his head. He grasped the coat, pulled it over his head, then proceeded to slash it to ribbons with the knife between his teeth. Throwing aside the strips of his heavy coat, he jumped back into the box as the audience roared its approval and cheered him on.

Down went Houdini, but this time for only ten minutes. With a dramatic flourish, he jumped from the box—wrists free—waving the bulky handcuffs over his head in triumph. Pandemonium exploded in London! Once again the showman had achieved the incredible—almost the *impossible*.

Afterward, Houdini was interviewed. Everyone wanted to know why he had to interrupt the process of his escape as often as he did. With a twinkle in his eyes, the magician freely admitted that he really didn't *have* to interrupt the process. He repeatedly explained that his ability to escape was based on knowledge.

"My brain is the key that sets me free!" he often declared. Then why did he keep standing up before he was loose? He confessed it was because he wanted the audience's applause to keep up his enthusiasm![61]

Two things, then set Houdini free: (1) his *knowledge* of what he knew to be true and (2) the cultivation of his own *enthusiasm*.

What an essential role enthusiasm plays in our lives! In many ways, it is the key ingredient that frees us from the cramping, dark, overheated confinement of a task. When the odds are against us, the hours are long, and the end is not yet in view, enthusiasm rescues us from the temptation to quit—or run away—or complain. It takes the grit and grind out of boredom. It calls in fresh troops when the battle gets long and the body gets weary.

Athletes feed on it. Salesmen are motivated by it. Teachers count on it. Students fail without it. Leadership demands it. Projects are completed because of it. Emerson's motto is as true today as the day he wrote it:

Nothing great was ever achieved without enthusiasm.[62]

Few characteristics are more contagious, more magnetic. I'm convinced that one of the reasons God gives us so many personal promises in His Word is to stir up our enthusiasm—to build a bonfire in the steam room of our souls.

Houdini had it right: Knowledge is essential—but knowledge without enthusiasm is like a tire without air . . . like a pool without water . . . like a bed without sheets . . . like a "thank you" without a smile. Remove enthusiasm from a church service on Sunday and you have the makings of a memorial service at a mortuary on a Monday. Remove enthusiasm from the daily whirl of family activities and you've made a grinding mill out of a merry-go-round. Enthusiasm acts as the oil on Saturdays in our home when it's cleanup day and the family machine needs a boost.

Two men were in a military prison. One was sad and depressed. The other was quite happy. The sad soldier lamented that he had gone AWOL and was in for thirty days. His smiling companion replied that he had murdered a general and was in for three days. Astonished, the gloomy GI complained, "That isn't fair! Your crime was far more serious. Why am I in for thirty days—and you for only three?" Still smiling, the other answered, "They're going to hang me on Wednesday."[63]

The difference? Enthusiasm.

Fun Is Contagious

A hurry-up lifestyle results in a throwaway culture. Things that should be lasting and meaningful are sacrificed on the altar of the temporary and superficial.

The major fallout in such a setting is the habit of viewing relationships casually. This cavalier attitude cripples society in various ways:

- Friends walk away instead of work through.
- Partnerships dissolve rather than solve.
- Neighbors no longer visit and relax together. They erect stone walls and exist on isolated islands.
- The aged are resented, not honored.
- Husbands and wives divorce rather than persevere.
- Children are brushed aside rather than nourished; used and abused rather than cherished and cultivated.

Caught in the vortex of all this, the most common response is to become negative and pessimistic. Everything begins to look dark. We start anticipating failure, impossibilities, and inevitable doom. We become rigid, much too serious. We start focusing on what *isn't* going well, and our whole frame of reference, to use Bunyan's vivid analogy, takes on the likeness of the "Slough of Despond." Indifference pokes a slow leak in our boat as Intensity and Anxiety climb aboard. How difficult it is to remain positive and encouraged in such a dismal context . . . yet how essential!

I heard recently about a man who was driving through North Carolina. As he approached one of the little towns nestled in the mountains, he noticed a large sign near the city limits marker. It read:

WE UNDERSTAND THAT A SERIOUS RECESSION IS SUPPOSED TO HAPPEN THIS YEAR, BUT WE'VE DECIDED NOT TO PARTICIPATE.

I love it! With an attitude like that, the place becomes an oasis of hope and joy in a desert of depression.

Let me encourage you to adopt a similar mind-set in your family. Let's stop taking our cues from the morning paper and the evening news. Let's decide not to be influenced by those grim statistics! I'm tired of the pessimism that dominates even the weather report. How about a switch? Instead of remembering that tomorrow will have a 20 percent chance of rain, what's wrong with thinking about the 80 percent chance of sunshine?

Call me crazy if you like (you won't be the first), but I am more convinced than ever that attitudes shape just about everything we do. Not facts, not a group of so-called authorities. Not some big, thick book spelling the demise of civilization . . . but *attitudes*. When those attitudes get refocused on God's power and His incredible purposes for living, hang on to your socks! Instead of running from each other in our relationships, we would be running toward one another. Before we realized it, people would become more important to us than status, fame, or fortune.

I believe it was writer Christopher Morley who said that if everybody had only five minutes to live, every phone booth in the world would be occupied by someone. Each would be sending out final words of affection and affirmation.

I may have questioned that before I endured an earthquake. Living here in southern California, you never know when "the big one" will hit. Little tremors and rock 'n' rollers keep us wondering. On October 1, 1987, I was in my study early in the morning. Suddenly, the movement of the floor gave me this strange sensation. Doors started to bump and windows rattled as an awful lot of shaking was going on.

Within seconds, I was partially covered with books from the shelves above my head. My desk lamp rocked back and forth. I stumbled across the room to stand in a doorway as the thought flashed through my mind, *If this isn't "The Big One," I can't imagine what IT will be like!* As you know, it wasn't. We still have it to look forward to. It's supposed to happen each year, but I've decided not to participate!

Guess the very first thing I did when the shaking calmed down. Like E.T., I picked up the phone and called home. First, I checked to see if Cynthia, Cols, and Chuck were okay. I then made two more calls . . . one to our son and his wife, Curt and Deb, and the other to our daughter and her husband, Charissa and Byron (mainly to check on the grandkids).

Relationships! When the quake hit, I never once thought, *I wonder who the church will get as my replacement.* Or, *Did we pick up the dry cleaning yesterday?* Or, *We probably ought to cancel our subscription to* Newsweek. Or, *Shoot! I forgot to get the car washed.* No way! My entire focus was on those people who bear my name, who complete the loop in my family circle.

Relationships! Never sell them short. If we'll slow down the hurry-up lifestyle for a moment and pause to catch our breath, we'll realize the need to call a halt to our throwaway culture.

FLEXIBILITY: IT IS ESSENTIAL

Uptight families cease to function properly. When Dad is tense and Mom is irritable, the kids have no trouble deciphering the message: Shut up and don't mess around. What happens down deep inside is tragic. Relationships break down. Feelings start getting internalized and confused. Negotiations are strained. Fear builds up as tension mounts. Communication is finally reduced to looks, frowns, shrugs, sarcastic jabs, and put-downs. Cooperation and teamwork fall by the wayside. Extremes emerge—long periods of silence periodically interrupted by shouting matches. Far from a haven of rest, such a home becomes a hell on earth.

FLEXIBILITY IN THE FAMILY SCENE

I offer no "series of steps" that will ultimately lead to a flexible family. I'm not writing of some sterile, theoretical technique but rather of a relational attitude. Wisdom, remember, must be given room to flow. It cannot be reduced to analytical formulas or computer programs. Growing wise in family life is a daily process, a trial-and-error, learn-as-you-go series of discoveries that has little to do with rigid rules and regulations . . . and everything to do with attitudes and actions.

My message is this: In order to grow, mature, and flourish, everyone needs room; let's provide plenty of it.

Watching other families over the years has confirmed what I've discovered in my own: The two entrenched enemies of flexibility are Hurry and Rigidity. Each results in family tension. Each, therefore, must be exposed.

WHAT'S THE HURRY?

The older I get, the more I appreciate the benefits of taking time. Woodwork done slowly and meticulously by a craftsman is beautiful and able to endure the test of the elements. Art—whether musical compositions, needlework, sculpture, or painting—requires time and attention to detail. Even the cultivation of our walk with God or some ministry skill requires a great deal of time to develop.

The psalmist realized this when he wrote, "Be still, and know that I am God" (Psalm 46:10, NKJV). The Hebrew does not suggest standing around and letting your mind wander—not that kind of being still. Rather, it means "Let go; relax." The New American Standard version renders this, "Cease striving." What a timely admonition!

If all this is true of other realms and responsibilities, it is certainly applicable to the home and family. Children were not created to be "jerked up" (as my mother used to put it), but to be cared for with gentleness and attention to detail. They require time . . . lots of it. Not all of it needs to be supervised, however.

Perhaps the best way to describe my early childhood world of play is with the word *relaxed*. Lots of friends in the neighborhood. Sandlot football down at the end of Quince Street in East Houston on an open field adjacent to St. Andrew's Methodist Church. Endless and exhausting hours of one-on-one or "horse" over at Eugene's house—with Freddie and Bruce—as the four of us shot hoops against the garage backboard. Then there was always "Hide-and-Seek" and "Kick the Can"—until suppertime. Weekends found me playing Cowboys and Indians, making scooters out of beat-up roller skates, runnir.g races and relays down the street, shooting my BB

gun in the woods down by the creek, and messing around with craw-
dads after a rain.

Plenty of time to grow up . . . easygoing, relaxing hours.

In the summer, there were family reunions down below Pala-
cios at my granddaddy's little bay cabin, plus fishing, floundering,
crabbing, swimming, driving the tractor, making rafts out of toesacks
and old inner tubes, seining for bait, and eating. My—*did we eat!* Fresh
shrimp, crab gumbo, fried gulf trout, barbecued beef cooked on
chicken wire stretched over an open pit of hickory coals, freshly
plucked watermelon, big brown eggs (laid that very morning), thick
slab bacon, homemade biscuits, gravy, hand-cranked ice cream . . .
I gotta stop!

Best of all, my brother, sister, and I were given room to be kids.
Just kids. I went to school barefoot until the fourth grade (when
Wanda Ragland and I fell madly in love), and I was still playing cops
and robbers in junior high. Nobody hurried me to grow up. I suppose everybody figured it would just happen. I can still remember
one hot summer afternoon sitting on the curb in torn blue jeans, licking a Popsicle, and thinking, *This is the life!* I had finished mowing
the grass, putting out the trash, mopping the bathroom floor, and
throwing my paper route (my major chores), and was about to head
down to the church with my well-worn football to play until my
daddy whistled, signaling supper.

I was just a kid. No big expectations drove me to excel or
achieve. Life was allowed to run its own course back then, like a lazy
river working its way down from the slopes to the sea. No big deal,
no adult pressure to perform, just down-home, easy livin', fun,
growin'-up stuff. And plenty of time. A lingering, relaxed childhood
was mine to enjoy.

No longer, it seems. Forty years removed from my laid-back
lifestyle, there is a new youngster in our city streets. Have you
noticed? Perhaps I'm overly sensitive because I've read David
Elkind's splendid book *The Hurried Child*, with the provocative sub-
title, *Growing Up Too Fast Too Soon*.[64] On the cover is a little girl, not
more than eleven or twelve . . . with earrings (pierced ears, of course),
plucked eyebrows, carefully applied cosmetics, teased and feath-
ered hair, and exquisite jewelry. I've looked at that picture dozens
of times, and on each occasion I see more. She bears the look of
bewildered innocence—almost like a helpless calf being pushed to

slaughter. She's afraid, but can't say so; it wouldn't be chic. She's into a role that deprives her the freedom to be simply a child. The problem? She is being hurried . . . like so many children and adolescents today. The luxury of childhood is no longer an option.

She reminds me of the seven-year-old whom Susan Ferraro mentioned in an article titled "Hotsy Totsy." It was the little girl's birthday party: ice cream and cake, a donkey poster with twelve tails waiting to be pinned, a door prize, the works:

> "Ooh," sighed seven-year-old Melissa as she opened her first present. It was Calvin Klein jeans. "Aah," she gasped as the second box revealed a bright new top from Gloria Vanderbilt. There were Christian Dior undies from grandma—a satiny little chemise and matching bloomer bottoms—and mother herself had fallen for a marvelous party outfit from Yves St. Laurent. Melissa's best friend gave her an Izod sports shirt, complete with alligator emblem . . . [65]

It's not the clothes. It's not those silly brand names that bug me. It's the message they announce. It's the subtle hurry-up woven through those threads and styles. It's the subliminal strokes and sensations a child in the second grade can wear but isn't equipped to handle.

The media isn't going to be outdone, either. Music, books, films, and of course, television increasingly portray the young as precocious and seductive. Kids are given scripts and scenes that present them in more or less explicit sexual and manipulative situations. "Such portrayals," writes Elkind, "force children to think they should act grown up before they are ready." This is certainly true in movies like *Little Darlings* where the two principals—teenaged girls—are in competition as to who will lose her virginity first. And I think I'll gag if I hear again "Take Your Time (Do It Right)" or "Do That to Me One More Time."

I'm no expert, understand, just a father and a concerned observer. From what I've read and heard on the subject, I understand that emotions and feelings are the most complex and intricate part of development. They have their own timing and rhythm and cannot be hurried. Children can grow up fast in some ways, but not in others. It is tough enough with nobody pushing, but I'm convinced it's bewildering, even confusing, when children's behavior and appearance are hurried to speak "adult" while their insides cry "child." It simply isn't fair!

One of America's most outstanding high school quarterbacks was written up in *Sports Illustrated* a while ago. His name is Todd Marinovich. His record of passing yardage (9,914) is all-time tops. His senior year, he threw for more yards than Jim Kelley or Dan Marino or John Elway did in theirs. Of 104 Division 1-A colleges and universities, no less than 100 of them were jumping through the hoop to have this young phenom. USC eventually snagged him as their number-one quarterback. The pros must already be salivating. We're talking *franchise*.

But before we get too impressed, let's back away a few feet, step into the time tunnel, and relive how this young fella, not yet twenty years old, arrived at this so-called enviable moment. It is a mouth-opening, mind-boggling account of parental fanaticism. Todd's dad, Marv, has been the primary force behind the boy's life. Trudi, his mother, has also cooperated. The article from which I quote has a telling title, "Bred to Be a Superstar."

> What's fascinating about Marinovich, a 6'4½", 212-pound left-handed redhead, is that he is, in a real sense, America's first test-tube athlete. He has never eaten a Big Mac or an Oreo or a Ding Dong. When he went to birthday parties as a kid, he would take his own cake and ice cream to avoid sugar and refined white flour. He would eat homemade catsup, prepared with honey. He did consume beef but not the kind injected with hormones. He ate only unprocessed dairy products. He teethed on frozen kidney. When Todd was one month old, Marv was already working on his son's physical conditioning. He stretched his hamstrings. Push-ups were next. Marv invented a game in which Todd would try to lift a medicine ball onto a kitchen counter. Marv also put him on a balance beam. Both activities grew easier when Todd learned to walk. There was a football in Todd's crib from day one. . . .
>
> Eventually Marv started gathering experts to work on every aspect of Todd's physical condition—speed, agility, strength, flexibility, quickness, body control, endurance, nutrition. He found one to improve Todd's peripheral vision. He enlisted a throwing coach and a motion coach and a psychologist. These days 13 different experts are donating their time in the name of science.

Tom House, the pitching coach for the Texas Rangers and a computer whiz, has analyzed Todd's form and found that while his balance is perfect, his arm is 4.53 inches too low throughout his delivery. Todd, who listens to everyone, is working on it. This Team Marinovich is the creation of Marv, who was a two-way lineman and a captain at USC in 1962, a marginal pro in the AFL with the Raiders and a sometime assistant coach for the Raiders, the Rams, the Cardinals and the Hawaiians of the defunct WFL.

Though Marv owns an athletic research center—a sort of high-tech gym—his true occupation has been the development of his son, an enterprise that has yet to produce a monetary dividend. And the Marinovich marriage ended last year after 24 years. "All Marv has done," says a friend, "is give up his entire life for Todd."

Which is fine with Marv. Father and son now live in a one-bedroom apartment. Todd has the bedroom, and Marv sleeps on the sofa in the living room. On weekends Todd visits Trudi, who has moved back in with her parents in Newport Beach.

"I think I'm a tyrant," says Marv. "But I think you have to be to succeed. The best thing about it is my relationship with my son. We wanted to have the healthiest possible mom and the healthiest possible child. It's fanatical, but I don't know if you can be a great success without being a fanatic." He pauses and then continues, "I suppose it was a little overdone."[66]

That, ladies and gents, is the understatement of the year! I cannot help but wonder if Todd will someday miss having been a child. Scripture clearly states, "There is an appointed time for everything" (Ecclesiastes 3:1). *How about time to be a child?* How about time to grow up slowly, carefully, yes, even protected, and dare I add, a little naive? How about time to "speak as a child, think as a child, reason as a child" (1 Corinthians 13:11)? It will take a lot of effort to make that happen. For a few, it is worth it to go against the trend and allow your children the joy of childhood—encouraging them simply to be what they are. But for most, it is too big a hassle. Maybe it's because we're too busy being what we're not and pushing our kids to do the same. Let's back off and start having fun again! Let's return to the psalmist's counsel to relax . . . to cease struggling.

Flexibility, folks, doesn't come easy! You and I are surrounded by peers who tend to pressure us by making what I call hurry-up comments. We hear them every day. They're about as subtle as a Mack truck.

"Our son is only seven, but you ought to see him on his PC. Wow! The kid's a whiz."

"We've decided that our preschooler needs to get serious about the future, so we've got her into dance and modeling classes. After all, the possibilities are endless once she gets into making commercials."

"We think Timmy has real athletic ability. We've talked him into that basketball clinic for nine-year-olds. The pros will want the kid before long!"

Don't get me wrong. I believe deeply in the importance of parents' seeing potential and being there as an encouragement . . . but to push for too much, too fast, too early takes away the fun of growing up . . . of being just a relaxed, tightly knit family with well-developed, close relationships.

Take it easy! Much of what parents push for will naturally flow in time. Put your energy into cultivating close relationships. Those high-powered goals have a way of emerging at the right time.

WHY THE RIGIDITY?

There is an equally disturbing concern of mine that is robbing fun from families—rigidity. What makes this one especially subtle is that it is present in homes of well-meaning Christian parents. Wanting to guard their children from the pitfalls of a permissive, godless society, they push the pendulum to the opposite extreme. For all the right reasons, these parents decide to put the clamps on all liberty. A willingness to listen, to reason, to give a little, to shrug and pass certain things off as part of growing up is considered too permissive. In place of all that is the erection of a brick fortress, where unbending rules are adhered to and nonnegotiables are regularly spelled out by super-intense parents.

Those who have bought into that family-fortress mentality won't like the following quotation. Unfortunately, those who need it the most tend to believe it the least.

> A rigid status quo orientation is indicative of pathology. . . . Given the continuing shifts in age, family composition and the need for redefinition of rules in families, a family locked into a rigid equilibrium . . . is in trouble.
>
> . . . The most viable family systems [are those where there is] a more free-flowing balance . . . successful negotiation; pos-

itive and negative feedback... with few implicit rules and more explicit rules.[67]

One major reason our family has remained close through each stage, and to this day continues to grow together and have fun together, has been our commitment to staying flexible. I hesitate to speak of this lest it all suddenly screech to a halt. I'm reminded of what one whale said to his mate, "Better watch it; when you get to the top and start to blow, that's when you get harpooned!"

My desire is neither to "blow" as if we've arrived, nor to shame those who are struggling through times of family turmoil. The only reason I return to the song of the Swindolls' close-knit family is to encourage you with the thought, *It can work! These things he is writing about have been proven over the years in their lives.* Trust me, we have made numerous mistakes and have frequently failed to carry out what we knew was best. Somehow we have survived, still walking in harmony. The grace of God is the main reason—plus children who have continued to forgive us, partly because they never had reasons to doubt their value in our eyes.

Let me return to this issue of domestic rigidity. Frankly, it cuts crossgrain with the magnificent grace and liberty of the gospel. Christ's death and resurrection provide the basis of the gospel. That "good news" has to do with our being liberated from bondage by His provision ... bondage to the law (which condemned us) and bondage to the power of sin (which intensified our guilt before God). Freed, we are now able to call our God *Father,* and our Savior *Friend.* What joy, what refreshing space this provides! It is like being set free from prison. Spiritually, we have moved into a realm of such ecstatic delight, the mere thought of being enslaved again is repulsive. To quote Jesus Himself:

> If therefore the Son shall make you free, you shall be free indeed (John 8:36).

Think of it! Free *indeed.* Totally and completely free in Him. At last, free to love, to serve, to laugh, to relax in His presence. Free to be all we were designed to be. Free to share openly ... free to think, to create, to call Him our Friend!

My question is obvious. If that is true of our condition in God's heavenly family, why shouldn't it be true in our earthly family? What keeps us from that level of spontaneity, closeness, and hilarious joy?

Who came along and stole the joy from the family . . . especially the Christian family? Who had the audacity to shove us back behind the bars of a relational prison? I say, *out* with such enemies of freedom!

If you know your Bible, you know which New Testament letter I have on my mind right now: Galatians. It is only six chapters long—less than 150 verses—but it packs a wallop. Paul wrote it because a group of Judaistic legalists had moved in on this congregation and stolen their liberty. He decided to expose the false teacher and exhort the Galatian Christians to break the bonds that were slowly but surely enslaving them.

Rather than my quoting passage after passage, I encourage you to take the time to read the Galatian letter in one sitting. You'll get the picture. My purpose in mentioning it is that there are several analogies between living in God's family strictly by tight rules and rigid regulations and living in our earthly family the same way. My observation is that neither works. The joy, the spontaneity, and the creativity dry up. So does the fun. In either place, people exist in fear, realizing the hammer may fall at any moment. Worst of all, life gets reduced to nothing more than a grim existence, best described by the one who pictured our hurry-up lifestyle in these vivid words:

> *This is the age of the half-read page,*
> *The quick hash and the mad dash,*
> *The bright night with the nerves tight,*
> *The plane hop with the brief stop;*
> *The lamp tan in a short span,*
> *The big shot in a good spot,*
> *The brain strain and the heart pain,*
> *The catnaps until the spring snaps;*
> *And the fun is gone.*[68]

Children are a lot like chickens . . . they need room to squawk, lay a few eggs, flap their wings, even to fly the coop. Otherwise, let me warn you, all that lid-sitting will one day explode, and you'll wish you had not taken such a protective stance.

HOW TO KEEP THE FUN IN THE FAMILY

Some of you are sincerely interested in changing. You see that what you have been doing isn't working. You want to lighten up and let the pressure off. You've had enough of protectionism and legal-

ism. Good for you! You're well on your way to happiness at home if
that is your attitude. Let me suggest several guidelines that will help
make it happen.

1. *Try to be absolutely authentic.* I know that seems like a threatening thought, but it is a giant step toward open communication.

How does authenticity reveal itself? It isn't that difficult.

- If you aren't sure of yourself, admit it.
- If you're afraid of the risk, say so.
- If you don't know the answer to a question your teenager asks
  you, use those wonderfully relieving words, "I don't know."
- If you were wrong, confess it.
- If you feel under pressure from others, own up to it.
- If your kids ask why, refuse to dodge behind that favorite of
  all parental clichés, "Because I said so." Be painfully honest
  with yourself. If you cannot think of a reason, maybe that's
  God's way of saying you need to bend and even give in.

Our youngsters (and oldsters) deserve to know the truth . . .
even if *we* were not raised in such a vulnerable environment. One
father describes it this way:

> The speech was finished and the audience had been generous
> with its applause, and in the car on the way home my fourteen-
> year-old son turned to me and said: "I really admire you, Dad,
> being able to get up there and give a speech like that. You always
> know what to say to people. You always seem to know what
> you're doing."
>
> I smiled when he said that. I may even have blushed mod-
> estly. But, at that moment, I didn't know what to say at all.
>
> After a while I thanked him and assured him that some day
> he would be comfortable speaking in front of an audience, that
> he would always know what to say to people, that he would
> always know what he was doing. But what I really wanted to say
> to my son was that his father was not at all what he appeared to
> be and that being a man is frequently a facade.
>
> It has taken me a long time to admit that—even to myself.
> Especially to myself. *My* father, after all, really *had* always known
> what *he* was doing. He was strong and confident and he never
> felt pain, never knew fear. There wasn't a leaky faucet he
> couldn't fix or an engine he couldn't manage to get running
> again. Mechanics never fooled him, salesmen never conned

him. He was always calm in emergencies, always cool under fire. He never cried.

For a long time I wondered how such a man could have produced such a weakling for a son. I wondered where the self-doubts and the fears I felt all the time had come from. I wondered why the faucets I fixed always dripped twice as fast after I got finished with them, why engines that sputtered before I started to work on them went stone-dead under my wrench. I dreaded the thought that some day my father would see me cry. I didn't realize that fathers are not always everything they seem to be.

It's different for fathers than it is for mothers. Motherhood is honest, close to the surface. Mothers don't have to hide what they feel. They don't have to pretend.

When there are sounds downstairs in the middle of the night, a mother is allowed to pull the covers over her head and hope that they will go away. A father is supposed to put on his slippers and robe and march boldly down the stairs, even if he's pretty sure that it's the Manson family waiting for him in the kitchen.

When the road signs are confusing and the scenery is starting to look awfully unfamiliar, it's perfectly natural for a mother to pull over to the side of the road and ask for directions from the first person who comes along. A father is supposed to know exactly where he's going, even if he has to drive two hundred miles out of the way to prove it.

Mothers can bang a new jar of peanut butter on the floor until the lid is loose enough to turn. Fathers are supposed to twist it off with their bare hands—without getting red in the face.

Mothers who lose their jobs are unfortunate. Fathers who lose their jobs are failures.

When a mother gets hurt she may want to swear, but she is only allowed to cry. When a father gets hurt he may want to cry, but he is only allowed to swear. . . .

I should have told him that the only reason his father, like lots of fathers, doesn't admit his weaknesses is because he is afraid that someone will think he is not a real man.

More important, what I should have said to my fourteen-year-old son in the car that night is that someday, when he's a father, he'll feel fear and self-doubt and pain, and that it's all right. But my father never told me, and I haven't told my son.[69]

2. *Keep the rules and policies to a bare minimum.* This is especially true as the children get older. Younger children need the securi-

ty of knowing where the boundaries are. That's the basis of discipline. But as little ones grow and begin to show healthy signs of exerting their independence, let it happen. Add more flex. Keep an open mind. I am not suggesting that you compromise on issues of integrity or purity. Of course not! There are limits.

I heard of a set of parents who decided they would take a hands-off policy once their son graduated from high school. He chose to stay home, commute to a local college, and continue to live off the folks' income. They agreed. He didn't work. They picked up the tab. Mom continued to make his bed and clean his room. Dad provided him with a car, a gasoline credit card, covered all his insurance expenses. It should not surprise you to read that by the end of his freshman year he was doing drugs ("just so you keep all that stuff in your room"), and bringing home one girl after another for overnight sex without once being confronted or told no. *That is ridiculous!* Giving room to grow is one thing. Giving up all moral restrictions and personal convictions for the sake of "peace at any price" is another thing entirely.

My point here has to do with adding the oil of wisdom to the gears of relationships. As children grow older and begin to think for themselves, wise parents realize that more rules and longer lists of policies only antagonize. Kids lose respect for parents who refuse to discuss reasons and never negotiate the rules.

As our children began to date, we found it necessary to establish times and places. They were expected to tell us where they were going and when they would be returning. We made it clear that if something kept them from getting to the previously stated place or being home by the agreed-upon time, a phone call was expected . . . even if it meant pulling off the freeway on the way home and finding a public phone to call us. Only on the rarest occasions was that simple policy unworkable. As they grew older, a later time to return home was permitted, but the phone call remained firm. We explained it was a matter of courtesy, not distrust. When two of our children married, we found it interesting that they were so accustomed to that communication accountability they continued the habit. They now call their mates when they are going to be later than expected. The "rule" has become a way of life, which is the mark of a workable rule.

3. *Unless it is absolutely impossible to do so, say yes.* That may sound like a funny statement until you think it through. The average parental reaction is no. Regardless of the question kids ask, most parents think *no* more often than *yes*. So Cynthia and I developed a policy early on that we'd think yes . . . and only when we found ourselves absolutely unable to say yes would we be forced to say no.

It is amazing how much of a positive influence that simple guideline provided for our home. I can testify that it revolutionized my attitude. Let me give you some examples.

"Can we sleep outside tonight?" Normally, like all dads, I would think and say no. In my mind would be all kinds of airtight reasons: "The mosquitoes . . ." or "You'll need to go to the bathroom and the door will be locked" or "What if it rains?" you know, dumb stuff. No longer. Sleeping outside became fine and dandy. I got to where I *preferred* 'em out there!

Another was "Can we sleep in our clothes?" Why not? (Who really cares *what* kids sleep in?) As my wife finally observed, once you have four, you're so grateful they're in bed, what they wear is of absolutely no consequence.

Another: "Can we have a party?" Sure. "How about a two-day party?" Have it! We taught them that the privilege of having a party included the responsibility of cleaning up after it . . . which was perfectly okay with them. The atmosphere became more and more fun, which is what family living is all about, right?

Say yes just as often as you can.

4. *A failure is not the end of the world.* When relationships are valued, when having fun is important, when saying yes is emphasized, there is risk involved. There will be times when a rule is inadvertently broken—a failure in the system occurs. So it goes. If it was accidental, welcome to the human race. Forgiveness follows confession. No grudges. And, I hope (if Dad stays quiet like he should), no lectures. If the rule was broken on purpose, that is another matter and is dealt with (privately) in a much more serious manner.

Nevertheless, any home that is run on the grace principle must have what our family calls "wobble room." Things don't always run to perfection, but the main issue is the attitude. A submissive, absolutely honest admission with a repentant spirit earns a lot of points in the Swindoll abode.

All of us mean well at the start of any plan, but the human element, being what it is, can't help but slip in occasionally. It's like the following diet plan someone passed on to me last year.

THE STRESS DIET
Breakfast
1/2 grapefruit
1 piece of whole-wheat toast
8 oz. skim milk

Lunch
4 oz. lean broiled chicken breast
1 cup steamed zucchini
1 Oreo cookie
Herb tea

Mid-afternoon snack
Rest of the package of Oreo cookies
1 qt. Rocky Road ice cream
1 jar hot fudge

Dinner
2 loaves garlic bread
Large mushroom and pepperoni pizza
Large pitcher root beer
3 Milky Ways
Entire frozen cheesecake, eaten directly from the freezer

That smile looks good on your face. Your family needs to see it more often!

FLEX THOSE FUN MUSCLES!
If you have stayed with me until now, you are to be commended. Ultra-rigid parents have probably stopped reading and have started writing me a letter of disagreement!

Would you like two or three ideas for developing your "flex" muscles? If so, here they are.

1. *When the family is young, balance the tighter rules with a strong emphasis on trust.* Our kids need to know we trust them, want only

the best for them, believe in them. Rather than viewing them with suspicion and sneaking around like a CIA spy, we need to convey our confidence in their loyalty. That's what grace is all about. Furthermore, children flourish in such a setting. This is a good time to add that the difference between "principles" and "rules" is radical. Rules can be made and therefore reshaped or broken. Principles cannot be arbitrarily made . . . they must never be broken. Rules are temporal, principles are eternal. Rules are helpful, principles are essential. Wise are the parents who understand those distinctions.

2. *As time passes, deliberately relax more and release the controls.* Yes, that's a risk. Yes, it's hard to do. But it won't get easier if you wait until they turn twenty! I think it would be great if parents would actually write out a "declaration of independence" for each one of the kids and hand it to them at a time when they reach a level of maturity and can handle it, like at graduation from high school or some such event.

3. *Throughout the process, cultivate and value the importance of close relationships.* Remember my earlier comment about every phone booth in the world being suddenly occupied if we had only five minutes to live? It's true. Nothing, absolutely *nothing* on this earth is more important to us when the chips are down than the members of our family. Do everything possible to cultivate those relationships.

Author J. Allan Petersen, writing on this very subject, tells of a traumatic experience he endured that drilled this fact home. It happened on an airplane.

> What do you think would be your last thought, your last unscheduled thought and word if you knew that in a minute or two your life was over. . . .
>
> Let's put this in context. . . .
>
> Every nook and cranny of the big 747 was crowded. It took off in the middle of the night in Brazil where I'd been speaking. As it moved into the night I began to doze. I don't know how long I slept, but I was starting to wake when I heard a strong voice announcing. "We have a very serious emergency." Three engines had gone because of fuel contamination, and the other engine would go any second.
>
> The steward said in English, "Now you must do exactly as we tell you. Don't anyone think of doing anything we do not suggest. Your life depends on us. We are trained for your safety, so you must do exactly as we tell you."

Then he rattled this off in Portuguese. Everybody looked soberly at one another.

The steward said, "Now pull down the curtains, in a few minutes we are going to turn off all the lights."

My thought exclaimed, "Lord."

The plane veered and banked, as the crew tried to get it back to the airport. The steward ran up and down the aisle and barked out orders, "Now take that card out of the seat pocket, and I want you to look at this diagram." You know, I've flown millions of miles over the world and here I thought I had the card memorized, but I panicked because I couldn't find the crazy card. Everybody looked stunned as we felt the plane plunge down.

Finally, the steward said, "Now tighten the seat belts as tight as you can, and pull up your legs and bury your head in your lap." We couldn't look out to see where we were—high or low.

I peeked around—the Portuguese were crossing themselves, and I thought, "This is it. This is serious. I can't believe this. I didn't know this was going to happen tonight. I guess this is it." And I had a crazy sensation.

Then the steward's voice broke into my consciousness, barking out in this machine-gun fashion, "Prepare for impact." Frankly, I wasn't thinking about the photocopier. I wasn't worried about the oil in my car. At times like that, involuntarily, from deep inside of us, something comes out that's never structured, planned or rehearsed. And all I could do was pray. Everybody started to pray. I found myself praying in a way I never thought of doing. As I buried my head in my lap and pulled my knees up, as I was convinced it was over, I said, "Oh, God, thank you. Thank you for the incredible privilege of knowing you. Life has been wonderful." And as the plane was going down my last thought, my last cry, "Oh, God, my wife! My children!"

Now I should say for the sake of you, the reader, that I survived! As I wandered about in the middle of the night in the airport with a knot in my stomach and cotton in my mouth, I couldn't speak. I ached all over.

I thought, *What did I do? What did I say? What were my last thoughts? Why did I think that?* I wondered, "What was the bottom line?"

Here's the bottom line: relationship.

When I . . . saw my wife at the airport, I looked at her and rushed to hold her hand. I just looked at her a moment, then threw my arms around her and said, "Oh, I appreciate you." And then with tears in my eyes, I looked at her again, and said, "I appreciate you so much. I didn't know if I'd ever see you again; oh, I appreciate you."

When I arrived home, I found my three sons and said, "I appreciate you. Boy, I'm glad you're in this house and I'm a part of you."

I am only one, you are only one. But because we are in a family we hold a piece of the puzzle in our own power. And what we can do, we should do. I trust that you will say with me, "And by the grace of God, I will do what I can do in my home."[70]

If you are getting caught in the squirrel cage of a hurry-up lifestyle, let me urge you to slow it down and get off. Your family deserves more than the leftovers of your time. By the grace of God do what you can do.

Start today. Please.

Acting Medium

The children worked long and hard on their own little cardboard shack. It was to be a special spot—a clubhouse—where they could meet in solemn assembly or just laugh, play games, and fool around. As they thought long and hard about their rules, they came up with three rather perceptive ones:

1. Nobody act big.
2. Nobody act small.
3. Everybody act medium.[71]

Not bad theology!
In different words, God says the very same thing:

... give preference to one another in honor (Romans 12:10).

... through love serve one another (Galatians 5:13).

... whoever wishes to become great among you shall be your servant, and whoever wishes to be first among you shall be your slave (Matthew 20:26–27).

Let another praise you, and not your own mouth; a stranger, and not your own lips (Proverbs 27:2).

Just "act medium." Believable, honest, human, thoughtful, and down-to-earth. Regardless of your elevated position or high pile of honors or row of degrees or endless list of achievements, just stay real. Work hard at counteracting the celebrity syndrome. Junk any idea that you deserve some kind of pat on the back or engraved wristwatch for a job well done. Who did you do it for, anyway? If you did it for God, He has an infinite number of unseen ways to reward you. If you did it for man, no wonder you're clawing for glory! But it's so subtle. So easy to draw out that praise for yourself, isn't it? Especially around the house when you do a few extras.

A certain firm has made headlines out of deflating overblown egos. Its well-trained employees accept contracts to squash juicy pies into the faces of various pompous individuals. In its first few months, over 60 hits were made at $35 per splash! All on disbelieving, immaculately dressed, prim-and-proper victims.

Imagine this scene: A dignified, well-tailored executive vice president waits for the elevator to open on the eighteenth floor. As he steps out, a stranger whips a pie out of a cardboard box and splosh! Giving the pie a professional twist, the hit man jumps into the elevator headed for the main floor. There stands Vice President Shmotz ... his once-spotless suit, matching vest, and tie now dripping with lemon meringue goo and crust.

An employee of the pie-tossing company said, "A pie in the face brings a man's dignity down to where it should be and puts the big guys on the same level with everyone else."[72]

Even Biola College weathered the pie-throwing rage. No one was safe from the meringue gang—neither the professors nor even the school's great-hearted president who took it on the chin like a champ. I'd hate to think how many college presidents would have responded with their superguarded, highly polished egos smeared with bright gold pumpkin pie and whipping cream. In about two and a half seconds, the whole school would know the truth, the whole truth, and nothing but the truth. I wonder how many profs would "act medium."

Again what was it the son of David said?

Let another praise you ... a stranger, and not your own lips.

Meaning what? Meaning no self-reference to some enviable accomplishment. Meaning no desire to manipulate and manufacture praise. Meaning authentic surprise when applauded. Genuine, rare humility—regardless.

Like the inimitable Principal Cairns, headmaster of an English school, who was walking onto the platform in a line of dignitaries. As he stepped up, a burst of spontaneous applause arose from the audience as an expression of their appreciation. In characteristic modesty, Cairns stepped back to let the man behind pass by as he began to applaud his colleague. He genuinely assumed the applause was for another.[73]

One final warning. Don't try to fake it. False humility smells worse than raw conceit. The answer lies not in trying to appear worthless and wormy. Folks in your family won't fall for that. Rather, be sensitive to the achievements, skills, and contributions of others. And say so. That's one way to serve others in love. Like Christ.

Got the rules memorized? They're really not that difficult. "Nobody act big. Nobody act small. Everybody act medium." Wise counsel from a cardboard clubhouse whose membership is pretty good at practicing what it preaches.

And they also laugh out loud when you get a pie in the kisser. Believe me, I know.

Running Scared

It happened over fifty years ago. The irony of it, however, amazes me to this day.

A mural artist named J. H. Zorthian read about a tiny boy who had been killed in traffic. His stomach churned as he thought of that ever happening to one of his three children. His worry became an inescapable anxiety. The more he imagined such a tragedy, the more fearful he became. His effectiveness as an artist was put on hold once he started running scared.

At last he surrendered to his obsession. Canceling his negotiations to purchase a large house in busy Pasadena, California, he began to seek a place where his children would be safe. His pursuit became so intense that he set aside all his work while scheming and planning every possible means to protect his children from harm. He tried to imagine the presence of danger in everything. The location of the residence was critical. It must be sizable and remote, so he bought twelve acres perched on a mountain at the end of a long, winding, narrow road. At each turn along the road he posted signs, "Children at Play." Before starting construction on the house itself, Zorthian personally built and fenced a play yard for his three children. He built it in such a way that it was impossible for a car to get within fifty feet of it.

Next . . . the house. With meticulous care he blended beauty and safety into the place. He put into it various shades of the designs he had concentrated in the murals he had hanging in forty-two public buildings in eastern cities. Only this time his objective was more than colorful art . . . most of all, it had to be safe and secure. He made sure of that. Finally, the garage was to be built. Only one automobile ever drove into that garage—Zorthian's.

He stood back and surveyed every possibility of danger to his children. He could think of only one remaining hazard. He had to back out of the garage. He might, in some hurried moment, back over one of the children. He immediately made plans for a protected turnaround. The contractor returned and set the forms for that additional area, but before the cement could be poured, a downpour stopped the project. It was the first rainfall in many weeks of a long West Coast drought.

If it had not rained that week, the concrete turnaround would have been completed and been in use by Sunday. That was February 9, 1947 . . . the day his eighteen-month-old son, Tiran, squirmed away from his sister's grasp and ran behind the car as Zorthian drove it from the garage. *The child was killed instantly.*

There are no absolute guarantees. No fail-safe plans. No perfectly reliable designs. No completely risk-free arrangements. Life refuses to be that neat and clean. Not even the neurotics, who go to extreme measures to make positively sure, are protected from their obsessive fears. Those "best-laid plans of mice and men" continue to backfire, reminding us that living and risking go hand in hand. Running scared invariably blows up in one's face. All who fly risk crashing. All who drive risk colliding. All who run risk falling. All who walk risk stumbling. All who live risk *something*.

> To laugh is to risk appearing the fool.
> To weep is to risk appearing sentimental.
> To reach out for another is to risk involvement.
> To expose feelings is to risk exposing your true self.
> To love is to risk not being loved in return.
> To hope is to risk despair.
> To try is to risk failure.

Want to know the shortest route to ineffectiveness? Start running scared. Try to cover every base at all times. Become paranoid over your front, your flanks, and your rear. Think about every possible peril, focus on the dangers, concern yourself with the "what ifs" instead of the "why nots?" Take no chances. Say no to courage and yes to caution. Expect the worst. Play your cards close to your vest. Let fear run wild. "To him who is in fear," said Sophocles, "everything rustles." Triple-lock all doors. Keep yourself safely tucked away in the secure nest of inaction. And before you know it (to borrow from the late author, E. Stanley Jones), "the paralysis of analysis" will set in. So will loneliness, and finally isolation. No thanks!

How much better to take on a few ornery bears and lions, as David did. They ready us for giants like Goliath. How much more thrilling to step out into the Red Sea like Moses and watch God part the waters. Sure makes for exciting stuff to talk about while trudging around a miserable wilderness for the next forty years. How much more interesting to set sail for Jerusalem, like Paul, "not knowing what will happen to me there," than to spend one's days in monotonous Miletus, listening for footsteps and watching dull sunsets. Guard your heart from overprotection!

Happily, not all have opted for safety. Some have overcome, regardless of the risks. Some have merged into greatness despite adversity. They refuse to listen to their fears. Nothing anyone says or does holds them back. Disabilities and disappointments need not disqualify! As Ted Engstrom insightfully writes:

> Cripple him, and you have a Sir Walter Scott. Lock him in a prison cell, and you have a John Bunyan. Bury him in the snows of Valley Forge, and you have a George Washington. Raise him in abject poverty and you have an Abraham Lincoln. Strike him down with infantile paralysis, and he becomes Franklin Roosevelt. Burn him so severely that the doctors say he'll never walk again, and you have a Glenn Cunningham—who set the world's one-mile record in 1934. Deafen him and you have a Ludwig van Beethoven. Have him or her born black in a society filled with racial discrimination, and you have a Booker T. Washington, a Marian Anderson, a George Washington Carver. . . . Call him a slow learner, "retarded," and write him off as uneducable, and you have an Albert Einstein.[74]

Tell your fears where to get off; otherwise, your quest for character will be interrupted. Effectiveness—sometimes greatness—awaits those who refuse to run scared.

Divorce

Some things are written with a lighthearted smile. Some with a forceful determination. Others with a desire simply to instruct and encourage. This, however, has been written with *a sigh*. A heavy heart has been my companion as I have forced myself to address a plague in our society that has reached epidemic proportions.

But closing my eyes and wishing it will go away isn't going to work. Nor is it best just to scream and shout against it. Cancerous tumors don't need Band-Aids.

Divorce is occurring—even in homes where both partners are Christians. Often in spite of good counsel, prayer by friends, and even against the desire of one of the partners. And very few are given any help *from the Scripture* as they struggle against the strong currents of guilt, depression, public put-downs, and rejection by fellow members of the body of Christ. We, unfortunately, have the sad reputation of being an organization that shoots our wounded.

Hopefully, these words will help as it holds out hope for many who have been "shot." My prayer is that you who read it will begin to hear God's voice over all others.

You'll be encouraged to know He is fresh out of Band-Aids.

Writing about marriage is enjoyable; writing about divorce is not.

When I wrote a book about marriage (*Strike the Original Match*), I struck an agreement with my readers. That agreement was to dig into the Scriptures and find out what wonderful things God says He can do in a marriage with two willing partners. We consulted the Architect of the home and discovered His original blueprint for getting it all together. We repaired the foundation by returning to that great passage in Genesis 2 and learning about severance, permanence, unity, and intimacy. We studied about those necessary bricks that build a marriage, how to keep our honeymoon from ending, ways to handle our conflicts, and even some tips on wise money management.

Written across every page of that book was the word HOPE. We openly admitted our imperfections and we willingly declared our need for divine assistance. Every major point and principle was affirmed by Scripture . . . so we did not build a case on human opinion. Time and again we returned to the "original match" to analyze, compare, observe, and learn. We were reassured that there was no marital problem so great that God could not solve it. Rebuilding and rekindling were the recurring themes. We found that no marriage—no matter how weak or scarred—need end.

I agree with a friend of mine in San Francisco. Two processes ought never be entered into prematurely: embalming and divorce. Time and again I suggested ways in which a marriage could be salvaged. Because I firmly believe there is *nothing* impossible with God. Because I have seen Him turn numerous husbands and wives around—180 degrees. Because it was never His original design that homes be destroyed. And because His Word is filled with promises that hold out hope to those who have blown it. But . . .

Divorce still occurs. Now, more than ever. Often against the desire of one of the partners. Often in spite of assistance, effort, and much prayer by friends. Often between two Christians—yes, often. And always where biblical principles were unknown, ignored, or openly violated. Yes, divorce happens. It's a fact we may hate (I confess, I really do!), but one we cannot deny.

And so, I want to strike a deal with you. Instead of dodging divorce and acting like it's not there, let's face it squarely. Even though I would much prefer not to, we haven't got that option.

I will be brief (there are entire *books* written on the subject), biblical, and compassionate. But in spite of these efforts, I'm sure some of you will be offended and others will misunderstand. Such is inevitable, unfortunately.

A CONTROVERSIAL SUBJECT

I'm convinced that there is no way any group of Christians picked at random would ever come to unanimity on this subject. I'll go further. I don't believe a busload of American evangelical theologians would be in unanimous agreement on divorce and remarriage even if they toured the United States an entire summer! It's a controversial issue, for sure. Therefore, no matter what I may conclude, I am confident some very reliable, competent, and equally sincere people will disagree. So save your cards and letters!

I am also confident of this: It's time some of us in the evangelical camp came up front and addressed the issue boldly. Many a divorced person is grinding out his or her life under an enormous load of unnecessary guilt. While I certainly would not desire to soften the penetrating blows of the Spirit of God (if, in fact, it *is* the Spirit producing conviction), I do hope that my words provide the breathing room God has allowed in certain instances. Of greatest concern to me is that someone might read these pages and *misinterpret* what I am saying. Disagreement is one thing; misinterpretation is another. And the emotions surrounding something as stressful as divorce have a way of playing tricks on one's mind, increasing the possibility of misinterpreting what one reads.

Let's make a deal. I promise to be as accurate, clear, and concise as I can possibly be with what I write if you will be equally as careful with what you read. Work hard at not reading into this something I am not saying . . . or take to an extreme something I am trying to keep in proper balance. In issues as controversial as this one, the vehicle of communication must be finely tuned. Let's both do our part, okay?

NOT IN GOD'S ORIGINAL BLUEPRINT

It should surprise no one that divorce was never in the original blueprint for the home. Not only is that implied in the Genesis account, it is clearly stated by Jesus:

"Because of your hardness of heart, Moses permitted you to divorce your wives; but *from the beginning it has not been this way*" (Matthew 19:8, emphasis mine).

The original match was simple and clear: one man (Adam) with one woman (Eve) joined together in a permanent union (marriage) throughout life. How perfect! Yes, and how innocent! Remember, sin was not yet present. Nor a carnal nature within human life. In the beginning days of the home (think of it!), there was absolute perfection.

Man was totally innocent. Uncontaminated. As we read in Genesis 5:1–2:

> . . . In the day when God created man, He made him in the likeness of God.
>
> He created them male and female, and He blessed them and named them Man in the day when they were created.

Clear enough, isn't it? Sinlessness. God's likeness infused into two human beings. The very image of God was stamped upon His creation.

SIN'S SHATTERING EFFECT ON MARRIAGE

But wait. Read on. In the same chapter, the very next verse, this is recorded:

> When Adam had lived one hundred and thirty years, he became the father of a son in his own likeness, according to his image, and named him Seth.

Notice the difference? The dad had originally been created in God's likeness, but when Seth came along, he was in Adam's likeness—"according to his [his father's] image." Why? Sin had invaded. Genesis 3 tells the grim story. And with the invasion of sin came all its horrible consequences, not the least of which was the beginning of strife, both internal (the root) and external (the fruit).

The disease impacted everything and everyone. Conflict replaced harmony. War replaced peace. Sorrow replaced joy. And things like disobedience, rebellion, argumentation, and even murder became the status quo. In nations. In cities. And in homes as well. Yes, marriages were not exempt. Unlike the original match, husbands and wives became selfish, demanding, brutal, unfaithful, angry, hateful, and competitive.

The nation Israel, God's chosen people, ultimately began to lose their distinction. They ignored God's directions and intermarried with foreigners—non-Israelites. The Jew-Gentile mixture was more than God would allow . . . so a compromise was provided by Moses. A "certificate of divorce" (Deuteronomy 24:1–4) was permitted due to the rampant epidemic that was threatening the uniqueness of Israel. Because of the stubborn, rebellious will of sinful people—Jesus called it "hardness of heart"—divorce evolved. But remember, it was not desired or designed in God's original arrangement for marriage. Sin polluted the plan.

Let's see if I can illustrate the problem another way. Pretend you and your family save enough money to buy a swimming pool. You meet with a builder and you discuss your design preferences. He smiles as he watches you sign the contract and give him your first check. The hole is dug, the reinforcement steel is installed, the cement is blown in, the plaster and tile are finished, and everybody is ecstatic. He kept his word and you paid the bill. Now, of course, the water needs to be added. As the pool begins to fill up, a strange color appears before your eyes—Green. Not crystal clear . . . not even bright blue. No, it's green. And the longer you watch, the greener it gets!

Now, you never intended to have green water. You envisioned a sparkling, clear, inviting pool . . . that was your original plan. But an enemy has come without invitation. Germs. And the longer that enemy stays, uncontested, the more putrid the pool appears. So you must make a concession. A compromise is essential, unless you choose to fill up the pool with dirt and forget all about swimming. You must add chemicals. Chlorine and acid and other materials must be placed into your lovely, once-white-and-ideal pool. They will burn your eyes and bleach your swimsuit . . . but if you're going to have a pool at all, chemicals must be used to counteract the germs. Like it or not (and you don't), you must compromise with the original plan.

And so it is with marriage. Because of the harsh presence and consequences of sin, divorce was permitted, lest marriage and the distinctives of a home that modeled Jehovah's character be completely nullified and destroyed. In that sense, divorce became a way of salvaging the believer's distinctives. But remember—it was never

God's original intention or desire. It was permitted once the ravages of sinfulness reached threatening proportions.

WHEN IS IT ACCEPTABLE TO REMARRY?

Enough of history. Let's come to the present. The question everyone wants answered is this: When is divorce permissible? Because of limited time and space, I will spare you a lot of verbiage and supportive quotations. Suffice it to say, I will answer the question with remarriage in mind. In other words, my answers assume that we are really asking, "Are there any biblical grounds for remarriage?"

I believe there are. I have searched the Scriptures, read everything I can get my hands on, and discussed this issue with my wife, my friends, fellow staff, and church board members, pastors, many theological professors, and other serious students of the Bible. I have talked with numerous divorced people, single persons, married couples, publishers, authors on the subject, and authorities in the field—both Christian and non-Christian. Here are my conclusions, simplified for the sake of clarity.

I believe the Christian has biblical grounds for remarriage when the divorce transpired under one of three situations.

A Marriage and Divorce Prior to Salvation

1. *When the marriage and divorce occurred prior to salvation.*
In 2 Corinthians 5:17 we read these words:

> Therefore if any man is in Christ, he is a new creature; the old things passed away; behold, new things have come.

I take this literally. I even take it to the extreme! I think "new" means "new." . . . So when God promises the believing sinner that he is "a new creature," then I take that to mean exactly that. A brand-new, fresh creation. Unlike before.

The Greek term "kainos" means . . . "that which is unaccustomed or unused, not new in time, recent, but new as to form or quality, of different nature from what is contrasted as old."[75] "Fresh" would be an acceptable synonym. It is used in the New Testament to describe Christ's "new commandment" to His disciples (John 13:34), the "new covenant" (Matthew 26:28–29), the sinner being made a "new man" (Ephesians 2:15), having a "new self" (Ephesians 4:24), our being given a "new name" in heaven (Revelation 2:17), and the "new heaven and a new earth" John the apostle saw (Revelation 21:1).

There can be no question about it, this has in mind the brand-new, fresh, unused creature one becomes at the moment of salvation. And if that isn't enough, Paul goes on to add "the old things passed away" at that same time. Again, I take that literally. The old life, with all its old characteristics and sins. They are, in grace, removed. The best word is *forgiven*. Totally and completely.

If that seems too extreme for you, perhaps it would help to read, slowly, those opening words in Ephesians 2:

> And you were dead in your trespasses and sins, in which you formerly walked according to the course of this world, according to the prince of the power of the air, of the spirit that is now working in the sons of disobedience.
>
> Among them we too all formerly lived in the lusts of our flesh, indulging the desires of the flesh and of the mind, and were by nature children of wrath, even as the rest.
>
> But God, being rich in mercy, because of His great love with which He loved us, even when we were dead in our transgressions, made us alive together with Christ (by grace you have been saved), and raised us up with Him, and seated us with Him in the heavenly places, in Christ Jesus, in order that in the ages to come He might show the surpassing riches of His grace in kindness toward us in Christ Jesus (vv. 1–7).

and just a few verses later in the same chapter:

> So then you are no longer strangers and aliens, but you are fellow citizens with the saints, and are of God's household, having been built upon the foundation of the apostles and prophets, Christ Jesus Himself being the corner stone, in whom the whole building, being fitted together is growing into a holy temple in the Lord; in whom you also are being built together into a dwelling of God in the Spirit (vv. 19–22).

Quite frankly, it is beyond my comprehension that passages such as these (there are dozens more) exclude divorce. If they do, then divorce is the only sin not covered by the blood of Christ. It is the one, permanent spot in our past that cannot be washed away. Furthermore, it is then questionable that we can take the words of David at face value when he writes:

He has not dealt with us according to our sins,
   Nor rewarded us according to our iniquities.
For as high as the heavens are above the earth,
   So great is His lovingkindness toward those who fear Him.
As far as the east is from the west,
   So far has He removed our transgressions from us.
(Psalm 103:10–12)

No, I believe "new" means "new." And when God promises the passing away of "old things," it surely includes divorce prior to salvation. After all, being alienated from God and at enmity with Him, how could any unbeliever possibly know His will regarding the choice of a lifetime mate? Having thought through this very carefully, I believe it falls within the context of God's superabundant grace to wipe our slate clean when we turn, by faith, to Christ the Lord.

When the marriage and divorce occurred prior to salvation, I believe God grants His "new creation" the freedom to remarry.

An Immoral and Unrepentant Partner

2. When one's mate is guilty of sexual immorality and is unwilling to repent and live faithfully with the marriage partner.

Much has been written on this particular issue, I realize. I repeat, I have read everything I can get my hands on, so I do not write these words hurriedly or superficially. I am fully aware of the difficulties connected with determining who is really the guilty party when it comes to sexual promiscuity. I also acknowledge the subjectivity involved in identifying "sexual immorality." Such matters must be carefully determined, usually with the help of a qualified counselor who can provide objectivity and wisdom in matters this serious. Each case *must* be considered independently.

Nevertheless, we cannot ignore or deny what Christ said in Matthew 19:9:

> "And I say to you, whoever divorces his wife, except for immorality, and marries another woman commits adultery."

All sorts of interpretations have been suggested to explain what our Lord was saying. Frankly, having examined every one of the suggestions and theories (some of them are incredibly forced and complicated), I return to the verse and accept it at face value.

Throughout my Christian life I have operated under a very simple—yet reliable—principle of interpretation: If the normal sense makes good sense, seek no other sense.

Let's do that here. Jesus is answering a question (it's in verse 3) asked by some Pharisees. It's a question related to divorce:

"Is it lawful for a man to divorce his wife for any cause at all?"

This leads to a second question (v. 7) having to do with the reason divorce was permitted in the first place:

"Why then did Moses command to give her a certificate and divorce her?"

His answer is clear:

He said to them, "Because of your hardness of heart, Moses permitted you to divorce your wives; but from the beginning it has not been this way."

And then, to clarify the matter even further, He adds:

"And I say to you, whoever divorces his wife, except for immorality, and marries another woman commits adultery."

This is Christ's personal counsel regarding justification for divorce and remarriage. That is the "normal sense" of the verse, hence we need not seek any other sense. The only thing that might help is to understand the meaning of the original term translated "immorality."

It is the Greek word *porneia*, from which we get the term "pornography." Throughout the New Testament it is used repeatedly as a term to describe illicit sexual activity. In the case of married partners, it would refer to intimate sexual involvement with someone other than one's mate—someone either of the opposite (heterosexual infidelity) or of the same sex (homosexual activity).

Our Lord has reaffirmed that in the beginning (Adam and Eve in the Garden of Eden), divorce was not present. But due to the "hardness of heart" permission was granted to allow divorce. Jesus spells out in detail when such a divorce and remarriage would be acceptable. When a spouse is guilty of immoral sexual conduct with another person and is unwilling to remain faithful to the innocent partner, the option is there for the faithful mate to divorce and remarry.

Before moving on to the third reason, let me ask you to reread that last sentence. I want to amplify it for a few moments. Two thoughts need to be emphasized. First, this is not simply a case of quickie sex on the sly—a one-time-only experience. This is *porneia*. I take this to mean an immorality that suggests a sustained unwillingness to remain faithful. I hesitate to use the term lest I be misinterpreted—but I think of the idea of an immoral *lifestyle*, an obvious determination to practice a promiscuous relationship outside the bonds of marriage.

Second, the faithful mate has the *option* to leave . . . but such is not mandatory. I have seen numerous marriages rebuilt rather than ended because the faithful partner had no inner peace pursuing a divorce. How much better to look for ways to make the marriage work rather than anxiously anticipate evidence that is needed to break off the relationship. But there are occasions when every attempt has been made to keep the marriage together . . . but sustained sexual infidelity won't allow it. It is in such cases our Lord grants freedom from that miserable and unbearable bond.

Desertion By an Unbeliever

3. *When one of the mates is an unbeliever and willfully and permanently deserts the believing partner.*

In order for us to understand this, we need to read 1 Corinthians 7:12–15 very carefully.

> But to the rest I say, not the Lord, that if any brother [a Christian] has a wife who is an unbeliever [a non-Christian], and she consents to live with him, let him not send her away.
>
> And a woman [a Christian] who has an unbelieving husband [a non-Christian], and he consents to live with her, let her not send her husband away.
>
> For the unbelieving husband is sanctified through his wife, and the unbelieving wife is sanctified through her believing husband; for otherwise your children are unclean, but now they are holy.
>
> Yet if the unbelieving one [a non-Christian] leaves, let him leave; the brother or the sister [a Christian] is not under bondage in such cases, but God has called us to peace

Paul is giving sound advice on marriage. He is offering counsel nowhere else revealed in Scripture. This passage is unique in that it addresses the very common problem of a mixed marriage, i.e., one partner is a Christian, the other is not. Interestingly, the counsel does not assume that such marriages are always unbearable. On the contrary, there are times when harmony and compatibility (to an extent) are possible. In such cases the Christian is strictly forbidden to walk away from the marriage. If the unbeliever desires to remain—stay put!

But there are occasions when "the unbelieving one leaves." *Please* take note that he or she is not forced out. No, the non-Christian mate willfully deserts, walks out, refuses to stay, chooses to leave. What's God's counsel to the Christian who is left? "...let him leave." In other words, the Christian is not under obligation to plead, to beg, to bargain, or to force the non-Christian partner to remain. Rather, "...let him leave."

But that is not the end of this counsel. Verse 15 goes on to say:

> ... the brother or the sister is not under bondage in such cases....

Of course, the key phrase is "not under bondage." Its meaning? Well, at the root of the Greek term is *doulos*, the New Testament term for "slave." Slaves were bound to their masters, inseparably linked to them. It is a strong word suggesting a firm, solid tie. I'm reminded of the verse in Genesis 2 that says the man "cleaves" to his wife. Remember, that word means "glue." Paul clearly has the marriage bond in mind here. Later in the chapter, he refers to this bond as being terminated at the death of one's mate:

> A wife is *bound* as long as her husband lives; but if her husband is dead, she is free to be married...(1 Corinthians 7:39, emphasis mine).

That verse clearly states that death frees us from the "bondage" of marriage, allowing the freedom of remarriage.

It is the term "bound" that interests us. Back in verse 15 we are told that the deserted Christian is *not* in bondage any longer. The normal sense of that term is clear. There is no need to seek some other sense. Being free of that "bondage" obviously means being free of the responsibility of that marriage. The desertion of the unsaved partner breaks the bond, thus freeing the believer to divorce and remarry.

Kenneth Wuest's *Expanded Translation* handles the thought quite capably:

"A [Christian] brother or [Christian] sister is not in the position of a slave, namely, bound to the unbelieving husband or unbelieving wife in an indissoluble union in cases such as these; but God has called us [to live] in peace"[76]

You probably don't need to be told that all sorts of suggestions have been made by sincere and qualified students of Scripture to explain what constitutes desertion ... and to spell out what "not under bondage" really means. Because I promised to spare you numerous quotations and tedious pages of verbiage, I'll not attempt to represent all the opinions that range from unbelievably conservative to downright crazy (in my opinion!). But perhaps a word of caution is needed.

When we read of the departure of the unbelieving partner, obviously Paul is not referring to a temporary, quick decision to chuck it all and bail out ... only to return in a little while. No, leaving means leaving. Permanence is definitely in mind. It implies a determined and willful decision that results in leaving the relationship with no desire to return, no interest in cultivating that home, no plan to bear the responsibilities, and no commitment to the vows once taken. That's "leaving." And the one being left has little doubt in such cases. The marriage is over. Finished. Ended.

It was in just such a case I became involved many, many years ago. The wife and mother of three (a Christian) was literally "left" by her husband, who happened to be a medical doctor. The man, an unbeliever, would no longer tolerate her relationship to Jesus Christ, even though she was exceedingly careful not to cram it down his throat. In fact, she remained a charming, affectionate, and gracious mate in spite of his obnoxious actions and cruel remarks. Ultimately, however, he walked away. No provision was made to help her financially or otherwise. Embarrassed and heartsick, *his* parents stepped in and generously assisted their daughter-in-law for an extended period of time. Still ... no word from her husband. He had definitely left. She remained faithful, but he was now gone.

A divorce followed. The woman walked with God through the whole painful experience. She was a remarkable model of patience and forgiveness. Bitterness never crept in. The marriage had ended, but by no means was her life finished.

Through a chain of events too lengthy to describe, she met the man who had been her high school sweetheart. He had never married, for in some strange way he was convinced the Lord would one day bring the two of them together. Although he had lost track of her whereabouts, he had this internal confidence they would someday marry. By the way, he was also a medical doctor . . . and had come to know Christ personally. Their courtship was beautiful to behold.

I had the privilege of officiating at the ceremony—an unforgettable delight. Just last year my wife and I saw them at a large Christian gathering. Their marriage is more solid than ever. Both are spiritually on target. And their family, now grown, is a close, harmonious unit of deep and meaningful affection. Even though her unbelieving mate had left, God kept His hand on her life. He came to her rescue and met her need. In grace. In abundance.

A SUMMARY AND A WARNING

I agree with John R. W. Stott that "[Divorce was] a divine concession to human weakness."[77] No Christian should aggressively seek the dissolution of his or her marriage bond. Some of the very best things God has to teach His children are learned while working through marital difficulties. Endless stories could be told of how God honored the perseverance of abused and ignored partners as they refused to give up.

But in certain extreme cases, against the wishes and efforts of the committed mate, the marriage bond is destroyed beyond any human ability to restore it. Scripture teaches that God's "divine concession to human weakness" is occasionally justified, allowing the Christian divorced person the right and freedom to remarry in the Lord. There are three such cases set forth in God's Word, each provided by His grace:

1. When the marriage and divorce occurred prior to salvation (2 Corinthians 5:17)
2. When one's mate is guilty of sexual immorality and is unwilling to repent and live faithfully with the marriage partner (Matthew 19:9)
3. When one of the mates is an unbeliever and willfully and permanently deserts the believing partner (1 Corinthians 7:15)

Before closing, a warning must be sounded. Being human and sinful and weak, we are all equipped with a remarkable ability to rationalize. Unless we consciously guard against it, when we experience marital difficulties, we'll begin to search for a way *out* instead of a way *through*. Given sufficient time in the crucible, divorce will seem our only option, our long-awaited and much-deserved utopia. And we will begin to push in that direction, at times ignoring the inner voice of God's Spirit and at other times violating the written principles of God's Word. Either is a grievous act.

I warn all of us against such thought and actions. To carry out that carnal procedure is to short-circuit the better plan God has arranged for His people and, worse than that, is to twist the glorious grace of God into a guilt-relieving excuse for giving us what we have devised instead of accepting what He has designed.

Where God permits divorce and remarriage, humbly let us accept it without fear or guilt. Let us not call "unclean" what He now calls clean. But neither let us put words in His mouth and make Him say what He, in fact, has not said. No matter how miserable we may be.

There is something much worse than living with a mate in disharmony. It's living with God in disobedience.

Monuments

Not far from Lincoln, Kansas, stands a strange group of gravestones. A guy named Davis, a farmer and self-made man, had them erected. He began as a lowly hired hand and by sheer determination and frugality he managed to amass a considerable fortune in his lifetime. In the process, however, the farmer did not make many friends. Nor was he close to his wife's family, since they thought she had married beneath her dignity. Embittered, he vowed never to leave his in-laws a thin dime.

When his wife died, Davis erected an elaborate statue in her memory. He hired a sculptor to design a monument that showed both her and him at opposite ends of a love seat. He was so pleased with the result that he commissioned another statue—this time of himself, kneeling at her grave, placing a wreath on it. That impressed him so greatly that he planned a third monument, this time of his wife keeling at *his* future grave site, depositing a wreath. He had the sculptor add a pair of wings on her back, since she was no longer alive, giving her the appearance of an angel. One idea led to another until he'd spent no less than a quarter million dollars on the monuments to himself and his wife!

Whenever someone from the town would suggest he might be interested in a community project (a hospital, a park and swimming pool for the children, a municipal building, etc.), the old miser would frown, set his jaw and shout back, "What's this town ever done for me? I don't owe this town nothin'!"

After using up all his resources on stone statues and selfish pursuits, John Davis died at ninety-two, a grim-faced resident of the poorhouse. But the monuments . . . it's strange. . . . Each one is slowly sinking into the Kansas soil, fast becoming victims of time, vandalism, and neglect. Monuments of spite. Sad reminders of a self-centered, unsympathetic life. There is a certain poetic justice in the fact that within a few years, they will all be gone.

Oh, by the way, very few people attended Mr. Davis' funeral. It is reported that only one person seemed genuinely moved by any sense of personal loss. He was Horace England . . . the tombstone salesman.[78]

Before we're too severe with the late Mr. Davis, let's take an honest look at the monuments being erected today—some of which are no less revealing, if not quite so obvious. A close investigation will reveal at least four:

- FORTUNE
- FAME
- POWER
- PLEASURE

Much the same as the Davis gravestone, these monuments are built in clusters, making them appear formidable . . . and acceptable. As the idols in ancient Athens, our society is saturated with them.

FORTUNE. How neatly it fits our times! Its inscription at the base is bold: "Get rich." The statuesque figures in the monument are impressive: a hardworking young executive; a clever, diligent businessman unwilling to admit to the greed behind his long hours and relentless drive.

FAME. Another monument tailor-made for Century Twenty. It reads: "Be famous." All its figures are bowing in worship to the popularity cult, eagerly anticipating the day when their desire to be known, seen, quoted, applauded, and exalted will be satisfied. Young and old surround the scene.

POWER. Etched in the flesh of this human edifice are the words: "Take control." These figures are capitalizing on every opportunity to seize the reins of authority and race to the top . . . regardless. "Look out for number one!"

PLEASURE. The fourth monument is perhaps the most familiar of all. Its message, echoed countless times in the media, is straightforward: "Indulge yourself." If it looks good, enjoy it! If it tastes good, drink it! If it feels good, do it! Like the line out of the Academy Award winning song "You Light Up My Life" that says:

It can't be wrong
If it feels so right. . . .

Conspicuous by its absence is the forgotten philosophy of Jesus Christ. He's the One who taught the truth about being eternally rich through giving rather than getting. About serving others rather than leaving footprints on their backs in the race for the farthest star. About surrendering rights rather than clamoring for more control. About limiting your liberty out of love and saying no when the flesh pleads for yes. You know—the whole package wrapped up in one simple statement . . .

> . . . seek first His kingdom, and His righteousness; and all these things shall be added to you (Matthew 6:33).

No elaborate set of statues. No sculptures done in marble—not even an epitaph for the world to read. And when He died, few cared because few understood. They were too busy building their own monuments.

We still are.

Dedication

Rare indeed are those folk who give of themselves with little regard for recognition, personal benefit, or monetary returns.

For some reason we are slowly eroding into a people that gauges every request for involvement from the viewpoint: *"What do I get out of it?"* or *"How can I get the most for the least?"* Tucked underneath that philosophy is a tremendous loss of plain old American dedication. Thanks to our lazy natures, we do not feel very uncomfortable getting by with the least amount of effort. Our former drive for excellence and quality control is now sacrificed on the altar of such rationalizations as:

"Well, nobody's perfect."

"That's good enough to get by."

"Don't worry, no one will even notice."

"Everybody's doing it."

As a result, our standard has become *mediocrity* and our goal, *maintaining the average.* The consecrated worker, the high achiever, the dedicated employee, the student who strives for excellence is often labeled a neurotic or shunned as a fanatic.

I find more encouragement from God's Word than any other source of information when it comes to the importance of personal dedication. The Lord assures me that His *glory* is my goal (1 Corinthians 10:31), not man's approval. Furthermore, when He tells me to love, He tells me to do it *fervently* (1 Peter 4:8). When maintaining a friendship, it is to be *devotedly* (Romans 12:10). When steering clear of evil, I am told to stay away from even *the appearance* of it (1 Thessalonians 5:22). When seeing a brother or sister in need, we are to bear his or her burden *sacrificially* (Galatians 6:1–2), not stay at a safe distance. When it comes to work, we are to be *disciplined* (2 Thessalonians 3:7–8) and *diligent* (1 Thessalonians 2:9). The Scriptures are replete with exhortations to go above and beyond the required call of duty—to a dedication of life that thrives on the challenge of doing a quality piece of work.

Lest you think this is too severe, let me share with you an excerpt from an actual letter written by a young communist to his fiancée, breaking off their engagement. The girl's pastor sent the letter to Billy Graham, who published it a number of years ago.

The communist student wrote:

> We communists have a high casualty rate. We are the ones who get shot and hung and ridiculed and fired from our jobs and in every other way made as uncomfortable as possible. A certain percentage of us get killed or imprisoned. We live in virtual poverty. We turn back to the party every penny we make above what is absolutely necessary to keep us alive.
>
> We communists do not have the time or the money for many movies, or concerts, or T-bone steaks, or decent homes, or new cars. We have been described as fanatics. We are fanatics. Our lives are dominated by one great overshadowing factor: the struggle for world communism. We communists have a philosophy of life which no amount of money can buy. We have a cause to fight for, a definite purpose in life. We subordinate our petty personal selves into a great movement of humanity; and if our personal lives seem hard or our egos appear to suffer through subordination to the party, then we are adequately compensated by the thought that each of us in his small way is contributing to something new and true and better for mankind.
>
> There is one thing which I am in dead earnest about, and that is the communist cause. It is my life, my business, my religion, my hobby, my sweetheart, my wife, my mistress, and my bread and meat. I work at it in the daytime and dream of it at night. Its hold on me grows, not lessens, as time goes on; therefore, I cannot carry on a friendship, a love affair, or even a conversation without relating it to this force which both drives and guides my life. I evaluate people, looks, ideas, and actions according to how they affect the communist cause, and by their attitude toward it. I've already been in jail because of my ideals, and if necessary, I'm ready to go before a firing squad.

That, my friend, is total dedication. The quest for character must include this rare, essential trait. Don't be afraid of it! Such commitment to excellence is not only rare, it's downright contagious.

Commitment

—◆—

Ours is a runaway world.
Runaway teenagers. Runaway athletes. Runaway students. Runaway wives and husbands. Unlike our forefathers—who toughed it out, regardless—when the going gets rough, we look for a way out, not a way through.

I want to offer you another plan. It isn't easy, but it *is* right. It upholds the sanctity of marriage. It highlights the permanence of those vows you took years ago. It stands against the popular plea: "If it feels good, do it!" But most of all, it assures you that God will give all the strength you need when you determine you are going to stand firm and let Him work when others around you are running away.

Listen again to the word: *commitment.* Since we don't hear it in our world, it's time we hear it from our God. May He provide you with all the strength you need to run to Him, in faith, instead of running away from Him in fear.

Commitment is the key.

◆

The 1980 Winter Olympics ended yesterday. As I write these words, Monday-morning sports pages all across America contain similar headlines to the *Los Angeles Times.*[79]

THE AMERICAN DREAM TURNS TO GOLD

A phenomenon has occurred. A bunch of no-name college kids and minor-league rejects have whipped the cream of international hockey—the Soviets, who had not lost an Olympic hockey game in *twelve years* . . . who have been wearing gold medals since 1964!

No longer. A group of kids (all in their teens and early twenties) have startled the athletic world. Everyone except a coach named Herb Brooks and this gang of hot dogs on skates said it couldn't be done. It was a silly, unattainable, impossible dream two weeks ago. Unlike the predictions of experts regarding speed skater Eric Heiden, who won five gold medals and emerged as the Olympic superstar, nobody gave this improbable little hockey team a second glance.

How did they do it? Honestly, now—what turned the American dream to gold? How was it possible for them to tie the Swedes, clobber the Czechs, beat the Russians, and come from behind to whip the Finns 4–2 for the final victory?

Well, if you are expecting a super-duper secret, you know, some hidden-surprise play they used, you obviously didn't watch the games. Those confident kids from the Midwest and East didn't rely on rabbit-in-the-hat tricks to win. They faced veteran finesse teams, one after another, with a game plan as old as hockey itself: Never back down, never quit, hang tough, keep hammering away, stay at it, regardless.

In a word: *commitment.*

In our permissive, irresponsible, escapism mentality, commitment is almost a dirty word. Those who would rather rationalize and run than stick with it and watch God pull off a miracle or two (not to mention shaping us in the process) resist this whole concept. If you, personally, are a runner, you are not going to like my words that follow.

A VOW IS A VOW

Marriage isn't begun in a context of vagueness and uncertainty. Two people, fully conscious and very much awake and aware, declare their vows. I realize vows may vary, but without exception, they include words like: "for better or for worse" and "'til death do us part."

Right? Remember those words you promised before God? Did He hear you? I'm being facetious—*of course He heard you!* Does He take such vows seriously? Read for yourself:

When you make a vow to God, do not be late in paying it, for He takes no delight in fools. Pay what you vow! (Ecclesiastes 5:4).

Yes, He not only takes them seriously, He remembers them permanently. A vow is a vow. A solemn promise by which one individual binds himself/herself to an act or service or another person. What is it God commands? "Pay what you vow!"

Now, listen very carefully. Read this slowly. No amount of psychological therapy, positive thinking (often dubbed "grace"), semantic footwork with the biblical text, alternative concepts, or mutual support from family and friends can remove your responsibility to *keep your vow.* Unless you are a victim of the conditions I talked about in my chapter on divorce, you are responsible for your marriage vow. I repeat—a vow is a vow.

Of course it's difficult! For sure, there will be times you are inwardly convinced you can't go on. But I remind you of your vow, your stated commitment: "For better, for worse."

What you are experiencing may be some of the "worse." And no marriage is exempt from such times.

I remember driving over to some friends' house quite a few years ago to pick up their daughter so she could go ice-skating with one of my children. The mom and dad were hanging wallpaper together. Now ... if you've ever done that as a husband-wife team, you know how tough that project is on a marriage. He and I laughed together as I shared with him the three stages couples go through when they hang wallpaper together:

First week: The couple considers separation.

Second week: The couple separates.

Third week: Divorce proceedings begin!

After the joke, he leaned over to me in the car and said something I wish I could hear every Christian husband and wife declare. With great sincerity, he stated these words:

"Chuck, do you know what makes our marriage work? One word: *commitment.* I am committed to that woman and she is to me— forever."

WHY SO LITTLE COMMITMENT?

What's happening? Why is the divorce rate skyrocketing? How come so many Christians are walking away from their commitment with no biblical justification?

I have boiled it down to four reasons. Perhaps there are many more, but these are the four I encounter most often.

Public Opinion

Ours is the "everybody's doin' it" craze. You know, the "don't sweat it" philosophy. The media ignores or, with a slick wave of the hand, glosses over the fact that a certain person recently walked away from his or her marriage. So does the press.

All this dulls the senses of the public. The edge of our discernment is dulled. By and by we tend to tolerate (and later *embrace*) the same compromise. No longer is it in vogue to be ashamed or embarrassed—certainly not to blush! Guilt is now an obscene term, something no one should bring on another by asking the hard questions.

This is nothing new. In Deuteronomy 6 God's people, the Hebrews, are just about to enter a vast, new territory. The Promised Land. Canaanite country. Sounds inviting, but it held numerous perils for those monotheistic, protected, sheltered people who had hovered around a cloud by day and a fire by night. Idolatry, humanism, and carnality in the raw awaited them in Canaan. And they would soon be living in that pagan culture where public opinion would be in conflict with their training under Moses. So God prepares them with this strong warning:

> Then it shall come about when the LORD your God brings you into the land which He swore to your fathers, Abraham, Isaac and Jacob, to give you, great and splendid cities which you did not build, and houses full of all good things which you did not fill, and hewn cisterns which you did not dig, vineyards and olive trees which you did not plant, and you shall eat and be satisfied, then watch yourself, lest you forget the LORD who brought you from the land of Egypt, out of the house of slavery. You shall fear only the LORD your God; and you shall worship Him, and swear by His name. You shall not follow other gods, any of the gods of the peoples who surround you, for the LORD your God in the midst of you is a jealous God (Deuteronomy 6:10–15a).

Without question, the Lord God stood against His people being dulled and lulled to sleep by the people who surrounded them. How relevant! Public opinion has a way of weakening our commitment.

Accommodating Theology

There is another reason Christian marriages are weaker in commitment. I call it "accommodating theology." This is nothing more than fitting the Bible into my lifestyle. In other words, I alter my theology instead of adjusting my life.

Ezekiel the prophet faced a group of people who did this. Jehovah warned him ahead of time so it wouldn't jolt him too severely. Read Ezekiel 33:30–33:

> But as for you, son of man, your fellow citizens who talk about you by the walls and in the doorways of the houses, speak to one another, each to his brother, saying, "Come now, and hear what the message is which comes forth from the LORD."
>
> And they come to you as people come, and sit before you as My people, and hear your words, but they do not do them, for they do the lustful desires expressed by their mouth, and their heart goes after their gain.
>
> And behold, you are to them like a sensual song by one who has a beautiful voice and plays well on an instrument; for they hear your words, but they do not practice them.
>
> So when it comes to pass—as surely it will—then they will know that a prophet has been in their midst.

The Living Bible says it straight:

> They hear what you say, but don't pay any attention to it (v. 32b).

Now, don't misunderstand. They are not obnoxious and ugly. No. In fact, they are gracious, flattering, and even good at listening. But down underneath, they *really* have no plans whatsoever to let biblical theology get in their way.

This requires great rationalization. It demands the ability to ignore some obvious things, reinterpret and explain away certain passages of Scripture, and to call upon grace (that vast dumping ground for every conceivable act of disobedience) to get them through. By accommodating one's theology, it is remarkable what the mind can do to remove even the slightest trace of guilt!

I write with emotion. I'm sure it shows through. Within the past three years I have watched about ten marriages dissolve. All Christian marriages. Yes, both husbands and wives. All very much involved in Christian activities and church ministries. In each case one of the mates in each marriage has willfully (and skillfully) accommodated his or her theology so that the Scriptures actually "approved" their plans to walk out.

There were no ugly fights or bold public announcements like, "I am denying the faith!" No need for that. Calmly and with reserved respectability, they simply left. That's it. Against my counsel and strong efforts to stop them. Against scriptural injunctions. Against their mates' desires. In spite of the certain damage to their children. And regardless of the shame it brought against the name of God and the Church of Jesus Christ.

Hang on—not one seems to be wrestling with much guilt or personal shame. In fact, several say they have never been happier. A few openly insist they are closer to the Lord than ever before in their lives. Some are still engaged in public ministries.

How? Accommodating theology, that's how.

Delayed Consequences

A third reason we see less commitment and an increasing number of broken marriages is a practical one—they get away with it without divine judgment.

Solomon once wrote about this:

> Because the sentence against an evil deed is not executed quickly, therefore the hearts of the sons of men among them are given fully to do evil (Ecclesiastes 8:11).

You've heard it before: "All God's accounts are not settled this month." I remember reading the words of a sixteenth-century saint similar to that one:

> God does not pay at the end of every day. But at the end, He pays.[80]

I'll be honest. This is one of the most difficult things for me to accept. It's beyond me why a holy and just God does not deal more quickly with disobedience among His wayward children. It would certainly do a lot to build a wholesome fear in the lives of those being tempted to disobey. But even though I cannot explain it, I must declare it: Delayed consequences cause couples to walk away from each other.

Funny, isn't it? Being here-and-now thinkers, we tend to deny the devastating effects divorce will ultimately have on us and, for sure, on our children. Because momentary relief is such a determined pursuit by an unhappy mate, the added "benefit" of little or no divine discipline provides the encouragement needed to carry out the plan.

Christian Approval

There is a fourth reason so many believers are breaking the bond of marriage. It ties in with the third one we just considered. For lack of a better way to say it, Christian approval encourages it.

Remember the Corinthian church? Remember how lax they were with the brother in their midst who was living in sin? Listen to the account:

> It is actually reported that there is immorality among you, and immorality of such a kind as does not exist even among the Gentiles, that someone has his father's wife.
>
> And you have become arrogant, and have not mourned instead, in order that the one who had done this deed might be removed from your midst.
>
> For I, on my part, though absent in body but present in spirit, have already judged him who has so committed this, as though I were present.
>
> In the name of our Lord Jesus, when you are assembled, and I with you in spirit, with the power of our Lord Jesus,
>
> I have decided to deliver such a one to Satan for the destruction of his flesh, that his spirit may be saved in the day of the Lord Jesus.
>
> Your boasting is not good. Do you not know that a little leaven leavens the whole lump of dough?
>
> Clean out the old leaven, that you may be a new lump, just as you are in fact unleavened. For Christ our Passover also has been sacrificed (1 Corinthians 5:1–7).

Church discipline is virtually unheard of in our day. The Corinthians were equally guilty of that same problem. They had a man who was guilty of incest. Rather than being ashamed, rather than applying discipline, they boasted about their tolerance and they were proud of how broad-minded they had become.

And so it is in America today. Precious few are the churches that take a stand against disobedience in their midst. How seldom do we hear of someone being disciplined because he or she breaks his marital vow! Such Christian approval has helped foster a shallow view of commitment in our day.

A Needed Clarification

It would be wise for us to pause a moment and clarify a matter seldom addressed in books on marriage, especially those that support commitment to the vows that were taken. There are unique occasions when it may be necessary for some couples to separate, temporarily. Due to various circumstances—all of them prompted either by emotional sickness or gross demonstrations of sin to the point of danger—there are times when life and health are seriously threatened. To remain together in such cases frequently leads to permanent damage and even tragedy in a home.

It is unrealistic and unfair to think that regardless of sure danger and possible loss of life, a godly mate and helpless children should subject themselves to brutality and other forms of extreme mistreatment. *At that point, commitment to Christ supersedes all other principles in a home.* I am not advocating divorce . . . but I do suggest restraint and safety via a separation.

It is one thing to be in subjection. It is another thing entirely to become the brunt of indignity, physical assault, sexual perversion, and uncontrolled rage.

At such crisis times, call for help! Seek out a Christian friend who can assist you. Talk with your pastor or a competent counselor who will provide both biblical guidance and emotional support. And pray! Pray that your Lord will bring about changes in the unbearable circumstances surrounding you. Ask for deliverance, safety, stability, and great grace to see you through, to settle your fears, to calm your spirit so you can think and act responsibly.

What is it David writes?

Be gracious, O God, for man has trampled upon me;
Fighting all day long he oppresses me,
My foes have trampled upon me all day long,
For they are many who fight proudly against me.
When I am afraid, I will put my trust in Thee.
In God, whose word I praise,
In God I have put my trust;
I shall not be afraid. What can mere man do to me?
All day long they distort my words;
All their thoughts are against me for evil.
They attack, they lurk,

They watch my steps,
As they have waited to take my life. . . .
Then my enemies will turn back in the day when I call;
This I know, that God is for me.
In God, whose word I praise,
In the LORD, *whose word I praise,*
In God I have put my trust, I shall not be afraid.
What can man do to me? (Psalm 56:1–6, 9–11).

Powerful words, waiting to be claimed!

PRINCIPLES THAT ENHANCE COMMITMENT

So far, much of what I have been writing has been more negative than positive. Now, I want to turn that emphasis in another direction. Let's consider several principles from 1 Corinthians 7 that enhance our marital commitment. To help make these thoughts stick, I will be brief and to the point. I find four principles in this great chapter.

1. *Christian marriages have conflicts, but they are not beyond solution.* Take a look at 1 Corinthians 7:28:

> But if you should marry, you have not sinned; and if a virgin should marry, she has not sinned. Yet such will have trouble in this life, and I am trying to spare you.

Writing with a compassionate heart, Paul says that he is trying to "spare us." One of his suggestions is that some not even marry (vv. 7, 26). But this is not God's will for most of us. So then, when we marry, we can be sure of this—times of disagreement, fleshly flare-ups, are bound to happen.

Remember this: There is no such thing as a home completely without conflicts. The last couple to live "happily ever after" was Snow White and Prince Charming. Even though you are committed to your mate, there will still be times of tension, tears, struggle, disagreement, and impatience. Commitment doesn't erase our humanity! That's bad news, but it's realistic.

The good news is this: With the Lord Jesus Christ living within you and with His Book, the Bible, waiting to be called upon for counsel and advice, *no conflict is beyond solution.*

Before moving on to the next principle, drop down to verses 32 through 35:

> But I want you to be free from concern. One who is unmarried is concerned about the things of the Lord, how he may please the Lord; but one who is married is concerned about the things of the world, how he may please his wife, and his interests are divided. And the woman who is unmarried, and the virgin, is concerned about the things of the Lord, that she may be holy both in body and spirit; but one who is married is concerned about the things of the world, how she may please her husband. And this I say for your own benefit; not to put a restraint upon you, but to promote what is seemly, and to secure undistracted devotion to the Lord.

Talk about realism! If you are married, there is no such thing as giving the Lord your "undistracted devotion" 100 percent of the time. Know why? Because you married a *distraction!* Just the difference between you and your mate—the male-female differences—have a way of keeping you trusting.

In our day of unisex and narrowing the gap between men and women, it is easy to pick up an erroneous idea that you and your partner are very much alike. No, that simply isn't true. Listen to one authority:

> An effort has been underway for the past few years to prove that men and women are identical, except for the ability to bear children. Radical feminists have vigorously (and foolishly) asserted that the only distinction between the sexes is culturally and environmentally produced. Nothing could be farther from the truth; males and females differ biochemically, anatomically, and emotionally. In truth, they are unique in every cell of their bodies, for men carry a different chromosomal pattern than women. There is also considerable evidence to indicate that the hypothalamic region, located just above the pituitary gland in the midbrain, is "wired" very uniquely for each of the sexes. Thus, the hypothalamus (known as the seat of the emotions) provides women with a different psychological frame of reference than that of men. Further, female sexual desire tends to be somewhat cyclical, correlated with the menstrual calendar, whereas males are acyclical. These and other features account for the undeniable fact that masculine and feminine expressions of sexuality

are far from identical. Failure to understand this uniqueness can produce a continual source of marital frustration and guilt.[81]

And never forget, those differences create conflicts . . . but in the Lord and under His control, none are unsolvable.

2. *Working through is harder than walking out, but it is God's way.* Again, listen to several verses from 1 Corinthians 7:

> Are you bound to a wife? Do not seek to be released. Are you released from a wife? Do not seek a wife (v. 27).

> Brethren, let each man remain with God in that condition in which he was called (v. 24).

> But to the married I give instructions, not I, but the Lord, that the wife should not leave her husband (but if she does leave, let her remain unmarried, or else be reconciled to her husband), and that the husband should not send his wife away.
> But to the rest I say, not the Lord, that if any brother has a wife who is an unbeliever, and she consents to live with him, let him not send her away.
> And a woman who has an unbelieving husband, and he consents to live with her, let her not send her husband away (vv. 10–13).

The obvious, underlying theme here is like our Olympic hockey team's game plan: Don't quit, hang tough, stay at it, regardless.

My wife and I declare our commitment to each other several times a year. We get alone, often for an overnight somewhere cozy and private. While there we look at each other and *verbalize* our promise to remain faithful. We actually declare aloud our commitment. Can't explain how or why it works, but there's something reassuring about putting things like that into words. As our ears hear what our mouths are saying (from our hearts, actually), our loyalty is reaffirmed.

Another fact is this: We have removed the term "divorce" from our vocabulary when we are working through a tough time. We do not refer to it, we do not use it as a threat, nor do we tuck it away in a safe place in our minds for some future use. The passages we just read pulsate with commitment:

"Do not seek to be released. . . ."

". . . remain. . . ."

"... the wife should not leave...."
"... the husband should not send his wife away."

Why? Why is it best to work through rather than walk out? I can think of several reasons:

- It is the continual counsel of Scripture.
- One's growth in Christ is strengthened.
- The testimony of Christ before the public is enhanced.
- Working through forces needed changes. To walk out means we take our same hang-ups into the next relationship.
- Children in the family remain more secure, stable, and balanced. They also learn to run if parents run ... or work out the difficulties if that's what Mom and Dad model.

I'm sure there are some who read these words and disagree—especially if you are thinking of walking out. Before you do, let me share with you a brief observation from an article out of a popular secular magazine:

> No Role Models: For better or worse, divorce continues to split families at an alarming rate. The number of children involved in divorce has tripled in the last twenty years. And though parents, children and professionals are struggling to deal with such new domestic realities as single-parent families, there are no long-standing precedents, no established role models to draw from. Divorce and its aftermath can be a labyrinth of confusion and conflict, some of which may never be resolved.[82]

There can be no denying it. Walking out may *seem to be* the solution. Even the secular authorities are beginning to question that now. No, there is a better answer than walking out. Work through!

3. *Being committed to one's mate is not a matter of demanding rights, but releasing rights.* Listen to these words:

> Let the husband fulfill his duty to his wife, and likewise also the wife to her husband.
>
> The wife does not have authority over her own body, but the husband does; and likewise also the husband does not have authority over his own body, but the wife does (1 Corinthians 7:3–4).

A couple of words in those verses pierce deeply, don't they? *Duty. Authority.* Selfishness within us *hates* terms like that! "I've got my rights!" says today's liberated woman. "Hey, don't tie me down!" yells today's macho man.

God has a better way: Surrender your rights. Lay down your arms. Release your grip on the things you've been fighting for. Commit the risk to God. Trust Him to defend you and keep you from being ripped off. I say that to husbands just as much as I do wives. Releasing rights, ideally, is a mutual thing—a duet, not a solo.

4. *The Christian's ultimate goal in life is not to be happy but to glorify God.* This is one of the greatest insights God ever gave me. If you will meditate on it long enough, deeply enough, it will literally revolutionize your life. It has mine. It is based on the last two verses in 1 Corinthians 6 and leads into these thoughts we've been considering on commitment:

> Or do you not know that your body is a temple of the Holy Spirit who is in you, whom you have from God, and that you are not your own?
>
> For you have been bought with a price: therefore glorify God in your body (vv. 19–20).

Two significant thoughts deserve our full attention. I will personalize them:

I AM NOT MY OWN.

I AM TO GLORIFY GOD.

If it were possible to set in concrete one all-encompassing truth from this chapter, those two statements would do it. Please read them again.

Our ultimate goal, our highest calling in life is to glorify God—not to be happy. Let that sink in! Glorifying Him is our greatest pursuit.

As I glorify Him, He sees to it that other essential needs are met … or my need for them diminishes. Believe me, this concept will change your entire perspective on yourself, your life, and your marriage.

A CONCLUDING THOUGHT ON COMMITMENT

We have thought about several reasons Christian marriages have grown weaker in our generation. We have also given consideration to some principles that strengthen our commitment to our mates. Every major point has been amplified from one or more biblical statements. And yet . . . I'm sure a few of you who read these words look upon your situation as an exception. Frowning, you sigh and think, *But you just don't know the person I'm married to. Our only answer is divorce. I just can't commit myself to this marriage. We're finished.*

For your sake, I share the following letter. It was written to me almost a year after I spoke on commitment in our church in Fullerton, California. The wife who wrote it understands what a difficult marriage is all about. Believe me, I know. Their home seemed beyond repair.

Dear Pastor Chuck:

Tonight, I commented to you about how much I appreciated your comments concerning your stand on divorce, remarriage, and commitment. I thank you for your supportive and compassionate understanding of this area of difficulty in many marriages.

I really wanted to tell you how I have been blessed since I last wrote you nearly ten months ago (after you gave your sermons on commitment). I decided to remain steadfast in commitment to my own marriage that was in the middle of a divorce action at that time. God has changed me. He has given me a new love for my husband and, in turn, my husband has been changing in his attitude toward me. He is still uncommitted about his relationship with Jesus—a miracle I am anticipating.

Six months ago we sat and listened to a psychologist (not a Christian) tell us to get on with the divorce because there was absolutely nothing left of our marriage and no basis upon which to build.

Well, God's grace has allowed the contrary. It's still a real struggle some days, but I have learned that as we "pull" toward each other rather than "push" at each other, the direction is more secure and sound. . . .

So, commitment is not just another word in my vocabulary. It has become a real part of my life.

In Him,
(signed)

No, commitment is not just another word. It is *the* watchword for a struggling, hurting, eroding marriage that seems destined to be locked up and closed forever.

Commitment is the key.

When Following Seems Unfair

They were sitting around a charcoal fire at the edge of the Sea of Galilee. Jesus and over half of His chosen disciples. It was dawn; quiet and cool. Smoke drifted lazily from the fire as well as the aroma of freshly toasted bread and smoked fish. Perhaps the fog hung low. No doubt small talk and a few laughs occurred as they breakfasted. Surely someone commented on how good it was to catch over 150 fish so *quickly*.

The sounds of these hungry men must have echoed across the placid waters of Galilee. How delightful it must have been to know they were reclining on the sand with the resurrected Savior in their midst.

Suddenly the conversation ceased. Jesus turned to Simon Peter. Their eyes met. For a few moments they talked together about the depth of Simon's love for his Lord. It must have been painful for the rough-hewn disciple, but he answered Jesus with honesty and humility.

Then, as abruptly as that conversation had begun, it ended—with a command. From Jesus to Peter. "Follow Me!" (John 21:19). Simple; easily understood; heard by everyone, especially Simon. The Lord wanted Simon's heart—without a single reservation. Jesus realized that His disciple was affectionately drawn to Him and greatly admired Him. But Jesus now told him to be totally available, fully committed with no strings attached. His command was perfectly calculated to get the fisherman off the fence.

Simon's response was classic. Verses 20 and 21 tell the story.

> Peter, turning around, saw the disciple whom Jesus loved [John] . . . and . . . seeing him said to Jesus, "Lord, and what about this man?"

Isn't that typical? The finger was on Peter and he attempted to dodge some of its pointed direction by asking Jesus about John. "What about John, Lord? You're asking me to follow you . . . how about *him?* Aren't you going to give him the same kind of command? After all, he's a disciple, too!"

Notice Jesus' reply in the very next verse. It must have stung.

Jesus said to him, "If I want him to remain until I come, what is that to you? You follow Me!"

This entire dialogue became permanently etched in Peter's memory. I am certain he *never* forgot the reproof.

Now what does this say to us—and what does it say to the members of our family? Simply this: Following Christ is an *individual* matter. The Lord saves us individually. He gifts and commissions us individually. He speaks to us and directs us individually. He maps our course and plots our path individually. Peter momentarily forgot this fact. He became overtly interested in the will of God for *John's* life.

Does that sound a little like you? It may be that God is putting you through an experience that seems terribly demanding, even humiliating. You are facing the rigors of an obedient walk . . . and you may be looking over the fence or across the dining-room table, wondering about *his* life, or *her* commitment. You're entertaining the thought, "It simply is not fair."

"What is that to you?" asks Christ. When it comes to this matter of doing His will, God has not said that you must answer for anyone else except yourself. Quit looking around for equality! Stop concerning yourself with the need of others to do what you are doing. Or endure what you have been called to endure. God chooses the roles we play. Each part is unique.

Some couples seem uniquely allowed by God to endure hardship—the loss of a child, a lingering and crippling illness, financial bankruptcy, a fire that levels everything to ashes, an unexplainable series of tragedies. While others are hardly touched by difficulty. It's so very easy for the Peter within us to lash out and bitterly lobby for an Equal Wrongs Amendment before the Judge. His response remains the same: "You just follow Me, my child. Remember, you're not John . . . you're Peter."

Has God called you to a difficult or demanding mission field . . . or occupation . . . or type of ministry . . . or home situation? Has He led you to live sacrificially . . . or pass up a few pleasures? If He has—*follow Him!* And forget about *John*, okay? If Jesus is big enough to prod the *Peters*, then He is also big enough to judge the *Johns*.

True Success

It doesn't say enough, but what it does say is good. I'm referring to Ralph Waldo Emerson's reflections on success.

> *How do you measure success?*
> *To laugh often and much;*
> *To win the respect of intelligent people*
> *and the affection of children;*
> *To earn the appreciation of honest critics*
> *and endure the betrayal of false friends;*
> *To appreciate beauty;*
> *To find the best in others;*
> *To leave the world a bit better*
> *whether by a healthy child,*
> *a redeemed social condition,*
> *or a job well done;*
> *To know even one other life has breathed*
> *because you lived—*
> *this is to have succeeded.*[83]

I'm impressed. I appreciate what *isn't* mentioned as much as what is. Emerson doesn't once refer to money, status, rank, or fame. He says nothing about power over others, either. Or possessions. Or a super-intimidating self-image. Or emphasis on size, numbers, statistics, and other visible nonessentials in light of eternity.

Read his words again. Maybe you missed something the first time around. Pay closer attention to the verbs this time: "to laugh ... to win ... to earn ... endure ... to appreciate ... to find ... to leave ... to know...." And all the way through, the major emphasis is outside of ourselves, isn't it? I find that the most refreshing part of all. It's also rare among success-oriented literature.

As I wade through the success propaganda written today, again and again the focus of attention is on one's outer self—how smart I can appear, what a good impression I can make, how much I can own

or how totally I can control or how fast I can be promoted or . . . or
. . . or. Nothing I read—and I mean *nothing*—places emphasis on
the heart, the inner being, the seed plot of our thoughts, motives,
decisions. Nothing, that is, except Scripture.

Interestingly, the Bible says little about success, but a lot about
heart, the place where true success originates. Small wonder
Solomon challenges his readers:

> Above all else, guard your heart, for it is the wellspring of life
> (Proverbs 4:23 NIV).

That's right—*guard* it. Put a sentinel on duty. Watch it carefully. Protect it. Pay attention to it. Keep it clean. Clear away the
debris. It's there, remember, that bad stuff can easily hide out, like:

> . . . evil thoughts, sexual immorality, theft, murder, adultery,
> greed, malice, deceit, lewdness, envy, slander, arrogance and folly
> (Mark 7:21–22 NIV).

You know, all the things that finally emerge once the heady,
sweet smell of success intoxicates us, causing "the wellspring of life"
to splash all around. How important is the heart! It is there that
character is formed. It alone holds the secrets of true success. Its treasures are priceless—but they can be stolen.

Are you guarding it? Honestly now, are you? Sin's ugly and poi-
sonous roots find nourishment deep within our hearts. Though we
look successful, sound successful, talk about success, and even dress
for success, all the while our hearts may be on a drift. It is possible
to be privately eroding from the very things our lips are publicly
extolling. It's called pretending. A harsher term is hypocrisy . . . and
successful people can be awfully good at that.

I have the late Joseph Bayly to thank for the following:

> Jesus warned His disciples, we must beware of hypocrisy—pre-
> tending to be something we aren't, acting with a mask cover-
> ing our face. Hypocrisy is a terrible sign of trouble in our
> hearts—it waits only for the day of exposure. For as John Mil-
> ton put it in *Paradise Lost*, "Neither men nor angels can discern
> hypocrisy, the only evil that walks invisible—except to God."[84]

Emerson's thoughts on success are profound, well worth being
memorized. But this business of the heart needs to be added. Guard-

ing it is essential, not optional. It isn't easy. It won't come naturally. It requires honesty. It calls for purity.

Successes can easily become failures. All it takes is letting our guard down.

Top Dog

If I were to ask you to describe someone who is lonely, chances are good you would not choose someone who is busy. It is also doubtful that you'd select someone in a top management position, the chief executive officer in a growing corporation, or the leading, well-paid salesperson in an aggressive, competitive organization. "Not them!" we think. "They're successful. They've got bucks. They're fulfilled. They've got it made. Furthermore, with all those people around, they haven't got *time* to be lonely!"

Don't bet on it. More often than not, those who find themselves approaching or at the top of the steep ladder of financial success have few friends (if any), struggle to keep peace at home, and live on the ragged edge of disillusionment, even despair.

Loneliness is the plague of the loner ... and, by and large, "top dogs" are loners. Either by design or by default, most executives operate in a very private world where happiness eludes them. Contentment and inner tranquility are seldom found in the penthouse. Instead, there is boredom and stark feelings of emptiness. As Thoreau states so well, these are people who "lead lives of quiet desperation."

It may interest you to know that there is a book in the Bible that addresses this relevant issue. It is named Ecclesiastes. Actually, it's more like a journal than a book: a blow-by-blow account of Solomon's futile search for happiness without God. Solomon's favorite term, which he constantly repeats as he admits his frustration, is "vanity." Again and again he exclaims, "All is vanity!" Even though he, the king of the land, had all the money and brains and resources and time to acquire or experience the zenith life could offer, he kept returning to that same heavy sigh, "All is vanity." Although busy, rich, and famous, Solomon was the personification of boredom and loneliness.

I strongly recommend that when you finish reading these pages, you get ahold of a Bible, locate the book of Ecclesiastes, and read it through at one sitting . . . especially if you are one who identifies with the lonely whine of the top dog.

◆

Then I looked again at all the acts of oppression which were being done under the sun. And behold I saw the tears of the oppressed and that they had no one to comfort them; and on the side of their oppressors was power, but they had no one to comfort them. So I congratulated the dead who are already dead more than the living who are still living. But better off than both of them is the one who has never existed, who has never seen the evil activity that is done under the sun.

And I have seen that every labor and every skill which is done is the result of rivalry between a man and his neighbor. This too is vanity and striving after wind. The fool folds his hands and consumes his own flesh. One hand full of rest is better than two fists full of labor and striving after wind.

Then I looked again at vanity under the sun. There was a certain man without a dependent, having neither a son nor a brother, yet there was no end to all his labor. Indeed, his eyes were not satisfied with riches and he never asked, "And for whom am I laboring and depriving myself of pleasure?" This too is vanity and it is a grievous task (Ecclesiastes 4:1–8).

Some things ought to be, but they never will be.

Take these words of Scripture from the ancient book of Ecclesiastes for example. These paragraphs from the Bible ought to be required reading at Harvard and Stanford business schools, but they never will be.

I'd also like to see this part of Solomon's journal appear just below the heading of every issue of the *Wall Street Journal*, so that business men and women around the world, upon picking up the *Journal*, would read Solomon's wisdom first. But that never will be.

If I had my way, I would see to it that all young executives, entrepreneurs, career-minded men and women climbing the corporate ladder of success hoping to fulfill their dreams for life would receive a postcard with this passage of Scripture printed on it—just as a reminder. That ought to occur annually, but it won't.

And since none of these things ever will occur, we're left to our own devices, assumptions, and observations. Our options are reduced to listening to the counsel of the world's system, watching our peers, observing our parents, taking note of those so-called "success models," and convincing ourselves that the dream is real. But it is not. It's hype—a bold-faced lie!

IDENTIFYING THE VICTIM

Let's understand that. Solomon doesn't have in mind, in these eight verses of Ecclesiastes 4, the little man who barely ekes out a living, who is satisfied with simplicity, and who is not worried too much about going beyond where he is—just willing to get along. That's not the person in the focus of Solomon's sights. No, not on your life.

These eight verses are directed to the senior executives, the high rollers, the top ranks in the military, the shakers and the movers . . . or to use some of today's slang, the "moguls," the "big cheeses," the "top dogs." Those are the ones who look successful and appear to have it made. But the truth is, they don't . . . even though most of them hide the truth rather well. And these are really the "victims" I want to address here . . . you who have arrived, as well as you who have hopes of being there someday.

Keep in mind, Solomon is a king. He's not looking from the ground up. His vantage point is from the top. He's looking around at others in those top positions. He certainly ought to know! His world is a world of elegance, opulence, and lavish affluence. His inability to find satisfaction in that realm is the subject of his journal named Ecclesiastes.

So he replaces the rose-colored glasses of idealism with crystal-clear glasses of realism as he informs his readers of the truth. He writes to physicians whose practice is growing and expanding. He writes to attorneys whose clients and personal finances are increasing. He writes to salesmen who are cleaning up financially. He talks to people who own their own businesses. He's talks to entrepreneurs . . . to presidents and would-be presidents of corporations. He says, "Let me tell you how it *really* is. Let me urge you to face the truth regarding where all this is leading."

A REALISTIC APPRAISAL

Now in this realistic view which, by the way, is a very empirical thing, all mysticism is removed. And as you'll see from verse 1, "I looked again," and from verse 4, "I have seen," *he's looking around.* He's not dreaming up something from a classroom. This isn't academia. This is real-life stuff, right from the office where you work, or from that privileged position where you sit or hope to sit someday.

As he looks around, he observes several categories of life. Three, as a matter of fact—not any one of which is satisfying. The first is enough to stop any of us in our tracks.

OPPRESSIVE CONDITIONS

I looked again at all the acts of oppression which were being done under the sun.

Here we are again at one of Solomon's favorite phrases throughout the book—"under the sun." You'll find it in verse 1. It appears at the end of verse 3 and again in verse 7. It's a phrase that emphasizes the horizontal dimension of life . . . existence *under* the sun, not above it.

Solomon says, in effect, "I looked all around my world. I observed the way people were being treated in Jerusalem. I observed Judea as well. I saw in all those places many, many people who were being controlled by a dominant few. I witnessed many caught in the grip of oppression."

What he really sees is a body of people who have the money, the influence, the power . . . and therefore the control of others. And what Solomon saw was anything but pleasant. Look carefully:

I saw the tears of the oppressed and that they had no one to comfort them; and on the side of their oppressors was power, but they had no one to comfort them.

It's a very vivid scene. Solomon says, "As I look around and see the tears and witness oppression, it's heartbreaking. I am caught up in despair." So his reaction to what he observes is equally vivid. He records it in verses 2 and 3:

> I congratulated the dead who are already dead more than the living who are still living.

As he looked upon those who had already died, he thought, *How fortunate you are to be gone from this earth, rather than to still be living under this oppression!* Solomon then makes a statement to the oppressors: "You have money. You have influence. You have the power to control others' lives. What do you do with that? Are you fair? Or do you oppress? Do you take advantage? Do you rob their freedom or do you release it? Are you a giver or a taker? One who enslaves or one who liberates? One who uses his money and power to wheel and deal? Only you can answer these questions."

King Solomon looks around and sees one who has taken away others' freedom. And he says, "They've no one to dry their tears, and so I congratulate you who are dead. I think you are better off than the living. In fact, better than both living and dead is the one who has never even been born!"

It's a strange moment in Scripture when the unborn are addressed:

> Better off than both of them is the one who has never existed, who has never seen the evil activity that is done under the sun (v. 3).

I'm sure you've thought about that at times: those of you who are married and have no children; those of you who have gone through the experience of losing your only child and now witness the times in which we live. On occasion, I'm sure you must think that maybe it is better they don't have to endure a society as insane as ours.

It just occurred to me that suicide probably never came to Solomon's mind. It was then considered such a heinous sin (an alien concept to the people of the Jews) that he wouldn't even offer it as a way out. But that's certainly not true in our day.

In my travels some time ago, I met a wonderful, well-educated Christian woman who has the vision to cultivate hospices in these United States to help those who are dying. She wants very much for us to be a model as a nation—even beyond what Europe is doing—for those who are terminally ill and find themselves in need of a place to die, a place of love and comfort, a place where they can be cared for and yet, at the same time, be surrounded by family love.

She said, "You know, Chuck, while I was completing my research, I came across a group of people who approached terminal illness from an altogether different slant. I attended one of their meetings, which happened to be held in a church in San Francisco. If you can believe it, it was a group that met to talk about ways to take one's own life. They discussed various methods of suicide, but especially ingesting dosages of medication that will affect your body so severely that you will die and die suddenly. And die quietly."

She told me that they even have a book on the subject, and she let me borrow it. It's called *Let Me Die Before I Wake*, and it is on what is called "self-deliverance" for the dying . . . over one hundred pages explaining how to take your own life. You see, in our times there is no longer a resistance against suicide. It is seriously considered an intelligent escape from pain.

Solomon says, "Those who have never been born are better off than those who have had to live through it and are now living, as well as those who have gone on ahead." He then continues his appraisal of the world around him, turning from oppressive conditions to a second observation.

COMPETITIVE DETERMINATION

And I have seen that every labor and every skill which is done
is the result of rivalry between a man and his neighbor. This too
is vanity and striving after wind (Ecclesiastes 4:4).

That's an interesting observation. This honest man says, "As I look at the act of business—buying and selling, as I watch people accomplishing their goals, as I look at the stream of success as it runs its course from the bottom of the ladder to the top, I observe a severe rivalry, a competitive determination, a 'dog-eat-dog' mentality."

He's not referring merely to healthy competition between corporations. That's necessary in business and helps keep a nation strong and great. He's talking about one-on-one rivalry. Fighting and devouring and clawing and pushing at one another. He's describing the outworking of carnal selfishness.

You see, he's got individuals in mind more than large businesses. He says, "I have seen such a determined and aggressive competition between individuals ... they fight against one another and, if necessary, assault each other!" It's sort of a maddening craze to outdo and outsell and outshine the other person.

You may be caught up in that. You may see yourself described in this scriptural scene. Verse 4 may be painting your portrait even though your name isn't stated. You're not the type that can easily take second place. You're not comfortable until you've captured that top position. You're making your moves and you're determined.

Several months ago I had occasion to look into the face of a frustrated, anxious forty-seven-year-old man. His life was strewn with the litter of the consequences of pressurized competition. In the process of becoming "successful," his relationship with his wife and children eroded. They were like a group of strangers living under the same roof. It must have been a hell-on-earth existence.

First, there was a son who would no longer speak to him. And a younger daughter who had said to him rather bluntly, "I don't like being with you anymore, Daddy." His wife was afraid of him. Now keep in mind, he had made it to the top of his profession. Six-figure salary, a lot of perks ... the whole package. At least up until the month before we talked. He had been caught stealing from his company—some $15,000. The company chose not to indict him and take him to court. Instead, he promised to pay it back, even though he was released from the organization. He had lost his job, lost his reputation, lost the one thing that gave him identity, the only thing he was comfortable "doing business with." And don't forget, his family was happier when he wasn't around.

He was adding, by the way, half-days on Sunday to his schedule of six days a week, so that toward the end he was working six-and-a-half days a week. He admitted to me, "Had I continued, it would have been a solid seven days a week—at least twelve to fourteen hours a day. I was on my way. Your classic workaholic."

As he looked at me, tears were streaming down his face. He sobbed, "How do I build back a home? How do I relate to a child that won't talk to me anymore? How do I go back and do it over?" He paced back and forth as we talked. A rather steady stream of profanity flowed from his tongue. One time, he reached up and swung in the doorway ... and hung there, full of anxiety, crying like a baby.

What a pathetic sight! He had served a cruel taskmaster—success at any price. Now he was like a leopard cornered in a cage.

I thought to myself, *There stands a product of "the system."* He confessed, "I bought into it all the way down to the soles of my shoes, but I couldn't handle it."

Now some would say, "Well, the reaction to that is to drop out. Just give up, you know. Drift. Become indifferent and complacent. Live off the land." Which is another way of saying, "Live off people who are working and let them pay your way through."

But Solomon says in verse 5, "That's not the answer." He calls that person a fool.

> The fool folds his hands and consumes his own flesh (Ecclesiastes 4:5).

No, dropping out of responsible living isn't the solution. A balance is what Solomon's pushing for. See the balance is verse 6? "One hand full of rest" (that's beautiful in the Hebrew; it says "quietness"—one hand full of quietness) "is better than two fists full of labor." That would be a pretty good thing to write on the visor of your car, where you could look at it every morning on the way to work. That'd be a pretty good thing to put on the mirror in your bathroom, where you get ready to face the day.

Did you get the picture? One hand full of contentment and responsible living as opposed to two fists clawing, striving, pushing, pounding their way to the top. It's better than that.

For a moment, let's go back to another book Solomon wrote, the Proverbs. Tucked away in chapter 15 is counsel worth some serious thought. First, Proverbs 15:16:

> Better is a little with the fear of the LORD, than great treasure and turmoil with it.

Isn't that the truth! Now look at the next verse. These are comparative proverbs—"better than, better than."

> Better is a dish of vegetables where love is, than a fattened ox and hatred with it.

"Better is a little bowl of vegetable soup, served at a table where there's a lot of love, than a big, thick prime rib thrown at you by somebody who can't stand you!"

Look next at chapter 16, verse 8, another comparative proverb:

Better is a little with righteousness than great income with injustice.

Pause and let that sink in! In our competitive world of more, more, more, we tend to forget the wisdom of these words. No income—I don't care how lucrative—no income is sufficient to clean up a guilty conscience.

But the push for success, no matter the compromise, leads to a terrible crisis. Disillusionment follows. As competition intensifies, we push for more . . . we start burning the candle at both ends, and we finally burn out. But instead of stopping, instead of evaluating, we simply run faster and farther without facing the music. We refuse to ask where it's all heading . . . what the ultimate result of this maddening pursuit will be. And our loneliness intensifies!

And then comes what our generation has termed the "midlife crisis." This has been described as a time of intense personal evaluation, when frightening and disturbing thoughts surge through the mind. We slowly begin to question who we are and why we're here and how come this matters so much. It is a period of self-doubt and disenchantment with everything . . . everything familiar and stable. It represents terrifying thoughts that can't be admitted or revealed even to those closest to us. And, I repeat, the loneliness intensifies.

There are enemies that fight within us at a midlife crisis. One is the body. The guy they called 'Joe College' just a few years ago is now growing older. His hair is falling out, despite desperate attempts to coddle and protect every remaining strand. Physical stamina decreases. He gets winded on escalators! And before long, words assume new meaning to 'Ol' Joe.' As one comic puts it, the Rolling Stones are in Ol' Joe's gallbladder. When he takes a business trip, the flight attendant now offers him coffee, tea, or milk of magnesia.

And then there's the man's work. It's no longer satisfying. It's now demanding. It's a slavery, in fact. It's disillusioning, and he hates it. But he can't get out of it, because he's got to keep paying the freight. And so the home becomes a part of the rivalry. And the whole thing goes up in smoke.

That's why Solomon says, "Better is a little . . . better is a hand full of contentment, love, and rest than two fists that keep fighting."

PERSONAL DISILLUSIONMENT

There's a third scene that Solomon observes in Ecclesiastes, chapter 4. Like the other two, it's a scene that is characterized by vanity. He says so in verse 7: "I looked again at vanity." He saw a personification of vanity in this "under the sun" observation. He saw emptiness in three-piece suits. He saw brokenness and disillusionment across the face of the career woman. He saw professional people with that tired-blood look, even though they possessed a pile of dough.

In this case, he saw a "certain man" (v. 8). Did you notice something? In the first view Solomon has of this old earth, there are *many* people: many oppressed and many doing the oppressing. In the second scene, there are *two* people. One against another in that scene of competitive rivalry. In this third scene, there's *one*—"a certain man." You see, as you climb higher on this ladder of so-called "success," you get increasingly lonely ... fewer friends, fewer personal contacts. While in the process of acquiring more stuff, you become a lonely man, a lonely executive.

I had a colonel in the military stop me shortly after I gave this talk several months ago. With great intensity he urged me, "Say it even stronger than you said it this time. The next time you talk about loneliness, don't forget the military officer. You're describing my life as a full-bird colonel." The top dog is again whining. He's crying for satisfaction, for companionship, because it's not there as he gets nearer the top.

"There was a certain man without a dependent" (here's a guy who is all alone), "having neither a son nor a brother ..." (v. 8a). Now you would think this man would say, "Since I don't have a lot of people to worry about, I'm going to enjoy myself. I've got this great position and I'm making more money than ever, so I'm going to lie back and take that hand full of quietness along with that fist full of work and I'm gonna balance the two. I'm gonna say, 'Enough is enough.'" Does he say that? Not according to Solomon's observation.

Even though he has no dependent, even though he has neither son nor brother, "...yet there was no end to all his labor." See, he doesn't know how to quit. He can't slow down. Indeed, his eyes were not satisfied with riches and he never asked, "And for whom am I laboring and depriving myself of pleasure?" (v. 8b). Isn't that something! This guy is such a driver that he isn't stopping and asking the obvious, such as "Why isn't this satisfying?" and "What's the outcome?" and "Why am I knocking myself out and enjoying so few pleasures?" Solomon exclaims, "This too is vanity and it is a grievous task" (v. 8c).

A PENETRATING ANALYSIS

See, the dream of the great society is that we work, work, work; fight, fight, fight; earn, earn, earn; sell, sell, sell; labor, labor, labor to get more, more, more! So it is at the top. It's crazy, but there's something so ego-satisfying about being at the top. It offers all of those perks that we didn't have down below. And by climbing in that cage at the top we think we'll then occupy our long-awaited dream: "I'm now in laid-back city . . . relax . . . rejoice. I have finally arrived!"

Stop and think about some of those super-duper perks. Your own parking spot. Your own bathroom attached to your office. A little thicker pad underneath your carpet. A chair you can lean way back in. Maybe a sofa! I mean, just think of a sofa in light of eternity! Drapes—big window. A company car. Tax write-offs. A boat to get in and pilot around a harbor twice a year. People calling you "president" or "doctor."

Solomon says, "It won't satisfy." Will you hear him? Will you be honest enough to pause in the middle of the ladder and think about stuff others refuse to think about? Hang on right there. Hang onto that rung and ask, "What do I gain by fighting to the next one?" And don't you climb until you can answer that. "If I'm not satisfied here, will I be satisfied there?"

AN ANCIENT, YET RELEVANT STORY

Let's think about one of Jesus' stories, since He has a way of telling them like no one else who has ever lived. This one is found in the twelfth chapter of Luke. It revolves around a sharp, very capable entrepreneur.

> And someone in the crowd said to Him, "Teacher, tell my brother to divide the family inheritance with me." But He said to him, "Man, who appointed Me a judge or arbiter over you?" And He said to them, "Beware, and be on your guard against every form of greed; for not even when one has an abundance does his life consist of his possessions." And He told them a parable, saying, "The land of a certain rich man was very productive. And he

began reasoning to himself, saying, 'What shall I do, since I have no place to store my crops?' And he said, 'This is what I will do: I will tear down my barns and build larger ones, and there I will store all my grain and my goods. And I will say to my soul, "Soul, you have many goods laid up for many years to come; take your ease, eat, drink and be merry."' But God said to him, 'You fool! This very night your soul is required of you; and now who will own what you have prepared?' So is the man who lays up treasure for himself, and is not rich toward God" (vv. 13–21).

Actually, the story unfolds as a dialogue between Jesus and a guy who feels he's getting ripped off. Look again at verse 13:

... Someone in the crowd said to Him, "Teacher, tell my brother to divide the family inheritance with me."

Now how's that for a rather practical place to begin? "The folks have died. My brother is the executor of the estate and he's taken it all, or most of it. Tell him to divide it with me." Jesus responds not to the actual statement, but to the motive behind it:

"Man, who appointed Me a judge or arbiter over you?" And He said to them, "Beware, and be on your guard against every form of greed ..." (vv. 14–15).

Not a bad warning to appear on the bottom of a diploma. Not a bad piece to mail annually to success-driven people—"Beware, and be on your guard against every form of greed; for not even when one has an abundance does his life consist of his possessions."

And He then told a story, a parable that began: "The land of a certain rich man was very productive." Now hold it! Chances are good that not too many farmers are reading this. If you *are* a farmer, you'll understand and you'll identify with the story. But you may be a white-collar professional. So let's paraphrase it this way: "The practice of a certain physician was increasing" or "The clients of a certain attorney were growing in number" or "The quota of a certain salesman was higher than before." That's the scene.

Now the man in Jesus' story talks to himself. Nobody else is around. He's alone at the top. The only guy to talk to is himself. The problem is, he doesn't give himself the right answers. He says, "What shall I do, since I have no place to store my crops?" (We could add,

"And the government is gonna eat my lunch!" to complete the idea.) He needs to do something with his profit.

"What am I gonna do about my taxes? What am I gonna do about my prosperity? What am I gonna do about my enlarged income? I've earned a bundle this year, and if I get more, I'll move up into another percentage bracket. If I get less, such and such is going to happen. What am I gonna do?"

> "This is what I will do: I will tear down my barns and build larger ones, and there I will store all my grain and my goods" (v. 18).

"I'll just plow it back into the company!" Sound familiar?

Familiar as the morning paper. "I'll just build it bigger. We'll just have another office down in Newport. We'll just go public. We'll make this thing one of the largest going." The implication is clear: " . . . because that's going to bring satisfaction!"

It doesn't right now, you understand; but he keeps hoping . . . he keeps enlarging . . . keeps feeding the ego. "Why, I've got a winner here! There's a market for it." Or the common rationalization, "This'll meet needs. My family will be happier because they'll have more things to enjoy. So naturally I'll tear down all those things and build more and more. I'll store more and more so I can enjoy (?) more and more." But then he goes one step too far:

> "And I will say to my soul, 'Soul, you have many goods laid up for many years to come; take your ease, eat drink, and be merry'" (v. 19).

"All these physical things are gonna satisfy all my deep, soul-level needs, right?" WRONG! Nothing physical touches the soul. Nothing external satisfies our deep needs within. Remember that! The soul belongs to God. He alone can satisfy us in that realm.

The soul possesses this God-shaped vacuum. And not until He invades and fills it can we be at peace within. Which is another way of saying, "If God isn't in first place, you can't handle success." Oh, if God fills your soul, if God fills your mind, if God satisfies your spirit, there is no problem whatsoever with prosperity. You've got it all put together. Your priorities will be right, and you will know how to handle your life so you can impact the maximum number of people. If He prospers you, if He entrusts you with material success and you continue walking with Him, God can use you mightily in His plan.

Now, I'm not attacking prosperity. I'm not saying, "Everyone take a vow of poverty. Stand with your arm raised and repeat after me: 'I swear to get out of business' or 'I promise never to make a profit.'" I am, rather, pleading—warning against losing a grip on right priorities.

Many of those who become successful, wealthy, and famous have a great struggle handling all that. Some are able to keep a clear perspective, but it's tough. It's like putting a camel through the eye of a needle. Remember Jesus' words? How seldom do we find the successful are genuinely humble!

The man in this story told himself to "eat, drink, and be merry." He could eat and he could drink, but he couldn't be merry, because being truly happy is a gift from God. And all of a sudden an angel steps into this man's scene—right into his office where he's talking to himself, leaning back in that soft chair—the death angel appears with his lips pursed, saying, "You fool! This very night your soul is required of you; and now who will own what you have prepared?" (v. 20). Great question! Every successful person owes it to himself to ask that question. "So is the man who lays up treasure for himself, and is not rich toward God," Jesus adds.

TWO HAUNTING QUESTIONS

When you boil all these words down to the bare essentials, two questions emerge: First, are you telling yourself the truth about possessions? Do you know what the truth will do? It will make you free. You can count on the truth to do that, my friend. So, are you telling yourself the truth about possessions?

Second, are you hearing God's warning about priorities? Just where is God in your business or your profession? As you climb that ladder, at which rung do you plan to meet Him and come to terms with things? Are you hearing God's warning about priorities?

It will help you if you never forget Yussif, the Terrible Turk—the three-hundred-and-fifty-pound wrestling champion in Europe a little over two generations ago. After he won the championship in Europe, he sailed to the United States to beat our champ, whose name was Strangler Lewis—a little guy who weighed just a shade over two hundred pounds.

Strangler had a simple plan for defeating his opponents. He'd put that massive arm of his around the neck of his opponent and he'd pump up that biceps and cut the oxygen off. Many an opponent had passed out in the ring with Strangler Lewis.

The problem he had when it came to fighting the Turk was that the European giant didn't have any neck! He just went from his head to those massive shoulders. Lewis couldn't ever get the hold, so it wasn't long before Yussif flopped Lewis down on the mat and pinned him. After winning the championship, the Turk demanded all $5000 in gold. After he shaped the championship belt around his vast, equatorlike middle, he stuffed the gold into the belt and boarded the next ship back to Europe. He was now the possessor of America's glory and gold. He had won it all . . . except immortality.

He set sail on the *SS Bourgogne*. Halfway across the Atlantic, it sank. Yussif went over the side with his gold still strapped around his body. The added weight was too much for the Turk, and he sank like an iron anvil before they could get to him with the lifeboats. He was never seen again.

"What a fool!" you think. I mean, he should've had a lot more class than that! Successful people don't wear their gold! But you know where yours is, don't you? You've got it stashed away. Whenever you need it, you can cash it in. Right?

But the bottom line is this: Gold won't get you into glory! Because it isn't going to help you. You see, you're not really ready to live until you're ready to die. If you aren't absolutely certain that heaven is your ultimate destination, then it is very doubtful you'll be able to handle earth's pressures.

Remember, some things ought to be, but they never will be. Possessions ought to satisfy, but they never will. Priorities ought to come automatically to smart people, but they never will. That's why we need God's Book, the Bible. No other book keeps bringing us back to the truth concerning possessions. No other book keeps bringing us back to the basics concerning priorities.

A FINAL WORD

Your problem is not your income. Solomon's words are addressed just as much to those who struggle to make ends meet as to those "top dogs" who have got it made financially. As a matter of fact, there are just as many envious people fighting their way up as there are top dogs whining in the penthouse of success. You can be just as greedy and lonely on your way up as those already at the top.

Are you telling yourself the truth about possessions? Are you hearing God's warning about priorities? If you haven't been doing that, do it now.

Jesus, the Authority of life—and life after death—once said, "But seek first His kingdom and His righteousness; and all these things shall be added to you" (Matthew 6:33). They'll fall into right perspective if Christ is first.

Has there ever been a time in your life when you've said this: "Jesus Christ, be the king. You be in first place. You take charge. You be the One who gives me counsel when I ask questions. Jesus Christ, You died for me. You have been raised from the dead. I lay my life before You: all the mess that I've made of it, all the competition, all the oppression, all the disillusionment of it. Take me. Save me. I come just as I am. As a sinner, I need Your forgiveness, Your life." If not—if you've never prayed such a prayer—do so now. Take the gift of eternal life which He offers you. Turn to Him in faith. Don't wait! This decision deserves top priority.

Loneliness in Leadership

There are times my heart really goes out to our president. Not only does he have the toughest job in the world, in addition to that he cannot win, no matter what he decides. Since doves and hawks will never coexist, there is no way he'll ever get them in the same cage together. There must be times when he begins to doubt his own value . . . times when he hears the footsteps of his critics and wonders if they may be right. The Oval Office has to be the loneliest place in America. The only comfort the man has is that *he is not unique.* Every president who preceded him experienced similar struggles. Being the Chief includes that occupational hazard.

I was reminded of this recently when I read of a television program aired on PBS on that most staid of subjects—a library. This library, however, was the Library of Congress, and the PBS's former chairman, Sir Huw Wheldon, was standing in a forest of card index files. The program had all the makings of a slow-moving, dull documentary until . . .

About halfway through, Dr. Daniel Boorstin, the Librarian of Congress, brought out a little blue box from a small closet that once held the library's rarities. The label on the box read: CONTENTS OF THE PRESIDENT'S POCKETS ON THE NIGHT OF APRIL 14, 1865.

Since that was the fateful night Abraham Lincoln was assassinated, every viewer's attention was seized.

Boorstin then proceeded to remove the items in the small container and display them on camera. There were five things in the box:

- A handkerchief, embroidered "A. Lincoln"
- A country boy's penknife
- A spectacles case repaired with string
- A purse containing a $5 bill—*Confederate money(!)*
- Some old and worn newspaper clippings

"The clippings," said Boorstin, "were concerned with the great deeds of Abraham Lincoln. And one of them actually reports a speech by John Bright which says that Abraham Lincoln is 'one of the greatest men of all times.'"

Today, that's common knowledge. The world now knows that British statesman John Bright was right in his assessment of Lincoln, but in 1865 millions shared quite a contrary opinion. The president's critics were fierce and many. His was a lonely agony that reflected the suffering and turmoil of his country ripped to shreds by hatred and a cruel, costly war.

There is something touchingly pathetic in the mental picture of this great leader seeking solace and self-assurance from a few old newspaper clippings as he reads them under the flickering flame of a candle all alone in the Oval Office.

Remember this: Loneliness stalks where the buck stops.

In the final analysis, top leaders pay a high price for their position. Think of some examples. Moses had no close chums. Nor did Joshua. You find David with Jonathan only in his earlier years—but when he became the monarch of Israel, his greatest battles, his deepest prayers, his hardest decisions occurred in solitude. The same with Daniel. And the other prophets? Loneliest men in the Old Testament. Paul frequently wrote of this in his letters. He informed his understudy, Timothy:

> . . . everyone in the province of Asia has deserted me (2 Timothy 1:15 NIV).

Ever thought about evangelist Billy Graham's life *apart from* his crusades and periodic public appearances? Or the president of a Christian organization or educational institution? Do that for a moment or two. They would qualify as illustrations of A. W. Tozer's statement: "Most of the world's great souls have been lonely."

Now don't misread this. It's not that the leader is aloof and unaccountable or purposely withdrawing or has something to hide—it's just the nature of the role. It is in lonely solitude that God delivers His best thoughts, and the mind needs to be still and quiet to receive them. And much of the weight of the office simply cannot be borne by others. Mystical though it may sound, it is absolutely essential that those whom God appoints to places of leadership learn to breathe comfortably in the thin air of the Himalayan heights where God's comfort and assurance come in the crushing silence of solitude. Where man's opinion is overshadowed. Where faith replaces fear. Where the quest for character deepens. Where (as F. B. Meyer once put it) vision clears as the silt drops from the current of our life.

It is there, alone and apart, true leaders earn the right to be respected. And learn the full meaning of those profound words, "Be still and know that I am God."

The Cure for Tunnel Vision

The splinter in my thumb this morning brings back pleasant memories of yesterday's diversion. Cranking up the old radial arm saw in my garage, I wound up with two pecky cedar window box planters. I plunged into the project with the zeal of a paratrooper, ecstatic over the airborne sawdust, delighting over every angle, every nail, every hammer blow, even the feel of the wood and the scream of the saw. I caught myself thinking about nothing but the next cut and its proper measurement . . . the exhilaration of accomplishment . . . the sheer joy of doing something totally opposite of my career and completely different from my calling. Periodically, I looked up through the sawdust and prayed, "Lord, I sure do like doing this!" In this terror-filled aspirin age, my saw and I gave each other wide, toothy grins.

It was Sir William Osler, the Canadian-born physician and distinguished professor of medicine at Johns Hopkins University, who once told an audience of medical men:

> No man is really happy or safe without a hobby, and it makes precious little difference what the outside interest may be— botany, beetles or butterflies; roses, tulips or irises; fishing, mountaineering or antiques—anything will do as long as he straddles a hobby and rides it hard.[85]

A worthier prescription was never penned. Diversions are as essential to our health and personal development as schools are to our education, or as food is to our nourishment. And it's funny— you can always tell when it's time to shift gears and change hats. The frown gets deeper . . . the inner spirit gets irritable . . . the jaw gets set . . . the mind gets fatigued—these are God's signals to you that say, "Don't abort, divert. Don't cave in, get away! Don't crumble, create!" The saddest believers I know—those most bored, most lonely, most miserable, most filled with self-pity—are those who have never developed interests outside the realm of their work.

The only vision they possess is tunnel vision, the most significant thing they've ever created is an ulcer, the only thing they can discuss in depth is their old nine-to-five routine. No thanks! That's not a career, it's a sentence. It may be fulfilling the demands of an occupation, but you'll never convince me it's the experience of "abundant life" our Lord Jesus talked about.

Give attention to such characters as Nehemiah or Job (when he was healthy) or David or Paul. Mark these names down on the ledger of guys who recognized the value and joy of involvement and accomplishment outside the boundaries of their "stated" occupations. One used his hands in construction, another composed music, another raised cattle.

Before you shelve this discussion, I challenge you to answer these four questions:

Can you name at least one area of interest (outside the limits of your "calling") that you are presently developing?

Do you experience as much satisfaction in your diversion as you do in your occupation (sometimes more!)?

Whenever you plunge into your diversion, is it without guilt and without anxiety?

Are you aware that your diversion is as significant to God and to your own happiness as your actual vocation?

If your answer to any of the above is no, you need a few splinters in your thumb. They may help you forget the worries in your head.

Leisure

Enjoying yourself, your life, and your Lord more—without feeling guilty or unspiritual—is no small task in our work-worshiping society. Many have cultivated such an unrealistic standard of high-level achievement that a neurotic compulsion to perform, to produce, to accomplish the maximum is now the rule rather than the exception. Enough is no longer enough.

Christians are not immune, especially vocational Christian workers. How many pastors or missionaries do you know who truly enjoy guilt-free leisure? How many Christian executives can you name who really take sufficient time to relax? On the other hand, how often have you heard someone boast about not having taken a vacation in several years? Or being too busy to have time to rest and repair?

Work is fast becoming the American Christian's major source of identity. The answer to most of our problems (we are told) is "work harder." And to add the ultimate pressure, "You aren't really serving the Lord unless you consistently push yourself to the point of fatigue." It's the old burn-out-rather-than-rust-out line.

I would like to offer a different rationale. One that says not only, "It's okay to relax," but also, "Relaxation is essential!" Without encouraging an irresponsible mentality, it says, "You can have fun and still be efficient." In fact, you will be *more* efficient!

◆

Pussycat, pussycat, where have you been?
I've been to London to look at the queen.
Pussy-cat, pussy-cat, what did you there?
I frightened a little mouse under the chair.[86]

Now there's a rhyme I'll never understand.

That little pussycat had the chance of her lifetime. All of London stretched out before her. Dozens of famous, timeworn scenes to drink in. Westminster Abbey. Trafalgar Square. Ten Downing Street, Churchill's old residence. The unsurpassable British Museum. That old Marble Arch at Hyde Park. She could have scurried up an old lamp-post and watched the changing of the guard. Or slipped in the side entrance and enjoyed an evening with the London Philharmonic. Or studied the immortal architecture at St. Paul's Cathedral.

She probably didn't even realize it was the historic Thames rushing by beneath that huge rusty bridge she scampered across, chasing more mice. After all, she didn't even take the time to scope out the queen as Her Majesty walked across the courtyard. Not this cat! She was such a mouseaholic that she couldn't break with the monotonous routine even when she was on vacation. Same old grind . . . even in London. *What a bore!*

Can you imagine the scene as her husband met her at the plane back in New York?

"Hi, Fluff. How was it? Didja have fun? What did ya' see? Tell me all about it."

"Well, Tom, uh, it all started when I went in the first day to see the queen. There was this little mouse under her throne. I darted after it . . . and, well, from then on, Tom, it was just like here. Do you realize how many mice there are in London?"

"You *what?* You mean to tell me you spent ten whole days in London and all you can say for it is this stuff about *mice?*"

That mouseaholic has a lot to say to *all* workaholics . . . and churchaholics, for that matter. Overcommitted, pushed, in a hurry, grim-faced, and determined, we plow through our responsibilities like a freight train under a full head of steam. What we lack in enthusiasm we make up for in diligence. And we ignore the stinging reality that monotony now follows us as closely as our own shadow.

IS FATIGUE NEXT TO GODLINESS?

Strangely, the one thing we need is the last thing we consider. We've been programmed to think that fatigue is next to godliness. That the more exhausted we are (and look!), the more spiritual we are and the more we earn God's smile of approval. We bury all thoughts of enjoying life ... for those who are really committed Christians are those who work, work, work. And preferably, with great intensity. As a result, we have become a generation of people who worship our work ... who work at our play ... and who play at our worship.

Hold it! Who wrote that rule? Why have we bought that philosophy? What gave someone the right to declare such a statement?

I challenge you to support it from the Scriptures. Or to go back into the life (and *lifestyle*) of Jesus Christ to find a trace of corroborating evidence that He embraced that theory. Some will be surprised to know that there is not one reference in the entire New Testament saying (or even implying) that Jesus intensely worked and labored in an occupation to the point of emotional exhaustion. No, but there are several times when we are told He deliberately took a break. He got away from the demands of the public and enjoyed periods of relaxation with His disciples. I'm not saying He rambled through His ministry in an aimless, halfhearted fashion. Not at all! But neither did He come anywhere near an ulcer. Never once do we find Him in a frenzy.

His was a life of beautiful balance. He accomplished everything the Father sent Him to do. Everything. And He did it without ignoring those essential times of leisure. If that is the way *He* lived, then it makes good sense that that is the way we, too, must learn to live.

THE PERSON TO IMITATE: GOD

Since most humans suffer from a lack of balance in their lives, our best counsel on this subject comes from God's Word, the Bible. In that Book, there appears a most unusual command:

> Be imitators of God, therefore, as dearly loved children ...
> (Ephesians 5:1 NIV).

Maybe you never realized such a statement was in the Bible. It seems unusual: "imitators of God"!

The Greek term translated "be imitators" is *MIMEOMAI*, from which we get the English word *mimic*. One reliable scholar says that this verb "is always used in exhortations, and always in the continuous tense, suggesting a constant habit or practice."[87]

In other words, this is neither a passing thought nor a once-in-a-blue-moon experience. The practice of our being people who "mimic God" is to become our daily habit. We are to do what He does. Respond to life as He responds. Emulate similar traits. Model His style.

But to do that, to be an imitator of God, requires that we come to terms with the value of quietness, slowing down, coming apart from the noise and speed of today's pace, and broadening our lives with a view of the eternal reach of time. It means saying no to more and more activities that increase the speed of our squirrel cage. Knowing God *requires* that we "be still" (Psalm 46:10).

It means if I'm a cat in London, I do more, much more, than frighten mice under chairs. Or if I'm a pastor, I do more than tend the sheep. I must—or I ultimately begin to walk dangerously near the ragged edge of emotional disintegration. It also means I refuse to be driven by guilt and unrealistic demands (mine or others). To be God-mimics, we must begin to realize that leisure is not a take-it-or-leave-it luxury.

Please understand that leisure is more than idle time not devoted to paid occupations. Some of the most valuable work done in the world has been done at leisure . . . and never paid for in cash. Leisure is free activity. Labor is compulsory activity. In leisure, we do what we like, but in labor we do what we must. In our labor we meet the objective needs and demands of others—our employer, the public, people who are impacted by and through our work. But in leisure we scratch the subjective itches within ourselves. In leisure our minds are liberated from the immediate, the necessary. As we incorporate leisure into the mainstream of our world, we gain perspective. We lift ourselves above the grit and grind of mere existence.

Interestingly, "leisure" comes from the Latin word *licere*, which means "to be permitted." If we are ever going to inculcate leisure into our otherwise utilitarian routine, we must give ourselves permission to do so.

But this calls for a close look. We need some specific guidelines to focus on what will help us imitate God and at the same time "permit" us to cultivate leisure in our lives.

FOUR GUIDELINES FROM GENESIS

If we are to imitate God as a daily habit of life, we need to nail down some specific guidelines. It occurred to me recently that an excellent place to locate those specifics in the Scriptures would be the first place He reveals Himself to us—the book of Genesis, especially the first two chapters.

If you were to take the time to read this familiar section, you would discover that God is involved in four activities:

He creates.

He communicates.

He rests.

He relates.

Let's limit our thoughts to those four guidelines. Each one fits perfectly into the cultivation of leisure. They form some excellent guidelines to follow as we begin to develop an accurate concept of leisure.

Creativity—Pens to Paintbrushes to Patios

First and foremost, God is engaged in the act of creation, according to Genesis 1 and 2. He begins with that which is "formless and void" (1:2), lacking meaning, beauty, and purpose.

He takes time to create with His own hands. In His mind were thoughts of a universe, indescribably beautiful. He mentally pictured vast expanses of land masses, deep oceans, colorful vegetation, an almost endless variety of living creatures . . . not to mention the stars, the planets, and the perfect motion of all. Finally, He creates mankind with a body and mind that still amazes students of physiology and psychology.

As He created, He added the music, harmony, and rhythm of movement—the miracle of birth and growth, the full spectrum of colors, sights, and sounds. He cared about details—from snowflakes to butterfly wings, from pansy petals to the bones of bodies, from the microscopic world of biology to the telescopic world of astronomy.

In doing all this, He set the pace. He, the first to create, announced its significance.

If I may suddenly jump forward to today, let me ask a penetrating question: *Are you taking time to create?* Obviously, you cannot create a solar system or bring forth an ocean from nothing, but you *can* make things with your hands. You can write things with your pen . . . or paint things with your brush . . . or compose things, using your piano or guitar or harmonica. You can dream things with your mind and then try to invent them or draw them or in other ways bring them to reality through some creative process.

There was a time when these words did not exist. They began as a dream, an idea that was mine which, by the way, occurred in one of my leisure moments. I gave myself permission to relax for several days on vacation, and this written material is the ultimate result of that occasion. These words have not been copied, nor does the flow of thought emerge from some required or forced structure. It has been a creative experience. One of my most enjoyable leisure activities is writing . . . something I would never have thought possible twenty years ago. But now I realize I've had this itch inside me most of my life. It wasn't until I began to let it out freely and fully that a whole new dimension of my life was added. And it is *such* fun!

All children have built-in creativity. Just look at the things they make and do (and say!) on their own. There is an enormous wealth of creative powers in the mind of a child. Walt Disney believed that and often spoke of it. But if we aren't careful, we adults will squelch it. We'll fail to encourage it or cultivate it or even let it out of its cage. Why? Well, it takes a little extra time and it often costs some money. I should add that it tends to be messy. Not many really creative people—in the process of creating—keep everything neat, picked up, and in its place.

There's a good motto to remember if you're determined to encourage and cultivate creativity:

A CREATIVE MESS IS BETTER THAN TIDY IDLENESS

If we are going to imitate God, we will need to find creative outlets in times of leisure. Yours may be music or one of the arts. It may be in the area of interior design. My wife enjoys houseplants and quilting. Yours may be gardening or landscaping projects, woodworking, or brick and stone work around the house. We had our patio enclosed during the remodeling of our house. Both the bricklayer and the carpenter we used employed a great deal of creativity in their skills. It's an added plus when you can create and even get paid for it! But regardless, our creativity needs expression.

Communication—To Self and to Others

If you read the Genesis account of creation rather carefully, you'll see that interspersed within the creative week were times of communication. He made things, then said, "That's good." After the sixth day, His evaluation increased to, "That's *very good.*"

The Godhead communicated prior to the creation of man, you may recall.

> Then God said, "Let Us make man in Our image, according to Our likeness; and let them rule over the fish of the sea and over the birds of the sky and over the cattle and over all the earth, and over every creeping thing that creeps on the earth" (Genesis 1:26).

And *after* creating man, He communicated with him, the highest form of life He had made.

> And God blessed them; and God said to them, "Be fruitful and multiply, and fill the earth, and subdue it; and rule over the fish of the sea and over the birds of the sky, and over every living thing that moves on the earth."
> Then God said, "Behold, I have given you every plant yielding seed that is on the surface of all the earth, and every tree which has fruit yielding seed; it shall be food for you; and to every beast of the earth and to every bird of the sky and to every thing that moves on the earth which has life, I have given every green plant for food"; and it was so (Genesis 1:28–30).

Again, I'd like to apply this to our times. Initially, in leisure, we take time to communicate with ourselves (as God did) and affirm ourselves, "That's good . . . that's *very* good." Do you do that? Most of us are good at criticizing ourselves and finding fault with what we have done or failed to do. I'd like to suggest an alternate plan— spend some leisure finding pleasure and satisfaction in what you have done as well as in who and what you are. Sound too liberal? Why? Since when is a good self-esteem liberal?

There are times we need to tell ourselves, "Good job!" when we know that is true. I smile as I write this to you, but I must confess that occasionally I even say to myself, "That's *very* good, Swindoll," when I am pleased with something I've done. That isn't conceited pride, my friend. It's acknowledging in words the feelings of the heart. The Lord knows that we hear more than enough internal put-downs!

Communicating in times of leisure includes self-affirmation, acknowledging, of course, that God ultimately gets the glory. After all, He's the One who makes it all possible.

Leisure also includes times of communicating with others who are important to us, just as God the Creator did with man the creature. Unless we are careful, the speed of our lives will reduce our communication to grunts, frowns, stares, and unspoken assumptions. Be honest. Has that begun to happen? Sometimes our children mirror the truth of our pace.

I vividly remember some time back being caught in the undertow of too many commitments in too few days. It wasn't long before I was snapping at my wife and our children, choking down my food at mealtimes, and feeling irritated at those unexpected interruptions through the day. Before long, things around our home started reflecting the pattern of my hurry-up style. It was becoming unbearable. I distinctly recall after supper one evening the words of our younger daughter Colleen. She wanted to tell me about something important that had happened to her at school that day. She hurriedly began, "Daddy, I wanna tell you somethin' andIwilltellyoureallyfast."

Suddenly realizing her frustration, I answered, "Honey, you can tell me . . . and you don't have to tell me really fast. Say it slowly."

I'll never forget her answer: "Then *listen* slowly."

I had taken no time for leisure. Not even at meals with my family. Everything was uptight. And guess what began to break down? You're right, those all-important communication lines.

God not only made man, He talked with him, He listened to him. He considered His creature valuable enough to spend time with, to respond to. It took time, but He believed it was justified.

There are entire books written on communication, so I'll not be so foolish as to think I can develop the subject adequately here. I only want to emphasize its importance. It is *imperative* that we understand that without adding sufficient leisure time to our schedule for meaningful communication, a relationship with those who are important to us will disintegrate faster than we can keep it in repair.

Take time to listen, to feel, to respond. In doing so, we "imitate God" in our leisure.

Rest—At Night, in the Day, or Mini/Maxi Vacations

Following the sixth day of creation, the Lord God deliberately stopped working.

> Thus the heavens and the earth were completed, and all their hosts. And by the seventh day God completed His work which He had done; and He rested on the seventh day from all His work which He had done. Then God blessed the seventh day and sanctified it, because in it He rested from all His work which God had created and made (Genesis 2:1–3).

He rested. Take special note of that. It wasn't that there was nothing else He could have done. It certainly wasn't because He was exhausted—omnipotence never gets tired! He hadn't run out of ideas, for omniscience knows no mental limitations. He could easily have made more worlds, created an infinite number of other forms of life, and provided multiple millions of galaxies beyond what He did.

But He didn't. He stopped.

He spent an entire day resting. In fact, He "blessed the seventh day and sanctified it," something He did not do on the other six days. He marked this one day off as extremely special. Like none other. Sounds to me like He made the day on which He rested a "priority" period of time.

- If we intend to "imitate God," we, too, will need to make rest a priority;
- A good night's rest on a regular basis;
- A full day's rest at least once a week;
- Snatch moments of rest here and there during the week;
- Vacation times of rest for the refreshment and repair of both body and soul;
- A release from the fierce grip of intense stress brought on by daily hassles.

I feel so keenly about declaring war on personal anxiety that I have written an entire booklet dealing specifically with stress,[88] and the toll it can take on our lives. Several things contribute to our lack of inner rest:

- A poorly developed sense of humor;
- Focusing more on what we *don't* have rather than on what we *do* have;

- Failure to give play, fun, rest, and leisure a proper place of dignity;
- Our strong tendency to compete and compare, leading to a wholesale dissatisfaction with things as they are;
- Preoccupation with always wanting more;
- Self-imposed guilt . . . unrealistic expectations;
- Longtime "heredity habit" of the all-work-and-no-play-will-make-me-happy philosophy of life.

And the result? Look around. Stretched across most faces of Americans driving to and from work is boredom. Not fulfillment. Not a deep sense of satisfaction. Not even a smile of quiet contentment.

Even though our workweek is decreasing and our weekend time is increasing, our country lacks inner peace. External leisure does not guarantee internal rest, does it?

For sure, our nation believes in the *theory* of leisure. I heard over a television documentary that we spend more on recreation each year than we do on education, construction of new homes, or national defense! The latest figures I've read show that Americans will spend more than $300 billion on leisure products and activities this year. But I question the Doublemint ads that tell us that if we double our pleasure, we'll automatically double our fun. Mental hospitals remain overcrowded . . . and most of the patients are not what we would call senior citizens.

Time on our hands, we have. But meaningful "rest" in the biblical sense of the term? No way!

I suggest that you and I do more than cluck our tongues and wag our heads at the problem. That helps nobody! Our greatest contribution to the answer is a radical break with the rut of normal living. My good friend, Tim Hansel of Summit Expeditions, suggests taking different kinds of vacations: midget vacations or mini-vacations (two minutes or more!) or, if you're able, maxi-vacations . . . or even, if possible, *super*-maxi-vacations where you take time to enjoy extended leisure, calling that year the "Year of Adventure" where we try our hand at sailing or rock climbing, skydiving, or learning karate. Or whatever.

Change your routine, my friend. Blow the dust of boredom off your schedule. Shake yourself loose and get a taste of fresh life. Need several suggestions to add "zip" to your leisure?

- Begin jogging and/or an exercise program;
- Buy a bicycle and start pedaling two or three miles each day;
- Get an album or two of your favorite music and lie down flat on your back, drinking in the sounds;
- Enroll in a local class and try your hand at painting;
- Start writing letters of encouragement to people you appreciate;
- Make something out of wood with your own hands;
- Dig around in the soil, plant a small garden, and watch God cooperate with your efforts;
- Take a gourmet cooking class;
- Spend some time at the library and pick up several good books on subjects or people of interest to you . . . then sit back, munch on an apple, and read, read, read;
- Plan a camping or backpacking trip soon with one of your children, your mate, or your friend, and spend a night or two out under the stars;
- Pull out all those old snapshots, sort them, and put them into albums;
- Write some poetry;
- Visit a museum or zoo in your area;
- By the way, don't miss those sunrises and sunsets, or the smells along with the sights.

Broaden your world. Kick away the thick, brick walls of tradition. Silence the old enemy Guilt, who will sing his same old tune in your ears. And work on that deep crease between your eyes. Look for things to laugh at . . . and *laugh out loud.* It's biblical!

> A joyful heart is good medicine, but a broken spirit dries up the bones (Proverbs 17:22).

Comedian Bill Cosby is right. There's a smile down inside of you that is just dying to come out! It won't until you give yourself permission. Rest releases humor.

One more glance at the Genesis passage will be worth our effort. Remember where we've been?

God created . . . in leisure; so do *we.*

God communicated . . . in leisure; so must *we.*

But He also *related* with the man and woman He made.

Relating—With Our Friends

The passage in Genesis 2 is so familiar. After God made man, He observed a need inside that life, a nagging loneliness that Adam couldn't shake.

> Then the LORD God said, "It is not good for the man to be alone; I will make him a helper suitable for him" (Genesis 2:18).

As a fulfillment to the promise to help Adam with his need for companionship, God got involved:

> So the LORD God caused a deep sleep to fall upon the man, and he slept; then He took one of his ribs, and closed up the flesh at that place.
>   And the LORD God fashioned into a woman the rib which He had taken from the man, and brought her to the man (Genesis 2:21–22).

Later we read that the Lord came to relate to His creatures "in the cool of the day" (Genesis 3:8). I take it that such a time must have been a common practice between the Lord God and Adam and Eve.

He considered them valuable, so the infinite Creator-God took time to relate with His friends in the Garden of Eden. He got personally involved. He observed their needs. He carved out time and went to the trouble to do *whatever* to help them. He cultivated that friendship. He saw it as a worthwhile activity.

I was amused at a cartoon that appeared in a magazine. It was the picture of a thief wearing one of those Lone Ranger masks. His gun was pointed toward his frightened victim as he yelled: "Okay, gimme all your valuables!"

The victim began stuffing into the sack all his *friends*.

How valuable to *you* are relationships? If you have trouble answering that, I'll help you decide. Stop and think back over the past month or two. How much of your leisure have you spent developing and enjoying relationships?

Jesus, God's Son, certainly considered the relationship He had with His disciples worth His time. They spent literally *hours* together. They ate together and wept together, and I'm sure they must have laughed together as well. Being God, He really didn't "need" those men. He certainly did not need the hassle they created on occasion. But He loved those twelve men. He believed in them.

They had a special relationship, a lot like Paul, Silas, and Timothy; David and Jonathan; Barnabas and John Mark; and Elijah and Elisha.

As the poet Samuel Taylor Coleridge once put it, "Friendship is a sheltering tree."[89] How very true! Whatever leisure time we are able to invest in relationships is time well spent. And when we do, let's keep in mind we are "imitating God," for His Son certainly did.

HOW TO IMPLEMENT LEISURE

The bottom line of all this, of course, is actually *doing* it. We can nod in agreement until we turn blue, but our greatest need is not inclination; it's demonstration.

Here are two suggestions that will help.

1. *Deliberately stop being absorbed with the endless details of life.* Our Savior said it straight when He declared that we cannot, at the same time, serve both God *and* man. But we try so hard! If Jesus' words from Matthew 6 are saying anything, they are saying, "Don't sweat the things only God can handle." Each morning, deliberately decide not to allow worry to steal your time and block your leisure.

2. *Consciously start taking time for leisure.* After God put the world together, He rested. We are commanded to imitate Him.

For the rest to occur in *our* lives, Christ Jesus must be in proper focus. He must be in His rightful place before we can ever expect to get *our* world to fall into place.

A bone-weary father dragged into his home dog tired late one evening. It had been one of those unbelievable days of pressure, deadlines, and demands. He looked forward to a time of relaxation and quietness. Exhausted, he picked up the evening paper and headed for his favorite easy chair by the fireplace. About the time he got his shoes untied, *plop!* Into his lap dropped his five-year-old son with a big grin.

"Hi, Dad . . . let's play!"

He loved his boy dearly, but his need for a little time all alone to repair and think was, for the moment, a greater need than time with Junior. But how could he maneuver it?

There had been a recent moon probe and the newspaper carried a huge picture of earth. With a flash of much-needed insight, the dad asked his boy to bring a pair of scissors and some transparent tape. Quickly, he cut the picture of earth into various shapes and sizes, then handed the homemade jigsaw puzzle over to his son in a pile.

"You tape it all back together, Danny, then come on back and we'll play, okay?"

Off scampered the child to his room as Dad breathed a sigh of relief. But in less than ten minutes the boy bounded back with everything taped in perfect place. Stunned, the father asked: "How'd you do it so fast, Son?"

"Aw, it was easy, Daddy. You see, there is this picture of a man on the back of the sheet . . . and when you put the man together, the world comes together."

And so it is in life. When we put the Man in His rightful place, it's amazing what happens to our world. And, more important, what happens to *us*. I can assure you that in the final analysis of your life— when you stop someday and look back on the way you spent your time—your use of leisure will be far more important than those hours you spent with your nose to the grindstone. Don't wait until it's too late to enjoy life.

Live it up *now*. Throw yourself into it with abandonment. Get up out of the rut of work long enough to see that there is more to life than a job and a paycheck. You'll never be the same!

To put it another way, when you forget all those mice in London, you'll start having the time of your life.

Operation
Relaxation

Some days start right, others end right. This one did both, for a change. During the daylight hours things fell into place and as the evening approached, it got better! As planned, I got home before Monday Night Football. The smell of homemade clam chowder was lingering inside the front door. After hugging the kids and kissing the cook, I settled into my favorite chair . . . loosened my tie and kicked off my shoes. Detecting a new aroma, our miniature schnauzer, Heidi, moved across the room.

Upstairs, our two youngest were fiddling around with a rabbit, two hamsters, and a guinea pig—the protesting squeals of man and beast wafting down the stairwell. Our older daughter (finally off the phone) was out front enjoying the companionship of a neighbor gal . . . and a couple of guys, if I'm not mistaken. Curt was on the floor in his room strumming out a few chords on his steel strings—singing "Raindrops Keep Fallin' on My Head" as a lazy California sun was saying good-bye for the day. In between chopped onions and diced potatoes, Cynthia had doubled over with laughter as she tried to finish a chapter of Erma Bombeck's *The Grass is Always Greener Over the Septic Tank*.

No amount of money could buy the feeling that swept over me—incredible contentment . . . an inner sense of fulfillment . . . a surge of release and relief as the noise and pace of the world were strangely muffled by the sounds and smells of home. The comfortable fingers of nostalgia wrapped themselves around me and warmed me within.

Although my "to do" list was mostly "yet to be done," the day was over. Tomorrow would usher in its own sets of needs and responsibilities, but that was tomorrow. We all enjoyed supper (at halftime, of course) then knocked out the cleanup in exactly five minutes . . . a new Swindoll world record . . . as we moved faster than six speeding bullets, laughing like mad.

What therapy! How essential! And yet, how seldom families really relax. It's almost as though we're afraid to shift into neutral and let the motor idle. With a drive that borders near the neurotic, we Americans hit the floor running at 6 A.M. then drop, exhausted, at 12 midnight . . . scarcely able to remember what transpired during that eighteen-hour episode of relentless actions and words. If God is going to get our attention, He'd better plan on (1) making an appointment, (2) taking a number, or (3) pulling us over with a flashing red light on the freeway—otherwise, forget it! Strange, isn't it, that we place such a high priority on achievement we actually feel guilty when we accomplish nothing over a period of several hours. Such an experience requires justification when others ask, "What did you do last night?"

I visited a small town during a recent trip through central Oregon. It was one of those places that was so relaxed I found myself getting antsy. Life moves along there about the speed of a glacier. You know . . . the type of town where people gather to watch hubcaps rust. I asked my friend:

"How do you stand it? Doesn't the slow pace drive you crazy?"

He responded with a smile. "Well, it took us about eight months to unwind. You gotta *learn* how to relax, Chuck. It isn't something that you do automatically. Now, we love it."

I've thought a lot about that. Relaxing isn't automatic. It's a skill that must be learned . . . cultivated. And since most of us don't live in a sleepy little town, here are a few suggestions to help you develop a workable plan.

1. Block out several evenings each month on your calendar. Make special plans to do *nothing*—except something you (or your family) would enjoy.

2. Loosen up the tight wires of your life by not taking yourself so seriously . . . nor your job. Sure, some things *are* terribly serious—but not everything.

3. Look for times during each day when something humorous or unusual makes laughter appropriate . . . then laugh out loud! That helps flush out the nervous system. Solomon tells us this is good medicine.

4. When you relax, *really relax* . . . blow it . . . enjoy the leisure
   . . . let out all the stops . . . ignore what some narrow-mind-
   ed, squint-eyed critic might think or say. For sure, you'll
   get flack from those who burn out.

I'm of the opinion that a relaxed, easygoing Christian is miles
more attractive and effective than the rigid, uptight brother who
squeaks when he walks and whines when he talks.

Restoration

When the twelve returned from a busy time of public ministry, they gave their reports and told Jesus all they had done and taught (Mark 6:30). I think it is extremely significant that our Lord *did not* push them right back into action or hurry them on to another assignment. Matter of fact, we never read that He "rushed" anywhere. Not on your life!

> He said to them, "Come away by yourselves to a lonely place and rest a while." (For there were many people coming and going, and they did not even have time to eat.) And they went away in the boat to a lonely place by themselves (Mark 6:31–32).

Renewal and restoration are not luxuries; they are essentials. Being alone and resting for awhile is not selfish; it is Christlike. Taking your day off each week or rewarding yourself with a relaxing, refreshing vacation is not carnal; it's spiritual. There is absolutely nothing enviable or spiritual about a coronary or a nervous breakdown, nor is an ultrabusy schedule necessarily the mark of a productive life.

Well . . . how's it going in *your* life? Let's take a brief appraisal. Pause long enough to review and reflect. Try to be honest as you answer these questions. They may hurt a little.

- Is my pace this year really that different from last year?
- Am I enjoying most of my activities or just enduring them?
- Have I deliberately taken time on several occasions this year for personal restoration?
- Are my meals choked down or do I take sufficient time to taste and enjoy my food?
- Do I give myself permission to relax, to have leisure, to be quiet?
- Would other people think I am working too many hours and/or living under too much stress? Am I occasionally boring and often preoccupied?
- Am I staying physically fit? Do I consider my body important enough to maintain a nourishing diet, to give it regular exercise, to get enough sleep, to shed those excess pounds?

- How is my sense of humor?
- Is God being glorified by the schedule I keep . . . or is He getting the leftovers of my energy?
- Am I getting dangerously close to "burnout"?

Tough stuff, huh? Yet what better time than *right now* to do a little evaluating . . . and, if necessary, some restructuring of our lives. We can learn a lesson from nature. A period of rest always follows a harvest; the land must be allowed time to renew itself. Constant production without restoration depletes resources and, in fact, diminishes the quality of what is produced.

Superachievers and workaholics, take heed! If the light on your inner dashboard is flashing red, you are carrying too much too far too fast. If you don't pull over, you'll be sorry . . . and so will all those who love you. If you are courageous enough to get out of that fast lane and make some needed changes, you will show yourself wise. But I should warn you of three barriers you will immediately face.

First, *false guilt.* By saying no to the people to whom you used to say yes, you'll feel twinges of guilt. Ignore it! Second, *hostility and misunderstanding* from others. Most folks won't understand your new decisions or your slower pace, especially those who are in the sinking boat you just stepped out of. No problem. Stick by your guns. Third, you'll encounter some *personal and painful insights.* By not filling every spare moment with another activity, you will begin to see the real you, and you'll not like some of those things you observe, things that once contaminated your busy life. But within a relatively brief period of time, you will turn the corner and be well on the road to a happier, healthier, freer, and more fulfilling life. Furthermore, your quest for character will get back on track.

Obviously, all this stuff on rest and renewal, taking some time off and relaxing, can be taken to a ridiculous extreme. I'm well aware of that. But for every person who will gravitate to that extreme and rust out, there are thousands more of us who have a much greater battle with burnout. Neither extreme is correct—either way, we're "out."

My desire is that all of us remain "in." In balance. In our right minds. In good health. In the will of God.

Are you?

Moral Purity

◆

I am well aware of the numerous written materials available today on the subject of moral purity. But I am even *more* aware of the enormous propaganda to which we are all exposed. Our minds and our emotions are easily lured off target by what I often call "the system." By that I mean the endless, relentless bombardment from the world in which we live. Its messages are subtle and bold, written and spoken, always attractive, remarkably convincing, and clever indeed.

Realizing the effectiveness of this sensual network, I am of the opinion that there needs to be a continual stream of information made available to the public that counteracts this force, presenting scriptural truth in an equally convincing manner. Erroneous thinking that leads to evil actions needs to be confronted. Because "the system" operates twenty-four hours a day, seven days every week, it is doubtful that Christians have come anywhere near overstating their position. With determination and diligence we must continue to make known a perspective that exposes "the system" and penetrates the moral fog which envelopes all who live on this planet.

As a pastor since the early 1960s, I have observed a tragic decline—a lowering of the standard of moral excellence—even within Christian circles. What was once confined to "the system" has now invaded the church. That fact alone is enough to justify an increase in our effort to publish materials that both uphold the need for personal holiness and declare the consequences of an immoral lifestyle.

If something I have written helps you to walk away from wrong that has held you in bondage and draws you back to the truth that will set you free, my purpose will have been achieved.

And may the Lord cause you to increase and abound in love for one another ... ; so that He may establish your hearts unblamable in holiness (1 Thessalonians 3:12–13a).

Holiness sounds scary. It need not be, but to the average American it is. Our tendency is to think that holiness would never find its way into the office of a salesperson; certainly not that of an aggressive and successful athletics coach. Nor would a mother of small children be that concerned about holiness, nor a teenager involved in a busy high school; to say nothing of some collegian pursuing a career with his or her eyes on great financial goals. Let's face it, holiness is something for the cloistered halls of a monastery. It needs organ music, long prayers, and religious-sounding chants. It hardly seems appropriate for those in the real world of the twentieth century. Author John White seems to agree with that:

Have you ever gone fishing in a polluted river and hauled out an old shoe, a teakettle, or a rusty can? I get a similar sort of catch if I cast as a bait the word *holiness* into the murky depths of my mind. To my dismay I come up with such associations as:

thinness
hollow-eyed gauntness
beards
sandals
long robes
stone cells
no sex
no jokes
hair shirts
frequent cold baths
fasting

hours of prayer
wild rocky deserts
getting up at 4 A.M.
clean fingernails
stained glass
self-humiliation[90]

Is that the mental picture you have when you think of holiness?
Most do. It's almost as though holiness is the private preserve of an
austere group of monks, missionaries, mystics, and martyrs. But
nothing could be further from the truth.

As a matter of fact, holiness *does* belong in the life of the teenager. Holiness *does* have a place in the office of the salesperson. It is,
indeed, appropriate in the world of the up-to-date, aggressive, even
successful individual.

I couldn't be in greater agreement with Chuck Colson's statement: "Holiness is the everyday business of every Christian. It evi-
dences itself in the decisions we make and the things we do, hour by
hour, day by day."[91]

THE FOG: AN ANALYSIS OF TODAY'S MORAL SCENE

Before going any further, let's back off a few feet and get a little perspective on the moral scene today. To penetrate the fog will
take some effort, I can assure you. Perhaps it will help to read the
writings of a sixth-century B.C. prophet named Habakkuk. His name
looks like a misprint, doesn't it? On the contrary, the man was a bold
voice for holiness in a day of compromise. A misfit, perhaps, but no
misprint. Had you lived in his day, you may have wondered about
his sanity! He was the kind of man who just wouldn't "get in line."
His world was corrupt, but he believed in personal purity, of all
things! How strange . . . yet how significant! We may not be familiar with him, but we surely understand his times.

He's a man who was surrounded by a moral fog. His book is an
ancient call for repentance. It is a holy cry to God for divine inter-
vention. And it's not just a cry; it's more like a scream. He says:

How long, O LORD, will I call for help, and Thou wilt not hear?
I cry out to Thee, "Violence!" yet Thou dost not save
(Habakkuk 1:2)

He saw immoral and brutal acts of violence. So, of course, he asked, "Why?" He also asked, "How long?" He struggled with God's lack of immediate action. Though the prophet prayed, God seemed unusually distant. "How long? Why?" The heavens were brass. "Why don't You act decisively? Why don't You unfold Your arms and get with it in this old, polluted world of ours? How long before You deliver Your people, Lord?" He continues:

> Why dost Thou make me see iniquity, and cause me to look on wickedness? Yes, destruction and violence are before me; strife exists and contention arises. Therefore, the law is ignored and justice is never upheld. For the wicked surround the righteous; therefore, justice comes out perverted (vv. 3–4).

> Art Thou not from everlasting, O LORD, my God, my Holy One? We will not die (v. 12a).

"I thought You were holy. Aren't You the Holy One? Then how in the world can You sit back and do so little about my unholy world?" "[Habakkuk] could not reconcile a bad world with a holy God."[92]

How bad was his world? As we just observed, it was a world of brutal violence (v. 2) so severe that the prophet screamed out his prayer. It was a world of personal iniquity and wickedness (v. 3). "Why dost Thou make me see *iniquity?*" The word includes lying, vanity, and idolatry. "Why do You cause me to look on *wickedness?*" That Hebrew term encompasses oppression, robbery, and assault.

There were crimes of homicide going on in the streets. "Aren't You Jehovah of Judah? Aren't You the God of this nation? Where are You, God?"

There were strife and relational wrangling. There were arguments in homes, fights between parents and kids as well as between marital partners—not to mention disputes between bosses and employees. And did you notice another relevant issue? The law was not being upheld. And when it was, it was being compromised. What a scene! It's going to sound familiar: brutal violence, personal iniquity, relational wrangling, legal compromise. You'd think Habakkuk lived in the inner city of some American metropolis.

I smiled when I was listening to a rather well-known Bible expositor several months ago. He said he'd just completed a serious study into the fourth, fifth, and sixth centuries B.C. and found himself intrigued to discover what they wrestled with back then.

He mentioned five issues that concerned those ancient people: (1) the imminent outbreak of international hostility; (2) the breakup of homes—weakening marriages; (3) the rebellion of youth and their lack of respect for parents or for the elderly; (4) the corruption in politics—integrity was undermined; and (5) the chuckholes in the public roads!

Does that sound familiar? Does it sound like something you could identify with? History certainly has a way of repeating itself!

That's what makes Habakkuk's complaint so timely. "I thought You were holy, God! Where are You? How can You allow this to happen? I'm surrounded by a fog of moral pollution and I'm tired of breathing it in. I'm tired of its diseased impact on my life. I'm beginning to wonder about a holy God in a world of people *this* unholy." Maybe those are your sentiments too.

Habakkuk cried aloud. Another prophet, named Jeremiah, just quietly sobbed. I have in mind his words as recorded in Jeremiah 6. He lived a little later than Habakkuk, though not by much. Habakkuk feared the nation's demise, but Jeremiah lived to see the nation destroyed.

That's why he wrote Lamentations, which is another name for *weeping*. Appropriately, Jeremiah is called "the weeping prophet." He doesn't scream. He doesn't fight. He doesn't even argue. He just sobs. He writes his prophecy while wiping tears from his eyes.

> Be warned, O Jerusalem, lest I be alienated from you; lest I make you a desolation, a land not inhabited (Jeremiah 6:8).

> To whom shall I speak and give warning, that they may hear? Behold, their ears are closed (v. 10a).

Understand, that's the result of living in the fog. "The system" takes its toll. Your ears slowly become closed, so much so that you can't hear the spiritual message God is giving. *"They cannot listen."* Observe the way Jeremiah puts it:

> The word of the LORD has become a reproach to them; they have no delight in it (v. 10b).

Do you want to know how that sounds in today's terms? "Aw, c'mon ... get off that stuff! Get up with the times, man! All that prophet-of-doom talk is old hat. This is where it's at!" In Jeremiah's words, "They have no delight in it"—that is, in hearing the truth about holiness.

> But I am full of the wrath of the LORD: I am weary with hold-
> ing it in (v. 11a).

"I'm boiling. I'm churning . . . I'm so tired, Lord."

> For from the least of them even to the greatest of them, every-
> one is greedy for gain (v. 13a).

Does that sound familiar?

Again, these verses describe life as it is lived in a moral fog. There is a constant fighting for gain. There's competition to get more and more. And to make matters worse:

> From the prophet even to the priest everyone deals falsely
> (v. 13b).

Jeremiah weeps, "It's bad enough that it's in the law courts, but it's now in the pulpits, my Lord. It's to the place where I can't trust the one who wears a collar, who says he speaks for You. I can't be sure that those who are robed with the mantle of God tell me the truth anymore. They deal falsely. They have healed the wound of Your people just slightly." Look at what he says! "They keep saying, 'Shalom, shalom!' when there is no shalom! There isn't any peace. But they keep saying, 'Don't worry. Don't worry. It's gonna be OK,' when it's *not* going to be OK."

And if you don't think *that's* bad, look at verse 15.

> Were they ashamed because of the abomination they have
> done? They were not even ashamed at all; they did not even know
> how to blush.

Honestly now, did you know the Bible spoke of a time in his-tory when people were so caught up in an immoral lifestyle that they no longer blushed? Jeremiah sobs, "I notice, God, that there are no more red faces. No one seems shocked anymore."

Today I suppose we could call it compensating or maybe ratio-nalizing. In order to handle the shock of our day, we compensate by remaining free of shock. I repeat, that's part of living in the fog.

Psychiatrist Karl Menninger took up the pen of a prophet when he wrote *Whatever Became of Sin?* In that searching book he admits,

In a discussion of the sin of *lust* we have to allow for a considerable shift in the social code during the past century. It has
been called a revolution, and perhaps it is. Many forms of sexual activity which for centuries were considered reprehensible,
immoral, and sinful *anywhere*, and their public exhibition simply *anathema*, are now talked and written about and exhibited
on the stage and screen.[93]

From *Honesty, Morality, and Conscience* by Jerry White, I find a
similar concern:

We live in the age of freedom of expression and freedom of
lifestyle. X-rated movies and magazines are available in every city.
Legislation to control pornography has failed in most places. The
sexual fiction of yesterday is the reality of today. Magazines displayed in supermarkets present articles featuring unmarried
couples living together. Sex manuals advocate extramarital affairs.
Fewer and fewer teenagers leave high school as virgins. Prime-
time television flaunts homosexuality and infidelity.[94]

Pitirim Sorokin, formerly professor of sociology at Harvard,
laments:

There has been a growing preoccupation of our writers with the
social sewers, the broken homes of disloyal parents and unloved
children, the bedroom of the prostitute, a cannery row broth-
el, a den of criminals, a ward of the insane, a club of dishonest
politicians, a street corner gang of teenage delinquents, a hate-
laden prison, a crime-ridden waterfront, the courtroom of a
dishonest judge, the sex adventures of urbanized cavemen and
rapists, the loves of adulterers and fornicators, of masochists,
sadists, prostitutes, mistresses, playboys. Juicy loves, ids,
orgasms, and libidos are seductively prepared and served with
all the trimmings.[95]

And to add Jeremiah's observation: Nobody blushes anymore.
It's all part of the moral pollution . . . the fog. "The system" may be
insidious, but it is effective.

In every major city today, with a turn of the television dial, you
can bring explicit sex right into your home for anybody to watch.
And nobody blushes.

You don't even have to go into an "adult" bookstore anymore
to find pornography. You can find it in quick-stop grocery stores or

in some large drugstores and supermarkets. You may have to look a little, but it's there. Again I remind you, nobody blushes.

The ultimate, telltale sign of a low view of personal holiness is that we no longer blush when we find wrong. Instead, we make jokes about it. We re-dress immorality and make it appear funny. And if we don't laugh, we're considered prudes ... we're weird ... we're kind of crotchety.

Maybe I don't like to laugh about that anymore because, as a minister, I am forced to deal with the consequences of it. And that's *never* funny. People in the backwash of a sensual lifestyle don't come to me and my staff to talk about the lasting joys of illicit sex. They wonder about their family; or what they should do about this disease; or how they can deal with this incestuous relationship that is tearing the home apart; or how they are going to tell their parents that she's pregnant out of wedlock, knowing it will break their parents' hearts.

It would be bad enough if it were limited to the world, but, as I mentioned in my introduction, it is now in the church—the place most people would consider to be the ultimate bastion of holiness.

THE TRUTH: GOD'S TIMELESS COUNSEL FOR CHRISTIANS

I am grateful that God talks straight when it comes to moral purity. I'm grateful He doesn't stutter or shuffle or shift His position. I'm even more grateful that He doesn't laugh. It's as if He is looking His people directly in the eye and lovingly, yet firmly, saying, "I want you to hear this very clearly. I'll make it brief and simple." And He then leaves us with a decision regarding personal holiness. Only one decision pleases Him—*obedience*.

As John Brown, a nineteenth-century Scottish theologian, once stated: "*Holiness* does not consist in mystic speculations, enthusiastic fervors, or uncommanded austerities; *it consists in thinking as God thinks and willing as God wills.*"[96]

That's what the apostle Paul is asking of the reader in chapter 4 of 1 Thessalonians. He got his foot in the door in the last part of chapter 3 when he set forth a foundational guideline on how to "really live" as we "stand firm in the Lord" (v. 8). And what does that include?

And may the Lord cause you to increase and abound in love for one another, and for all men, just as we also do for you; so that He may establish your hearts unblamable in holiness (vv. 12–13a).

What a great way to live—"unblamable in holiness"! Confident living is directly linked to being "unblamable." It's better than knowing the answers to all the questions on a test, or having plenty of money, or earning an advanced degree. There's no security like being free of blame. When we are established in holiness, living unblamable lives of moral purity, we can smile at life. We can take its pressures and enjoy its pleasures. And then when marriage comes along, we can enjoy the partnership of the opposite sex, including all the joys of sexual delights.

Make no mistake about it, God is pleased when married partners enjoy a healthy sex life in marriage. He applauds it. And why shouldn't He? He invented it. His Word clearly states that marriage is to be held in honor and that the marriage bed is to be undefiled—free of blame (Heb. 13:4). But the implied warning is clear: If we remove sex from its original, God-given context, it becomes "sexual immorality," "lustful passion," and "impurity."

IN YOUR WALK, EXCEL!
1 Thessalonians 4:1–2

Finally then, brethren, we request and exhort you in the Lord Jesus, that, as you received from us instruction as to how you ought to walk and please God (just as you actually do walk), that you may excel still more (v. 1).

We have other ways of saying "excel" today: "Go for it. Give it your best shot. Don't just drift; pursue!" Or, as many parents often say, "Get with it!" Paul says, in effect, "Just as we have written you and have served as models before you, I encourage you to excel in your walk. *Get with it!* Make something happen in your life. Don't just drift along in a fog of mediocrity. Go the second mile. Excel!"

If you're a C student, try your best for a B. If you tend to be rather laid back in life, now is the time to go beyond your normal level. I exhort you to give yourself to diligence. Overcome that tendency toward laziness. All of that and more is involved in excelling.

While advocating an excelling lifestyle, Paul zooms in on one specific area that needs constant attention: moral purity.

IN YOUR MORALS, ABSTAIN!

1 Thessalonians 4:3–6

For this is the will of God, your sanctification; that is, that you abstain from sexual immorality (v. 3).

Paul has written strong and emotional words regarding our spiritual walk. We are to excel in it. Now he specifies our moral life. Whoever wishes to excel in his or her spiritual walk must come to terms with an inner battle: sexual lust. Yes, it's a battle … a vicious, powerful, relentless fight that won't suddenly stop when we turn fifty. And it won't end just because we may lose our mate. Nor will it decrease because our geography changes, or because we are well educated, or because we may be isolated behind prison walls, or because we remain single, or even because we enter the ministry. The struggle to be morally pure is one of those issues from which no one is immune. That includes *you!* Now let's understand what God is saying here.

"This is the will of God." Very seldom will you find such straight talk in Scripture. When it comes to remaining morally pure, you don't need to pray and ask whether it is God's will. "This is the will of God … abstain from sexual immorality." When I discussed the issue of divorce earlier, I stated that the word *immorality* is translated from the Greek word *porneia*, from which we get our words *pornography* or *pornographic*. It refers to any kind of intimate, sexual encounter apart from one's marital partner. It would include, of course, intimate encounters with the opposite sex or with the same sex. Fornication, adultery, or homosexuality would be included in *porneia*. Clearly, the command is that we are to *abstain*. Abstain means exactly that—*abstain*. Outside marriage, have nothing to do with sexual involvements with others.

Now in the fog of horizontal standards, you will be left with any number of options. You will be told by some to be discreet, but certainly not to abstain. "I mean, let's not be fanatical about this." A few may even counsel you, "It would be dangerous for you to play around with somebody else's mate, so don't do that. And, for sure, you need to watch out for disease." But wait. "Abstain," in Scripture, doesn't simply mean "watch out" or "be discreet." It means "have *nothing* to do" with something. Others' advice continues: "It's unwise for you to cohabit with a partner in your family. That's incest." (It is not only unhealthy, but it is illegal.) "If you're a teacher, you shouldn't be intimate with your students. That's not professionally wise, so don't do that," some would caution. But again I remind you: Scripture clearly states that it is God's will that we abstain. Moral purity is a matter of abstaining, not simply being careful.

How relieving it is to know exactly where we stand with our holy God! Now then, let's be very specific: If you are not married, there are no sexual exceptions provided for you. It is the will of God that you not be sexually intimate with any other person until marriage. That's what Scripture teaches both here and elsewhere. That is how to walk in obedience. It is God's best. Furthermore, it is for our good and it enhances God's glory.

I am pleased to add that we are not left with simply a stark command. Amplifying counsel follows in verses 4 and 5:

> That each of you know how to possess his own vessel in sanctification and honor, not in lustful passion, like the Gentiles who do not know God.

It is God's will that we abstain from moral impurity. It is *also* His will that we know how to do that. I suggest that you must become a student of *yourself* in order to know how to handle your battle with sexual lust. Those who fail to know themselves will lose the battle and ultimately become enslaved to lust. In order for one to "possess his own vessel," there must be a practical, working knowledge of one's own tendencies.

You know what kind of student you are, academically, in order to pass the course. You have to apply what you know will work in order to pass the test, and accomplish the course, and get the degree or the diploma, correct? In the realm of your intimate life, there must be another equally diligent application of knowledge. Each of us is to know how to "possess his own vessel"—meaning, maintain purity in one's own body.

The point? In order to abstain from *porneia*, we must become alert and disciplined students of our bodies; how they function, what appeals to them, and what weakens as well as strengthens them. We are to know how to control our inner drive, how to gain mastery over it, and how to sustain ourselves in a life of purity rather than yielding to lustful passions.

Let me amplify that by putting it in practical words no one can possibly misunderstand. Within the media there are certain things

that you and I cannot handle. We are to know ourselves well enough
to admit that and to face the fact that certain sensual stimuli weaken
us. We simply cannot tolerate those things and stay pure. The obvious conclusion is this: We are wrong to traffic in them. There are certain magazines you and I should not read. There are certain films, television programs, and late-night channels we have no business
watching. There are certain people who, by their suggestive conversation, weaken us. There are settings too tempting, touches too personal, and liberties that are too much for us to handle. We are fools to
play around with them. They create appealing temptations we simply
cannot control. So, if we are committed to abstain, we stay clear of them.

Such decisions are difficult to make and even more difficult to
implement, but it is all part of our knowing how to "possess [our ves-
sels] in sanctification and honor." Remember this: No one automatically remains morally pure. Abstention from sexual immorality is never an easy-come, easy-go issue. As I said earlier, it's a battle.
We're talking *warfare!*

The battle rages in the realm of sexually stimulating activities.
Even some parties, places, kinds of music, and pastimes can weak-
en us. Again, we are fools to tolerate those things. A person who is
trying to recover from alcoholism realizes he is fighting a losing battle if he chooses to live on the second floor above a bar. No question
about it, it will lead to failure. There is more:

> And that no man transgress and defraud his brother in the mat-
> ter because the Lord is the avenger in all these things, just as we
> also told you before and solemnly warned you (v. 6).

Some would get around total sexual abstention by saying,
"Well, what we could do is just keep this within the family. It's OK
if it's between two family members or among Christians." But He
corners us here as well. He adds that "no [one] transgress and defraud
his brother in the matter, because the Lord is the avenger in all these
things."

This verse refers not only to members in the family of God but
to individual family members—the indecent practices of relating inti-
mately to one's daughter or daughter-in-law, son or son-in-law,
mother, stepmother, father, stepfather, and on and on, covering the
whole realm of incest. Such indecent, unlawful acts defraud our family members!

Now to state it painfully straight: God clearly and unequivo-cally stands against extramarital sex, homosexual sex, and sexual encounters with individuals outside of marriage under ANY situa-tion. I repeat, the command is direct and dogmatic: *"Abstain from sexual immorality."*

As I write this, I realize I am not the only one saying these things. But, I confess, sometimes I feel like a lonely voice in our day. And because some illustrations could appear as gossip, I choose not to use anyone else but myself as an example. Allow me to tell you *my* story.

My wife and I were married in June of 1955. We both were quite young. I finished my schooling and then faced the need to ful-fill my military obligation. Back in the 1950s the military was not an option to choose but a requirement to be fulfilled. Because their time requirement best suited my particular situation, I chose the Marine Corps . . . an outfit not known for its moral purity.

I received the promise from my recruiting officer that if I joined, I would not have to serve my military duty overseas. And since I was married, that certainly was appealing to me because I was enjoying life with my bride, and the last thing we wanted was a forced sepa-ration from each other. I really wanted to be with her. But, through a chain of events too lengthy to explain, I wound up eight thousand miles from home. Stationed in the Orient for over a year, I was sud-denly faced with sexual temptation as I had never known it.

Before I ever dropped the seabag off my shoulder on the island of Okinawa, I was faced with a tough decision. I was going to make my home in a barrack that was characterized by a godless lifestyle. Venereal disease was not uncommon among those on the island. Living with a woman in the village was as common as breathing smog in southern California. If you lived in Okinawa, you slept around. And it wasn't uncommon for the chaplain, who was supposed to lecture incoming marines about purity, to ultimately joke his way through and tell you where to go to get penicillin shots. Welcome to the real world, Swindoll.

I realized, especially since I had known the joys of intimacy in marriage, that temptation would be incredibly strong. Surrounded by men who couldn't have cared less about the things of God, away from my home and free from physical accountability to my wife and my family, I would soon become another nameless marine on the back streets of Okinawan villages. But I was a Christian. I determined then and there to *"abstain from sexual immorality."* How I praise my Lord for His sustaining strength!

By the grace of God, the decision that I made back in the late 1950s allows me to speak and write today with confidence. Had I not been preserved from unfaithfulness, I would have to pass rather hurriedly and embarrassingly over this passage and similar sections of Scripture. I sincerely doubt that I would have pursued the ministry had I fallen into sexual lust.

Candidly, I had to be tough on myself. There were times when I had to be downright *brutal* with my emotions. I had to make some tough, Spartan decisions . . . unpopular decisions among a bunch of guys who tried everything in the book to tempt me. I was determined to be different so that I could reach those fellow marines with a message that had integrity. Let me clarify something, lest you misunderstand. God showed me it wasn't my job to clean up the goldfish bowl; it was my job to fish. I wasn't called to lead a flag-waving crusade for moral purity across the Orient. It was my job to live clean whether anybody else did or not. To put it bluntly, I was not to put my hands on someone who wasn't my wife. I wasn't even to *talk* about such things. Today I can speak from experience when I write these words: Sexual abstention works. It pays rich and rewarding dividends. It works . . . even in the life of a young, red-blooded marine surrounded by endless opportunities to yield.

And God made it clear to me that if I would abstain from sexual immorality, He would honor that. And His Spirit came to my rescue time and again. I had no corner on strength. I was often in the path of temptation, as anyone reading these words right now would understand, but I refused to surrender. Those were lonely days away from home for almost eighteen months. I was often burning with desire for my wife. But, thank God, I was committed to abstaining from immorality.

How did I make it? I involved myself in things that were wholesome, things that paid off, things that kept me busy, active, and fulfilled. I cultivated my musical abilities by becoming much more proficient in several instruments. I also was involved in an aggressive athletic program, spending most of my spare time with men who were committed to the same wholesome objectives. In my mind, the village was "off-limits." I didn't even drop in and get a soft drink in the village bars. I couldn't handle it. When I got off the bus that took me to my destination, I looked straight ahead and walked fast. That little island had physically attractive women and over five thousand places of prostitution. I never touched one of them. Obviously, I saw them . . . but I refused to yield.

In my heart I knew that once I broke, once I stepped into that sensual world, I would not stop. I knew the drive that was inside me *couldn't* be stopped once I yielded. And I probably would not even have wanted to stop it. It's like breaking with a diet. Once you take off the restraint, it's much easier to say, "Who cares?" Once you've eaten a little chocolate cake following lunch, that night it's *half a pie!*

Perhaps you are thinking, "That just mocks me, because my lifestyle isn't there. I've compromised sexually . . . I'm not walking in purity." Wait! My message to you isn't complicated—*start today!* It's time to take charge, my Christian friend. Telling yourself it won't work is the very thing that keeps you from a life of moral purity and its rewards. Stop lying to yourself! If you are born from above, if you are a child of God, then this passage is addressed to *you.* Your name belongs at the beginning of these verses.

See verse 1 of 1 Thessalonians 4? "Finally then, *brethren* . . ." Put your name there. This is specific instruction for you, child of God. No one else has the power. To be very frank with you, it's beyond me how an unsaved person can stay morally pure. Only by the power of the living Christ and His Spirit can this kind of life be carried out. If you really want to live in moral purity, yet you are not a Christian, then put first things first. You need to come to Christ. Becoming a Christian precedes cleaning up your moral act. Trusting in the Lord Jesus Christ is primary. Only then can you call upon the power you will need to walk in personal holiness.

Even then, I remind you, it won't be easy or automatic. You'll still need to apply the techniques I've mentioned to sustain your commitment to purity. I have found there are times when temptation is so fierce I have to be almost rude to the opposite sex. That may not sound very nice, but that's the price I'm willing to pay. It is worth it, believe me.

Some of you are husbands and fathers. The habits of fidelity you are forming directly affect your wife and children at home. How careful are you with personal holiness? How consistent? How tough are you on yourself? You cannot depend on anyone else to provide you with a moral standard. YOUR moral standard is the one that's going to keep you pure . . . or lead you astray. Isn't it time you became serious about moral purity?

You may be single, attractive, and capable. You may have entered a fine career. That's great . . . but it is also possible that you have begun to compromise your morals. You may find yourself saying, "It feels so good, and I am so lonely, and it is so accessible, so secret." Wait . . . it *isn't* secret! There is no "secret sin" before God. Furthermore, it won't remain a secret on earth forever.

See what it says in verse 6? It's not often that the Lord calls Himself the *Avenger*, but He does in this case. The meaning? "One who satisfies justice by punishing or disciplining the wrongdoer." Not all of that avenging will wait until the judgment day. Some of it happens now in the form of anxiety, conflict, guilt, disease, insanity . . . even death.

By the way, 1 Corinthians 6:18 is a pretty significant verse. In a context much like the one we've been considering, the writer exhorts the reader not to compromise morally. The verse says:

> Flee immorality. Every other sin that a man commits is outside the body, but the immoral man sins against his own body.

Practically speaking, all other sins can be fairly well managed in an objective manner. But this one comes in on you. In today's terms, it's an "inside job." In many ways, sexual sins take a personal toll on the victim, leaving the person in bondage, increasingly less satisfied, and on a downward spiral which only results in greater tragedy.

Few have ever said it better than Evangelist Billy Graham:

> In every area of our social life we see operating the inevitable law of diminishing returns in our obsession with sex. Many do something for a thrill only to find the next time that they must increase the dose to produce the same thrill. As the kick wears off, they are driven to look for new means, for different experiences to produce a comparable kick. The sex glutton is tormented by feelings of guilt and remorse. His mode of living is saturated with intense strain, unnatural emotions, and inner conflicts. His personality is thwarted in its search for development. His passions are out of control, and the end result is frustration. In his defiance of God's law and society's norm, he puts a death-dealing tension on his soul. His search for new thrills, for new kicks, for exciting experiences keeps him in the grip of

fear, insecurity, doubt, and futility. Dr. Sorokin says: "The weakened physical, emotional, and spiritual condition of the sex glutton usually makes him incapable of resisting the accompanying pressures, and he eventually cracks under their weight. He often ends by becoming a psychoneurotic or a suicide."[97]

When just a small boy, I remember memorizing the following:

Sow a thought, and you reap an act;
Sow an act, and you reap a habit;
Sow a habit, and you reap a character;
Sow a character, and you reap a destiny.

How true! And we never come to the place where we can call a halt to the sowing-reaping process.

I heard of a Christian leader who interviewed a veteran missionary who was then in his eighties. The interviewer asked, "Tell me, when did you get beyond the problem with lust?" In candor the godly gentleman answered, "It hasn't happened yet. The battle still goes on!" If you're waiting to outgrow the battle, don't hold your breath.

IN YOUR REASONING, REMEMBER!

1 Thessalonians 4:7–8

For God has not called us for the purpose of impurity, but in sanctification (v. 7).

Paul uses "sanctification" for the third time in this passage. It's a theological term referring to our pilgrimage, our progress from earth to heaven. Perhaps we could call it our growth pattern.

Remember this: You and I have been called to operate in the sphere of spiritual progress. God has called us to be in a spiritual growth pattern. Sometimes we're up . . . sometimes down. Sometimes we're more victorious than other times. But the progress is a movement forward and higher. God certainly has *not* called us for the purpose of impurity, even though we continue to live in a world socked in by a moral fog.

Consequently, he who rejects this is not rejecting man but the God who gives His Holy Spirit to you (v. 8).

The second thing to remember is: To reject a lifestyle of holiness is to reject the God who empowers you to live it. Holy living is inseparably linked to believing in a holy God.

THE CHOICE: A DECISION ONLY YOU CAN MAKE

Let me conclude my thoughts by simplifying your options. Actually, you have two. First, you can choose to live your life in a horizontal fog. If that is your choice, the results are predictable. You will continue to drift in a fog of moral uncertainties. Your disobedience will result in a series of rationalizations that will leave you empty. Guilt and grief will be your companions. You can choose to live like that. If you do, you open up a door of misery for yourself. You'll play at church. You'll toss around a few religious words. But before very long, your lifestyle will match the atmosphere around you. Your eyes will no longer tear up. Your conscience will no longer sting. Your heart won't beat faster. You may even stop blushing. A jaded, horizontal lifestyle is an option. But it has those consequences . . . those terrible consequences.

Why? The Avenger. God doesn't let His children play in the traffic without getting hurt. Your disobedience will result in increasing personal misery.

Second, you can choose to live your life vertically on target. The benefits? You will honor the God of moral absolutes. And your obedience will result in greater personal confidence and habits of holiness. It will begin to come supernaturally. You'll find yourself stronger, more secure, possessing a healthy self-image.

Internally, we're a little like an automobile. The God who made us built us with all the right lights on our internal dashboard. I don't know of anybody who after purchasing a new car also buys a little hammer for the glove compartment. Let's imagine a weird scene. Let's say that as two men are driving along, one of the lights on the dashboard starts flashing red. The driver says to his friend, "Hand me that hammer in the glove compartment, OK? Thanks." Tap . . . Tap . . . Bamm . . . Bamm . . . Pow! "There! Now we've gotten rid of *that* light." Smoke is coming out of the hood, yet the guy keeps driving along.

How foolish! And yet, it isn't difficult to find people who will hand out hammers. As they do, they say, "Aw, that's needless guilt. We're in an age where guilt is no longer considered important. You need to get rid of all that stuff." But wait . . . that's NECESSARY guilt!

God help us when we don't have it! It's the conscience that bites into us deep within and stings us when we compromise our moral purity. When we sin, it's *supposed* to hurt. We are *supposed* to be miserable when we compromise morally. That's the red light flashing down inside. It's God's way of saying, "Pull over . . . stop. Lift the hood. Deal with the real problem."

Jonathan Edwards, one of the great preachers of early American history, once made this resolution: "*Resolved*, Never to do any thing, which I should be afraid to do if it were the last hour of my life."[98]

You have available to you the power that's necessary to solve the real problems of your life. He is Jesus Christ. And once you have the Savior, you also have the Holy Spirit. He will come inside not to mock you but to help you; not simply to cry with you over how strong the temptation is but to empower you to overcome it. You can do all things through Him who keeps on pouring His power into you. Even if you have never done it in your life, you can begin a life of power today. There's no checklist. There's no probation period. There's no long list of responsibilities that you must fulfill before God will give you the power. If you've never met the Savior, holiness begins at the Cross, where Christ paid the penalty for sin. Take Him now.

Group Numbing

Tell me, where were you the morning of March 16, 1968? I can't remember either. But there is a group of men who can't forget. Even though they'll never be together again, *that* morning will never be forgotten.

The guys had a tough assignment . . . one of those search-and-destroy missions, a combat element of *Task Force Barker*, assigned to move into a small group of hamlets known collectively as MyLai (Me-Lie) in the Quang Ngai province of South Vietnam. Hastily trained and thrown together, most were inexperienced in battle. For a whole month prior to MyLai, they had achieved no military success. Although unable to engage the Vietcong in actual combat, they had nevertheless sustained a number of demoralizing casualties from land mines and nasty booby traps. Add to this poor food, thick swarms of insects, oppressive heat, jungle humidity and rain, plus loss of sleep, and you've got the makings of madness. And confusion as to the identity of the enemy didn't help either. Vietnamese and Vietcong looked the same. Since so few wore uniforms, distinguishing combatants from noncombatants was more than difficult. Would you believe *impossible?*

Looking back across the years since 1968, with the calm objectivity time and history provide, it's not an exaggeration to say that the instructions given to both enlisted men and junior officers the night before the assault were at best incomplete and ambiguous. All troops were supposed to be familiar with the Geneva Convention, which makes it a crime to harm any noncombatant (or, for that matter, even a combatant) who has laid down his arms because of wounds or sickness. It's probable that some of the troops were also unfamiliar with the "Law of Land Warfare" from the *United States Army Field Manual*, which specifies that orders in violation of the Geneva Convention are illegal and not to be obeyed. Period.

When "Charlie" Company moved nervously into the MyLai region that morning, they discovered not a single combatant.

Nobody was armed. No one fired on them. There were only unarmed women, children, and old men.

The things that then occurred are somewhat unclear. No one can reproduce the exact order of events, but neither can anyone deny the tragic results: Between five hundred and six hundred Vietnamese were killed in various ways. In some cases, troops stood at the door of a village hut and sprayed into it with automatic and semi-automatic rifle fire, killing everyone inside. Others were shot as they attempted to run away, some with babies in their arms. The most large-scale killings occurred in the particular hamlet of MyLai 4 where the first platoon of "Charlie" Company, under the command of a young lieutenant named William L. Calley, Jr., herded villagers into groups of twenty to forty or more, then finished them off with rifle fire, machine guns, and/or grenades.

The killing took a long time, like the whole morning. The number of soldiers involved can only be estimated. Perhaps as few as fifty actually pulled triggers and yanked grenade pins, but it is fairly accurate to assume that about two hundred directly witnessed the slaughter. We might suppose that within a week at least five hundred men in *Task Force Barker* knew that war crimes had been committed. Eventually, you may remember, charges were to be considered against twenty-five, of whom only six were brought to trial. Finally, only one was convicted, Lieutenant Calley . . . though, if we got specific about it, many were guilty. I remind you, failure to report a crime is itself a crime. In the year that followed, guess how many in *Task Force Barker* attempted to report the killings. Not one.

The fact that the American public learned about MyLai at all was due solely to a letter that Ron Ridenhour wrote to several congressmen three months after his return to civilian life at the end of March 1969 . . . over one year after the massacre.

So much for March 16, 1968. It happened. It's over. It's not my desire to set myself up as judge and jury, to point a finger of guilt at a few more of those soldiers trying to survive on the ragged edge. The men don't need further condemnation (frankly, I admire them for even *being* there, trying to do their duty), but we can all benefit from a brief evaluation.

To me, MyLai is a classic illustration of what one professional has called "psychic numbing," which often occurs within a group . . . sort of an emotional self-anesthesia. In situations in which our emotional feelings are overwhelmingly painful or unpleasant, the group aids in the capacity to anesthetize one another. It is greatly encouraged by being in the midst of others doing the same thing. Instead of crisp thinking, distinctly weighing the rightness and wrongness of an act, we find it possible—even easy—to pass the moral buck to some other part of the group. In this way, not only does the individual forsake his or her conscience, but the conscience of the group as a whole becomes so fragmented and diluted that it becomes almost nonexistent. As Dr. Scott Peck describes so vividly in his book *People of the Lie*, "It is a simple sort of thing ... the horrible becomes normal and we lose our sense of horror. We simply tune it out."[99]

That explains why peer pressure is so powerful, so potentially dangerous. It's a major motivation behind experimentation with drugs or sexual promiscuity or wholesale commitment to some cult or cooperation with an illegal financial scheme. The smirks or shouts of the majority have a way of intimidating integrity. And if it can happen to soldiers in Southeast Asia it can just as surely happen to folks like you and me. So be on guard! When push comes to shove, think independently. Think biblically. Do everything possible to lead with your head rather than your feelings. If you fail to do this, you'll lose your ethical compass somewhere between longing to be liked and desiring to do what is right.

"Do not be misled," warns the apostle who often stood alone, "bad company corrupts good character" (1 Corinthians 15:33 NIV). Group numbing has the possibility of hovering almost indefinitely in a conscienceless and evil holding pattern.

You question that? Consider Jonestown. Or Watergate. Or the LSD experiments conducted by the CIA. Or the Holocaust. Or the Inquisition. Or the group that screamed, "Crucify Him."

Tell me, is some group numbing you?

Gentleness

Tough and tender."[100]

That's the way my friend Joyce Landorf describes what every woman wants in a man. Her plea is for a balanced blend, an essential mixture of strong stability *plus* consideration, tact, understanding, and compassion. A better word is *gentleness*. But for some peculiar reason, that idea seems alien to the masculine temperament.

Observe the media-myth man. The man portrayed on the tube is rugged, hairy, built like a linebacker, drives a slick sports car, and walks with a swagger. In the beer ads he's all out for grabbing the gusto. With women he is a conqueror . . . fast and furious. In business he's "bullish." Even with a razor or hair dryer he's cocky, super-confident. If you don't believe it, *ask him*. The media-myth is, basically, *tough*. Spanish-speaking people would say he is known for his *machismo*. To the majority of young men—that's their hero, their masculine model.

Now let's understand something. A man *ought* to be a man! Few things are more repulsive than a man who carries himself like a woman . . . or wears stuff that suggests femininity. And we are living in an era when the roles are definitely eroding. I heard about a preacher who was conducting a wedding ceremony for a couple like this—both bride and groom having the same length hair and dressed in similar attire. Confused over their identity, he closed the ceremony with, "Would one of you kiss the bride?"

The right kind of toughness—strength of character—ought to mark the man of today . . . but not only that. Tenderness—gentleness—is equally important.

God considers gentleness so important He places it on the list of nine qualities He feels should mark the life of His children:

> But the fruit of the Spirit is love, joy, peace, patience, kindness, goodness, faithfulness, gentleness, self-control; against such things there is no law (Galatians 5:22–23).

There it is . . . number eight. The Greek word translated "gentleness" is *Prautes*, and it brims with meaning. In secular writings, the Greeks used it when referring to people or things that demonstrated a certain soothing quality—like an ointment that took the sting out of a burn. They also used this word to describe the right atmosphere that should prevail during a question-answer period in a classroom; the idea of discussing things without losing one's temper or becoming strongly defensive.

And think about this one. *Prautes* described the controlled conduct of one who had the power to act otherwise. Like a king who chose to be gracious instead of a tyrant. Like a military commander who patiently trained an awkward squad of soldiers. Plato called *Prautes* "the cement of society" as he used this word in the sense of politeness, courtesy, and kindness.

Gentleness has *three close traveling companions* in the New Testament:

1. It keeps company with agape-love (1 Corinthians 4:21).
2. It is a friend of meekness (2 Corinthians 10:1).
3. It is attached to humility (Ephesians 4:2).

Similarly, according to the New Testament, gentleness is the proper attitude when faced with *three difficult assignments:*

1. When faced with the need to exercise discipline in the Body of Christ (Galatians 6:1).
2. When faced with personal opposition (2 Timothy 2:25).
3. When faced with the truth of God's Word—being open and teachable (James 1:21).

Remember, our goal is balance . . . always balance. Not either-or, but both-and. Not just *tough*. That, alone, makes a man cold, distant, intolerant, unbearable. But tough *and* tender . . . gentle, thoughtful, teachable, considerate.

Both.

Like Christ.

Prayer

Here is a nontraditional, fresh approach to a subject all of us have read about throughout our Christian lives. But don't worry, from start to finish Scripture will be used as a basis of each major point . . . but the principles will surprise you.

Interestingly, when the Bible is examined and its truths are allowed to speak on a given subject, people are usually surprised. We are all too enamored of human opinion. Long enough have we allowed man's tradition to replace God's revelation! Especially on the subject of prayer.

If you are seeking a meaningful prayer life, if you long to break away from the imitations of intercession and come to terms with a genuine relationship with God where the two of you connect, these pages will help. They have been written with the hope that somehow you can see your way clear to pray—*really* pray—in an effective manner.

May God replace your formal struggle with an ease in His presence. And may He use these words to get you back where you belong in order to operate in the realm of His power . . . on your knees.

I should tell you up front that this is not going to be your basic religious-sounding discussion on prayer. Sorry, I just don't have it in me.

No, I'm not sorry.

To be painfully honest with you, most of the stuff I have ever read or heard said about prayer has either left me under a ton-and-a-half truckload of guilt or wearied me with pious-sounding clichés and meaningless God-talk. Without trying to sound ultracynical, I frequently have walked away thinking, "Who needs it?" Because I didn't spend two or three grueling hours a day on my knees as dear Dr. So-and-So did . . . or because I failed to say it just the "right way" (whatever that means) . . . or because I wasn't able to weave several Scripture verses through my prayer . . . or because I had not been successful in moving mountains, I picked up the distinct impression that I was out to lunch when it came to this part of the Christian life. It seemed almost spooky, mystical, and (dare I say it) even a little superstitious. A lot of verbal mumbo jumbo laced with a secret jargon some people had and others didn't. And I definitely *didn't*.

If you had asked me twenty or more years ago if prayer was one of the essentials in an aimless world like ours, I would surely have said no. At least, not the brand of prayer I had been exposed to. It wasn't that I was unaware of the high profile prayer plays in the Bible. I was simply turned off by the exposure I had had. So I pretty well tuned it out.

Maybe you have too. It is quite possible, therefore, that you have put off reading anything about prayer for awhile. I fully understand. And I do not blame you. On the contrary, I admire you for plunging in! Let's see if there is something I can say that will help put prayer in a better light for you. Hopefully, you will see rather soon that it isn't *authentic* prayer you've been struggling with, but rather a caricature, a distortion, a pitiful imitation of the genuine item.

PERSPECTIVE FROM PAUL

In the fourth chapter of Philippians, a small first-century letter Paul wrote that found its way into the New Testament, he mentions a series of things all of us want:

We all *want* to stand firm in our faith (v. 1).

We all *want* to have a joyful attitude through the day (v. 4).

We all *want* to have minds that dwell on beneficial things (v. 8).

We all *want* to apply God's principles so completely that we are flooded with His peace (v. 9).

For sure, we all *want* contentment and satisfaction (vv. 10–12).

Yes, we all *want* these things, but few of us experience them on a regular basis.

So? Our anxiety level rises higher and higher. Worries multiply. Cares increase. Irritation often invades, making us feel resentful and confused. We can't even crank it out. We struggle with thoughts like "I'm a hypocrite, I'm a poor Christian example." What's most interesting is this: THE FIRST AND ONLY THING THAT WILL WORK IS THE LAST THING WE TRY ... PRAYER. Take a look at this:

> Be anxious for nothing, but in everything by prayer and supplication with thanksgiving let your requests be made known to God. And the peace of God, which surpasses all comprehension, shall guard your hearts and your minds in Christ Jesus (Philippians 4:6–7).

Most Christians are so familiar with those words, I fear they may have lost their punch. To guard against that, let's read them from another translation—the Amplified Bible:

> Do not fret or have any anxiety about anything, but in every circumstance and in everything by prayer and petition [definite requests] with thanksgiving continue to make your wants known to God. And God's peace [be yours, that tranquil state of a soul assured of its salvation through Christ, and so fearing nothing from God and content with its earthly lot of whatever sort that is, that peace] which transcends all understanding, shall garrison and mount guard over your hearts and minds in Christ Jesus (Philippians 4:6–7).

Now *that's* a mouthful! If I understand this correctly, the anxiety that mounts up inside me, the growing irritation and the struggles that make me churn, will be dissipated—and, in fact, replaced with inner peace plus all those other qualities I want so much—if I will simply talk to my God. Prayer is the single most significant thing that will help turn inner turmoil into peace. Prayer is the answer.

But, wait! Why, then, is it such a struggle? What is it about prayer that makes even the great and the godly (those we admire so much) so guilty? So dissatisfied? So unhappy with their own prayer life?

In no way do I wish to be disrespectful by saying the following things, but I believe it's time somebody declared them to help clarify the barrier that keeps us from entering into authentic prayer. That barrier is the traditional wrappings that have been placed around prayer. Not even the grand models of church history admitted to much joy or peace or satisfaction in their prayer lives!

Dietrich Bonhoeffer, for example, once admitted that his prayer experience was something to be ashamed of. The German reformer, Martin Luther, anguished in prayer, saving three of the best hours of the day to pray . . . and yet he seldom seemed satisfied. Go down through the list and we find one after another working hard at prayer, but frequently we'll find they're dissatisfied, some of them even *woefully* unhappy about their prayer lives.

E. M. Bounds, Alexander Maclaren, Samuel Rutherford, Hudson Taylor, John Henry Jowett, G. Campbell Morgan, Joseph Parker, Charles Haddon Spurgeon, F. B. Meyer, A. W. Tozer, H. A. Ironside, V. Raymond Edman, William Culbertson, and on and on. Great men, strong Christian examples, magnificent models, yet you can hardly find one of that number who was satisfied with his prayer life. Oh, they labored in prayer, they believed in prayer, they taught and preached prayer . . . but why the dissatisfaction? Why the guilt? Or disappointment? Or, for some, embarrassment? I ask you—why?

At the risk of sounding downright heretical, I'm convinced that for centuries Christians have forced prayer into a role it was never designed to play. I would suggest we have *made* it difficult, hard, even painful. The caricature that has emerged through years of traditional (not biblical) modeling is now a guilt-giving discipline, not an anxiety-relieving practice. It is self-imposed. It doesn't come from God.

Remember Philippians 4:6–7? Paul's perspective on prayer was this: It *results* in peace, it doesn't take it away. It *alleviates* anxiety, it isn't designed to create it! But, you see, we have been led to believe that in order for prayer to be effective, it must be arduous, lengthy, even painful. And we must stay at it for hours on end . . . pleading, longing, waiting, hurting.

Are you ready for a shocker? You don't find any of that in the Scriptures. Except in very few and extreme cases, prayer is neither long nor hard to bear. And I cannot find any biblical characters who struggled with guilt because they didn't pray long enough or because they weren't in enough pain or because they failed to plead and beg sufficiently. Check it for yourself. It isn't there.

During my years in seminary, there was an upperclassman who believed God was calling him to the mission field. He was a sincere, careful student who read numerous biographies of great men and women who served Christ throughout their lives. The more he read, the more convinced he became that commitment required an infliction of bodily pain, sleepless nights spent in prayer. He even slept on the floor instead of his bed. He became increasingly more masochistic in his pietism, firmly dedicated to his self-imposed lifestyle of rigorous denial. A marked fanaticism characterized the man's attitude. He became more distant and defensive, less tolerant and balanced in his whole view of life. He was a driven man who, by the way, often spoke of his lack of enough time spent in prayer and his need for greater devotion to Christ. I recall, on one occasion, asking him to show me the biblical basis of his enough-is-never-enough mentality. I'm still waiting for his answer.

A warning: Let's be careful about making the extreme our standard. When it comes to prayer, let's get rid of all the traditional garbage and come back to the original model our Savior gave to us when He walked and talked among us.

INSTRUCTION FROM JESUS

Religious people in Jesus' day took their cues from the leaders of the synagogue—the Pharisees, the Sadducees, and the scribes. Didn't *they* believe in prayer? Yes, indeed. They had a saying, "He who prays within his house surrounds it with a wall that is stronger than iron." They only regretted they couldn't pray all day long. And it was this intensity that caused prayer to degenerate from a flowing spontaneity to a rigid, packaged plan, dispensed routinely by the religious leaders. Prayer changed from a privilege to an obligation. From pleasure in God's presence to man-made requirements. To help us understand what Jesus had to face, let's examine for a few minutes the impact of tradition on first-century Judaism.

How Prayer Had Degenerated

Anyone who makes a serious study of the life of Christ in the first four books of the New Testament (Matthew, Mark, Luke, John) quickly picks up the idea that Jesus' teachings were different from the official leaders of Judaism. He was, in every sense of the term, a radical revolutionary in their eyes, ultimately a threat to their system. In other words, He blew them away! This is evident when we read His now-famous "Sermon on the Mount" which is punctuated with a repeating of the same statement: "You have heard . . . but I say to you. . . ." Time after time He addressed the teaching they had received from the Pharisees and then offered a fresh and much-needed alternative. Take, for example, prayer.

In those days prayer had degenerated in five specific areas.

1. *Prayer became a formal exercise rather than free expression.* There were stated prayers for all occasions. Prayer was liturgical, standardized, a cut-and-dried routine.

> . . . Certain faults had crept into the Jewish habits of prayer. It is to be noted that these faults are by no means peculiar to Jewish ideas of prayer; they can and do occur anywhere. And it is to be noted they could only occur in a community where prayer was taken with the greatest seriousness. They are not the faults of neglect; they are the faults of misguided devotion. . . .
>
> . . . Jewish liturgy supplied stated prayers for all occasions. There was hardly an event or a sight in life which had not its stated formula of prayer. There was prayer before and after each meal; there were prayers in connection with the light, the fire, the lightning, on seeing the new moon, comets, rain, tempest, at the sight of the sea, lakes, rivers, on receiving good news, on using new furniture, on entering or leaving a city. Everything had its prayer. Clearly there is something infinitely lovely here. It was the intention that every happening in life should be brought into the presence of God. But just because the prayers were so meticulously prescribed and stated, the whole system lent itself to formalism, and the tendency was for the prayers to slip off the tongue with very little meaning.[101]

2. *Prayer was ritualistic, not spontaneous.* There were set times to pray, much like the Muslims of today who bow toward Mecca at specific times daily. In Jesus' day the "required" hours were 9:00

A.M., 12 noon, and 3:00 P.M. There were certain places to pray as well; the most preferred were the synagogues.

3. *Prayers were long, and filled with verbiage.* It was actually believed that whoever was longest in prayer was heard more readily by God. And the more flowery, the better. One well-known prayer had no less than sixteen adjectives preceding the name of God! There was this strange subconscious idea that whoever banged long and hard enough on the doors of heaven was granted God's attention.

4. *There were repetitious words and phrases.* We remember reading about this among Gentile idol-worshipers ("O Baal, hear us! O Baal, hear us!" in 1 Kings 18—Living Bible, for example), but by the first century the same tendency crept into the synagogue. Prayer led to an almost intoxication with words as those engaged in the practice fell under the spell of meaningless repetition.

5. *Praying became a cause for pride rather than the humble expressions of one in need.* It was a legalistic "status symbol" to pray well. The religious system, when followed to the letter, led to an ostentatious public display with hands outstretched, palms up, head bowed, three times a day . . . out on a public street corner!

Is it any wonder prayer had lost its value? As it degenerated into an insignificant routine marked by overt hypocrisy and meaningless terms, coupled with a judgmental spirit, prayer hit the skids. Such high expectations that became impossible for the common person to achieve resulted in the entire act becoming a fleshly display proudly performed by the religious hotshots. This explains why our Lord took them to task in His immortal sermon. It also helps us understand why He says what He does about prayer and other religious attitudes in Matthew 6.

How Prayer Can Be Effective

Jesus makes three strong statements (all of them negative) as He suggests a plan to follow if we want a satisfying and God-honoring prayer life.

1. *Don't be hypocritical.*

Beware of practicing your righteousness before men to be noticed by them; otherwise you have no reward with your Father who is in heaven. When therefore you give alms, do not sound a trumpet before you, as the hypocrites do in the synagogues and in the streets, that they may be honored by men. Truly

I say to you, they have their reward in full. . . . And when you pray, you are not to be as the hypocrites; for they love to stand and pray in the synagogues and on the street corners, in order to be seen by men. Truly I say to you, they have their reward in full. . . . And whenever you fast, do not put on a gloomy face as the hypocrites do, for they neglect their appearance in order to be seen fasting by men. Truly I say to you, they have their reward in full (Matthew 6:1–2, 5, 16).

Jesus reserved some of His strongest comments for hypocrisy. It is safe to say He *despised* it. The comment He repeats (for the sake of emphasis) is that those who do their thing to be seen get all the reward they will ever get *now*. He makes it clear there will be nothing gained later. Rather than making a cheap show of it, Jesus says:

But you, when you pray, go into your inner room, and when you have shut your door, pray to your Father who is in secret, and your Father who sees in secret will repay you (Matthew 6:6).

Prayer is never something we do to be seen. It loses its whole purpose if it becomes a platform to impress others. It is a private act of devotion, not a public demonstration of piety. According to Jesus, it belongs in the closet of our lives, an act done in secret.

The story of Daniel is familiar to all of us. Remember the decision of the king and how Daniel continued to pray three times a day? Do you recall where he went to pray?

Now when Daniel knew that the document was signed, he entered his house (now in his roof chamber he had windows open toward Jerusalem); and he continued kneeling on his knees three times a day, praying and giving thanks before his God, as he had been doing previously (Daniel 6:10).

No big public demonstration, just a quiet retreat to his room where he met, in secret, with his Lord. And you'll note he had done it many times before. This was a regular habit with Daniel. The absence of hypocrisy impresses us.

2. Don't use a lot of repetition.

And when you are praying, do not use meaningless repetition, as the Gentiles do, for they suppose that they will be heard for their many words. Therefore do not be like them; for your

Father knows what you need, before you ask Him (Mathew 6:7–8).

Even a casual reading of these words will lead us to realize that Christ never saw prayer as pleading or begging or hammering away at the throne of God. No, the Father knows His children, He knows what we need. Therefore, there is no reason to think that connecting with Him requires special words excessively repeated.

Now, let me be even more specific. Today, just as in that day, there is no part of the Christian life more in need of freshness and spontaneity than prayer. Whether it is prayer from a pulpit or church group meeting for prayer or prayer before meals or before a meeting gets started, meaningless repetition abounds! Tired, overworked words and phrases keep returning. Break loose from those old bromides! For starters, I dare you to pray without using "bless" or "lead, guide, and direct" or "help so-and-so" or "Thy will" or "each and every" or any number of those institutionalized, galvanized terms. I dare you!

On one occasion, evangelist Dwight L. Moody had been the recipient of numerous blessings from the Lord. In his abundance, he was suddenly seized with the realization that his heavenly Father was showering on him almost more than he could take. Encouraged and overwhelmed, he paused to pray. With great volume he simply stated, "Stop, God!" Now *that's* spontaneous. It is also a beautiful change from "Eternal, almighty, gracious Father of all good things, Thy hand hath abundantly and gloriously supplied our deepest needs. How blessed and thankful we are to come to Thee and declare unto Thee . . .," and on and on and on, grinding into snore city. Can you imagine one of your kids approaching you like that? I'll tell you, if one of mine did, I would stare directly at him and wonder, "What in the world is wrong?"

Listen to brand-new Christians pray. You know, those who are fresh from birth, who haven't learned "how to do it" yet, thank goodness. They talk to God like He's their friend, they use street terms anybody can understand, and they occasionally laugh or cry. It's just beautiful. Another tip that may add a new dimension to your prayer is the use of music. Sing to your God. We've started doing more and more of that in our church family . . . even the pastoral prayer often includes a chorus of worship. Or when you have prayer before your meals, have each person pray for one thing or pray for the specific food, naming the vegetables or the meat dish. Occasionally, our family will spend a few minutes before supper telling one thing that happened that day, then the one who prays mentions two or three of those matters before God. The point is clear: Guard against meaningless verbiage.

3. *Don't harbor anything against another.*

> For if you forgive men for their transgressions, your heavenly Father will also forgive you. But if you do not forgive men, then your Father will not forgive your transgressions (Matthew 6:14–15).

Before God will forgive us, we must be certain that our conscience is clear. A familiar verse from Psalms frequently pops into my mind when I begin to pray: "If I regard wickedness in my heart, the Lord will not hear" (Psalm 66:18). If I want cleansing, I must be certain things are right between myself and others.

Prayer includes praise and thanksgiving, intercession and petition, meditation, and confession. In prayer we focus fully on our God; we capture renewed zeal to continue, a wider view of life, increased determination to endure. As we strengthen our grip on prayer, it is amazing how it alters our whole perspective.

The late Dr. Donald Barnhouse, greatly admired American pastor and author of the last generation, once came to the pulpit and made a statement that stunned his congregation: *"Prayer changes nothing!"* You could've heard a pin drop in that packed Sunday worship service in Philadelphia. His comment, of course, was designed to make Christians realize that God is sovereignly in charge of everything. Our times are literally in His hands. No puny human being, by uttering a few words in prayer, takes charge of events and changes them. God does the shaping, the changing; it is He who is in control. Barnhouse was correct . . . except in one minor detail. Prayer changes *me*. When you and I pray, *we* change, and that is one of the major reasons prayer is such a therapy that counteracts anxiety.

A FINAL ENCOURAGEMENT

Prayer was never intended to make us feel guilty. It was never intended to be a verbal marathon for only the initiated . . . no secret-code talk for the clergy or a public display of piety. None of that. Real prayer—the kind of prayer Jesus mentioned and modeled—

is realistic, spontaneous, down-to-earth communication with the living Lord that results in a relief of personal anxiety and a calm assurance that our God is in full control of our circumstances.

I encourage you to start over. Form some brand-new habits as you fight off the old tendency to slump back into meaningless jargon. Get a fresh, new grip on prayer. It is essential for survival.

Many years ago I decided to do that very thing. I was fed up with empty words and pharisaical phrases. In my search for new meaning, I came across this brief description of prayer, which I set on my desk and carried in the front of my Bible for years. I cannot locate the book from which it was taken, but I do know the author, a seventeenth-century Roman Catholic Frenchman named François Fenelon. Although written centuries ago, it has an undeniable ring of relevance:

> Tell God all that is in your heart, as one unloads one's heart, its pleasures and its pains, to a dear friend. Tell Him your troubles, that He may comfort you; tell Him your joys, that He may sober them; tell Him your longings, that He may purify them; tell Him your dislikes, that He may help you to conquer them; talk to Him of your temptations, that He may shield you from them; show Him the wounds of your heart, that He may heal them; lay bare your indifference to good, your depraved tastes for evil, your instability. Tell Him how self-love makes you unjust to others, how vanity tempts you to be insincere, how pride disguises you to yourself and to others.
>
> If you thus pour out all your weaknesses, needs, troubles, there will be no lack of what to say. You will never exhaust the subject. It is continually being renewed. People who have no secrets from each other never want for subjects of conversation. They do not weigh their words, for there is nothing to be held back; neither do they seek for something to say. They talk out of the abundance of the heart, without consideration they say just what they think. Blessed are they who attain to such familiar, unreserved intercourse with God.

The Tongue of the Wise

Wisely labeled "the saving virtue," tact graces a life like fragrance graces a rose. One whiff of those red petals erases any memory of the thorns.

Tact is like that.

It's remarkable how peaceful and pleasant it can make us. Its major goal is avoiding unnecessary offense . . . and that alone ought to make us *crave* it. Its basic function is a keen sense of what to say or do in order to maintain the truth *and* good relationships . . . and that alone ought to make us *cultivate* it. Tact is *savoir faire* on the horizontal plane. It is incessantly appropriate, invariably attractive, incurably appealing, but rare . . . oh, so rare!

Remember the teacher you had who lacked tact? Learning was sacrificed daily on the altar of fear. You wondered each session if *that* was the day you'd be singled out and embarrassed through some public put-down.

Remember the salesman you encountered who lacked tact? Once you found out (and it usually doesn't take sixty seconds), you wanted only one thing—to get *away!*

Remember the boss you worked for who lacked tact? You never knew if he *ever* understood you or considered you to be a valuable person.

And who could forget that tactless physician? You weren't a human being, you were Case No. 36—a body with a blood pressure of 120/70 . . . height 5'7" . . . weight 160 . . . a chronic history of diarrhea . . . stones in your gallbladder—*"and you need radical surgery immediately!"* All this was spoken in perfect monotone as he glared grimly at a folder stuffed with X-rays, charts, and long sheets of paper covered with advanced hieroglyphics. Brilliant, capable, experienced, dignified, respected . . . but no tact.

Perhaps you heard about the husband who lacked tact. Early one morning his wife left for a trip abroad . . . and that very day their poodle died. When she called home that evening, she asked how everything was—and he bluntly blurted out, "Well, the dog died!" Shocked, she chided him through tears for being so tactless, so strong.

"What should I have said?" he asked.

"You should've broken the news gently, perhaps in stages. When I called you from here in New York, you could have said, 'The dog is on the roof.' And the next day when I called you from London, 'He fell off the roof.' The following day from Paris, you could have told me, 'He is at the vet's . . . in the hospital.' And finally, from Rome, I could have then been informed, 'He died.'"

The husband paused and thought about the advice. His wife then asked, "By the way, how is mother?"

He responded, "She's on the roof!"

Ah, that's bad. But it isn't the worst. The classic example of tactless humanity, I'm disappointed to declare, is the abrasive Christian (so-called) who feels it is his or her calling to fight for the truth with little or no regard for the other fella's feelings. Of course, this is supposedly done in the name of the Lord. "To do anything less," this tactless individual intones with a pious expression, "would be compromise and counterfeit." So on he goes, plowing through people's feelings like a clumsy John Deere tractor, leaving them buried in the dirt and, worst of all, deeply offended. For all his rapid-fire Scripture quotations, you will rarely find Proverbs 18:19 on the lips of this armored crusader:

> A brother offended is harder to be won than a strong city, and contentions are like the bars of a castle.

His favorite plan of attack is either to overlook or strongly demand, and the backwash is a back alley strewn with the litter of broken hearts and bitter souls. Unfortunately, the preacher himself is often the greatest offender, who seems to delight in developing a devastating pulpit that scourges rather than encourages, that blasts rather than builds. His murder weapon is that blunt instrument hidden behind his teeth.

"The heart of the righteous ponders how to answer," wrote Solomon. That which turns away wrath is "a gentle answer."

The wise person uses his tongue to "make knowledge accept-able," the king added. And who could ever forget the impact of the proverb that says: "The tongue of the wise brings healing" . . . or "a man has joy in an apt answer and how delightful is a timely word!"

There's a TV ad for a first-aid ointment that says, "Stop hurt-ing . . . start healing." Another offers a bandage that takes the "ouch" away. That's good counsel. Let's be gentle and sensitive when we are touching the tender feelings of others. Moms and Dads, it's hard to exaggerate the value of tact within the walls of your home. Soften the blows a little! You'll preserve some very valuable self-esteem while gaining respect, believe me.

By the way, no facts need be subtracted when tact is added. I used to sell shoes years ago. With a twinkle in his eye, my seasoned employer instructed me not to say, "Lady, your foot is too big for this shoe!" Instead, I was taught to say, "I'm sorry, ma'am, but this shoe is just a little too small for your foot." Both statements expressed the facts, but one was an insult and the other a tactful compliment. Same facts, different words.

It didn't shrink her foot, but it did save her face.

And that's what tact is all about.

Finishing the Course

Not enough is said or written today about *finishing* well.
Lots and lots of material is available on motivation to get started and creative ways to spark initiative. Plenty of advice is floating around on setting goals and establishing priorities and developing a game plan. All of it is insightful and needed. Getting off the dime is often a herculean task. Starting well is Plan "A," no doubt about it.

But let's hear it for the opposite end, for a change. Let's extol the virtues of sticking with something until it's *done*. Of hanging tough when the excitement and fun fade into discipline and guts. You know, being just as determined eight minutes into the fourth quarter as at the kickoff. Not losing heart even though the project has lost its appeal. Eugene Peterson, sounding a lot like the late A. W. Tozer, in his fine book, *A Long Obedience in the Same Direction*, expresses the same concern with these insightful words:

> Our attention spans have been conditioned by thirty-second commercials. Our sense of reality has been flattened by thirty-page abridgments.
>
> It is not difficult in such a world to get a person interested in the message of the gospel; it is terrifically difficult to sustain the interest. Millions of people in our culture make decisions for Christ, but there is a dreadful attrition rate.... In our kind of culture anything, even news about God, can be sold if it is packaged freshly; but when it loses its novelty, it goes on the garbage heap. There is a great market for religious experience in our world; there is little enthusiasm for the patient acquisition of virtue, little inclination to sign up for a long apprenticeship in what earlier generations of Christians called holiness.[102]

I fear our generation has come dangerously near the "I'm-getting-tired-so-let's-just-quit" mentality. And not just in the spiritual realm. Dieting is a discipline, so we stay fat. Finishing school is a hassle, so we bail out. Cultivating a close relationship is painful, so we back off. Getting a book written is demanding, so we stop short. Working through conflicts in a marriage is a tiring struggle, so we walk away. Sticking with an occupation is tough, so we start looking elsewhere. This reminds me of something my sister recently passed along to me, entitled *Six Phases of a Project:*

- Enthusiasm
- Disillusionment
- Panic
- Search for the guilty
- Punishment of the innocent
- Praise and honors for the nonparticipants

By the time a project has run its crazy course, confusion has replaced accomplishment. Participants have changed to spectators. The "let's-just-quit" mentality is upon us.

Ignace Jan Paderewski, the famous composer-pianist, was scheduled to perform at a great concert hall in America. It was an evening to remember—black tuxedos and long evening dresses, a high-society extravaganza full bore. Present in the audience that evening was a mother with her fidgety nine-year-old son. Weary of waiting, he squirmed constantly in his seat. His mother was in hopes that her boy would be encouraged to practice the piano if he could just hear the immortal Paderewski at the keyboard. So—against his wishes—he had come.

As she turned to talk with friends, her son could stay seated no longer. He slipped away from her side, strangely drawn to the ebony concert grand Steinway and its leather tufted stool on the huge stage flooded with blinding lights. Without much notice from the sophisticated audience, the boy sat down at the stool, staring wide-eyed at the black and white keys. He placed his small, trembling fingers in the right location and began to play "Chop Sticks." The roar of the crowd was hushed as hundreds of frowning faces turned in his direction. Irritated and embarrassed, they began to shout:

"Get that boy away from there!"
"Who'd bring a kid that young in here?"
"Where's his mother?"
"Somebody stop him!"

Backstage, the master overheard the sounds out front and quickly put together in his mind what was happening. Hurriedly, he grabbed his coat and rushed toward the stage. Without one word of announcement he stooped over behind the boy, reached around both sides, and began to improvise a countermelody to harmonize with and enhance "Chop Sticks." As the two of them played together, Paderewski kept whispering in the boy's ear: "Keep going. Don't quit, Son. Keep on playing ... don't stop ... don't quit."

And so it is with us. We hammer away on our project, which seems about as significant as "Chop Sticks" in a concert hall. And about the time we are ready to give it up, along comes the Master, who leans over and whispers: "Now keep going; don't quit. Keep on ... don't stop; don't quit," as He improvises on our behalf, providing just the right touch at just the right moment.

Do I write today to a few weary pilgrims? Is the road getting long and hope wearing a little thin? Or to a few parents who are beginning to wonder if it's worth it all—this exacting business of rearing children, which includes cleaning up daily messes and living with all that responsibility? Or to you who have a dream, but seeing it accomplished seems too long to wait? Listen to the Master's whispering:

> "Let us not lose heart in doing good, for in due time we shall reap if we do not grow weary"(Galatians 6:9).

> "Therefore ... be steadfast, immovable ... your toil is not in vain in the Lord" (1 Corinthians 15:58).

> "Be of sober spirit, be on the alert.... And after you have suffered for a little while, the God of all grace ... will Himself perfect, confirm, strengthen and establish you" (1 Peter 5:8, 10).

So many start the Christian life like a lightning flash—hot, fast, and dazzling. But how many people (aged sixty and over) can you name who are finishing the course with sustained enthusiasm and vigor? Oh, there are some, I realize, *but why so few?* What happens along the way that swells the ranks of quitters? I really wish I knew that answer. If I did, I'd shout warnings from the pulpit Sunday after Sunday. No, better than that, I'd stoop over and whisper them to every discouraged person I meet. Before it's too late.

Before he quits, and, instead of mastering the *Minuet* or *Concerto in A Minor*, settles for "Chop Sticks."

Stress

Whoever dubbed our times "The Aspirin Age" didn't miss it by very far. It is correct to assume there has never been a more stress-ridden society than ours today. For many, gone are the days of enjoying bubbling brooks along winding pathways or taking long strolls near the beach. The relaxed bike ride through the local park has been replaced with the roar of a motorcycle whipping its way through busy traffic. And the easy-come, easy-go lifestyle of the farm has been preempted by a hectic urban family going in six different directions . . . existing on instant dinners, shouting matches, strained relationships, too little sleep, and too much television.

Add financial setbacks, failure at school, unanswered letters, obesity, loneliness, a ringing telephone, unplanned pregnancies, fear of cancer, misunderstanding, materialism, alcoholism, drugs, and an occasional death; then subtract the support of the family unit, divide by dozens of opinions, multiply by 365 days a year, and you have the *makings of madness!* Stress has become a way of life; it is the rule rather than the exception.

There is an old Greek motto that says:

YOU WILL BREAK THE BOW IF YOU KEEP IT ALWAYS BENT.

Wise words, but how do we loosen the strings? Even when we make every effort to slow down and relax, others place high demands on us. Their "shoulds" and "oughts" and "musts" hit us like strong gusts of wind, driving our lives onto shallow reefs of frustration and even desperation.

Suicide is now a viable option to many who once would have never tolerated the thought. Every day in the United States, over eighty people take their lives—that's more than three each hour, twenty-four hours every day. The suicide rate for Americans under thirty years of age has increased three hundred percent in the past decade! For many, the bow has already broken.

A BIBLICAL STRESS CASE

To the surprise of some people, the Bible often speaks directly to key issues. Let's step into the time tunnel to find a perfect example of stress. It is the classic story of Mary and Martha, two unmarried sisters whom Jesus visited in their home at Bethany. The account is recorded in the last several verses in Luke 10 as follows:

> Now as they were traveling along, He entered a certain village; and a woman named Martha welcomed Him into her home. And she had a sister called Mary, who moreover was listening to the Lord's word, seated at His feet (vv. 38–39).

A lovely scene, Jesus dropped by, probably unexpectedly, for a brief visit. Mary, the younger, realized how privileged they were, so she decided to sit down and really make the most of it. She sat at His feet, drinking in His every word.

But Martha? Well, she was neither sitting down nor drinking in. She was under a great deal of stress.

> But Martha was distracted with all her preparations; and she came up to Him, and said, "Lord, do You not care that my sister has left me to do all the serving alone? Then tell her to help me" (v. 40).

We read that Martha was "distracted." Instead of relaxing and enjoying the Lord's presence, Martha was in a mild frenzy over all her preparations. The lady was trying to fix a nice meal, get everything done on time, arrange the table, and be a good hostess ... while her sister sat in the room and never offered to help. As her anxiety reached the breaking point, she reacted strongly.

- She assumed the Lord Jesus didn't care—"Lord, do You not care . . . ?"
- She blamed Mary for being irresponsible—" . . . my sister has left me to do all the serving alone . . ."
- She tried to work things out her way—". . . tell her to help me."

It was okay for Martha to want to serve Jesus something to eat. Commendable, in fact. She was like that—active, energetic, diligent, thoughtful, and determined. All fine qualities. But her problem grew out of hand when she attempted to do more than was necessary. Then a critical glance was cast at Mary because she chose not to spend her time in the same way, hustling, bustling, and fussing.

It is interesting that anxiety-prone people frequently blame others for their plight. Rather than realizing that their stress is self-appointed, they often criticize others for causing it to happen.

Does that sound unfair? Read on:

> But the Lord answered and said to her, "Martha, Martha, you are worried and bothered about so many things; but only a few things are necessary, really only one, for Mary has chosen the good part, which shall not be taken away from her" (vv. 41–42).

Can't you just hear Jesus? "Marthaaaa . . . Martha!" Then He quickly analyzed her stress in two words—"worried" and "bothered." The term Dr. Luke uses for "worried" is the one that means "to be pulled in different directions." The root verb in Greek means "to divide into parts." Martha was being pulled apart from within. Her stress was caused by this internal tearing. The word *bothered* suggests originally the idea of "noise, tumult, trouble." She was agitated, ripped apart in turmoil.

Unfortunately, it's a familiar sight.

Jesus noticed she was worried and disturbed about "so many things"—the meat, the napkins, the timing, the rolls, the setting of the table, the way things looked, the numerous other picky details. She was no longer able to focus on the big picture. The single most important thing she *should* have chosen got lost in the shuffle. And remember, there was nothing wrong with her desire to serve Him, but before long, as worry stole away her perspective, she lost sight of the important.

Charles Hummel calls this "the tyranny of the urgent,"[103] a fitting description. For Martha, who allowed herself to get caught in the sticky web of stress, the important got replaced by the urgent.

THE PERSPECTIVE OF JESUS

The night Jesus was placed under arrest and later subjected to a series of mock trials, which ultimately led to His crucifixion, He had been praying to the Father. In that prayer He said:

> I glorified Thee on the earth, having accomplished the work which Thou hast given Me to do (John 17:4).

When you think that through, you will be surprised. He said that He had completed the job. Mission accomplished. Yet there were still regions which had not heard. There were still hundreds of blind and sick and lame people as yet untouched and unchanged. There were still millions of slaves in the Roman Empire being mistreated, yet He said He had accomplished what the Father had for Him to do. Even though there were still numerous needs, our Savior was free of stress. Unlike His nervous friend Martha, Jesus maintained the right perspective.

OVERCOMING WORRY

We have seen a couple of New Testament examples (one negative, the other positive) of people under stress. Let's now go back to the Old Testament and lift out some familiar words that hold out hope to those who are clenched in the vice grip of worry. Let's learn how we can cope with anxiety today. If you have a Bible nearby, turn to Proverbs 3:5–6.

The passage is so well-known to most Christians that we have perhaps missed its significant message. Read slowly the words of Solomon:

> Trust in the LORD with all your heart, and do not lean on your own understanding.
>
> In all your ways acknowledge Him, and He will make your paths straight.

Go back and read them again, please; this time *aloud*.

MY PART, GOD'S PART

Let's do a little digging. I'd like to suggest three important observations I see in what we just read.

1. *There are four verbs—words of action—in these two verses:*

- trust
- do not lean
- acknowledge
- make straight

A closer look will reveal that the first three verbs are commands. They are directed to the child of God, the Christian. They represent *our* responsibility.

Trust . . . do not lean . . . acknowledge. . . .

The fourth verb is a promise. It declares God's part in the transaction, *His* responsibility.

. . . He will make your paths straight.

Putting this observation in the form of a simple diagram looks like this:

My Responsibility God's Promise

Trust!   He will make straight . . .

Do not lean!

Acknowledge!

2. *The same term is used no less than four times.* Can you find it? Look again at the verses. Circle the word *your*. God is really emphasizing the personal nature of this truth. He is also telling us that we must enter into it individually—no one else can apply it for us.

Your responsibility in your circumstances is to trust with all *your* heart . . . and to refuse to lean on *your* own understanding . . . acknowledging Him in all *your* ways . . . so that He might make straight *your* paths.

Get the picture? Responding to life's situations is *your* choice. No one else can do it for you.

3. *The first phrase is linked to the last phrase, giving us the main idea.* (Trust . . . He will make straight.) The two middle phrases merely amplify the main idea. (Do not lean . . . acknowledge.) Let me explain.

I am to trust in my Lord without hesitation and without reservation—with all my heart—so that He might step in and take control, making my way meaningful and straight. And what is involved in trusting with all my heart? Two particular decisions—one negative, the other positive:

- Negatively, I am not to lean on my own understanding.
- Positively, I am to acknowledge Him in the whole battleground.

DEFINING SOLOMON'S WORDS ABOUT WORRY

So much for the observations. To make them even more meaningful, let's uncover several of the significant terms.

Trust. At the root of this original Hebrew term is the idea of throwing oneself down and lying extended on the ground, casting all hopes for the present and the future upon another, finding shelter and security there. We are *commanded* by our Lord to cast ourselves fully and absolutely at His feet. Remember: It is with *all* our hearts that we do this.

Heart. Obviously, Solomon is not referring to the organ in the chest that pumps blood. He's using the Hebrew term that appears throughout the Old Testament in reference to one's "inner person" ... that part of us which is the very center of our intellect, emotion, and will. In other words, we are commanded to cast upon our God our total trust, not holding back in any area of our mind or feeling or volition. No reservations whatsoever.

Understanding. The term appears first in the Hebrew text for the purpose of emphasis: " ... and upon your understanding do not lean." It is referring to *human* understanding. The thought is this: "Don't turn first to your own limited viewpoint; don't try to work things out on your own."

Lean. The Hebrew term means "to support oneself, as though leaning for assistance." It's used in Judges 16 where blind Samson leaned on the huge pillars supporting the Philistine temple. Think of resting your weight on a crutch. It's that idea ... except it is a *negative* command. "Do not" rest on your own ingenuity. Quit chasing down all the possibilities you can think of. Stay out of the way, guard against fear and panic, scheming and manipulating, worrying and hurrying.

Acknowledge. Here's the positive part. Literally, it means "recognize." In the midst of the whole scene, recognize, mentally call to mind, God's presence and control.

Make straight. It's the thought of making something smooth, straight, right. It includes the idea of removing obstacles that are in the way, as when a road is being built through a mountain pass. The Hebrew verb appears in this verse in a particular stem that denotes *intensity.* In other words, when the Lord is fully relied upon to handle a given situation. He will do a thorough, complete job of smoothing out our part.

THE SWINDOLL AMPLIFIED VERSION

We have taken a deep look into these verses and examined the vital parts. Now we need to put the thought back together and see the whole picture in a new light.

Throw yourself completely upon the Lord—that is, cast all your present and future needs on Him who is your intimate Savior-God . . . finding in Him your security and safety. Do this with all your mind and feeling and will. In order to make this possible, you must refuse to support yourself upon the crutch of human ingenuity. Instead, recognize His presence and concern in each one of your circumstances. Then He (having taken full control of the situation) will thoroughly smooth out and straighten your paths, removing each obstacle along the way.

What a magnificent promise to all the "Marthas" reading this!

APPLYING YOUR PERSONALIZED VERSION

As I think all this through, several specific truths seem to bounce off the pages of Scripture:

- This is a personal promise for anxiety-prone people to claim right now. God has preserved this statement just for you. Claim it!
- God will do His part, but first we must do our part. He will keep His promise if we obey His commands. And keep in mind that our response to His commands *precedes* His part in the transaction.
- Our God wants our total trust. Yes, total. Nothing held back. No games. No empty, pious-sounding words. No, He commands our total trust.

- There is no area that He is unable to handle. Did you note the twice-repeated "all"? God is a specialist in *every* circumstance . . . and that includes yours today.
- Since this promise is to be personally applied, how about filling in the blank with your current stress right now? Instead of reading:

  . . . in all your ways recognize Him, and He will smooth out your path, removing all necessary obstacles . . .

  you fill in the space:

  . . . in _____ recognize Him . . .

Right this moment, take that worry that is eating away at you like a rapidly growing cancer, and turn it over to Him as you write it in that blank space. Refuse to brood over it any longer! Cast aside doubt and fear and leave it *all* with Him. Then stand back and watch Him work.

On the authority of His own Word, I can assure you, He *will* go to work on your behalf. And on top of all that, He will "loosen your strings" so your bow won't break.

SPREADING OUT THE WORKLOAD

There is another side of stress that is easily overlooked, and that is trying to do too much ourselves. All of us have a limit. If those huge freight trucks on the highway have a load limit, you can be sure each one of us does, too. When we try to do more than we were designed to do, our level of anxiety immediately begins to rise. This is a common problem among strong natural leaders who assume too much responsibility rather than delegate the tasks to others who could help shoulder the load. When we don't do that, the bow stays bent and occasionally snaps. Even Christians can crack up!

MOSES: AN OVERWORKED SERVANT-LEADER

To the surprise of many people, Moses is an example of one who fell into this very trap. He was surrounded by an endless number of needs, people demands, requests for decisions, and problems to solve. On one occasion, his father-in-law, Jethro, paid him a visit and witnessed the load Moses was living under. Exodus 18 tells the story:

And it came about the next day that Moses sat to judge the people, and the people stood about Moses from the morning until the evening. Now when Moses' father-in-law saw all that he was doing for the people, he said, "What is this thing that you are doing for the people? Why do you alone sit as judge and all the people stand about you from morning until evening?" And Moses said to his father-in-law, "Because the people come to me to inquire of God. When they have a dispute, it comes to me, and I judge between a man and his neighbor, and make known the statutes of God and His laws." And Moses' father-in-law said to him, "The thing that you are doing is not good. You will surely wear out, both yourself and these people who are with you, for the task is too heavy for you; you cannot do it alone" (vv. 13–18).

The classic account of an ancient workaholic! This wise father-in-law comes right out and faces Moses with the truth: "It isn't good . . . you'll wear yourself out." Jethro saw the whole thing objectively. He saw his son-in-law on the raw edge of exhaustion. The anxiety brought on by that much work was soon to take a toll on Moses. He couldn't continue doing it all alone.

Before we proceed, let me ask you: Does this sound like *your* biography? Are you the type who tends to take on too much . . . to handle the demands all alone . . . to hang in there without much thought of passing the load around? To quote Jethro's counsel, "The thing that you are doing is not good." Perhaps this is the bottom-line reason you have become so anxious in recent days. Be honest enough to admit it if it's true. That's the first (and most important) step in the process of change.

As Moses listened, Jethro continued:

"Now listen to me: I shall give you counsel, and God be with you. You be the people's representative before God, and you bring the disputes to God, then teach them the statutes and the laws, and make known to them the way in which they are to walk, and the work they are to do. Furthermore, you shall select out of all the people able men who fear God, men of truth, those who hate dishonest gain; and you shall place these over them, as leaders of thousands, of hundreds, of fifties and of tens. And let them judge the people at all times; and let it be that every major dispute they will bring to you, but every minor dispute they themselves will judge. So it will be easier for you, and they will bear the burden with you. If you do this thing and God so commands you, then you will be able to endure, and all these people also will go to their place in peace." So Moses listened to his father-in-law, and did all that he had said (vv. 19–24).

Moses was smart to listen. He was hearing the advice of a wise man.

Now don't misunderstand. The plan was not that he should back out of the scene completely. No, that wouldn't have been best. His presence was still extremely valuable. But he was to determine those things he should handle—the really weighty issues—then pass around to qualified people the balance of the workload.

And did you notice that those who were to help him needed to be well-qualified? Read again the specifics in verse 21:

- Able men who fear God
- Men of truth
- Those who hate dishonest gain
- Leader types

Had Moses chosen the wrong kind of delegates to help handle the workload, his stress would have *increased*, not decreased.

He did as Jethro had suggested:

And Moses chose able men out of all Israel, and made them heads over the people, leaders of thousands, of hundreds, of fifties and of tens. And they judged the people at all times; the difficult dispute they would bring to Moses, but every minor dispute they themselves would judge (vv. 25–26).

This, no doubt, enabled him to have many more effective years of meaningful leadership . . . and we would do well to follow his example.

YOU: AND WHAT ABOUT YOU?

The real issue, however, is not the stress of Moses. It is *you* and *your* load of anxiety. What is it that makes you think you are capable enough to handle more than you should? Why do you feel the need to continue living under the heavy weight of anxiety when it seems so natural to spread the work among several others?

I challenge you: Release your grip on all those details! Find a few qualified people to help you get the job done. This same principle works when you are under the pressure of an intense trial in your life. No need to tough it out alone. Share it. Let a few people enter into that lonely experience with you. They can stand by you and provide an enormous amount of support, thus relieving much of the stress you would otherwise be enduring alone.

SHIFTING THE STRESS BY PRAYER

Prayer is another relief—an *essential* therapy during stressful times. I'm reminded of David on one occasion. He and a group of his men returned home after a wearying three-day journey. They found that while they were away an enemy tribe had made a raid on their homes and had burned them to the ground. On top of that, their wives and children had been taken captive by the enemy. It wasn't very long before their morale hit bottom.

> Then David and the people who were with him lifted their voic-es and wept until there was no strength in them to weep (1 Samuel 30:4).

What stress! And to make matters even worse, mutiny broke out. The men spoke of stoning David because they were embittered against him. They indirectly blamed their leader for what was hap-pening (that still goes on, by the way). We read of David's response:

> Moreover David was greatly distressed because the people spoke of stoning him, for all the people were embittered, each one because of his sons and his daughters. But David strength-ened himself in the LORD his God (v. 6).

In the depth of discouragement and the height of stress, "David strengthened himself in the Lord his God." He got alone and prayed. He shifted the pressure from his own shoulders to Jehovah's. He knew that the stress was too big a load for him to carry alone, so he "trust-ed in the Lord with all his heart," and God immediately began to push away the obstacles.

ENTERING INTO REST

We've thought about overcoming worry by leaning totally and consistently on the Lord, refusing to rely on our own strength and ingenuity. We've talked about delegating your workloads that pro-duce anxiety. We've also considered the value of prayer; simply calling on God for relief and wisdom. These are essential techniques in keeping ourselves out from under the weight of anxiety.

But there is one more scriptural insight on stress that is not mentioned very often. It has to do with cultivating a lifestyle that is characterized by rest—a mental and emotional rest, virtually free of the tyranny of the urgent.

The biblical basis of this inner rest is found in Hebrews 4, a chapter that has its roots in the Old Testament:

> Therefore, let us fear lest, while a promise remains of entering His rest, any one of you should seem to have come short of it. For indeed we have had good news preached to us, just as they also; but the word they heard did not profit them, because it was not united by faith in those who heard. For we who have believed enter that rest (vv. 1–3a).

THE REST AVAILABLE TODAY

The Hebrew people, to whom these words were originally addressed, understood that the writer had their forefathers in mind . . . those people who came out of Egyptian captivity under Moses' leadership. And what does he say of them? Look back at the verses you just read. The truth they heard "did not profit them." Why? Because it remained merely truth—sterile, theological, unrelated information—unmixed with their faith. They heard *about* God's provisions, they heard *about* how He would give them the Promised Land, but they did not take all of it personally. His truth and their faith remained two distinct and separate factors. They failed to enter into the rest He made available. They continued to operate on the basis of sight, which led them into fear, then stress, finally open unbelief.

Does that mean there's no more "rest" available for God's people today? Quite the contrary.

> There remains therefore a Sabbath rest for the people of God. For the one who has entered His rest has himself also rested from his works, as God did from His. Let us therefore be diligent to enter that rest, lest anyone fall through following the same example of disobedience (Hebrews 4:9–11).

God continues to hold out to all His children a peaceful, worry-free lifestyle that we can enter into on a moment-by-moment basis.

Will it happen automatically? No, we are instructed to "be diligent to enter that rest." What does that mean? Simply this:

1. *We acknowledge that our God is in full control of our lives.* No accidents or surprises occur. He calls the shots.

2. *We take Him at His word.* We believe His promises (the Bible is full of them—by the *hundreds*).

3. *We claim them by faith.* We apply them to our particular circumstance almost as if God were speaking directly to us this very moment.

4. *We rest in Him.* We consciously refuse to worry or fret over how He is going to work things out. By entering into that rest, we cease from our own works just as deliberately as our Creator-God ceased from His works on the seventh day of the creative week.

5. *We continue in that calm frame of mind until God sovereignly intervenes and solves the problem.* We keep trusting in Him with *all* our hearts. And every time an alien thought of anxiety flits through our minds, we turn it over to the Lord in prayer.

This is perhaps the best way to explain the verse,

Cease striving and know that I am God (Psalm 46:10a).

The marginal reference suggests the alternative rendering, "Let go, relax." What a beautiful, refreshing thing it would be to see most of God's people *relaxing* in Him! Really, thoroughly at peace as we lean on Him.

AGAIN: WHAT ABOUT YOU?

When are you going to do this, my friend? That's the key question. What is it going to take to make you "let go, relax"? He is your Lord, longing to take the burden and carry it for you; but He won't force you to let go. You must do that yourself. You must take the risk and, in faith, entrust it all into His care. He says to you, "Then and *only* then will you know that I am God."

It's like the familiar yet descriptive story of the tightrope walker who stretched his cable across the vast expanse of a section of Niagara Falls. He walked across and back with his balancing pole as the mist of the falls sprayed all around him. Next he walked across and back without the aid of his pole. Everyone burst into loud applause. His next trip was with a wheelbarrow. To the amazement and delight of the crowd, he went all the way across, pushing the clumsy wheelbarrow with no difficulty at all.

A wide-eyed little five-year-old boy was standing near the acrobat. Suddenly, the man looked right at the boy, smiled, and said: "Son, I'm going to push this wheelbarrow back across the rope. Do you believe I can do it?"

"Yes, sir, I sure do!"

"You mean to tell me that you have that kind of faith in me? You *really* believe I can do it?"

"Yeah, I really do!"

"Okay, Son, get in the wheelbarrow."

That's another story entirely, isn't it? But not until we "get in" do we really entrust ourselves to God's care. Not until then do we "cease striving" and enter into His rest.

The removal of stress is not automatic. It is the cooperative effort of the Christian and his God. In the past few pages, you have been exposed to biblical truth. You have had brief visits with Mary and Martha, plus Moses and Jethro. You have also dug into John 17:4, Proverbs 3:5–6, and Hebrews 4:1–11. You've identified with David in his moment of despair, and you've even felt the chill of fear that ran up the back of a five-year-old boy at Niagara Falls. May our God be allowed entrance into your mind and be given the reins of your life so completely that all your stress is replaced with peace as all your fear is removed by faith.

The Tailor's
Name Is Change

When you boil life down to the nubbies, the name of the game is *change*. Those who flex with the times refuse to be rigid, resist the mold, and reject the rut—ah, *those* are the souls distinctively used by God. To them, change is a challenge, a fresh breeze that flows through the room of routine and blows away the stale air of sameness.

Stimulating and invigorating as change may be—it is never easy. Before you get all jazzed about some quick and easy change you plan to carry out, better read that sentence again, pal. Changes are especially tough when it comes to certain habits that haunt and harm us. That kind of change is excruciating—but it isn't impossible.

Jeremiah pointed out the difficulty of breaking into an established life pattern when he quipped:

> Can the Ethiopian change his skin or the leopard its spots?
> Neither can you do good who are accustomed to doing evil
> (13:23 NIV).

Notice the last few words, "accustomed to doing evil." The Hebrew says, literally, "learned in evil." Now that's quite an admission! We who are "learned in evil" cannot do good; evil habits that remain unchanged prohibit it. Evil is a habit that is learned; it is contracted and cultivated by long hours of practice. In another place, Jeremiah confirms this fact:

> I warned you when you felt secure, but you said, "I will not listen!" This has been your way from your youth; you have not obeyed me (22:21 NIV).

All of us have practiced certain areas of wrong from our youth. It is a pattern of life that comes "second nature" to us. We gloss over our resistance, however, with the varnish of excuse:
"Well, nobody's perfect."

"I'll never be any different; that's just the way I am."
"I was born this way—nothing can be done about it."
"You can't teach an old dog new tricks."

Jeremiah tells us why such excuses come so easily. We have become "learned in evil" . . . it has been our way from our youth. In one sense, we have learned to act and react in sinful, unbiblical ways with *ease* and (dare we admit it?) with a measure of *pleasure*. Admittedly, there are many times we do it unconsciously; and, on those occasions, the depth of our habit is more revealing.

It is vital—*it is essential*—that we see ourselves as we really are in the light of God's written Word . . . then be open to change where change is needed. I warn you, the number one enemy of change is the hard-core, self-satisfied sin nature within you. Like a spoiled child, it has been gratified and indulged for years, so it will not give up without a violent temper tantrum. Change is its *greatest* threat, and a confrontation between the two is inevitable. Change must be allowed to face and conquer the intimidations of inward habit—and I repeat the warning that a nose-to-nose meeting will never be an easy one.

The flesh dies a slow, bitter, bloody death—kicking and struggling all the way down. "Putting off" the clothes of the old man (the old, habitual lifestyle) will not be complete until you are determined to "put on" the garment of the new man (the new, fresh, Christian lifestyle). The tailor's name is Change, and he is a master at fitting your frame. But the process will be painful . . . and costly.

Change—real change—takes place slowly. In first gear, not overdrive. Far too many Christians get discouraged and give up. Like iceskating or mastering a musical instrument or learning to waterski, certain techniques have to be discovered and developed in the daily discipline of living. Breaking habit patterns you established during the passing of *years* cannot occur in a few brief days. Remember that. "Instant" change is as rare as it is phony.

God did not give us His Word to satisfy our curiosity; He gave it to change our lives. Can you name a couple of specific changes God has implemented in your life during the past six or eight months? Has He been allowed, for example, to change your attitude toward someone . . . or an area of stubbornness . . . or a deep-seated habit that has hurt your home and hindered your relationship with others for a long, long time . . . or a pattern of discourtesy in your driving . . . or a profane tongue . . . or cheating . . . or laziness?

Perhaps a better question would be, "Exactly what changes do you have on your personal drawing board?"—or—"What are you asking the Lord to alter and adjust in your life that needs immediate attention?"

The tailor's real name is the Holy Spirit. You can count on Him to dispose of your old threadbare wardrobe as quickly as He outfits you with the new. By the way, He's also on call twenty-four hours a day when you have the urge to slip into the old duds "just one more time." If you ask Him, He'll help you remember what you looked like on the day you first walked into His shop. His has a mirror with memories—the Bible.

'Nuff said.

Starting Over

Instant replays have become old hat. We now expect them in all televised sports. Whether it's a tennis pro's impressive backhand or an NBA center's slam dunk or a heavyweight boxer's smashing jab, we never have to worry about missing it the first time around. It'll be back again and again and probably *again*.

It occurred to me recently that I'd enjoy (for lack of a better title) *delayed* replays of some of the more significant times in my life. But these would be different from fixed frames on film. In "delayed replays" I'm fantasizing the possibility of going back and being given another chance to relive a particular experience that could have been handled differently. More wisely. With greater tact. In better taste. You know, all those "if-I-had-that-to-do-over-again" thoughts. What a second chance that would be!

Just think of all the things we'd refrain from saying that we blurted out the first time around. And consider the different attitudes we would have toward unexpected interruptions, unplanned babies, unrealistic expectations, unimportant details. I really think we would take a lot more things a lot less seriously, don't you?

Fun times form great memories . . . so let's hear it for fewer frowns and more smiles. Laughter lingers. It soaks into the walls of a home, coming back to encourage us many years later.

Bob Benson captures all this so well in his piece, "Laughter in the Walls."

> *I pass a lot of houses on my way home—*
> *some pretty,*
> *some expensive,*
> *some inviting—*
> *but my heart always skips a beat*
> *when I turn down the road*
> *and see my house nestled against the hill.*
> *I guess I'm especially proud*
> *of the house and the way it looks because*

I drew the plans myself.
It started out large enough for us—
I even had a study—
two teenaged boys now reside in there.
And it had a guest room—
my girl and nine dolls are permanent guests.
It had a small room
Peg had hoped would be her sewing room—
two boys swinging on the dutch door
have claimed this room as their own.
So it really doesn't look right now
as if I'm much of an architect.
But it will get larger again—
one by one they will go away
to work,
to college,
to service,
to their own houses,
and then there will be room—
a guest room,
a study,
and a sewing room
for just the two of us.
But it won't be empty—
every corner
every room
every nick
in the coffee table
will be crowded with memories.
Memories of picnics,
parties, Christmases,
bedside vigils, summers,
fires, winters, going barefoot,
leaving for vacation, cats
conversations, black eyes
graduations, first dates,
ball games, arguments
washing dishes, bicycles
dogs, boat rides

getting home from vacation
meals, rabbits and
a thousand other things
that fill the lives
of those who would raise five.
And Peg and I will sit
quietly by the fire
and listen to the
laughter in the walls.[104]

Yes, if we had the benefit of "delayed replays," we would gain a lot of perspective on life we often miss the first time around.

But, unfortunately, second times around don't happen. We cannot rerear our children. I cannot repastor my first church. Initial impressions cannot be remade. Cutting remarks cannot be resaid. Scars can't be completely removed. Tear stains on the delicate fabric of our emotions are, more often than not, permanent. Memories are fixed, not flexible.

"You mean God won't forgive?"

You know better than that.

"And people can't overlook my failures?"

Come on, now. That's not the issue at all. Most people I know are amazingly understanding. Our biggest task is forgiving *ourselves*.

The main message is clear: Think before you speak. Pause before you act.

Another chance? No chance. It's absolutely impossible to go back and start over. Today is tomorrow's yesterday . . . and "delayed replays" will never occur. Today is memory in the making, a deposit in the bank of time. Let's make it a good one!

In the now-or-later battle for priorities, it's clear where the secret lies. Let's take care of the biggies now—today. It's amazing how the incidentals will fade away when we focus fully on the essentials. And that's impossible unless we put the important ahead of the urgent.

Tell me, what will be yesterday's replays in the tomorrows of your life? The answer is not that complicated. They will be the things your "walls" are absorbing today.

Destiny

"**H**ow can I know God in a meaningful way?"

"What must I do to guarantee eternal life with my Maker?"

"Is there some way I can be certain that I will go to heaven?"

"Will you explain in simple, nontechnical terms what it means to be born again?"

"I'm guilty because I haven't lived a clean life. How can the Lord forgive me?"

"I have been a fairly religious person, but I lack a deep and abiding peace with God . . . why?"

"What does the Bible say about life after death?"

"Did Jesus actually die for me?"

"What, exactly, is 'the gospel'?"

Whether or not these questions are verbalized, they are the ones that most people think about, especially when death seems near. They are good questions that deserve an answer. They are also searching questions that have to do with an issue of utmost importance—receiving eternal life from God. Forgiveness forever. This is not something that calls for a lot of opinions or theological double-talk. The insights must come from the Bible, and they need to be so clear that anybody can understand them. They also have to make sense.

Here is a scriptural, simple, sensible answer for those who wonder about the single most significant subject in all of life: salvation.

◆

Being lost is a terrifying experience. A person's head spins as panic creeps up, shouting threats like, "You'll never find your way!" or "It's impossible!" Fear clutches at you.

When I was about eight years old, I remember being lost in the busy downtown metropolis of Houston, Texas. My mother had told me to stay in the toy department of a store while she went down the street to pick up a package she was having gift-wrapped. I continued to play for a few minutes, but I soon lost interest. So I decided to leave the store and walk down to where my mom had gone. Poor decision. I turned the wrong way, so I was going in the opposite direction, all the time being absolutely sure it was the right way.

I must have walked four long blocks before I realized my mistake. I thought, *Maybe it's across the street.* My heart began beating faster as I trotted over to the other side, but I still couldn't find the store. By then I had run four, five, six blocks . . . still no sign of that familiar storefront.

By then I was crying. I didn't know whom to ask for help . . . everybody seemed so unconcerned. My mind was seized with such fear that I couldn't even remember the name of the store where she said she was going *or even the store I had left twenty minutes before.* I circled back toward the direction I began—or so I thought—but in my bewildered state, I had made yet another miscalculation, for nothing looked at all familiar now.

To this day I distinctly recall the awful sense of desperation and confusion. Guilt assaulted me as I said to myself again and again, *Why didn't I do as Mama told me? Why didn't I obey?*

The strange part of it all was that there were people all around me—hundreds of them—and within a few feet there were cars moving in both directions. There was also a policeman at each intersection, as well as numerous employees and merchants inside every store I passed. There I was darting here and there amongst all that humanity, but I could not have felt *more* lost in the thick jungles along the Amazon!

Through the kindness of a total stranger who saw my plight and took the time to escort me back to the original toy department, I was rescued and reunited with my concerned, loving mother. Although I am fifty years removed from that horrible episode, I vividly remember how terrifying it was to be lost.

Several strange things are true about being lost. One is that we can think we really aren't when we are. Sincerity is no guarantee we're on the right road. Furthermore, we don't have to be alone to be lost. We can be surrounded by a lot of folks—even a large group of nice people—and be totally offtrack. And running faster doesn't help either. Speed, like sincerity, is no friend to the bewildered.

One more thought: We can't trust our feelings or our hunches to solve our dilemma. We need help from something or someone outside ourselves. A map. A person who knows the way. Whatever or whoever . . . we must have accurate assistance.

HURTLING TOWARD A DESTINY . . . UNAWARE

It is interesting to note that one of the terms the Bible uses to describe people who don't know God in a personal and meaningful manner is "lost." That doesn't necessarily mean they are immoral or lawless or bad neighbors or financial failures or emotionally unstable or irresponsible or even unfriendly folks. Just lost. As we've already observed, they may be sincere, involved, and in touch with many people, moving rapidly (and successfully) through life. They may even feel good about themselves—confident, secure, enthusiastic . . . yet still lost. Physically active and healthy, yet spiritually offtrack. Sincerely deluded. Unconsciously moving through life and out of touch with the One who made them. Disconnected from the living God.

Take a close look at this statement I have copied from the old, reliable book of Proverbs in the Bible.

> There is a way which seems right to a man, but its end is the way of death (Proverbs 14:12).

Isn't that penetrating? The "way" a person is going through life may *seem* right. It may have the appearance of being okay. It may also have the approval and admiration of other rather influential individuals . . . but its end result is the ultimate dead-end street.

All this reminds me of a true yet tragic World War II story. The *Lady-Be-Good* was a bomber whose crew was a well-seasoned flight team, a group of intelligent and combat-ready airmen. After a successful bombing mission, they were returning to home base late one night. In front of the pilot and copilot was a panel of instruments and radar equipment they had to rely on to reach their final destination. They had made the flight many times before, so they knew about how long it took to return.

But this flight was different. Unaware of a strong tailwind that pushed the bomber much more rapidly through the night air than usual, the men in the cockpit looked in amazement at their instruments as they correctly signaled that it was time to land.

They refused to believe those accurate dials and gauges, though. Confident that they were still miles away from home, they kept flying and hoping, looking intently for those familiar lights below. The fuel supply was finally depleted. The big olive-drab bomber never made it back. It was found deep in the desert many miles further and many days later. Its fine crew had all perished, having overshot the field by a great distance . . . because they followed the promptings of their own feelings, which "seemed right" but proved to be wrong. Dead wrong.

What happened in the air back in the early 1940s is happening in principle every day on earth. There are good, sincere, well-meaning, intelligent people traveling on a collision course with death, yet totally unaware of their destiny. That's why we read that Jesus, God's great Son, came " . . . to seek and to save that which was lost" (Luke 19:10). His coming to earth was God's rescue plan—a seek-and-save mission designed to help those who are lost find the right way home.

That needs some explanation.

Think of the Bible as the absolutely reliable instrument panel designed to get people (and to *keep* people) on the right track. We won't be confused if we believe its signals and respond to its directions, even though we may not "feel" in agreement at times. In this Book we find a bold yet true statement:

> . . . God has given us eternal life, and this life is in His Son. He who has the Son has the life; he who does not have the Son of God does not have the life.
>
> These things I have written to you who believe in the name of the Son of God, in order that you may know that you have eternal life (1 John 5:11b–13).

Read that again, this time a little more slowly and, if possible, aloud:

> ... God has given us eternal life, and this life is in His Son. He who has the Son has the life; he who does not have the Son of God does not have the life.
>
> These things I have written to you who believe in the name of the Son of God, in order that you may know that you have eternal life.

SALVATION OFFERED—FREE

It doesn't take a Ph.D. in English Literature to observe that God is offering a gift. The gift is eternal life, which is directly connected to His Son. Now let's be clear and cautious. Becoming a member of a church is not mentioned here—just believing in the Son of God, Jesus Christ. Neither does God require a long list of heavy-duty accomplishments. Nor vast sums of money. God is coming to the rescue of those who are lost by offering the free gift of eternal life to those who will simply believe. Those who do may *know* they have been rescued.

No mumbo jumbo, no tricks, no divinely hidden agenda, no cleverly concealed conditions. The lost can *know* they are on the right road by trusting what God is signaling from His panel of truth. Believe Him!

"But it seems too easy," you say. "Something as vital as eternal salvation seems far more valuable than that." Don't misunderstand. It *is* valuable ... the most priceless possession one can have. But because we don't have to work for it or pay for it does not mean it's cheap or that nobody paid a handsome price. Someone did. His name? Jesus. Perhaps you already forgot that this gift of salvation is directly connected to God's Son, Christ Himself. Because He paid the full price, because He opened the way for us, we are able to take it as a gift.

It's funny, but most of us are suspicious of free gifts. "There ain't no such thing as a free lunch" is more than a line out of a comedian's script. We have too much skepticism (or pride) to believe we can get something for nothing. Anytime we are approached by an individual who promises, "Here, take it; it's yours, *free*," we are wary— we usually don't reach out and accept it. So it's understandable that we'd be reluctant to accept a gift as important as eternal salvation if it has the appearance of a "free lunch," right?

THE COST OF ETERNAL SALVATION

To say that God's rescue offer costs nobody anything is misleading, in all honesty. It costs *us* nothing today, but it cost His Son's life. That's the part we forget about.

When sin first reared its ugly head on earth, the holy God of heaven could no longer enjoy a close relationship with the human race. And the longer mankind practiced his or her wicked ways, the wider the gap grew between man and God. This sin disease, contracted at birth and inescapably contagious, spread like wildfire from one generation to the next. With sin came death, as this verse of Scripture declares:

> When Adam sinned, sin entered the entire human race. His sin spread death throughout all the world, so everything began to grow old and die, for all sinned (Romans 5:12 TLB).

Yes, everything. In fact, this universal sin disease impacted every part of our being. Hard as it may be to read these words, please do so:

> As the Scriptures say, "No one is good—no one in all the world is innocent."
> No one has ever really followed God's paths, or even truly wanted to.
> Every one has turned away; all have gone wrong. No one anywhere has kept on doing what is right; not one.
> Their talk is foul and filthy like the stench from an open grave. Their tongues are loaded with lies. Everything they say has in it the sting and poison of deadly snakes.
> Their mouths are full of cursing and bitterness.
> They are quick to kill, hating anyone who disagrees with them.
> Wherever they go they leave misery and trouble behind them, and they have never known what it is to feel secure or enjoy God's blessing.
> They care nothing about God nor what he thinks of them (Romans 3:10–18 TLB).

Talk about descriptive! But that's the way we are in God's sight. Being lost, we are in such a miserable spiritual condition that we have no hope of finding our way to Him on our own. Sin separates us from our Creator. His rightful requirement is that sin *must* be punished. Someone who is qualified must rescue mankind by satisfying God's wrath against sin. Someone must pay the awful price, dying as our substitute, taking our place and bearing our sin before God.

Jesus Christ did just that.

Don't simply believe my words . . . believe the words from the Bible:

> For God took the sinless Christ and poured into him our sins. Then, in exchange, he poured God's goodness into us! (2 Corinthians 5:21 TLB).

> We aren't saved from sin's grasp by knowing the command-ments of God, because we can't and don't keep them, but God put into effect a different plan to save us. He sent his own Son in a human body like ours—except that ours are sinful—and destroyed sin's control over us by giving himself as a sacrifice for our sins (Romans 8:3 TLB).

> For God loved the world so much that he gave his only Son so that anyone who believes in him shall not perish but have eter-nal life.

> And all who trust him—God's Son—to save them have eternal life; those who don't believe and obey him shall never see heaven, but the wrath of God remains upon them (John 3:16, 36 TLB).

> Christ also suffered. He died once for the sins of all us guilty sinners, although he himself was innocent of any sin at any time, that he might bring us safely home to God (1 Peter 3:18 TLB).

> Under this new plan we have been forgiven and made clean by Christ's dying for us once and for all. Under the old agreement the priests stood before the altar day after day offering sacri-fices that could never take away our sins.

> But Christ gave himself to God for our sins as one sacri-fice for all time, and then sat down in the place of highest honor at God's right hand (Hebrews 10:10–12 TLB).

THE ONLY UNRESOLVED ISSUE ABOUT SALVATION

Yes, it certainly cost somebody something. It cost Jesus Christ His life. But because *He* paid the price in full on our behalf, we are able to accept God's offer free and clear of any cost to us. The pay-ment has been made. The ransom has been provided in full.

The only issue that remains is this: Will you accept the gift God offers you today? Now that the remedy for sin has been provided, all that remains is receiving it ... not having every related question answered.

Picture a person helplessly trapped on the sixth floor of a burning hotel. The elevators no longer function, the stairways are flaming infernos. To live, the person must leap into a net that firemen down below are holding ready. Imagine the trapped man screaming from his broken window, "I will not jump until you give me a satisfactory explanation of several things: (1) How did this fire get started? (2) Why has it spread so quickly? (3) What happened to the sprinkler system? and (4) How do I know for sure that net will hold me? Until you guys can come up with some pretty substantial answers, I'm staying right here in Room 612!"

In like manner, the question as to why God allowed sin to enter the world or the need for airtight convincing proof is comparatively unimportant, even irrelevant, as we find ourselves lost, moving rapidly toward the grave, and destined for eternal condemnation. Slice it up and analyze it any way you wish, when we reduce our response to God's offer of salvation, it comes down to *faith:* being willing to abandon oneself, without reservation, to the eternal net God has spread ... leaping while believing with absolute confidence that He will do as He promised. Remember, the other options are reduced to zero, according to God's plan.

WHAT ABOUT LIFE AFTER DEATH?

A discussion on this vital subject would be incomplete if nothing were said about life beyond the grave. Thanks to such authorities as Dr. Elizabeth Kübler-Ross and Raymond A. Moody, Jr., the issue of life after death is now being discussed openly. Numerous books—Christian and non-Christian—are now available, ranging from the bizarre to the skeptical. For the sake of space and dependability, let's limit our thoughts to the biblical record.

Jesus spoke openly about both heaven and hell. So did several others in Scripture. It is clear to all who read the Bible that everyone has an eternal soul ... *everyone* has eternal life ... but the real question is where will we spend it? Read the following verses carefully:

> And inasmuch as it is appointed for men to die once and after this comes judgment (Hebrews 9:27).

And I say to you, that every careless word that men shall speak, they shall render account for it in the day of judgment. ... And these will go away into eternal punishment, but the righteous into eternal life (Matthew 12:36; 25:46).

But you, why do you judge your brother? Or you again, why do you regard your brother with contempt? For we shall all stand before the judgment seat of God (Romans 14:10).

Jesus said to her, "I am the resurrection and the life; he who believes in Me shall live even if he dies, and everyone who lives and believes in Me shall never die. Do you believe this?" (John 11:25–26).

The Reality of Hell

A particular story Jesus once told comes to my mind every time I think of life after death. Because it is descriptive and brief, we are able to get a fairly uncomplicated picture in our minds of this subject.

Now there was a certain rich man, and he habitually dressed in purple and fine linen, gaily living in splendor every day. And a certain poor man named Lazarus was laid at his gate, covered with sores, and longing to be fed with the crumbs which were falling from the rich man's table; besides, even the dogs were coming and licking his sores.

Now it came about that the poor man died and he was carried away by the angels to Abraham's bosom; and the rich man also died and was buried.

And in Hades he lifted up his eyes, being in torment, and saw Abraham far away, and Lazarus in his bosom.

And he cried out and said, "Father Abraham, have mercy on me, and send Lazarus, that he may dip the tip of his finger in water and cool off my tongue; for I am in agony in this flame."

But Abraham said, "Child, remember that during your life you received your good things, and likewise Lazarus bad things; but now he is being comforted here, and you are in agony.

"And besides all this, between us and you there is a great chasm fixed, in order that those who wish to come over from here to you may not be able, and that none may cross over from there to us."

And he said, "Then I beg you, Father, that you send him to my father's house—for I have five brothers—that he may warn them, lest they also come to this place of torment."

But Abraham said, "They have Moses and the Prophets; let them hear them."

But he said, "No, Father Abraham, but if someone goes to them from the dead, they will repent!"

But he said to him, "If they do not listen to Moses and the Prophets, neither will they be persuaded if someone rises from the dead" (Luke 16:19–31).

Much of what you just read needs no explanation. It is the story of two men. While alive, their statuses could hardly have been more different. And when they died, again a contrast. One found himself in heaven; the other, in hell. Our attention falls upon the rich man who is pleading for relief and removal from his torturous surroundings. The scene is unpleasant to imagine, but it is nevertheless real. Neither here nor elsewhere does Jesus suggest this was merely a fantasy.

The man in hell is in conscious torment. He is crying out for mercy. Being "far away" (v. 23) and permanently removed by "a great chasm" (v. 26), he is desperately alone, unable to escape from hell, as we read, "none may cross over" (v. 26). The horror is painfully literal, unlike the jokes often passed around regarding hell. Haunted with thoughts of other family members ultimately coming to the same place, the man begs for someone to go to his father's house and warn his brothers "... lest they also come to this place of torment" (v. 28).

This is only one of many references to an eternal existence in hell. The New Testament, in fact, says more about hell than it does about heaven. Here are just a few characteristics of hell set forth in the New Testament:

- It is a place of weeping and gnashing of teeth (Matthew 8:12).
- It is a place where people scream for mercy, have memories, are tormented, feel alone, cannot escape (Luke 16:23–31).
- It is a place of unquenchable fire (Mark 9:48).
- It is a place of darkness (Revelation 9:2).
- It is a place of eternal damnation (Mark 3:29 KJV).
- It is a place where God's wrath is poured out (Revelation 14:10).
- It is a place of everlasting destruction (2 Thessalonians 1:9).

The finality of all this is overwhelmingly depressing. We have little struggle believing that heaven will be forever, but for some reason, we ignore that hell will be equally everlasting. To deny the permanence of hell is impossible without also removing the permanence of heaven. Each is a reality and each is ultimate finality.

Many views try to explain away or bypass hell. One attempt is annihilation. This says that the righteous will live eternally, but the wicked will ultimately be judged and destroyed. Nice idea but a theological cop-out. It cannot be maintained by a serious and intelligent study of Scripture . . . for example, the whole issue of a bodily resurrection. What purpose is the resurrection if the lost are to be extinguished forever?

Another attempt at bypassing hell is universalism, which teaches that all humanity will ultimately be saved. This position offers a comforting "redemptive mercy" that will eventually include all mankind. If this were true, what did Jesus mean when He talked about the very real possibility of being lost forever? "Should not perish," in John 3:16, implies that some will indeed perish. And how could His comment be taken seriously when He says to the unsaved, "Depart from me, accursed ones, into the eternal fire" (Matthew 25:41)? Count on it, friend, eternal means eternal.

The Reality of Heaven

The same Bible that develops the subject of hell also reveals the truth about heaven. What is heaven like? Playing harps all day? Lounging around on Cloud Nine? Living in enormous mansions along solid gold streets? Does it mean we'll all have long white robes with matching sandals, glowing halos, and big flapping wings? *Hardly!*

Heaven is an actual place. A prepared place, designed for God's redeemed people, those who have accepted God's free gift of His Son.

> Let not your heart be troubled; believe in God, believe also in Me. In My Father's house are many dwelling places; if it were not so, I would have told you; for I go to prepare a place for you. And if I go and prepare a place for you, I will come again, and receive you to Myself; that where I am, there you may be also (John 14:1–3).

According to this and other New Testament verses, heaven will be a place of beauty, peace, constant health and happiness, filled with people from all the earthly ages who have one thing in common—faith in the Lord Jesus Christ, the Lamb of God, who took away the sin of the world.

Think of it! Characters from the Old Testament like Moses, David, Rahab, Elijah, Abraham, Joseph, Esther, Job, Daniel, and the other godly prophets will converse with John, Peter, Matthew, James, Paul, Silas, Barnabas, Mary, Elizabeth, Lydia, and Andrew. We'll be able to enjoy close conversations with church history's great Christians, like Augustine, Livingstone, Hudson Taylor, Martin Luther, Calvin, Knox, Spurgeon, Moody, Wycliffe, and Huss (to name only a few), plus those unknown martyrs, missionaries, pastors, authors, statesmen, politicians, poets, and leaders from every generation since time began. Stupendous thought!

And in heaven we'll have a face-to-face, exclusive relationship with our Savior, gloriously enjoyed without interruption or heartache or grief or sin or the threat of death.

> And I saw a new heaven and a new earth; for the first heaven and the first earth passed away, and there is no longer any sea. And I saw the holy city, new Jerusalem, coming down out of heaven from God, made ready as a bride adorned for her husband. And I heard a loud voice from the throne, saying, "Behold, the tabernacle of God is among men, and He shall dwell among them, and they shall be His people, and God Himself shall be among them, and He shall wipe away every tear from their eyes; and there shall no longer be any death; there shall no longer be any mourning, or crying, or pain; the first things have passed away." And He who sits on the throne said, "Behold, I am making all things new." And He said, "Write, for these words are faithful and true." And He said to me, "It is done. I am the Alpha and the Omega, the beginning and the end. I will give to the one who thirsts from the spring of the water of life without cost" (Revelation 21:1–6).

There it is again, "without cost." Heaven will be the destiny of those who take God at His Word, believing in His Son, Jesus Christ, and coming, by faith, to salvation . . . without cost.

Can something this good really be free? Even free of works? You decide after reading these Scripture verses.

For by grace you have been saved through faith; and that not of yourselves, it is the gift of God; not as a result of works, that no one should boast (Ephesians 2:8–9).

Being justified as a gift by His grace through the redemption which is in Christ Jesus (Romans 3:24).

Now to the one who works, his wage is not reckoned as a favor but as what is due. But to the one who does not work, but believes in Him who justifies the ungodly, his faith is reckoned as righteousness (Romans 4:4–5).

He saved us, not on the basis of deeds which we have done in righteousness, but according to His mercy, by the washing of regeneration and renewing by the Holy Spirit, whom He poured out upon us richly through Jesus Christ our Savior, that being justified by His grace we might be made heirs according to the hope of eternal life (Titus 3:5–7).

Knowing that you were not redeemed with perishable things like silver or gold from your futile way of life inherited from your forefathers, but with precious blood, as of a lamb unblemished and spotless, the blood of Christ (1 Peter 1:18–19).

Nevertheless knowing that a man is not justified by the works of the Law but through faith in Christ Jesus, even we have believed in Christ Jesus, that we may be justified by faith in Christ, and not by the works of the Law; since by the works of the Law shall no flesh be justified (Galatians 2:16).

... who has saved us, and called us with a holy calling, not according to our works, but according to His own purpose and grace which was granted us in Christ Jesus from all eternity, but now has been revealed by the appearing of our Savior Christ Jesus, who abolished death, and brought life and immortality to light through the gospel (2 Timothy 1:9–10).

Yes, salvation comes to us "free and clear" of any hidden charges or religious deeds or human effort. We come to God through Christ ... lost, sinful, without hope, and deserving of hell. In grace, He sees us in Christ and in grace loves us, forgives us, accepts us into His family, and promises us an eternal home with Him in heaven, the ultimate destination of all His people.

YOUR FINAL DESTINATION: WHERE?

Salvation is the single most important issue in all of life. And yet, if we are not careful, we'll put it off until later; we'll even put it completely out of our minds. Salvation is an urgent matter. We dare not postpone our decision! In review:

1. We are lost.
2. We are sinful.
3. We need help.
4. God is holy.
5. Christ has died.
6. Salvation is free.
7. Hell is horrible.
8. Heaven is available.
9. We must believe.

For I delivered to you as of first importance what I also received, that Christ died for our sins according to the Scriptures, and that He was buried, and that He was raised on the third day according to the Scriptures (1 Corinthians 15:3–4).

. . . God has given us eternal life, and this life is in His Son. He who has the Son has the life; he who does not have the Son of God does not have the life. These things I have written to you who believe in the name of the Son of God, in order that you may know that you have eternal life (1 John 5:11b–13).

You can know.
Will you believe?
I read these words recently:

The reality of life beyond the grave should make every one of us ponder our eternal destination, because the Bible teaches only two possibilities, heaven and hell.

We take care to provide for the relatively short span of retirement after 65. How foolish not to plan for the endless ages of eternity. Confrontation with what comes after death caused one young man to prepare for the hereafter by receiving Jesus Christ as his Savior. He was looking at a large estate one day and said to a friend, "Oh, if I were lucky enough to call this estate mine, I should be a happy fellow. It's worth a quarter million."

"And then?" said his friend.

"Why, then I'd pull down the old house and build a mansion, have lots of friends around me, get married, have several fine cars and keep the finest horses and dogs in the country."

"And then?"

"Then I would hunt, and ride, and fish, and keep open house, and enjoy life gloriously."

"And then?"

"Why, then, I suppose like other people, I should grow old and not care so much for these things."

"And then?"

"Why, in the course of nature I should die."

"And then?"

"Oh, bother your 'and then.' I have no time for you now!"

Years later the friend was surprised to hear from him, "God bless you. I owe my happiness to you."

"How?"

"By two words asked at the right time—'And then?'"[105]

Salvation is yours for the taking. I ask you, will you do so today?

Someday

SOMEDAY WHEN THE KIDS ARE GROWN, things are going to be a lot different. The garage won't be full of bikes, electric train tracks on plywood, sawhorses surrounded by chunks of two-by-fours, nails, a hammer and saw, unfinished "experimental projects," and the rabbit cage. I'll be able to park both cars neatly in just the right places, and never again stumble over skateboards, a pile of papers (saved for the school fund drive), or the bag of rabbit food—now split and spilled. Ugh!

SOMEDAY WHEN THE KIDS ARE GROWN, the kitchen will be incredibly neat. The sink will stay free of sticky dishes, the garbage disposal won't get choked on rubber bands or paper cups, the refrigerator won't be clogged with nine bottles of milk, and we won't lose the tops to jelly jars, catsup bottles, the peanut butter, the margarine, or the mustard. The water jar won't be put back empty, the ice trays won't be left out overnight, the blender won't stand for six hours coated with the remains of a midnight malt, and the honey will stay *inside* the container.

SOMEDAY WHEN THE KIDS ARE GROWN, my lovely wife will actually have time to get dressed leisurely. A long hot bath (without three panic interruptions), time to do her nails (even toenails if she pleases!) without answering a dozen questions and reviewing spelling words, having had her hair done that afternoon without trying to squeeze it in between racing a sick dog to the vet and a trip to the orthodontist with a kid in a bad mood because she lost her headgear.

SOMEDAY WHEN THE KIDS ARE GROWN, the instrument called a "telephone" will actually be available. It won't look like it's growing from a teenager's ear. It will simply hang there ... silently and amazingly available! It will be free of lipstick, human saliva, mayonnaise, corn chip crumbs, and toothpicks stuck in those little holes.

SOMEDAY WHEN THE KIDS ARE GROWN, I'll be able to see *through* the car windows. Fingerprints, tongue licks, sneaker footprints, and dog tracks (nobody knows how) will be conspicuous by their absence. The backseat won't be a disaster area, we won't sit on jacks or crayons any more, the tank will not always be somewhere between empty and fumes, and (glory to God!) I won't have to clean up dog messes another time.

SOMEDAY WHEN THE KIDS ARE GROWN, we will return to normal conversations. You know, just plain American talk. "Gross" won't punctuate every sentence seven times. "Yuk!" will not be heard. "Hurry up, I gotta go!" will not accompany the banging of fists on the bathroom door. "It's my turn" won't call for a referee. And a magazine article will be read in full without interruption, then discussed at length without mom and dad having to hide in the attic to finish the conversation.

SOMEDAY WHEN THE KIDS ARE GROWN, we won't run out of toilet tissue. My wife won't lose her keys. We won't forget to shut the refrigerator door. I won't have to dream up new ways of diverting attention from the gumball machine . . . or have to answer "Daddy, is it a sin that you're driving 47 in a 30-mile-an-hour zone?" . . . or promise to kiss the rabbit goodnight . . . or wait up forever until they get home from dates . . . or have to take a number to get a word in at the supper table . . . or endure the pious pounding of one Keith Green just below the level of acute pain.

YES, SOMEDAY WHEN THE KIDS ARE GROWN, things are going to be a lot different. One by one they'll leave our nest, and the place will begin to resemble order and maybe even a touch of elegance. The clink of china and silver will be heard on occasion. The crackling of the fireplaces will echo through the hallway. The phone will be strangely silent. The house will be

quiet . . .
and calm . . .
and always clean . . .
and empty . . .
and filled with memories . . .
and lonely . . .

and we won't like that at all. And we'll spend our time not looking forward to *Someday* but looking back to *Yesterday*. And thinking,

Maybe we can baby-sit the grandkids and get some life *back in this place for a change!*

Could it be that the apostle Paul had some of this in mind when he wrote:

> . . . I have learned to be content in whatever circumstances I am (Philippians 4:11).

Maybe so. But then again, chances are good Paul never had to clean up many dog messes.

God, Give Us Models

An usher met me as I was leaving our church several years ago. He had been involved in counting the morning offering. He smiled as he walked up to me, stuck out his hand, and said, "I've got something for you. It came in the offering."

Here was a little hand-scribbled note from a child who had been in our worship service. It read:

TO PASTER CHUCK SWINDOL

    I don't think you know me, but I shure know you. You are a very good speeker for Jesus Christ, I think your neet.

    I even understand what you are saying and that's how it should be.

I LOVE YOU!

Guess what was attached to the note. A chocolate sucker, all wrapped in cellophane, ready to be enjoyed.

Now, friend, that's admiration. When a darling little kid will surrender his prized possession ... wow! That sucker meant more to me than most any honor I could ever receive, because it represented something no amount of money could buy. A child's respect. Personal admiration. To some busy, active youngster tucked away in our vast congregation, I represented somebody he or she looks up to. And believes in.

I'm honest, it chokes me up. It also keeps me on my toes. Somewhere out there is a child whose eyes are on me ... whose ears are tuned in ... who's also pretty choosy. After all, the sucker was wrapped in cellophane, tied with ribbon ... and it hadn't even been licked (so far as I could tell).

Admiration. There's not much of it today. Maybe that explains the inordinate hunger for fantasy heroes like Batman, Superman, Jack Ryan, and James Bond. There has never been a day when the athletic prima donnas have had larger fan clubs or weird musical groups bigger crowds. There was a time when patriotism provided us with all the models we needed. Remember? Why, who ever had the audacity to suggest a hint of suspicion against MacArthur . . . or "Ike" . . . or the local police department or the *FBI*, for that matter? The cop on the corner may have been stared at, but it was out of respect, not rebellion. Physicians were also admired. So were teachers. And lawyers. And preachers. And hard workers. And mothers.

What's happened? Why the low regard for leaders? Especially the outspoken ones who stand for decency and integrity and love for country, the flag, human dignity, and a wholesome respect for the family.

Has Watergate, the Iran-Contra affair, and Whitewater raped everyone's trust in anyone? Are all the police officers suspect? Must every preacher prove he's not an Elmer Gantry? Is it necessary for every surgeon to conduct his profession more concerned about a malpractice lawsuit than the gallbladder operation? Is corruption now so prevalent in government that young men and women with integrity no longer consider political science a viable major? Has the Vietnam thing soured everybody against the military? I mean, where are the heroes?

Hymn-writer Isaac Watts' question should be changed from, "Are there no foes for me to face?" to, "Are there no models for me to follow?" And it would be a right-on query. Foes to face we have. Models to admire, we don't. At least it seems that way. Now we are like the best-sellers a few years back—*Looking Out for #1* and *Pulling Your Own Strings*.

Funny thing, when you write stuff like this, you feel a little dated . . . somewhat soapboxish. You sense there's a whole gang of quasi-sophisticates thinking, "There's the old *Marine* coming out in Swindoll again. Shades of Guadalcanal gung-ho . . . Americanism on parade." Well, if a confession will help, I openly admit I still get a chill down my spine when they play our national anthem at the Olympics. I also confess getting a little misty when I recall standing at ramrod attention saying the pledge of allegiance as a barefoot fourth-grader in Southmayd Elementary . . . then praying for a crippled president I had never seen, but admired more than words could say.

Our cynical, self-centered society would do well to restore an invaluable antique that has been cast aside, forgotten like a dust-covered treasure: admiration. As that restoration occurs, so will the *esprit de corps* of our nation, the morale that once gave us pride to pull together and passion to stand alone. Our children need it. So do our youth, as well as adults. Individuals we hold in high esteem, in whom the qualities of greatness are incarnated. People who mirror the bedrock principles of solid Christian character. Those things can neither be purchased nor inherited. Slowly, almost unawares, admiration becomes the carbon paper that transfers character qualities by the rubbing of one life against another.

Like Christ with His guys. Like a godly coach with the team. Like an authentic Christian businessman with his peers. Like a faithful dad with his family. Usually the model doesn't even consider himself such until something little happens.

Something as little as a chocolate sucker in the church offering plate on Sunday morning.

My Dad
and His Death

My dad died last night.

He left like he had lived. Quietly. Graciously. With dignity. Without demands or harsh words or even a frown, he surrendered himself—a tired, frail, humble gentleman—into the waiting arms of his Savior. Death, selfish and cursed enemy of man, won another battle.

As I stroked the hair from his forehead and kissed him goodbye, a hundred boyhood memories played around in my head.

- When I learned to ride a bike, he was there.
- When I wrestled with the multiplication table, his quick wit erased the hassle.
- When I discovered the adventure of driving a car, he was near, encouraging me.
- When I got my first job (delivering newspapers), he informed me how to increase my subscriptions and win the prize. It worked!
- When I mentioned a young woman I had fallen in love with, he pulled me aside and talked straight about being responsible for her welfare and happiness.
- When I did a hitch in the Marine Corps, the discipline I had learned from him made the transition easier.

From him I learned to seine for shrimp. How to catch flounder and trout and redfish. How to open oyster shells and fix crab gumbo . . . and chili . . . and popcorn . . . and make rafts out of old inner tubes and gunny sacks. I was continually amazed at his ability to do things like tie fragile mantles on the old Coleman lantern, keep a fire going in the rain, play the harmonica with his hands behind his back, and keep three strong-willed kids from tearing the house down.

Last night I realized I had him to thank for my deep love for America. And for knowing how to tenderly care for my wife. And for laughing at impossibilities. And for some of the habits I have picked up, like approaching people with a positive spirit rather than a negative one, staying with a task until it is finished, taking good care of my personal belongings, keeping my shoes shined, speaking up rather than mumbling, respecting authority, and standing alone (if necessary) in support of my personal convictions rather than giving in to more popular opinions. For these things I am deeply indebted to the man who raised me.

Certain smells and sounds now instantly remind me of my dad. Oyster stew. The ocean breeze. Smoke from an expensive cigar. The nostalgic whine of a harmonica. A camping lantern and white gas. Car polish. Fun songs from the '30s and '40s. Freshly mowed grass. A shrill whistle from a father to his kids around suppertime. And Old Spice aftershave.

Because a father impacts his family so permanently, I think I understand better than ever what the Scripture means when Paul wrote:

> Having thus a fond affection for you, we were well-pleased to impart to you not only the gospel of God but also our own lives, because you had become very dear to us . . . just as you know how we were exhorting and encouraging and imploring each one of you as a father would his own children, so that you may walk in a manner worthy of the God who calls you into His own kingdom and glory (1 Thessalonians 2:8, 11–12).

Admittedly, much of my dad's instruction was indirect—by model rather than by explicit statement. I do not recall his overt declarations of love as clearly as I do his demonstrations of it. His life revolved around my mother, the darling and delight of his life. Of that I am sure. When she left over nine years ago, something of him died as well. And so—to her he has been joined and they are, together, with our Lord. In the closest possible companionship one can imagine.

In this my sister, my brother, and I find our greatest comfort—they are now forever *with the Lord*—eternally freed from pain and aging and death. Secure in Jesus Christ our Lord. Absent from the body and at home with Him. And with each other.

Last night I said good-bye. I'm still trying to believe it. You'd think it would be easy since his illness had persisted for more than three years. How well I remember the Sunday he suffered that first in a series of strokes as I was preaching. God granted him several more years to teach many of us to appreciate the things we tend to take for granted.

He leaves in his legacy a well-marked Bible I treasure, a series of feelings that I need to deepen my roots, and a thousand memories that comfort me as I replace denial with acceptance and praise.

I await heaven's gate opening in the not-too-distant future. So do other Christians, who anxiously await Christ's return. Most of them anticipate hearing the soft strum of a harp or the sharp, staccato blast of a trumpet.

Not me. I will hear the nostalgic whine of a harmonica . . . held in the hands of the man who died last night . . . *or did he?* The memories are as fresh as this morning's sunrise.

Notes

[1]David Blankenhorn, *Fatherless America* (New York: HarperCollins, 1995), 2.

[2]From the Brut/Yankelovich National Survey quoted in "The '90s Man," *Good Housekeeping Magazine*, vol. 218, no. 4, April 1994, 66.

[3]Ibid.

[4]Margery Williams, *The Velveteen Rabbit* (New York: Doubleday, 1958), 16–17. Reprinted by permission.

[5]Giora Dilberto, "Invasion of the Gender Blenders," *People Weekly*, 23 April 1984.

[6]Alvin Toffler, *The Third Wave* (New York: Bantam Books, 1982), 123.

[7]Gerhard Friedrich and Gerhard Kittel, eds., *Theological Dictionary of the New Testament*, vol. 3 (Grand Rapids: Eerdmans, 1964), 176.

[8]Richard Halverson, *Perspective* (Grand Rapids: Zondervan, 1957).

[9]*Saint Augustine's Confessions*, trans. with an introduction by R.S. Pine-Coffin (Harmondsworth, Middlesex, England: Penguin Books, Ltd., 1961), 45.

[10]Dan Benson, *The Total Man* (Wheaton, Ill.: Tyndale House, 1977).

[11]Charlie W. Shedd, *You Can Be a Great Parent*, formerly titled *Promises to Peter* (Waco, Tex.: Word, 1970), 12–13.

[12]William B. Franklin, from *A Father's Love*, Peter S. Seymour (Kansas City, Mo.: Hallmark Cards, Inc., 1972).

[13]"Ships" by Ian Hunter, copyright 1979 SBK April Music Inc. and Ian Hunter Music Inc. All rights controlled and administered by SBK April Music Inc. All rights reserved. International copyright secured. Used by permission.

[14]Jay E. Adams, *Christian Living in the Home* (Grand Rapids: Baker, 1972), 91–92.

[15]Gordon MacDonald, *The Effective Father* (Wheaton: Tyndale House, 1977), 13–14.

[16]Edith Schaeffer, *What Is a Family?* (Old Tappan, N.J.: Fleming H. Revell, 1975), 119.

[17]Jerry White, *Honesty, Morality, and Conscience* (Colorado Springs: NavPress, 1978), 49.

[18]Leo Rangell, M.D., *The Mind of Watergate* (New York: W. W. Norton & Company, 1980), 24–25.

[19]William Shakespeare, *Familiar Quotations*, ed. John Bartlett (Boston: Little, Brown and Company, 1955), 191.

[20]Anthony Campolo, *Who Switched the Price Tags?* (Waco, Tex.: Word, 1986), 69–72. Used by permission.

[21]Dale E. Galloway, *Dream a New Dream* (Wheaton, Ill.: Tyndale House, 1975), 59.

[22]Mark Kram, "The Face of Pain," *Sports Illustrated* 44, no. 10 (8 March, 1976): 60.

[23]Philip Yancey, *Where Is God When It Hurts* (Grand Rapids: Zondervan, 1978), 142.

[24]Douglas Colligan, "That Helpless Feeling: The Dangers of Stress," *New York*, 14 July, 1975, 28.

[25]Charles R. Swindoll, *Improving Your Serve* (Waco, Tex.: Word, 1981).

[26]"Murphy's Law" (231 Adrian Road, Millbrae, Calif.: Celestial Arts, 1979).

[27]Bruce Larson, *There's a Lot More to Health Than Not Being Sick* (Waco, Tex.: Word, 1981), 46.

[28]Horatio G. Spafford, "It Is Well with My Soul," copyright 1918 The John Church Co. Used by permission of the publisher.

[29]T. H. Holmes and R. H. Rahe, "The Social Readjustment Rating Scale," *Journal of Psychosomatic Research* II (1967): 213–18. Copyright 1967 Pergamon Press, Ltd.

[30]Bruce Larson, *The One and Only You* (Waco, Tex.: Word, 1974), 84–85. Adaptation by permission of Word Books, Publisher, Waco, Texas 76703.

[31]"Got Any Rivers" © 1945. Renewal 1973 by Oscar Eliason. Assigned to Singspiration, Inc. All rights reserved. Used by permission.

[32]Mary A. Thomson, "O Zion, Haste," *Worship and Service Hymnal* (Chicago: Hope Publishing Co., 1966), 430.

[33]Howard G. Hendricks, *Say It with Love* (Wheaton, Ill.: Victor Books, 1973), 91–92.

[34]"Olympic Hockey Hero Craig Paid Price for Fame: an Ulcer," *Los Angeles Times*, 10 August 1980, Sec. 3, p. 2.

[35]F. B. Meyer, *Joseph* (Fort Washington, Penn.: Christian Literature Crusade, 1955), 30.

[36]Dietrich Bonhoeffer, *Temptation* (London: SCM Press, 1964), 33.

[37]Charles R. Swindoll, *Killing Giants, Pulling Thorns* (Portland, Ore.: Multnomah Press, 1978; Grand Rapids: Zondervan, 1995), 27.

[38]Robert M. Pirsig, *Zen and the Art of Motorcycle Maintenance* (New York: Bantam Books, 1974), 272–73.

[39]Ibid.

[40]Thomas Jefferson, "A Decalogue of Canons for Observation in Practical Life" (21 February, 1825), reprinted in *Familiar Quotations*, ed., John Bartlett, 376.

[41]Mark Twain, "Pudd'nhead Wilson's Calendar," Ch. 3, *Familiar Quotations*, ed., John Bartlett, 678.

[42]Washington Irving, "The Sketch-Book (1819–1820)," reprinted in *Familiar Quotations*, ed., John Bartlett, 446.

[43]David Augsburger, *Caring Enough to Confront* (Glendale, Calif.: Regal Books, 1973).

[44]A.W. Tozer, *Root of the Righteous* (Harrisburg, Penn.: Christian Publications, Inc., 1955), 137.

[45]Gail MacDonald, *High Call, High Privilege* (Wheaton: Tyndale House, 1981), 29.

[46]M. Scott Peck, *The Road Less Traveled: A New Psychology of Love, Traditional Values, and Spiritual Growth* (New York: Touchstone Books, 1978), 50–52, 56.

[47]Thomas Carlyle, *Familiar Quotations*, ed., John Bartlett (Boston: Little, Brown and Company, 1955), 599.

[48]C. S. Lewis, *Screwtape Letters* (New York: Macmillan, 1942), 62.

[49]Ibid., 124.

[50]Hazel Werner, *Quote Unquote*, ed. Lloyd Cory (Wheaton: Victor Books, 1977), 154.

[51]Socrates, *Familiar Quotations*, ed. John Bartlett (Boston: Little, Brown and Company, 1955), 20.

[52]Harold S. Kushner, *When Bad Things Happen to Good People* (New York: Schocken Books, 1981), 6.

[53]Leighton Ford, "Yes, God Is Good," Decision, 5 June 1982.

[54]Ibid.

[55]Walter A. Henrichsen, *After the Sacrifice* (Grand Rapids: Zondervan, 1979), 83.

[56]Kushner, *When Bad Things Happen to Good People*, 26.

[57]Source unknown.

[58]From the song "In His Time" by Diane Ball, © 1978 by Maranatha Music. All rights reserved. International copyright secured. Used by permission.

[59]J. Oswald Sanders, *Spiritual Leadership* (Chicago: Moody Press, 1967), 59–60. Used by permission.

[60]Ibid., 60.

[61]Bruce W. Thielemann, *There Is a Way Out* (Glendale, Calif.: Gospel Light Publications [Regal Books], 1975), 39–43.

[62]Ralph Waldo Emerson, *Familiar Quotations*, ed., John Bartlett (Boston: Little, Brown and Company, 1955), 502.

[63]Thielemann, *There Is a Way Out*, 39.

[64]David Elkind, *The Hurried Child* (Menlo Park, Calif.: Addison-Wesley Publishing Co., 1981).

[65]Susan Ferraro, "Hotsy Totsy," *American Way*, inflight magazine of American Airlines, April 1981, 61. Used by permission of the author.

[66]Reprinted courtesy of *Sports Illustrated* from the 22 February 1988 issue. © 1988, Time Inc. "Bred to Be a Superstar" by Douglas S. Looney. All rights reserved. Used by permission.

[67]David H. Olson, Douglas H. Sprenkle, and Candyce Russell, "Circumplex Model of Marital and Family Systems," *Family Process* 18 (March 1979): 12–13.

[68]From an unpublished message by Ray Stedman, senior pastor, Peninsula Bible Church, Palo Alto, Calif.

[69]D. L. Stewart, "Why Fathers Hide Their Feelings," *Redbook*, January 1985, 32. Used by permission of the author.

[70]J. Allan Petersen, "Expressing Appreciation," *Family Building*, ed. Dr. George Rekers (Ventura, Calif.: Regal Books, 1985), 103–6.

[71]Leslie B. Flynn, *Great Church Fights* (Wheaton: Victor Books, 1976), 105.

[72]Ibid., 104.

[73]Ibid., 105.

[74]Ted Engstrom, *The Pursuit of Excellence* (Grand Rapids: Zondervan, 1982), 81–82.

[75]W. E. Vine, *Expository Dictionary of New Testament Words*, 4 vols. (Old Tappan, N. J.: Fleming H. Revell, 1940), 3:109.

[76]Kenneth S. Wuest, *The New Testament, An Expanded Translation* (Grand Rapids: Eerdmans Publishing Company, 1961), 394.

[77]John R. W. Stott, *Christian Counter-Culture* (Downers Grove, Ill.: InterVarsity Press, 1978), 95.

[78]Charles L. Allen, *You Are Never Alone* (Old Tappan, N. J.: Fleming H. Revell, 1978), 145–46.

[79]*Los Angeles Times*, 25 February, 1980, sec. 2, p. 1.

[80]Ann of Austria.

[81]Dr. James Dobson, *What Wives Wish Their Husbands Knew About Women* (Wheaton, Ill.: Tyndale House, 1975), 114.

[82]Linda Bird Francke and others, "Children of Divorce," *Newsweek* [New York], 11 February, 1980, 58–63.

[83]Poem by Ralph Waldo Emerson quoted in *Freedom for Ministry* by Richard John Neuhaus (San Francisco: Harper & Row, 1956), 90.

[84]From an unpublished speech by Dr. Josephy Bayly entitled "Guarding Our Hearts." Presented at West Suburban Ministerial Fellowship in Wheaton, Illinois, April 1986. Used by permission.

[85]Sir William Osler, *Familiar Quotations*, ed., John Bartlett (Boston: Little, Brown and Company, 1955), 744.

[86]*The Real Mother Goose* (Chicago, Ill.: Rand, McNally & Company, 1916), 26.

[87]W. E. Vine, *An Expository Dictionary of New Testament Words*, Vol. II (Westwood, N. J.: Fleming H. Revell, 1940), 248.

[88]Charles R. Swindoll, *Stress* (Portland, Ore.: Multnomah Press, 1981; reprint, Grand Rapids: Zondervan, 1995).

[89]Samuel Taylor Coleridge, "Youth and Age," Stanza 2, *Familiar Quotations*, ed. John Bartlett (Boston, Mass.: Little, Brown and Company, 1955), 425a.

[90]John White, *The Fight* (Downers Grove, Ill.: InterVarsity Press, 1976), 179.

[91]Charles W. Colson, *Loving God* (Grand Rapids: Zondervan, 1983), 131.

[92]Kyle Yates, *Preaching from the Prophets* (North Nashville: Broadman Press, 1953), 152.

[93]Karl Menninger, *Whatever Became of Sin?* (New York: Bantam Books, Inc., 1978), 138.

[94]Jerry White, *Honesty, Morality, and Conscience* (Colorado Springs: NavPress, 1979), 184.

[95]Graham, *World Aflame* (New York: Doubleday., 1965), 21–22.

[96]John Brown, *Expository Discourses on 1 Peter* (Edinburgh: Banner of Truth, reprint edition, 1848), 1:106. Italics in original.

[97]Billy Graham, *World Aflame*, 23.

[98]*The Works of Jonathan Edwards*, 2 vols., revised and corrected by Edward Hickman (Carlisle, Pa.: The Banner of Truth Trust, reprint edition, 1976), 1:XX. Italics in original.

[99]M. Scott Peck, *People of the Lie* (New York: Simon & Schuster, 1983), 221.

[100]Joyce Landorf, *Tough and Tender* (Old Tappan, N.J.: Fleming H. Revell, 1975), 156.

[101]William Barclay, *Gospel of Matthew*, 2 vols., The Daily Study Bible (Edinburgh: The Saint Andrews Press, 1956), 1:191, 193.

[102]Eugene Peterson, *A Long Obedience in the Same Direction* (Downers Grove, Ill.: InterVarsity Press, 1980), 11, 12.

[103]Charles E. Hummel, *Tyranny of the Urgent!* (Downers Grove, Ill.: InterVarsity Christian Fellowship, 1967), 5.

[104]Bob Benson, "Laughter in the Walls," in *Laughter in the Walls* (Nashville: Impact Books, 1969). Used by permission.

[105]Leslie B. Flynn, *Man: Ruined & Restored* (Wheaton, Ill.: Victor Books, 1978), 100–101.

New International Version
The Living Insights Study Bible
Charles R. Swindoll, General Editor
Available September 1996

Solid, relevant, application-oriented Bible teaching. Inspirational, energizing encouragement. Dr. Charles Swindoll, experienced pastor, masterful Bible teacher, and now president of Dallas Theological Seminary, provides both teaching and encouragement throughout this complete New International Version Bible.

Dr. Swindoll informs and uplifts with his extraordinary ability to communicate the truths of Scripture. Accurately and clearly he shows how biblical truths apply to real life.

- Extensive book introductions are like a Bible survey course.
- In-depth articles explore the themes and doctrines of the faith.
- Section and chapter summaries give a clear understanding of the big picture.
- "Living Insights" illuminate the truth of Scripture in fresh and inspiring ways.
- Also includes character profiles, charts, concordance, glossary of key doctrinal terms, and more.

Available editions include:

Regular Size 6 1/2 x 9 1/4		Personal Size 5 1/2 x 8 1/2	
Hard Cover	0-310-91870-7	Softcover	0-310-91882-0
Bonded Leather			
Burgundy	0-310-91872-3		
Forest Green	0-310-91874-X		
Navy	0-310-91876-6		
Top-Grain Leather			
Burgundy	0-310-91878-2		
Black	0-310-91880-4		

ZondervanPublishingHouse
Grand Rapids, Michigan

A Division of HarperCollins*Publishers*